Ian A. Fraser

Oct 1995.

ENGLISH PLACE-NAME SOCIETY

VOLUME LXX FOR 1992-93

General Editor

VICTOR WATTS

THE PLACE-NAMES OF SHROPSHIRE

PART TWO

THE SURVEY OF ENGLISH PLACE-NAMES
UNDERTAKEN WITH THE APPROVAL AND SUPPORT OF
THE BRITISH ACADEMY

THE PLACE-NAMES OF SHROPSHIRE

By

MARGARET GELLING
in collaboration with
H. D. G. FOXALL

PART TWO

THE HUNDREDS OF FORD AND CONDOVER

NOTTINGHAM
ENGLISH PLACE-NAME SOCIETY
1995

Published by the English Place-Name Society

Registered Charity No. 257891

ISBN 0 904889 43 2

The camera-ready copy for this volume
has been prepared by Mrs E. Pattison
on equipment provided by
Allied Breweries plc
and
Advent Desktop Publishing Ltd

Printed in Great Britain
by Woolnough Bookbinding, Irthlingborough, Northants

CONTENTS

The collection from unpublished documents of material for the Shropshire volumes has been greatly assisted by grants received from the British Academy.

INTRODUCTION

Ford and Condover Hundreds were chosen for the first of the regional volumes of the Shropshire place-name survey because they had been treated in Volume VIII of the Victoria History of Shropshire (1965). In addition to the VCH's printed accounts of parishes in these hundreds I was able to consult notes and transcripts from the collection of material on which Vol. VIII was based. These collections, and the editing of Vol. VIII, were the work of the late A.T. Gaydon, and I am deeply indebted to him and to the later VCH team, G. Baugh, D.C. Cox and P.A. Stamper. The place-name survey will continue to run parallel with the VCH topographical volumes. *The Place-Names of Shropshire* Part 3 will deal with an area south and east of Condover Hundred, part of which is treated in VCH XI (1985) and the rest in VCH X (in the final stages of compilation at the time of writing). The enormous advantages of this collaboration will outweigh the disadvantage of departing, in Part 3, from the usual EPNS practice of basing parts of its surveys on the areas of medieval hundreds. A further debt to VCH VIII is the use of maps from the volume as the basis of those here numbered Maps 1-5.

The topography of Ford Hundred is succinctly described in VCH VIII, 178. There is mountainous country to the west, where the hundred takes in part of the Breiddens and the Long Mountain, and to the south, where its boundary crosses the northern foothills of the Stiperstones and the Long Mynd. The main features of the area between these blocks of high ground are the broad valley of the Rea Brook and the belt of heathland between that and the valley of the R. Severn. The heathland stretches from Shrewsbury to the Long Mountain.

The Rea Valley is said in the VCH account to be the most densely settled part of the hundred, and "probably always the most prosperous", and the only large villages, Pontesbury and Minsterley, overlook the river. The apparent loss of the pre-English name for this river is a striking instance of the phenomenon discussed in the Introduction to Part 1 of general loss of British names in the county, though it should be noted that the OE derivation suggested for Meole, the earlier name of Rea Brook, may not meet with universal acceptance. It is, however, certain that for Rea Brook there was no survival of one of the well-evidenced, recurring pre-English river-names, like that of the parallel tributary, Cound Brook. There are, in fact, no identifiable names of pre-English origin in the whole area of Ford Hundred, and no names containing *Walh* 'Welshman'. For the most part the Welsh names of the western part of the hundred like Trefnant in Wollaston, are not likely to be pre-English, though simplex names, like Bulthy and Glyn, could be so.

A point clearly brought out by the place-name survey is that there was much woodland along the Rea Brook when the English names were being formed. From Leigh in Worthen (just beyond the southern boundary of Ford Hundred) to Pulley (in Condover Hundred) eleven names with *lēah* as generic are found by the river or its tributary streams. Two of the places (Habberley and Minsterley) are ancient parishes, the others (Asterley, Farley, Lea, Leigh, Plealey, Pulley, Westley, Whitley, Winsley) are townships. Four of them (Farley, Minsterley, Pulley, Winsley) are named in DB, the rest are first recorded at dates ranging from 1199 (Leigh in Worthen) to 1306-7 (Whitley, S. of Shrewsbury). It is reasonable to conclude that these are pre-Conquest names, probably dating from the Middle Saxon period, when *lēah* was regularly used for settlements in forest clearings. It is impossible to say whether these were settlements already established when English-speaking people arrived, or whether they result from the clearing of woodland after that incursion. What is certain, however, is that until the end of the Anglo-Saxon period English speakers would only use *lēah* in naming settlements which had a wooded environment.

Some other names in the basin of the Rea Brook denote woods. Malehurst and Little Hanwood are townships of Pontesbury, while Great Hanwood is a parish in Condover Hundred. Hurst in Winsley is *Wynnesleyeshurst* 1334, and there is a *Woodhouse* (later Wood Hall) in Pontesbury. Hinwood in Pontesbury adjoins the late-recorded Wigley in Westbury. Hargrave, on the north edge of the medieval Forest of Hayes, may refer to a coppiced wood.

The woodland of Ford Hundred which survived into the Middle Ages is shown on the map on p.182 of VCH VIII. Most of it is peripheral to the Rea basin, and it may be suggested that a good deal of woodland closer to the river was cleared soon after eastern Powys became open to English settlement.

Between the Rea basin and the Severn flood-plain lay a

wedge-shaped area of heathland, marked by Bicton Heath, Ford Heath, Stretton Heath and Wattlesborough Heath. A number of settlements on the fringes of this have names in *-tūn*, which was the generic regularly used in the Middle Saxon period for settlements in open (as opposed to wooded) land. These are Amaston, Braggington, Cardeston, Cruckton, Eyton, Loton, Rowton, Stoney Stretton, Vennington, Whitton, Winnington and Wollaston. The separation of *tūn* and *lēah* is not absolute. Halston and Hinton, townships of Pontesbury, lie directly beside the Rea Brook, and Poulton in Minsterley is by a tributary, while Bausley (just in Montgomeryshire) is a *lēah* name beside the Severn; but most of the *lēah* names are in the valley of the Rea and most of the *tūn* names are north-west of it. So in spite of the survival into the Middle Ages of woods on the south bank of the Severn, as marked on the VCH map, the place-name evidence suggests that a woodland environment was the norm for settlements by the Rea, and an open environment for those between the Rea and the Severn at the time when the settlement-names evolved.

There are few references in settlement-names to wet ground or to the broad flood-plains of the Severn and the Rea Brook. The main roads ran east/west, between the flood-plains, and crossings of small tributaries were important. Ford probably refers to a made-up crossing-place at Welshman's Ford, where the Welshpool/Shrewsbury road crosses Cardeston Brook. Stanford in Wattlesborough township may refer to a causeway over wet land, and Pontesford is at a stream crossing. An area of marshy ground away from the main rivers is referred to in the names Marche (or Marsh) and Wigmore, adjacent settlements on either side of the upper course of a tributary of Rea Brook, and Vennington ('fenny settlement') is on a parallel stream a short distance to the south. For the most part, however, the people of the region seem to have taken for granted the meadowland resources and the ways in which rivers and streams were negotiated by travellers.

There are some apt topographical names, such as Edge and Wallop. As regards habitative names, the main alternative to *tūn* is *cot* (Arscott, Boycott, Sascott, Sibberscot). The solitary Newnham must represent use of this compound for a late, minor settlement, rather than being an instance of *hām* in its full dignity as an early habitative generic.

A very striking feature of the place-names of Ford Hundred is the use of *byrig* in the names of the three great parishes, Alberbury, Pontesbury and Westbury, which dominate the area. The three settlements are situated on roads which run west from Shrewsbury, and Westbury is at the junction of several routes. At Pontesbury and Westbury the morphology of the villages clearly suggests fortified areas dating from before the period of the Norman castles which (as can be seen from Map 2) are a notable feature of the post-Conquest landscape in this hundred. For Alberbury, which has a feminine personal name as qualifier, the 'military' sense of *byrig* seems less compelling, but here, too, a Norman castle was placed. It seems likely that these three parishes, with their numerous townships (each of which acquired its own field-system), represent pre-English composite estates in which the component parts were renamed by English speakers. After eastern Powys became part of Mercia the principle sites in the three land-units may have been perceived as places of military importance guarding the routes of entry from western Powys. The system (if such there was) may have included Wattlesborough, where the 'fort' term occurs in the nominative, *burh*. This component of Alberbury parish overlooks the road which runs between those dominated by Alberbury and Westbury, and here, also, there was a Norman Castle. The interpretation adumbrated here contradicts the discussion of Alberbury and Wattlesborough in Part 1: inconsistency of this sort is unavoidable in a project carried out over a long period.

The landscape of Condover Hundred resembles that of Ford Hundred in several ways. It has the Severn as part of its northern boundary, and it takes in a little mountainous ground - in this case part of Hoar Edge and the northern slopes of the Long Mynd. Similar, also, is the manner in which the area is traversed by the Cound Brook, a somewhat larger tributary than the Rea Brook, flowing roughly parallel with it and entering the Severn at Cound. Unlike the Rea Brook, however, Cound Brook does not have a broad flood-plain.

Cound Brook kept its pre-English name, but there is no other certain linguistic trace of pre-English nomenclature. Church Hill in Pontesbury probably contains *crūc*, but this loan word from Primitive Welsh was used freely by Old English speakers.

The woodland names along the Rea Brook extend into the western part of Pulverbatch, but otherwise the names in this hundred which denote ancient forest are notably concentrated in the south of the hundred, at the junction of plain and hills. Here are the parishes of Harley, Kenley, Ruckley, Langley, Frodesley and Leebotwood, and Longnor was *Lege* in DB. Lydley Hays is in Leebotwood parish, and in both these places there are references to the making of assarts by Haughmond Abbey and the Knights Templars in the second half of the 12th century. Botwood, which occupied the southern half of Leebotwood parish, was enclosed in the 17th and 18th centuries. Micklewood was situated in the northern half of the parish.

In addition to these major names there are minor names containing *lēah* in this area, and it is possible that here the sense 'woodland clearing' survived till the end of the Anglo-Saxon period. The position of Acton Burnell on the north edge of this woodland is consistent with the suggestion made in Part 1 that the recurrent name Acton may refer to a special function in relation to supplies of oak timber.

By contrast with the Rea Brook, the Cound Brook is fringed by *tūn* settlements. Norton, Betton and Stapleton overlook the river, Ryton and Dorrington are by one of its headwaters, and Moreton stands on a tributary. Berrington and Boreton (for which a special significance was suggested in Part 1) are on either side of Cound Brook. Eaton Mascott refers directly to the river, using the term *ēa*, which indicates that the status of the watercourse was felt to be higher than is implied by modern 'brook'. It may fairly be concluded that the Cound valley was clear of woodland when the English names evolved. Other *tūn* names, Brompton and Chilton, are by the Severn. The only *tūn* name eccentric to this distribution is Woolstaston, which marks the S.W. edge of the woodland belt in the southern part of the hundred.

As regards habitative generics other than *tūn* there is one *worðign* (Belswardine) and a cluster of *cot* names - Smethcott, Betchcott, Cothercott, Picklescott and the lost *Hollycot* - on the northern foothills of the Long Mynd. These last may be settlements established in the latter part of the Anglo-Saxon period.

Condover Hundred is richer than Ford Hundred in topographical settlement-names. Bayston, Condover, Golding, Harnage, Huglith, Longden, Lyth and Pitchford are in this category. Cressage offers, in the nearby Lady Oak, a valuable indication of the manner in which a tree might receive special treatment enabling it and its descendants to mark a settlement for centuries. Cantlop and Preen are, unfortunately, not amenable to classification, as the significance of both is obscure.

It may be significant that the largest parishes, Condover and Cound, both use the British river-name. It is impossible to make any case for linguistic continuity in the area south of Shrewsbury, but administrative continuity from pre-English times is another matter. It is a reasonable assumption that much of the settlement pattern was established long before the area became part of Mercia, and that most of the settlement-names represent re-naming in the language of the Mercian administrators. In the south of Condover Hundred, however, the *cot* and *lēah* names are likely to represent expansion of arable cultivation in the late Anglo-Saxon period.

Parish, village and hamlet names throw light on settlement history. The history of land-use is illustrated (albeit with tedious repetitiveness) in the field-names.

Treatment of field-names for the place-name survey of Shropshire is a much more rewarding exercise than usual because of the availability of the set of maps prepared for the VCH by George Foxall. Mr Foxall redrew all the available Tithe Award maps for the county to a uniform 6" scale, and wrote the names from the schedules in the individual fields whose outlines were drawn on the originals. I am the first English Place-Name Survey editor to have such a tool at my disposal, and all comments on size, shape and position in the field-name sections of this volume derive from my set of copies of the Foxall maps. The 6" scale enables geographical information from an early set of OS 6" maps to be taken easily into account.

The interest and pleasure of studying field-names in this manner cannot, unfortunately, be conveyed to the reader, because of the alphabetical arrangement of the field-name lists. This is an inescapable requirement, since the field-name material could not be organised for philological study without it. The connection between the name and the piece of land is obscured by alphabetisation, but it is a major development that the interpretations offered for the names are matched to the actual fields, and this provides a sounder basis than would otherwise have been available in a vast number of cases. The lists provided here for each township will be of interest to local readers. For the philologist they will provide useful cumulative evidence for dialect terms and dialectal senses of words, and embedded in the repetitive names of lesser interest are the occasional gems which constitute serious additions to our knowledge of the English language. Some of the more significant field-names are noted in the Index, and an excellent overview of the field-names of the whole county can be obtained from George Foxall's book *Shropshire Field-Names.*

Acknowledgements of help in the collection of material, the production of the volume, and the provision of organisational background to the enterprise are as stated in the Introduction to *The Place-Names of Shropshire* Part 1, except that to the names listed there should be added that of Victor Watts, now Director of the EPNS Survey in succession to Professor Cameron, and that of Anne Tarver, who has drawn the maps for Part 2.

July 1994 Margaret Gelling
Birmingham

ABBREVIATIONS and BIBLIOGRAPHY

Abbreviations printed in roman type refer to printed sources and those in italic to manuscript sources.

a.	*ante.*
Abbr	*Placitorum Abbreviatio* (RC), 1811.
acc.	accusative.
AD	*Catalogue of Ancient Deeds* (PRO), 1890 and in progress.
AddCh	Additional Charters in BM.
adj.	adjective.
APW	*Calendar of Ancient Petitions relating to Wales,* ed. W. Rees, Cardiff 1975.
ASC	*The Anglo-Saxon Chronicle.*
Ass	Assize Rolls (PRO).
ASWills	*Anglo-Saxon Wills,* ed. D. Whitelock, 1930.
Ave.	Avenue.
Baugh	*Robert Baugh's Map of Shropshire 1808,* Shropshire Archaeological Society 1983.
BBCS	*The Bulletin of the Board of Celtic Studies.*
Bd	Bedfordshire.
Berks	Berkshire.
Bk	Buckinghamshire.
BL	Documents in British Library.
Blome	Richard Blome, *A General Mapp of Shropshire with its Hundreds* (c.1675).
BM	*Index to the Charters and Rolls in the Department of Manuscripts, British Museum,* ed. H.J. Ellis and F.B. Bickley, 2 vols, 1900-12.
Bowcock	E.W. Bowcock, *Shropshire Place-Names,* Shrewsbury 1923.
Burton	*Charters of Burton Abbey,* ed. P.H. Sawyer, *Anglo-Saxon Charters* II, British Academy 1979.
c.	*circa* 'about'
Ca	Cambridgeshire.
Cant	*The Register of Thomas de Cantilupe,* Canterbury and York Society II, 1907.

CartAntiq	*The Cartae Antiquae Rolls* 1-10, PRS NS 17, 1939; 11-20, PRS NS 33, 1960.
cent.	century.
Ch	Cheshire.
Ch	*Calendar of Charter Rolls* (PRO), 1903-27.
Ch 1, Ch 2	regnal dates, t. Charles I or II.
ChanR	*Calendar of various Chancery Rolls*, A.D.1277-1326 (PRO), 1912.
Charles	B.G. Charles, 'The Welsh, their Language and Place-Names in Archenfield and Oswestry', in *Angles and Britons. O'Donnell Lectures*, University of Wales Press 1963, pp. 85-110.
ChR	*Rotuli Chartarum*, ed. T.D. Hardy (RC), 1837.
Cl	*Calendar of Close Rolls* (PRO), in progress.
ClR	*Rotuli Litterarum Clausarum*, ed. T.D. Hardy (RC).
Co	Cornwall.
Coin(s)	spellings taken from coin-legends.
Corn.R.O.	Buller MSS in Cornwall Record Office, Truro.
Craven	Surveys of the Craven Estates in Shrewsbury Public Library (Class M.S.Accession 2480-3).
Ct	Court.
Cu	Cumberland.
Cur	*Curia Regis Rolls* (PRO), in progress.
CurR	*Rotuli Curia Regis* (RC), 1835.
D	Devon.
dat.	dative.
Db	Derbyshire.
DB	Domesday Book.
Denb	Denbighshire.
DEPN	E. Ekwall, *The Concise Oxford Dictionary of English Place-Names*, 4th ed., 1960.
Do	Dorset.
Du	County Durham.
Dugdale	W. Dugdale, *Monasticon Anglicanum*, 6 vols. in 8, 1817-30.
Duignan	W.H. Duignan, *Notes on Staffordshire Place-Names*, London 1902.
e.	early.
E.	east.
ECWM	H.P.R. Finberg, *The Early Charters of the West*

	Midlands, Leicester 1972.
Ed 1, Ed 2 etc.	regnal dates, t. Edward I, t. Edward II, etc.
el.	place-name element.
Eliz	regnal date, t. Elizabeth I.
EPN	A.H. Smith, *English Place-Name Elements,* Parts 1 and 2 (EPNS 25, 26), Cambridge 1956.
EPNS	publications of the English Place-Name Society.
ERN	E. Ekwall, *English River-Names,* Oxford 1928.
ERY	East Riding of Yorkshire.
Ess	Essex.
et freq	*et frequenter* : and frequently (thereafter).
et seq	*et sequenter* : and subsequently.
Eyton	SRO 665/37-8, an uncatalogued collection of 16th, 17th and e.18th cent. indentures from the Condover estate which came to SRO from the Eyton family.
Eyton	R.W. Eyton, *Antiquities of Shropshire,* London 1854-60.
FA	*Feudal Aids* (PRO), 1899-1920.
Fees	*The Book of Fees* (PRO), 1920-31.
Feilitzen	O. von. Feilitzen, *The Pre-Conquest Personal Names of Domesday Book,* Uppsala 1937.
fem.	feminine.
ff.	and the pages following.
FF	*Feet of Fines* (PRSoc 17, 20, 23, 24), 1894, 1896, 1898, 1900. Some FF forms have been taken from SAS vols; these are referenced (e.g.) SAS 2/X(FF).
FFW	*Fouke Fitz Warin, Roman du XIVe Siècle* ed. Louis Brandon, Paris 1930.
Fine	*Calendar of Fine Rolls* (PRO), in progress.
Fli	Flintshire.
Fm	Farm.
f.n., f.ns.	field-name(s).
FN	H.D.G. Foxall, *Shropshire Field-Names,* Shrewsbury 1980.
For	*Select Pleas of the Forest,* ed. J.G. Turner, Selden Soc. 13, 1901.
ForProc	Forest Proceedings in PRO.
Fr	French.
freq	*frequenter,* frequently.
G	German.

Gazetteer	H.D.G. Foxall, *A Gazetteer of Streets, Roads and Place Names in Shropshire*, 2nd ed., Shrewsbury 1967.
gen.	genitive.
GeolSurv	T.H. Whitehead and R.W. Pocock, *Dudley and Bridgnorth*, Memoirs of the Geological Survey of England and Wales, HMSO 1947.
Gir	*Giraldi Cambrensis Opera* (RS), 1861-91.
Gl	Gloucestershire.
G.R.	national grid reference.
Ha	Hampshire.
HAC	*The Cartulary of Haughmond Abbey*, ed. Una Rees, Cardiff 1985.
Harl 433	*British Library Harleian Manuscript 433*, ed. Rosemary Horrox and P.W. Hammond, 4 vols., Richard III Soc. 1979-83.
He	Herefordshire.
Ho	House.
Hobbs	J.L. Hobbs, *Shrewsbury Street-Names*, Shrewsbury 1954.
Howard	C. Howard, *The Roads of England and Wales*, 1883.
Hrt	Hertfordshire.
HTR	*The Shropshire Hearth-Tax Roll of 1672*, ed. W. Watkins-Pitchford, Shrewsbury 1949.
Hu	Huntingdonshire.
Hunt	*Henrici Huntendunensis Historia Anglorum* (RS), 1879.
Hy 1, Hy 2 etc.	regnal dates, t. Henry I, t. Henry II etc.
ib, *ib*	*ibidem* (referring respectively to published and unpublished sources).
InqMisc	*Calendar of Inquisitions Miscellaneous* (PRO), in progress.
Ipm	*Calendar of Inquisitions Post Mortem* (PRO), in progress.
Jas 1, Jas 2	regnal dates, t. James I, t. James II.
JEPN	*Journal of the English Place-Name Society.*
John	regnal date, t. John.
K	Kent.
Kelly	*Kelly's Directory of Shropshire*, 1934.
Kynnersley Brown	Letter from W.J. Kynnersley Brown, The Hall, Leighton, date 31st Jan. 1933, filed in E.W. Bowcock's material.
l.	late.

L	Lincolnshire.
La	Lancashire.
LCA	*Index to Llyfr Coch Asaph, Archaeologia Cambrensis* 3rd series, Vol. 14, 1868.
LDR	Glebe terriers in Lichfield Diocesan Registry.
Lei	Leicestershire.
Leland	*Leland's Itinerary in England and Wales,* ed. L. Toulmin Smith, 5 vols., London 1964.
LHEB	K. Jackson, *Language and History in Early Britain,* Edinburgh 1953.
Lib	*Calendar of Liberate Rolls* (PRO), in progress.
Lil	Lilleshall Cartulary, BL AddMS 50121.
Lilco	Records of the Lilleshall Company.
m.	mid.
Margary	I.D. Margary, *Roman Roads in Britain,* 2 vols., London 1955-7.
masc.	masculine.
ME	Middle English.
MemR	*The Memoranda Roll of the King's Remembrancer for* 1230-31 (PRS NS 11), 1933; - *for the Michaelmas Term of the First Year of the Reign of King John* (PRS NS 21), 1943.
MGS	C.H. Drinkwater, *The Merchants' Gild of Shrewsbury* : a series of articles in SAS. Most of these are bound in a volume in the Local Studies Library, Shrewsbury, (D 36.1 Acc No 1695).
MHG	Middle High German.
Mills	A.D. Mills, *Dorset Place-Names: Their Origins and Meanings,* Wimborne 1986.
MinAcc	Ministers' Accounts (PRO).
MM	*Mappa Mundi* in *The Historical Works of Gervase of Canterbury,* ed. W. Stubbs, Vol. II (RS), 1880.
ModE	Modern English.
Mont	Montgomeryshire.
Morden	*The County Maps from William Camden's Britannia 1695* by Robert Morden. A Facsimile (1972).
MorganTs	R. Morgan, *Welsh Place-Names in Shropshire* (typescript) 1988.
MS, MSS	Manuscript(s).
Mx	Middlesex.

N.	North.
Nb	Northumberland.
NCPNW	B.G. Charles, *Non-Celtic Place-Names in Wales*, London 1938.
n.d.	undated.
NED	*A New English Dictionary*, ed. J.A.H. Murray and others, Oxford 1888-1933.
Nf	Norfolk.
NLW	MSS in the National Library of Wales.
nom.	nominative.
Norwich	*The Valuation of Norwich*, ed. W.E. Lunt, Oxford 1926.
NRY	North Riding of Yorkshire.
NS	New Series in a run of publications.
Nt	Nottinghamshire.
Nth	Northamptonshire.
O	Oxfordshire.
obl.	oblique case.
OE	Old English.
Ogilby	J. Ogilby, *Itinerarium Angliae*, London 1675.
OHG	Old High German.
OLG	Old Low German.
ON	Old Norse.
OrdVit	*The Ecclesiastical History of Ordericus Vitalis*, ed. M. Chibnall, 6 vols., Oxford 1968-80.
OS	Ordnance Survey.
p.	page.
p.	*post.*
(p)	place-name used in a person's surname.
P	Pipe Rolls (PRS), in progress.
part.	participle.
Pat	*Calendar of Patent Rolls* (PRO), in progress.
pers.n.	personal name.
P.H.	Public House.
Pk	Park.
pl.	plural.
Pltn	Plantation
Plymley	J. Plymley, *General Survey of the Agriculture of Shropshire*, London 1803.
pn., p.ns.	place-name(s).
PN	EPNS survey of the county indicated by the

	abbreviation which follows.
PR	*Shropshire Parish Registers,* Shropshsire Parish Register Society. (H) Hereford Diocese; (L) Lichfield Diocese; (StA) St Asaph Diocese.
PRAlveley etc.	MS transcripts of parish registers in Shrewsbury Borough Library.
PrGerm	Primitive Germanic.
PRO	Public Record Office, London.
PRS	Pipe Roll Society.
PrW	Primitive Welsh.
PW	*The Parliamentary Writs and Writs of Military Summons* - - - (RC), 1827-30.
QW	*Placita de Quo Warranto* (RC). 1818.
R.	River.
R 1, R 2 etc.	regnal dates, t. Richard I, t. Richard II etc.
Rad	Radnorshire.
RB	Romano-British.
RBE	*The Red Book of the Exchequer,* ed. H. Hall (RS), 3 vols., 1896.
RC	Record Commission.
Rd	Road.
Redin	M. Redin, *Studies on Uncompounded Personal Names in Old English,* Uppsala 1919.
RentSurv	Rentals and Surveys in PRO.
RH	*Rotuli Hundredorum* (RC), 1812-18.
RS	Rolls Series.
Ru	Rutland.
S	P.H. Sawyer, *Anglo-Saxon Charters, an annotated list and bibliography,* Royal Historical Society, 1968.
S.	South.
s.a.	*sub anno.*
Sa	Shropshire.
SAC	*The Cartulary of Shrewsbury Abbey,* ed. Una Rees, 2 vols., National Library of Wales, 1975.
Saints	*Die Heiligen Englands,* ed. F. Liebermann, Hanover 1889.
SAS	*Transactions of the Shropshire Archaeological Society.* The series is numbered in arabic figures, the volume in roman, e.g. 1/IX, 4/III. If no series is given the ref. is to the current series,

	and the volume no. is in arabic.
Saxton	Saxton's *Map of Shropshire*, 1577.
SBL	A collection of Shropshire documents in the Local Studies Department of Shropshire Libraries, Shrewsbury.
Searle	W.G. Searle, *Onomasticon Anglo-Saxonicum*, Cambridge 1897.
Sf	Suffolk.
ShelveMap	Map of 1650 displayed in Shelve church.
sing.	singular.
Slack	*The Lordship of Oswestry 1393-1607*, ed. W.J. Slack, Shrewsbury, 1951.
s.n.	*sub nomine*.
So	Somerset.
SNQ	*Shropshire Notes and Queries* Vols I and II, Shrewsbury 1886 (items collected from *The Shrewsbury Chronicle* 1884-86).
Sr	Surrey.
SR	*The Shropshire Lay Subsidy Roll of 1 Edward III, 1327*, ed. W.G.D. Fletcher, reprinted from SAS, Oswestry 1907. *The Lay Subsidy Roll of 1334*, ed. R.E. Glasscock, British Academy 1975.
SRO	Documents in Shropshire Record Office.
St	Staffordshire.
Strange	*Le Strange Records*, ed. Hamon le Strange, London 1916.
StRO	Documents in Staffordshire Record Office.
s.v.	*sub voce*.
Swin	*Registrum Ricardi de Swinfield, Episcopi Herefordensis*, ed. W.W. Capes, Canterbury and York Society VI, 1909.
Sx	Sussex.
t.	*tempore*.
TA	Tithe Award.
TAMap	Map accompanying *TA*.
Templars	*Records of the Templars in England in the Twelfth Century*, ed. B.A. Lees, British Academy 1935.
Tengstrand	E. Tengstrand, *A Contribution to the Study of Genitival Composition in Old English Place-*

	Names, Uppsala 1940.
TN	*Taxatio Ecclesiastica Angliae et Walliae, auctoritate Papae Nicholai IV, c.1291*, ed. S. Ayscough and J. Caley, London 1802.
Tong	G. Griffiths, *A History of Tong, Shropshire*, Newport 1894.
Townson	R. Townson 'A Sketch of the Mineralogy of Shropshire' in *Tracts and Observations in Natural History and Physiology*, London 1799.
TRE	*tempore Regis Edwardi*, the DB term for 'on the day that King Edward the Confessor was alive and dead'.
VCH	*The Victoria History of the County of Shropshire*, in progress.
VCH	Victoria County History notes, held at Shropshire Record Office. Sometimes followed by note of ultimate source, e.g. *VCH(Longleat)*, *VCH(Hereford)*.
VE	*Valor Ecclesiasticus*, ed. J. Hunter (RC), 1810-34.
W	Wiltshire.
W.	West.
WATU	M. Richards, *Welsh Administrative and Territorial Units*, Cardiff 1973.
Wd	Wood.
We	Westmorland.
WMidl	west-midland.
Wo	Worcestershire.
Wom	Wombridge Cartulary, *BL EgMS 3712*.
WRY	West Riding of Yorkshire.
WSax	West-Saxon.
Wt	Isle of Wight.
Y	Yorkshire.
*	a postulated form.

Words printed in bold type, e.g. **āc**, **tūn**, are recognised place-name elements. Most of these are discussed in EPNS XXV-XXVI; some are to be found in the Elements sections of later volumes.

Dates such as '1271-2 *Ass*' indicate that the spelling cannot be precisely dated within those limits. Dates such as '1347,54 Ipm' indicate that the same spelling occurs in 1347 and 1354.

Long and short vowels are indicated thus: **ā**, **ă**

Abbreviations used in Field-Name Sections

Fd	Field
Flg	Furlong
Lsw	Leasow
Mdw	Meadow
Pce	Piece
Yd	Yard

Field-names are arranged in lists headed (a) and (b), the former containing those names known to have been in use in the 19th century or later.

Capitalisation in field-names has been rationalised; the use in sources of small or capital initials has not been reproduced.

PHONETIC SYMBOLS

p	*p*ay	j	*y*ou	ɔ	p*o*t
b	*b*ay	x	lo*ch* (Scots)	ɔ:	s*aw*
t	*t*ea	h	*h*is	ɔi	*oi*l
d	*d*ay	m	*m*an	e	r*e*d
k	*k*ey	n	*n*o	ei	fl*ay*
g	*g*o	ŋ	si*ng*	ɛ	jam*ai*s (Fr.)
ʍ	*wh*en	r	*r*un	ɛ:	th*ere*
w	*w*in	l	*l*and	i	p*i*t
f	*f*oe	ʧ	*ch*ur*ch*	i:	b*ea*d
v	*v*ote	ʤ	*j*u*dg*e	ou	l*ow*
s	*s*ay	ɑ:	f*a*ther	u	g*oo*d
z	*z*one	ɑu	c*ow*	u:	b*oo*t
ʃ	*sh*one	a	m*a*nn (German)	ʌ	m*u*ch
ʒ	a*z*ure	ai	fl*y*	ə	ev*er*
þ	*th*in	æ	c*a*b	ə:	b*ir*d
ð	*th*en			?	wa*t*er (Cockney, glottal stop)

Phonetic symbols are enclosed in square brackets: [ ].

The symbols used in the expression of Brit and PrWelsh forms are those used in LHEB.

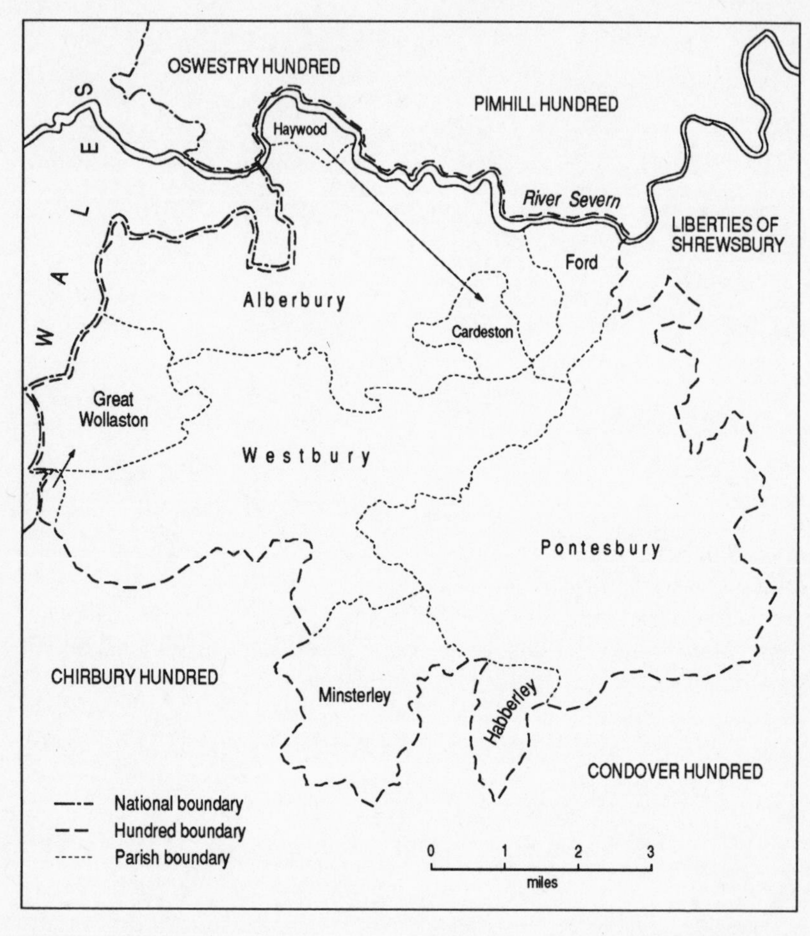

Map 1. The Hundred of Ford

FORD HUNDRED

Ford' 1203-4 *Ass, Forda* 1221 Fees, *Forde* 1284-5 FA *et freq, Ford* 1346 FA
La Forde 1255-6, 71-2 *Ass*

Named from the manor of Ford, which replaced Alberbury as the *caput.*

In DB the hundred which belonged to Alberbury is called *Ruesset* (4), *Reweset,* which means 'settlers by the hill'. In this name OE **sǣte** has been added to Welsh *rhiw,* the Welsh word being perhaps a general term for the belt of high ground traversed by the county boundary on the west side of the hundred, rather than a reference to a specific mountain.

Rhiwsǣte is an item in a line of *-sǣte* names extending along Offa's Dyke from the R. Wye in Herefordshire to Oswestry. These are mapped and discussed in M. Gelling, *The West Midlands in the Early Middle Ages* (1992). They may result from an administrative reorganisation of this belt of territory at the time of the building of the Dyke.

The history of the hundred is set out in VCH pp.178-81. (All references to VCH in this section of the place-name survey are to Vol. VIII except where otherwise stated).

Alberbury with Cardeston

Alberbury ('manor-house of a woman named Aluburg') and Cardeston ('Card's estate') are discussed in Part 1.

The parish is divided into the townships of Alberbury, Amaston, Benthall, Braggington, Cardeston, Eyton, Ford-in-Alberbury, Hayes, Loton, Rowton, Little Shrawardine and Wattlesborough; and the map on p.188 of VCH, reproduced here on p. 17, shows the areas of these. (Great Wollaston, included on the VCH map, is here treated as a separate parish).

1. ALBERBURY (SJ 358144)

ALBERBURY CASTLE, probably built by Fulk Fitz Warin III in early 13th (VCH 196). ALBERBURY PRIORY, *La Novele Abbeye - - - pres de Alberburs, en le boschage sur la rivere de Sauverne* c.1320 FFW, *New Abbey by Alburbury* 1356 Pat, *Nova Abbia* 1390 Pat. For names used after the dissolution *v.* White Abbey *infra.* BOOT PLANTATION, shaped like a boot. DEER PARK, *Loton Park* 1842 *TA, Ye Park* 1716 PR(H) 6. VCH 184 says that the part of this park which lies S. of the road from Alberbury to Coedway corresponds roughly with the area of an earlier wood called *Rew Wood*, for which *v.* f.ns. The portion N. of the road, in Loton township, was probably formed in early 18th when the Leighton family moved from Wattlesborough to Loton Hall. LOWER WOOD, 1836 OS, *The Lower Wood* 1657, 17th PR(H) 6. This was near *Alberbury Wood*, which was enclosed in 16th (VCH 183). PARK LODGE, *v.* Deer Park *supra.* RED ABBEY, 1836 OS, a short distance S.W. of White Abbey. ROCK PLANTATION, 1842 *TA, Upper Rock* 1836 OS. SUNNYBANK. WHITE ABBEY, 1836 OS, *Album Monasterium by Albertbyri* c.1540 Leland, *Blacke Abbey* 1574-5 PR(H) 6, *Black Abbeye als. White Abbey* 1633 ib, *The Abey* 1656-7 ib, *White Abby* 1683 ib, *Black Abby* 1686 ib, *Ye Abby* 1688 ib. Alberbury Priory was a house of Grandmontine Monks founded by Fulk Fitz Warin III. The monks wore black habits. The account in VCH II, pp.47-50, says that the house was called New Abbey or Black Abbey in the Middle Ages, but was known as White Abbey, from the building stone, since Leland's time. References in parish registers indicate, however, that *Black Abbey* and *White Abbey* alternated throughout the 17th.

Field-Names

Forms in (a) are 1842 *TA*. Earlier forms for which no source is given are PR(H) 7, except for those dated 1500, which are *VCH*. Some of the 1500 names are furlongs.

(a) Abbey Fd (near Red Abbey *supra*); Alders; The Banks; Beggars Bank; Big Fd; Black Mdw; Bradys Fd, Far and Near; Brickkiln Mdw and Pce, Far Brickkiln Fd; Brickyard, Middle and Upper; Britch, - Mdw (*v.* **bryce**); Broomhill;

Calves Lsw and Mdw; Castle Garden; Close (3); Close beyond the Park; Big Clover Pce; Coppice Pce; Corner Pce; Cow Pasture, Far, Lower and Upper - -; Crabtree Lsw and Pce; Croft (*freq*); Crow Wall; Davies's Mdw; Dukes Mdw; Eight Days Math (meadow by R. Severn); Eyton Fd and Mdw (adjoining Eyton township); Far Pasture; Far Patch; Ferny Bank; Fold (3); Fourteen Acres; Gallants Lane and Pce; Garden (*freq*); Garden by Paddock; Garden Pce; Gittins Pce; Gorse Cover; Green Fd; Gritty Flg (this and Sour Butts *infra* are in the area of a common field called Cross Fd mentioned VCH 186); Harries's Mdw; Hoops, Far and Near; Jones's Yd; Lambs Well; Limepit Lsw; Upper Limetree Lsw; Little Mdw; Loton Garden, Lawn and Park; Loton Lime Rock; Lower Ground; Meadow (*freq*); Middle Fd; Moat (near Alberbury Priory); Mug Ground, Far - -; Near Mdw (2); Near Patch; New Drain; New Lsw; New Mdw; Oak Lsw; Olive Bank; Orchard (*freq*); Orchard Fd; Osiers; Oval Pltn in Park; Paddock (2); Park Pool and Island; Perkins Lsw; Piece between Roads; Piggs Pce; Plantation (*freq*); Pltn adjoining Lawn; Pltn by Boundary; Pltn on Lime Rock; Pltn open to Park; Pool Fd (pools shown on *TAMap*); Potato Patch; Pound Pce (2); Powells Pce; Pwll (a small stream running into the Severn, *Pulth Brook* 1585 *VCH*, Welsh **pwll** 'pool'); Rough, - on Road Side; Round Pltn; Rue Fd (*Rye Feeld* 1597 *VCH*, *Rue Feild* 1664 *ib*, said VCH 185 to be a common field, but only a small area on *TAMap*, *v.* *Rywood* in (b)); Lower Ryegrass; Sandhole (2); Sandy Bank; School Pce; Severne Mdw; Shop Lsw (no building marked on *TAMap*); Shrubberies; Smiths Mdw (2); Sour Butts; Stable Pce; Stackyard, - Fd; Stone Quarry; Turnpike House and Lsw (*Turnpike House* 1780, on the Shrewsbury road); Upper Patch; Webbs Lsw and Wood; White Fd; Yard.

(b) *Birches* 16th VCH 183 (apparently near Britch in (a), perhaps the same name); *Bradmed* 1232 Eyton ('broad meadow', VCH 206 says on the boundary of Alberbury and Eyton townships); *Broke Forlong* 1500 (*v.* **brōc**); *Bryn a Coone* 1664 *VCH* (a Welsh name, perhaps 'hill of the dogs'); *The Casting, The Quisting* 1500; *County Brook* 1810; *Cover Wood* 1765; *Cross Field* 1593 *VCH* (a common field, there is a reference 1652 *VCH* to a cross in this field); *Dadenhill* 1500; *Drakewood* 1758 ('dragon wood', *v.* **draca**); *The Fescan* 1780; *Field House* 1782; *The Folly* 1759, *The Folley* 1776 (*v.* **folie**); *The Haugh* 16th VCH 183 (*v.* **halh**); *The Held, Held Cop* 1500 (*v.* **helde**, **copp**); *The Hollowey, Holoweys Brink* 1500; *The Limekiln Bank* 1774; *The Marsh* 1500; *Mecisson* 1666; *Moorgate* 1500; *Rew Wood* 1539 *VCH, Rye Wood* 1597 *VCH, Rywood* 1614, *Ryewood* 1624, *The Reewood* 1656, *Rue Wood* c.1660 *VCH, Ree Wood* 1667, *Rie Wood* 1720 *VCH, The Rea Wood* 1754 *VCH* (Rue Fd in (a) may be abbreviated from Ruewood Field: VCH 178 suggests association with the DB hundred-name *Ruesset*, discussed *supra*: the *Rue-*, *Rew-* spellings support this, but the *Rye-*, *Ree-*, *Rea-* ones do not, and in the absence of ME spellings the etymology is best left open: the position of the wood is shown on the map in VCH, p.182); *The Sheppoles* 1500; *Sidwall Gate* 1500; *Vernylie* 1500 VCH 183 (*v.* **fearn**, **lēah**); *Ye Vroughes* 1768; *Wilesyarde, Willsyate* 1649; *The Winding* 1500.

2. AMASTON (SJ 378112)

The township-name, which means 'Ēanbald's estate', is discussed in Part **1**. An additional spelling is *Emboldeston* 1208 SAS 2/X (FF).

GRANGE FM, ORCHARD FM. These lie close together in the vicinity of *Wollaston Farm* 1848 *TA*. This last represents the settlement of Little Wollaston, for which *v.* Part **1**. HAYFORD FM, *Heyford* 1348 InqMisc, *Hafod Farm, Homestead and Mill* 1848 *TA*. A road crosses a stream here. OE **Hēgford*, 'hay ford', perhaps misinterpreted in 19th as Welsh *hafod* 'summer dwelling'. VCH p.192 says the place is recorded in 1281, when there was a mill and a single farm, and these are the assets recorded in 1348. HEATH FM probably represents the settlement of Amaston, *v.* Part **1**. ROUGH BURROWS, *Rough and Smooth Burrows, Rough Burrows Meadow* 1848 *TA*, referring to rabbits.

Field-Names

Forms in (a) are 1848 *TA*.

(a) Badleys, East, Great, Little and West (*Badlees* 1537 VCH 185, *Badlee, -lie* 1625-34 PR(H) 6); Barnyard, Lower and Upper; Barnyard Fd; Bog Side, East and West; Briery Bank; Brook Flg; Broomy Lsw; Calves Yd (2); Cockshut Bank (*v.* ***cocc-sciete**); Cooks Lsw; Cow Pasture; Crabtree Lsw; Croft (*freq*); Crow Wood, Big and Little, Crow Wood Croft; Deep Ditches, Further and Hither; East Croft; The Feg, Feg Cover, Big, Little, Lower and Upper Feg (dialect *feg* 'long, rank grass', the names are spread over a wide area and Feg may have been a district-name); Firtree Pce; Fishpond Lsw (by the brook which forms the N. boundary of the township); Flat Lsw; Further Croft; Further Lsw; Further Leys; Golden Lsw; Groves, Far, Near and Little; Hamsleys, Big and Little (perhaps *Ambashegh'* c.1380 *SBL 6172*, the correct reading may be *Ambasliegh'* but is not *-lyegh* as in VCH 185; the early name is 'enclosure' or 'clearing of Amaston', with *-ton-* dropped from the compound, *v.* **(ge)hæg, lēah**); Heath Ground, Lsw and Wood; Home Croft (by Amaston Fm); Horleys, Lower and Upper (*Horleys* 1703 *SBL 6042*); Horse Pce; James's Square (a square field); Kiln Croft; Long Lsw; Millers Croft, East and West; Mill Mdw, North and South (by Hayford Mill); Moor Meadow (*More Meadow* 1637 PR(H) 6, *v.* **mōr**); Morris's Pce, Big and Little; Near Lsw, Big and Little; Park Fd, East and West (by Cardeston Park); Pit Lsw; Rail Yd; Rogers Piece, Far and Near; Rough Chambers; Round Wood; Rushy Coppice and Mdw; Ryegrass Fd and Pce; Slang (a comparatively narrow field); Spout Mdw (*v.* **spoute** 'mouth of a water-pipe'); Wainhouse Mdw ('cart-house'); Walters Lsw; Well Mdw; West Croft; Wet Mdw (2); White Fd; White Lsw.

(b) *Ambaston Wode* c.1380 *SBL 6172* (*v.* **wudu**); *Espe Field* 1634 VCH 186 (said to be a common field near Little Wollaston, probably **æspe,** Mercian *espe*, 'aspen'); *Stocketlond'* c.1380 *SBL 6172* (*v.* ***stoccett** 'place with tree-stumps').

3. BENTHALL (SJ 394139)

The township-name, which means 'bent-grass nook', is discussed in Part 1.

Field-Names

Names in (a) are 1842 *TA*.

(a) Barn Pce; Barretts Fd (adjoins Shrawardine township, *v.* S. f.ns. *infra*); Big Mdw; Close; Coppice; Dovehouse Yd; Flog Moor, Long - - (probably *flag*, used of marsh plants); Footway Lsw; Garden; Hollands; Horse Pasture; Long Lsw; Long Moor; Middle Fd; New Lsw; New Mdw; Orchard; Paddock (2) (cf. *Ye Paddock* 1776 PR(H) 7); Patches; Plantation; Severne Pasture, Near - -; Shirkleg (*Shirtley Furlong* 1646 VCH 186); Shrawardine Fd (by Little Shrawardine); Smithy Fd (*Smythfild* 1463 *SBL 127*, *Smithyfielde* 1612 PR(H) 6, *Smithy Filds* 1682 ib, *v.* **smiððe**, no building is shown on *TAMap*); Stocks Fd, Little - - (see Eyton township); Stych Mdw (perhaps referring to hurdles, *v.* PN Berks 907, it is a large field); Towns Fd; White Fd.

4. BRAGGINGTON (SJ 333137)

Braginton 1255 Pat *et freq* to 1610 PR(H) 6, *Bragyntone* 1289 Swin, *-ton* Hy 6 *SBL 6173*, *Bragginton* 1651 PR(H) 6
Bragyton 1322 Pat
Bregington 1682 PR(H) 6, *Breginton* 1695 Morden
Bragington 1752 *SBL 6253*, *Braggington* 1842 *TA*

This is almost certainly an **-ingtūn** formation, perhaps with a Welsh personal name as base. There is no OE name or word which would suit.

The history of the former hamlet is traced in VCH, p.192.

BRAGGINGTON HALL was built in 1675.

Field-Names

Names in (a) are 1842 *TA*.

(a) Ash Coppice; Bank Fd, Great and Little (Bank 1836 OS); Brick Mdw; Bridleway Pce; Coalpit Coppice (19th cent. OS shows the Coppice and also Coal Pits, see VCH 211 for an account of the "somewhat desultory" coal-mining at the N.W. end of the Hanwood Coalfield); Cockshutt Mdw (*v.* ***cocc-scīete**); Cowhouse Mdw; Cow Lsw, Upper; Croft (several); Dingle; Gorsty Bank, Big and Little; Green Fd; Hoar Lsw and Mdw, Far Hoar Lsw (perhaps preserving the first element of an earlier 'hoar-stone' name, the fields are on the township boundary); Lady Fd (*v.* **hlǣfdige**); Middle Fd; Mill Mdw; Old House Lsw; Olive Mdw; Ox Pasture; Paddock; Patch; Ryegrass Fd; Big Shade Lsw and Mdw, Little Shady Fd; Sheepcote Lsw; Shotton Mdw, Upper Shotton (the farm called Shotten is in the salient of Montgomeryshire which lies E. of Braggington); Vetches Lsw.

5. CARDESTON (SJ 395123)

Cardeston, 'Card's estate', is discussed in Part 1. The civil parish was united with that of Alberbury in 1886. As depicted on the *TAMap* of 1847, Cardeston consisted of three separate areas. One of these included the greater part of Wattlesborough township, and another lay in a loop of the R. Severn, N. of Hayes. For the purposes of this study, the Wattlesborough land has been dealt with under that township, but the land by the Severn (which was probably ancient detached meadow) has been treated as part of Cardeston.

CARDESTON PARK, *Cardiston Park* 1847 *TA.* VCH 185 says the park to which the house-name refers was formed before 1374, and (204) that it may have replaced an earlier enclosure described as 'old park' in 1379. HEATH FM is *Upper Farm* 1847 *TA, Heath Meadow* and *Great Heath* being adjacent fields. LORD'S PLANTATION occupies one of three fields called *Lords Meadow* 1847 *TA*, in the detached land by the Severn.

Field-Names

Forms in (a) are 1847 *TA.* Those in (i) are in the area surrounding the hamlet of Cardeston, those in (ii) are in the detached land in a loop of the R. Severn. Early forms dated 1379 are *SBL 6172.* VCH 186 gives information about open fields called *Edge Field* and *Whiston Field.*

(a) (i) Ash Tree Lsw; Bake House; The Bank, The Far -; Banky Fd, Far Banky Pce; Barn Yd; Big Lsw; Bridge Patch (by a bridge); Brook Furlong; Brook Lsw; Broomy Croft; Broomy Lsw, Little - -; Calves Croft; Calves Patch; The Chircles; Cockshutt Mdw (*v.* **cocc-scīete**); Coppice, Lower and Upper; Corbetts Crofts; Cow Lsw; Croft; Cuckoos Nest (a very small field on S. boundary of township, cf. *Kucoacre* 1379, perhaps originally a literal reference to the bird, but *cuckoo* often has fanciful meanings in f.ns. as in the later name here); Deal Yd (perhaps *dial*, i.e. sundial); Far Lsw; The Far Yd (2); Field Pce; Flat Mdw; The Furlongs (these are furlong-shaped fields on the Cardeston/ Westbury boundary, VCH 186 says *Black Furlong* e.17th lay here); Garden; Glen Park (2 fields S.E. of the village); Gorsty Lsw; Grass Lsw, Great and Little; Green Fd; Green Yd; Gully Patch; The Hill; Hockley Lsw, Hockleys Crofts (*Hockley* 1774 PR(H) 7, Foxall's Gazetteer notes Hockley Cottages as a modern name); Hoggins Lane, Far and Near Hoggins Lsw; Inclosure; Jockey Lsw; Lady Croft (*v.* **hlǣfdige**); Leasow, Big, Long and Lawrences; The Leasows; Limerock Pce and Waste (by Quarry Lsw *infra*); Little Mdw; Little Yd; Long Lsw; Long Mdw; Long Pce; Long Slang (a narrow field); Lower Farm (the field is ½ mile

N.W. of Upper Farm, see Heath Fm *supra*, 6" map shows a large building-complex here); Lower Pce; The Meadow (by the village); Middle Pce; New Lsw; The Moors, Moors Mdw; Morris's Yd; Near Bank; New Garden; Orchard Pce; Park Side (*v.* Cardeston Park *supra*); Patch (*freq*, the term for the smallest enclosures); Patch along Road; The Pools (on either side of a stream); Preeces Fd, Mdw and Patch; Quarry Lsw (by Old Quarries on 6", fields called Rocks on *TAMap* occupy the site of the quarries); Road Pce; Rough Lsw, Near - -; Rowley (by Upper Fm, probably *Roulow(e)* 1379, *v.* **rūh**, **hlāw**); Shed Patch; Slang (a narrow field); Squire Lsw; Swan's Nest, Big and Little (in the bend of a brook); Turnpike Pce; Upper Fm (*v.* Heath Fm *supra*); Upper Park; Warrings Lsw; Weir Lsw; Well Mdw; Well Yd; Wet Mdw (*Wetemedwe* 1379, *v.* **wēt**, **mǣd**); Whistone Lsw (not adjacent to Whistone in Ford-in-Alberbury); Wigwall.

(ii) Barn Pce; Boathouse Pce; Bridge Lsw; Burrow Bank; Buskillian Bank; Butchers, Great and Little; Clemley Park (*v.* PN Ch **3**, 47, where a number of examples of this and related names in Ch and Db are discussed, with the suggestion that the base is an OE ***clǣme** 'muddy place', there is another example in Yockleton *infra* and (The) Clemley occurs in Acton Pigott and Harnage); Coppice; Hoggins, Great and Little; House Pce; Hunt Pce; Little Mdw; Maes Issa, Great and Ceverne (*Maes Issa* 1655 VCH 199, Welsh 'lower field', *Ceverne* from R. Severn); Moor Mdw; The Perches (a very small field by Clemley Park); The Ridges (a large field, perhaps named from plough ridges); Rushy Lsw; Shafty Kerring (*v.* Hayes f.ns. *infra*); Squires Mdw; Slang (a narrow field); Stocking Bank (*v.* ***stocking**); Waste Bog (a small area in the large field called Stocking Bank); Wernog Gornys (a Welsh n., first el. *gwern* 'alder swamp'); Wet Mdw, Far and Near.

(b) *Le Bruche* 1379 (*v.* **bryce**); *Haderug'* 1379 (possibly 'heath ridge'); *Le Knill* 1379 (*v.* **cnyll**); *Longmoor Brook* 17th (VCH 224 says this was the n. of Cardeston Brook); *Lynacresende* 1379 (*v.* **līn**, **æcer**, **ende**); *Le Mullepole* 1379 ('mill pool'); *Pechemedwe* (*v.* **mǣd**, first el. possibly a surname).

6. EYTON (SJ 377140)

The township-name, which means 'island settlement', is discussed in Part 1.

EYTON GORSE (a wood). Two areas of woodland called *Lower Woods* and *Green Woods* occupy this space on *TAMap*. VCH 184 identifies the place with *Ley Gors* 13th, and suggests that it is a surviving remnant of medieval woodland. *v.* **lēah, gors(t).**

STOCKSFIELD. A hamlet here is believed to be the second manor of *Etune* listed in DB (VCH 191). The place is called *Eytonstok* 1276 Cl, *Le Stockes* 13th VCH 191, *Eyton Stokkes* 1376 Pat. It is *Stokkes Fild* 1463 *SBL 127 et seq* with a variety of spellings (*Stocksfilde, Stoksfield, Stookfield, Stockesfild, Stockfild, Ye Stocks-Field*). *v.* **stoc** 'dependent settlement', perhaps later associated with *stock* 'tree-stump'.

Field-Names

Forms in (a) are 1842 *TA*.

(a) Abbey Lsw, Far - - (near Alberbury Priory); Appletree Lsw; Beavens Pce; Big Pce (2); Bridleway Pce; Broom Hill, Lower and Upper; Burnt House Pce; Chapel Bank; Cop Tree Hill, Long - - -; Cow Pasture, Lower and Upper; Croft (*freq*); Great Ditches, Upper Lower Ditches (N.E. of the village, perhaps indicating earthworks of a larger settlement); Embreys Pce; Ferny Bank; The Flats, Little Flats (adjacent, furlong-shaped fields, *flats* probably used of strips in a field-system); Gallantry Bank (probably 'gallow tree'); Garden; Gorsty Lsw (by Eyton Gorse, *supra*); Hunger Hill (probably inferior land); Lady Fd (*v.* **hlǣfdige**); Leasow; The Leys (*Eyton's Leyes* c.1549 VCH 184, *v.* **lēah**, this adjoins Woods *infra*); Limekiln Fd, Lower and Upper; Little Fd; Lockleys, Lower and Upper; The Meadow (a tiny field on the E. boundary of the township); Netchells Lsw, - Mdw, - Severne Mdw (3 separate fields, probably from a surname); New Lsw; Oak Mdw; Orchard; Ox Pasture; The Parks (a field of equivalent size to its neighbours); Park Mdw (adjoins preceding); Patch; Patch by side of Road; Pleck (Pleck and Patch are tiny adjoining fields on the village edge); Rye Corner; Severne Mdw (2); Westmoor, Little - (other parts of the 'west marsh' are in Little Shrawardine township); Wet Mdw; Woods, Green, Little, Lower, Middle and Upper (these occupy and adjoin the area of Eyton Gorse *supra*, VCH 183-4 defines Eyton Wood as occupying the northern part of the township, it is *Eyton's Wood* 1612 PR(H) 6); Woodmoor Coppice and Mdw ('wood marsh', in the area of Eyton Wood, VCH 184 says this was granted to Alberbury Priory in 13th, the Coppice is named 1833 OS).

7. FORD-IN-ALBERBURY

The discrepancy between the area of the civil parish of Ford and the ancient township is explained in VCH, p.223. The township, which was larger than the parish, included an area west of Ford village which was in the parish of Alberbury, and this is treated here as a township of Alberbury.

BENTHALL CROSS, BENTHALL STONE FM. This is a road junction at which a road to Benthall (*supra*) leaves the Shrewsbury/Alberbury road. VCH 225 says that the base of a sandstone cross was formerly known as Maiden Cross, and this name occurs as *The Maidens Cross* 1796 *SBL 1374*. In 1848 *TA* the cross is called *Benthall Stone*, and *Maidens Cross* is shown twice as the name of fields on either side of the road. BENTHALL STONE FM is shown on *TAMap*, but not named; *Benthall Stone Piece* is adjacent to *Maidens Cross* on the S. of the road. BROADWAY, FAR and NEAR, *Broadway* (a house) 1848 *TA*. BURD'S COPPICE, from a 19th-cent. owner of Whiston Priory (VCH 224-5). COPPY HO, 1699 VCH 228, *Coppice House* 1836 OS, 1848 *TA*. CROSSGATES P.H., *Cross Gates* 1848 *TA*. This is ½ mile E. of Benthall Cross. There was a railway station called Ford and Crossgates. VCH 227 says the inn was so called in 17th cent. DODLEE, *Close called Dodz Lee* 1601 *SBL 12706, Dolley* 1721 PR(H) 6, *Dodley* 1796 *SBL 1374, Doddlee Corner* 1847 *TA, Dodlee* (a house), *-Piece, East Dodlee Close* 1848 *TA*. LONGMORE COTTAGE. WHISTON COTTAGES, FM, PRIORY and VILLA, *The Whistones, Long -, Whistone Piece and Plantation, - Priory* 1848 *TA*. The house called W. Priory was built 1834-51 (VCH 225). Whiston Field was a common field. No early spellings have been noted, but the name may be 'white stone'.

Field-Names

Forms in (a) are 1848 *TA*.

(a) Annus Fd; Banky Lsw; The Beans Hill, Docky and Yewtree - -, Bean Sylt, Beans Hill (*Beanshull'* 1631 *SBL 11047, Beant Hills* 1796 *SBL 1374*, a common field, VCH 225 says alias Deepdale, which is *Depz Dale* 1601 *SBL 12706*, the hill and dale are both slight, Sylt represents Welsh pronunciation); Big Mdw (2); Birchley Mdw (VCH 224 says Birchley Coppice is recorded a.1272, 'birch wood'); Breeches Mdw (*v.* **brēc**); Brickkiln Fd; Brooks Furlong (two fields probably enclosed from Whistones common field); Brook Lsw; Clover Fd; Cockpit Lsw (by Crossgates P.H.); Common, Far and Near; Common Land (*freq*); Coppice Bank, Lsw, Pce (all S. of Coppy Ho); Cottage Pce, Big and Little; Cow Pasture (several); Dukes Camp (a large field S. of Coppy Ho); Evans Mdw; Far Common; Far Lsw; Far Mdw; Far Pce; Flat Lsw; Four Turning Patch (by a crossroads); Fox Croft; Garden (*freq*); Garden Fd; Gorsy Ground, Big and Little; Half Lsw (two fields); Hog More (*Hogamores* 1796 *SBL 1374*, 'hog marsh'); Howells Patch; Lawn (a large field by Whiston Priory); Leechmoor, Little - (*The Three Letchmores* 1796 *SBL 1374*, a common minor place-name, from **mōr** and either **læcc** 'stream, bog' or **lǣce** 'leech'); Little Mdw (2); Long Parks (*Long Park Field* 1796 *SBL 1374*); Meadow (3); Middle Pce; Near Common; Near Lsw; New Pce, Far, Near, Middle and Gough's; Novers Bank, Rough and Tenement (*The Novers* 1764 PR(H) 7, *Novers* 1791 ib, the 250' contour runs along the Severn here, the name is probably OE *æt þæm ofre* 'at the ridge', see Wentnor in Part I for a discussion of ***ofer**); Old House Lsw and Yd; Orchard; Piece by Jones's; Plantation (2); Potato Patch; Quancums, Quankhams (*Quonkerne* 1575 VCH 224, *The Quanquam* 1796 *SBL 1374*); Rough Pce; Rushy Fd; Sandy Lsw; Severne Pasture; Sidelong Patch (between a road and R. Severn); Slang (two adjacent narrow fields); Stone Horse Patch (i.e. stallion); Sytch Mdw (*v.* **sīc**); Wainhouse Fd ('waggon house'); Warings Coppice (for the Waring family *v.* VCH 231ff); White Gate Fd, Far and Near; Wood.

8. HAYES (SJ 352155)

The Haye 1278 Eyton, *Haya de Lockton'* 1291-2 *Ass, Le Hay* 1322 Pat
Hey 1381 Cl, 1430 Fine, *Heye* 1382, 1474 Cl, Hy 6 *SBL 6173*
The Hayes Farm 1770 *SBL 6203*

The earliest reference is in DB, where *una haia* is listed as a property of Loton. VCH 190 says that the 1278 reference in Eyton is the first to a settlement here. Probably Medieval Latin *haia* 'part of a forest fenced off for hunting', rather than OE **(ge)hæg** 'enclosure'. There was woodland on the S. bank of the R. Severn in this area.

VCH 190 suggests that *La Hope* e.13th, said to be in the field of Loton, was an earlier name for the settlement. **hop** is here used in the sense 'enclosure in waste or marsh'. The e.13th reference is from All Souls muniments. Richard *de Hope* witnesses a Rowton deed 1303 *SBL 75*.

Field-Names

Forms in (a) are 1842 *TA*. Names in (b) for which no date or source is given are c.1380 *SBL 6172*. Forms dated 1784 are from an unnumbered *SBL* document in the box numbered 6181-6241.

(a) Barn Lsw, Lower - -; Barnyard; Battlefield; Cote Lsw; Croft; Five Acres; Footway Pce (1784); Pentre Pce (*Pentry* - 1784, adjoins Pentre in Mont); Stable Pce; Weir Lsw and Mdw (*Wear Leasow* 1784, *Old Weir* 1836 OS).

(b) *Balesleyesbrok/* (*v.* **brōc**, from Bausley, Mont); *Corn Stubble or Greenfields* 1784; *Feggy Pce* 1784 (*feg* is coarse grass); *Fynchestockyng'* (*v.* **stoccing**, *Fynche* is probably a surname); *Green Pce* 1784; *Grontislond'*; *Hathorne* 1784 ('hawthorn'); *Hondelyegh'* (*v.* **lēah**); *House Pce* 1784; *Hugyneslye* (*v.* **lēah**)); *Hunts Pce* 1784; *Phybbestyle* (probably a surname plus 'stile'); *Rotelondesmor' als' voc' Merchyehessmore* (*v.* **mōr**, both first elements are probably surnames); *Rough Pce* 1784; *Rushy Pce* 1784; *Shafty Herrings* 1784 (corresponds to Shafty Kerring in Cardeston *TA*, on the boundary between Hayes and the detached Cardeston meadow-land).

9. LOTON (SJ 356147)

The township-name, which means 'lake settlement', is discussed in Part **1**.

PARTNER'S COPPICE. *Partons Ground* 1842 *TA*. THE WOOLLERS, 1836 OS, 'the alders', *v.* **alor**; *Aldery Leasow and Meadow* adjoin on *TAMap*, where the wood is called *Plantation*. THE SPAWNS, *Little Spawns* 1836 OS, *Spawns, Little Spawns, Spawns House* 1842 *TA*. VCH 186 says this is *Spone* 1599, so the source is probably **spōn** 'wood-shaving'.

Field-Names

Forms in (a) are 1842 *TA*.

(a) Aldery Lsw and Mdw (cf. The Woollers *supra*); Bare Mdw; Brook Fd; Calves Close; Cow Lsw; Davies's Mdw; Little Mdw; Loton Lawn (Loton Park is divided into three fields, each with this name, cf. Rowton Lawn *infra*); Lower Pasture; Meadow; Mill Mdw; New Tining (*v.* **tȳning** 'enclosure'); Paddock; Park Pce; Plantation (several); Round Mdw (by no means circular); Stockings (*v.* **stoccing**); Tining, Upper and Lower (not near New Tining, *q.v.*); Under Park (by Loton Park); Wall Croft (probably referring to the park enclosure); Well Mdw.

10. ROWTON (SJ 365124)

The township-name, which means 'settlement in rough ground', is discussed in Part **1**.

THE DAIRY, *Dairy Field* 1848 *TA*. ROWTON CASTLE, VCH 189 says that a motte-and-bailey castle stood on the site of the present house. SMITHY, *Smithy Field and Plantation* 1848 *TA*. SNOD COPPICE, 1848 *TA*, *wood called Le Snodde* 1318,19 Ipm. OE **snād** 'detached piece of woodland'. The regular development in a simplex name would be to *Snoad, but there can be little doubt of the etymology. SPRING COTTAGE. WINDMILL P.H., *Windmill Inn* 1848 *TA*.

Field-Names

Forms in (a) are 1848 *TA*. VCH 186 identifies open fields called *Quere Field* (*infra*), Bean Field and Snod Field (*v. supra*).

(a) Barnyard, Big and Little; Brand Yard (a triangular field, probably *brandart* 'trivet'); Clover Pce; Croft (*freq*); Cross Lsw (by a T-junction); Devil's Dream; Dogkennel Pce; Evans Pce; Garden (*freq*); Golden Croft; Griffiths Pce; Hoggins Lsw; Home Croft (by Windmill Inn); Johns Lsw; Further Leys; Limekiln Lsw (adjoins Lime- names in Alberbury township); Long Lsw; Millingtons Pce, Far, Near and Middle; Mount Pleasant (adjoins Devil's Dream *supra*); Near

Mdw; Orchard and Fishponds (by Rowton Castle); Outlet (a tiny croft in the village); Ox Croft and Lsw; Park Side; Peplows, Far, Near and Great (a surname from Peplow in Hodnet); Pinfold Mdw; Plantation (*freq*); Potato Croft; Poultry Yard; Towton Lane (in the park by Rowton Castle, VCH 184); Sandy Lsw; Sawyers Croft; Sheep Pasture, Lower and Upper; Shop Lsw, East, Middle and West; Stackyard; Well Pce; Yewtree Lsw.

(b) *Byshopes Orchard* c.1380 *SBL 6172*; *Dole Butt* 1737 *SBL 6527* (*v.* **dāl, butte**); *More Medwe* c.1380 *SBL 6172* (*v.* **mōr, mǣd**); *Park Lee* 1375 VCH 184 (*v.* **lēah**, an assart by the park); *Quere Field* 15th VCH 186 (an open field, probably belongs to the class of f.ns. referring to the upkeep of the church, in which choir - i.e. chancel - often appears as *Quere, Quire*); *Shertfforlong'* c.1380 *SBL 6172* ('short furlong').

11. SHRAWARDINE (LITTLE) SJ 393151

The township-name is discussed in Part 1, in the article on Great Shrawardine, which is a parish on the N. bank of the R. Severn.

WEIR HOUSE, 1833 OS.

Field-Names

Forms in (a) are 1842 *TA*. VCH 186 says that the common fields, *Little Field, Cross Field* and *Barrett Field* (*Le Barret Feild* 1635 *SBL 152*) were enclosed by agreement c.1636.

(a) Bank (2); Banky Green; Barn Fd; Big Lsw; Boat Lsw and Mdw (by R. Severn, *boat* in the sense 'ferry'); Bound Mdw; Broad Lsw; Calves Croft; Docky Lsw; Garden (3); Green, Far and Near; Middle Lsw; Mount Fd; Westmoor, Flat, Further, Lower, Middle and Near; Wet Mdw; White Acre; Withy Mdw.

12. WATTLESBOROUGH SJ 355126

The township-name, which means 'Wæcel's fort', is discussed in Part **1**.

BRETCHEL

Bradeshull' 1220 Cur *et freq* with variant spellings *-hull(e)* to 1430 Fine, *Magna Bradeshull'* 1291-2 *Ass, Great Braddeshill* 1474 Cl
Bredeshull 1242 SAS 4/VI (FF) *et freq* with variant spellings *-hul(e)* to c.1388 *SBL 6172*
Parva Prechhill (*sic*) 1534 BM, *Brechill Parva* 1617 PR(H) 6, *Bretchell* 1644 ib, *Little Brechell* 1671 ib, *Brechil* 1778 PR(StA) I
Little Brichell 1658 PR(H) 6, *Brichell* 1660 ib, *Britchel* 1800 ib
Brichall 1664 PR(H) 6, *Brichhale* 1668-9 ib, *Brichnoll* 1676 ib, *Little Brichhall* 1677 ib

Probably a compound of **hyll** with a pers.n. *Brægd* occurs in Breaston and Breadsall in Db, and this may be the name we have here. The material set out in PN Db 430-1 and 539 shows, however, that while *Brades-, Bredes-* are well-represented from the early 13th cent. on, spellings such as *Braides-, Breides-* are to be expected in addition to those, and such spellings have not been found for Bretchel. A name *Brǣd* might be postulated as a side-form of the recorded *Brāda*.

VCH 192 speaks of Great and Little Bretchel, but only one large farm has the name Bretchel on OS maps.

DOVASTON PLANTATION, *Dovaston Patch and Ground* 1847 *TA*, the actual wood is *Plantation* on *TAMap.* THE HOLE, this farm is *Lower Stanford* 1842 *TA, v. infra.* IVYEND (a house), *Ivy End* 1847 *TA.* POUND, *Pound Corner and Piece* 1847 *TA.* STAG'S HEAD, *Nags Head* 1675 Ogilby, 1847 *TA.* STANFORD, *Stursford* 1609 PR(H) 6, *Stanford* 1610 ib, 1752 *SBL 6482, Little Stanford* 1738 PR(H) 7, *Stamford* 1758 ib, *Lower Stanford* 1842 *TA.* The ford was perhaps a causeway over wet ground rather than a crossing-place on the tiny stream near The Hole. 'Stone ford', a common name. Lower Stanford is shown as a small township on the 19th cent. 1" map. WATTLESBOROUGH HALL, 1833 OS, the building is described in VCH 197-8. W. HEATH, *Wattlesbro Heath formerly presented as Kings Marsh, Wattlesbro Heath or Rosse y Drevreth* 1583-4 *VCH, Ye Heath* 1662 PR(H) 6, *Watleburgh Heath* 1675 Ogilby, *Kings Marsh* 1705 *SBL 6042.* The Welsh name in **ros** has an obscure qualifying element. VCH 193 says the Heath was enclosed c.1780, and the settlement along the Welshpool road probably dates from then. W. LAWNS, 1847 *TA*, a group of fields, probably an enclosed park. W. PLANTATION. WINDMILL FM, *Ye Windmill* 1668 PR(H) 6, *Windmill* 1847 *TA.* VCH 210 says the mill was called 'Many Fingers' in 1579.

Field-Names

Forms in (a) are 1842 and 1847 *TA*. The 1847 *TA* is for Cardeston, and the treatment of names in that award is explained under Cardeston *supra.* The area surrounding Lower Stanford (The Hole) is shown on an 1842 award. Most of Wattlesborough and Bretchel lay in the civil parish of Cardeston, which explains the discrepancy in the *TA*s.

(a) Aldery Fd (cf. Aldery ns. in Loton); Ash Coppice (2); Backhouse Fd (possibly 'bakehouse'); Balls Pce; Bank Pce; Bank Yd; Banky Patch; Barley Fd; Barn Lsw; - Patch; - Pce; - Yd; Big Lsw (2); Big Pce; Bowling Green; Brick Kiln; - - Fd; Brickkiln Lsw; Brick Mdw; Broad Mdw (*Brademedwe* 1242 SAS 4/VI (FF), *v.* **brād, mǣd**); Brook Fd; Calves Close; - Croft; Cherry Orchard; Close; Closure; Clover Lsw; Coal Pit Bank, Coppice, Patch and Pce (cf. Braggington f.ns.); Cockshutt Lsw (*v.* **cocc-sciete**); The Common; Common Fd; - Patch; Coppice; Coppy Mdw; Counds Fd; Cow Pasture; Crabtree Pce; Cunneries, Far and Near (rabbit warrens, *v.* **coninger**); Dove House Croft; Daisy Mdw; Everlasting (one of a group of small fields, the others have unremarkable ns.); Fair Place Pce, Heath Fair Place (cf. Market Pce *infra*); Far Close; Far Lsw; Far Mdw; Far Pce; Fegg (2) (coarse grass); Finger Post Pce; Fish Pool Pce; Five Acres; The Flakes (perhaps a reference to flax, this and Long Ridges adjoin each other by Lower Stanford; they look like enclosed furlongs); Flower Garden; Fold (3); Foot Road Pce; Foxholes, Far, Middle and Near; Ganders Patch; Garden Mdw; Gorsty Fd (*v.* ***gorstig**); - Yd; Gravel Hole Pce; Green Fd; Guide Post Fd (across the road from Finger Post Pce); Hardens Furlong; Heath Pce; House Close; - Fd; - Pce; Lane Lsw; Little Mdw (*freq*); Little Wood; Long Lsw;

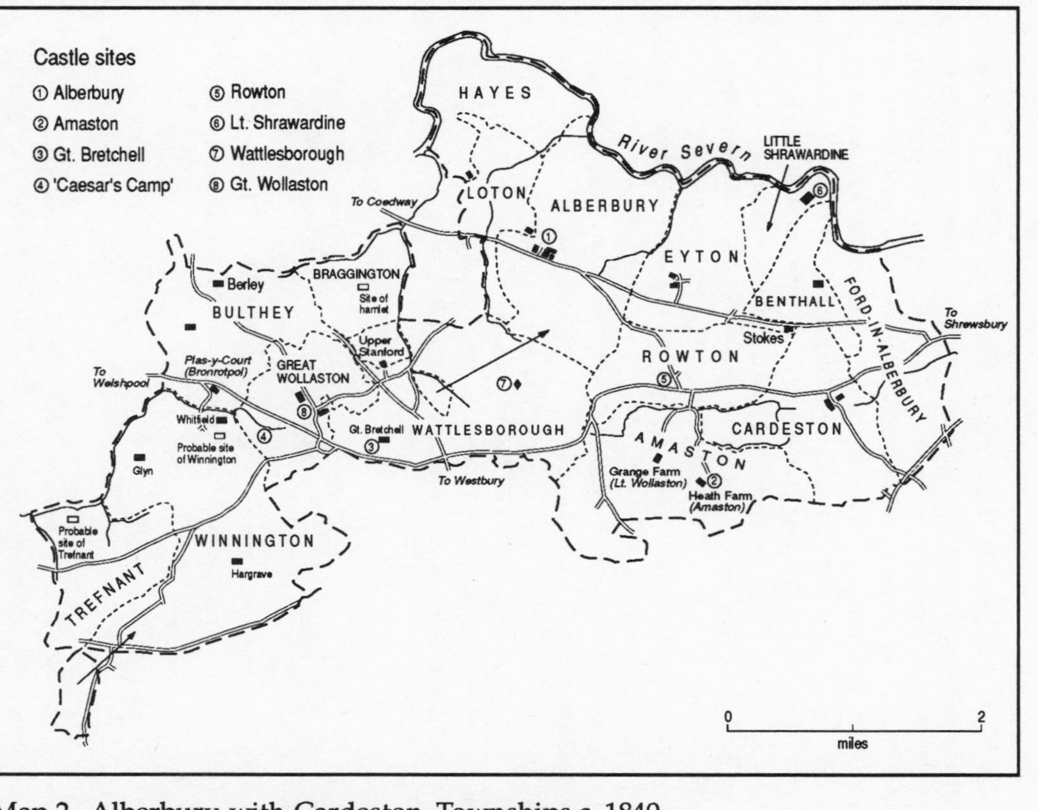

Map 2 Alberbury-with-Cardeston, Townships c. 1840
(Based on tithe apportionments and maps, 1840-8)

- Mdw (2); - Ridges (*v.* The Flakes *supra*); Lunns Mdw; Malthouse Pce; Market Pce (2, VCH 211 says that until 1857 a fair was held annually in the Market Pce S.E. of Wattlesborough Hall; *TAMap* shows a second Market Pce N.W. of this and also Fair Place Pce on the Welshpool road); Mauls Mdw; Middle Fd; - Mdw; - Patch; - Pce; Millards Lsw; Mount Pleasant; Muncorn Fd (a mixture of wheat and rye); Near Fd; Near Mdw; Newfound Well; Nut Patch; Orchard Patch; Over Yd; Ox Lsw; Ox Mdw; Paddock, Far -; Pant Lees, Nether and Further (by a small stream); Patch (*freq*); Pearces Patch; Pecknall Fd (Pecknall is in Mont); Phillips Pce; Piece before the Door (2); Piece by Numps; Plovers Patch; Pool Mdw; Pool Pce; Potato Patch; Pound Pce and Corner; Pritchard's Yd; Red Heart (several fields adjoining a building); Road Pce; Roundabout (there are roads on two sides); Round Pce (adjoins preceding, and is entirely enclosed by roads); Rye Grass; Slad (probably here a patch of ground too wet to plough); Slang (several, all narrow strips); Square Patch (3); - Pce (2); Stackyard Pce (2); Taques Patch and Mdw; (The) Triangle (3); Well Fd (2); - Mdw; - Patch; Wern Mdw and Pce (Welsh *gwern* 'swamp'); Wet Stone Patch; Wigmore Fd (by Wigmore in Westbury); Wilde Rough (OE **wilde** 'uncultivated', as in Weald Moors); Williams Lsw; Windsors Patch.

(b) *Le Brode Pole* c.1380 *SBL 6172* (*v.* **brād**, **pōl**); *Hullesacres ib* (perhaps from a surname); *Kenalesmede ib* (probably 'meadow of the kennel'); *More Medwe ib* (*v.* **mōr**, **mǣd**); *Le Mot' de Bredeshull' ib* (VCH 198 equates this with the moated enclosure by Wattlesborough Hall);

Ford

The parish-name ('ford') is discussed in Part 1. From 1283-1807 the place was frequently referred to as *Fordesham*, later *Fordeshome*. Spellings are:

Fordesham 1283 Ipm, 1322 Fine, 1342 Pat, 1491 Ipm
Forthesham 1322 Pat
Fordeshome 1366 Cl *et freq* to 1807 *SBL 1695*, *-hom* 1409 Pat, *Foordshome* 1518 *SBL 86*, 1635 *SBL 151*, *Fowrdisholme* 1575 *SBL 68*, *Fordshome* 1613 *SBL 6814*
Ford als Fordeshome 1601 *SBL 12706*, 1699 *SBL 87*, *Ford or Fordhome* 1772 *SBL 1134*, *Ford otherwise Fordshome* 1807 *SBL 1691*

In many of these references, the *-ham, -home* forms refer specifically to the manor. The 1283 inquisition gives an extent of the manor of *Fordesham* in which reference is made to the township of *Forde.* The longer name was probably not an alias, though perceived as such in 17th and 18th cents. The manor of Ford differed in extent from the township, as is noted under Ford-in-Alberbury *supra,* and a need may have been felt for a name which took account of this discrepancy. The addition is **hām**, one of the OE senses of which was 'manor'. There are other Sa instances of this usage: Astley Abbots is *Asteleyhome* 1429,30 Fine, and Worfield is *Worfeldhome* Eliz *SBL MS292, Worfield Home* 1699 PR(L) 8. It does not appear to have been noted in other counties, however.

FORD HEATH, *Ford's-Heath* 1747 PR(H) 18, was earlier *Boscus de Espeleg', - de Aspel'* 1255-6 *Ass, Espele* 1272 Cl, *-leye* 1308 Ipm. 'Aspen wood', *v.* **æspe**, **lēah**. There is another instance in Espley in Hodnet. VCH 248 says that 'Aspley Wood' was the name of Ford Heath until the 16th cent., and that Gough's Coppice (*infra*) is a remnant of the wood.

SHOOT HILL, 1785 PR(H) 7, 1808 PR(H) 1, SHOOTHILL FM. Cf. *La Shute* 1271-2 *Ass* (p). OE ***scēot** 'steep slope', perhaps 'projecting hill'. The identification of the early form is not certain, as the full reference is to *Will. de La Shute de Albrythton',* and Albrighton is six miles N.E. of Ford. ***scēot** is rare in this area, however. A 13th-cent. *Serthul'* is identified with Shoot Hill in VCH 224, but this is much more likely to be Shorthill in Lea township, Pontesbury, *q.v.*

BUT LANE, BUTLANE HEAD, *Butt Lane* 1848 *TA, Buttlane Head* 1847 VCH 227. CHAVEL, *Chaville* 1776 VCH 227, *Chavil* 1783 PR(H) 7, *Chavel Field and Patch* 1848 *TA*, perhaps a name in **-feld**. CRUCKFIELD, 1848 *TA*, near the boundary with Cruckton. DINTHILL COTTAGE, adjoining Dinthill in Bicton. FAIRFIELD HOUSE. FORD HALL, HOUSE and VILLA. GOUGH'S COPPICE, *Moor Coppice* 1848 *TA*. KADER COTTAGE. Probably named from *Kittahoe Lane* 17th VCH 225, *Kit-y-hook, Kity Hook Piece, Kite Hook Piece* 1848 *TA, Kittyoak Lane* modern VCH 225. Cardeston Brook has a squiggly course here, and *hook* may refer to the stream-bends. MOOR HOUSE, 1672 VCH 228, 1836 OS, *v.* **mōr** and cf. f.ns. NED'S COPPICE, 1836 OS. NEW HOUSE. PAVEMENT GATES P.H., *Pavement Gate* 1796 *SBL 1374*, 1836 OS, - *Gates* 1848 *TA*. VCH 227 says the inn was so called in 17th cent. It is on the same road as Crossgates P.H. in Ford-in-Alberbury. It has now been renamed the Owen Glendower. TITHE BARN, see VCH 228. WELSHMAN'S FORD, 1836 OS, *Welshman's Foord* 1641-2 *SBL 155*, perhaps the stream-crossing from which Ford is named. *Welshman's Patch* 1848 *TA* is nearby. WHITE HOUSE.

Field-Names

Forms in (a) are 1848 *TA*. Earlier forms for which no date or source is given are 1796 *SBL 1374*. Those dated 1573 are *SBL 5952*, 1601 are *SBL 12706*.

(a) Ashtree Coppice; The Bank; Banky Lsw (2); Barn Pce; Barn Yd (6); Beans Hill (the fields with this name straddle the township boundary and are discussed under Ford-in-Alberbury); Big Fd; Big Lsw; Birch Hill; Black Mdw; Black Pce; Botany Bay (two fields on the bank of R. Severn); Brandart ('trivet', a triangular field); Breeches, Long, Lower and Upper, Breeches Mdw (*v.* **brēc**, probably in this case drained marshland); Brickkiln, - Fd, - Mdw (in different parts of the parish); Briery Lsw (2); Broad Lsw; Butcher Croft; Butchers Pce; Butt Land Pce (not near But Lane); The Bylett (the Sa term for islands in R. Severn formed by cutting channels for boats, but this field is not by the river); Cats Hill (VCH 225 says this is the name of the sand and gravel ridge on which the church stands, perhaps earlier *Catsbrain Hill, *v.* ***cattes-braȝen**); Clay Furlong; Clemson's Croft; Coppice Lsw; Coppice Pce, Far, Lower, Middle, Near and Upper; Corner Fd; Cow Lsw; Cow Pasture (8); Crabtree Pce; Croft (4); Crossgates Pce (not adjacent to Crossgates in Ford-in-Alberbury); Crow Mdw, Big and Little; Daffy Lsw; Dale Hone; Dinthill Fd and Patch (adjoins Dinthill in Bicton); The Fallow; Far Mdw; Far Patch (4); Field Pce; Fir Plantation; First Patch (Patch is the term for the smallest enclosures); Five Turning Patch and Pce (five roads meet here, Four Turning Patch in Ford-in-Alberbury is nearby); Four Cornered Pce (a square field); Fox Croft; The Gladstones; Glovers Mdw; Good Pool, Squires - - (a series of fields by a road); Gravel Hole; Gravel Lsw;

Green Lsw; Hagrey Breeches; Hare Pce; Heath Fd and Pce; Hell Wickett; Hem Ley (not on parish boundary); Holly Lsw; Hop Bank; House Mdw (2); Hoval Pce (perhaps a squatter's house on Ford Heath); Irongrass Fd (a type of grass, *Aira caespitosa*); Lane Patch; Lawn (by Ford Hall); The Leys, Long Leys, Lower - (*v.* **lǣs**); Little Lsw (2); Little Mdw (2); Little Patch; Long Ground; Long Lsw (3); Long Mdw (2); Long Slang (2, one narrow the other not); Lower Mdw (2); Marsh Reans, Far - - (*rean* is the Sa word for a drainage furrow); May Pools (*The May Pool*, a series of fields by R. Severn); Meadow (3); Middle Fd, Far and Near; Middle Patch (3); Milking Bank; Mills Lsw; Mirey Wickett (a short distance from Hell Wickett); Mountford (by R. Severn, which is the boundary with Montford); Moor Coppice, Lsw and Mdw (by Moor House *supra*); Near Croft; Near Fd; Near Mdw; Near Patch; New Lsw; New Pce, Big, Middle and Near - -; Oak Fd; Oaktree Lsw; Orchard Pce; Park Mdw; Patch (*freq*); Pell Beggar (on the edge of Ford Heath, probably land which would repel a beggar, there is no house so it is not a reference to uncharitable people); Penlands Patch; Piece by Smith's Shop; Pinkins Footway, - Pitt Fd; Pit (*Pit Meadow*); Plantation (3); Pool Lsw; Porting Mdw (the Shrewsbury/Welshpool road was *Portway* 1607 *SRO 1709/106/2*); Potato Lsw or Slang (a rectangular field); Pretty Pce; Quay's Patch; Rhonsmoor (*Ramsmores*); Robins Yd; Rookery Mdw; Rowton's Pce; Shady Mdw; Shop Yd; Slang (3, all narrow strips); Sleve (sleeve-shaped); Square Pce (rectangular, but not square); Stackyard (2); Stony Lsw; Tailors Yd; Three Cornered Patch, - - Pce (both triangular); Top Pce; Townsend (on village outskirts); Triangle (so-shaped); Turnip Lsw (2); Upper Mdw; Wainhouse Fd ('carthouse'); Wall Hill, Far and Near - - (these fields occupy an area immediately S.W. of the village: they may record an ancient earthwork, but there was a Wall family at Ford House, VCH 226); Way Lsw; Weavers Patch; Wet Mdw; Wheat Fd or Long Ground; White Fd; White Gate Fd and Pce; White Lsw; Willow Alder; Wood; The Yard.

(b) *Aldermans Croft*; *The Anpolls* 1573; *The Barn Yard*; *Brimshill*; *The Bromyfelde* 1573 (*v.* **brōmig**); *Buddiegreves Coppey* 1641-2 *SBL 156*, *The Buddy Groves* (*v.* **grǣfe**); *Clover Pieces*; *The Conygree* 1573 (*v.* **coninger**); *Cox's Piece*; *Creeks Pool*; *The Crosse Hill* 1573; *The Fogge Leasowe* 1573 (*v.* ***fogga** 'long grass'); *Gammons Poole* 1601, 1796; *Gorsty Leasows* (*v.* ***gorstig**); *Hall Yate Nooke* 1601; *The Holly Tree Croft*; *The Heath* 1601; *Marsh Lane* 1745 VCH 225; *Maynards Nooke* 1601; *The Moelie* 1601; *Oldfield* 1601 (VCH 225 says Lower Field or Oldfield was one of the open fields of Ford); *Parkefield, Over and Nether* 1573; *The Post Way* (Posting or Post Way was used in 1936 for the road earlier called Port Way, *v.* Porting Mdw *supra*); *Prestons Croft*; *The Rough*; *Le Stockinge Yate* 1631 *SBL 11047* (*v.* ***stoccing**, **geat**); *Westley Meadows, Great and*

Little, Westmoores 1635 *SBL 151*; *Le Whittichars ib*; *The Whitton Leasow*, *Wildymoor Field*.

Habberley

The parish-name, which consists of a feminine pers.n. with **lēah** 'clearing', is discussed in Part **1**. It is first recorded in 1242, and VCH (pp.238, 242) conjectures that the area became an independent parish in the 12th cent., as the church contains features of that date. It was probably part of the DB manor of Worthen.

HABBERLEY BROOK: no trace has been noted of an earlier name for this stream. HABBERLEY HALL, *ye Hall-house of Habberly* m.17th PR(L) 6. VCH p.240 says that the low mound on which the house stands is likely to be a castle-site. LEES COPPICE: this is *Plantation* 1839 *TA*, the adjoining field being *Leas Piece*, *v.* **lǣs**. MARSLEY, so named 1839 *TA*. This has been suggested as an identification for DB *Marsetlie*, mentioned in connection with customs when the king was hunting from Shrewsbury. A more likely identification is perhaps Marsley Park in Allington, Denb (NCPNW 195). The DB place was a *parcus*, and Marsley Denb is consistently a 'park' in refs. from 14th-16th cents. WESTCOTT, LOWER: Westcott is in Ratlinghope parish.

Field-Names

Forms in (a) are 1839 *TA*. Forms in (b) are c.1380 *SBL 6172* unless otherwise stated.

(a) Appletree Fd; Audley, Big, Smith's Lower, and Square (*The Audley* 17th VCH 238, perhaps **ald** + **lēah**); Bank Lsw, Lower and Upper; Banky Lsw (2); Barn Yds; Bens Bank, Further and Near; Betty Humphreys Patch; Big Mdw; Boggy Mdw; Brandy Croft (perhaps cleared by burning, *v.* **brand**); The Brinks (beside Habberley Brook); Broad Flgs; Broad Lsw; Bromley's Lsw; Bromy Patch; Brook Lsw; Brook Mdw (2); The Brooks; Callow Hill Lsw and Rough (*v.* **calu**); Calves Croft and Yd; Clarons Fd; Clawdy Patch (perhaps dialect *clarty* 'sticky'); Claypits; Cockshut Lsw (*v.* ***cocc-sciete**); Cote Lsw (*v.* **cot**); Cow Pasture

(2); Cross Lane Pce; Cuckoo Mdw, Big and Little, Far and Near; Darnford, Upper ('secret ford', *v.* **derne**); Dovehouse Yd, Upper and Lower; Emsley (*Elmondeslye* c.1380 *SBL 6172*, *v.* **lēah**, first element possibly a ME surname); The Fanstages; Far Bank; Far Lsw; Field below the Meadow; The Five Oaks; Flat Lsw, Lower and Upper; Footway Fd; Forge Mdw; Forked Bridge Lsw; Gander's Leg (adjoins Goose's Foot *infra*); Garden (2), Goddin Knowles; Goose's Foot (from the shape, but the adjoining Gander's Leg is not distinctive); The Gowdens; Hales, Little (*v.* **halh**); Hawthorn Lees (*v.* **lǣs**); Higley's Lsw, Lower and Upper, Higley's Park; Horny Mdw; Horse Pce; The Knowles (*v.* **cnoll**); Lincadines; Little Fd, Far and Near; Long Flg; Lower Lsw (2); Lower Mdw (3); Lower Pasture; Manks Lea; Meadow (4); Melverley (the parish of Melverley is 10 miles N.W.); Middle Patch; Millers Bank and Pce; Mill House; Mills Pce; Minsterley Mdw (adjoining Minsterley parish); Monument Mdw; The Moor, Lower -, - Croft and Mdw (*v.* **mōr**); Morris's Mdw; Near Patch; New Mdw; New Pce; Orchard; Parsons Mdw; Pea Fd; Pce above Little Marsh; Pce below the Garden; Pigs Patch; Pitchell, Far and Near (*Pedeshull'* c.1380 *SBL 6172*, *v.* **hyll**, first element uncertain, VCH p.238 says this was a common field); Primrose Bank; Quarry Hole Pitchell; Rick Lsw; Roberts Yd; Rough (3); Rough Lsw; Rough Mdw; Sandy Hole Pce; Sandy Lees (*v.* **lǣs**); Schoolhouse Mdw; Shop Croft, Lower and Upper Shop Yd (*v.* **sceoppa**, probably 'shed'); Long Sideland Pce (a very narrow strip by a road); Six Days Math (i.e. 'mowing'); Slaid Mdw, Big and Far Slaid (*v.* **slæd**, the road into the village dips sharply here); Slang (a long, narrow strip); Small Slang (not near preceding); Small Pce at Brook; Smith's Pce; Stable Bank; Stackyard; Sucky's Patch; The Three Oaks; Turnip Fd; Upper Lsw; Upper Mdw; Upper Pasture; Waterage (by Habberley Brook); Wheat Fd, Flg and Pce; Yewtree Lsw.

(b) *ye Black-sitch* m.17 PR(L) 6 (*v.* **sīc**); *Le Bryches* (*v.* **bryce**); *Crouesmere or Crouesmore* 1540 SAS 54; *Galoneslye* (probably a surname with the ME derivative of **lēah**); *Greneweysmore* c.1380 *SBL 6172*, *Grynewysmore* 1540 SAS 54 (*v.* **grēne**, **weg**, **mōr**); *Hartbeach* 17th VCH (*v.* **heorot**, **bæce**); *Holymoresacre* (*v.* **hālig**, **mōr**, **æcer**); *Hokynshe* 1540 SAS 54; *ye Lady Meadow* m.17 PR(L) 6 (*v.* **hlǣfdige**); *Litle Medow* ib; *Lolleshethe* 1540 SAS 54; *Le Marleputt'* ('marlpit'); *ye New Leasow* m.17 PR(L) 6; *Poleacre* ('pool acre'); *Pullende* (p) (perhaps 'pool end'); *Le Rowe* 1540 SAS 54 (*v.* **rāw**); *Rowemores* ('rough marshes'); *Russelleslyes* (cf. *Galoneslye supra*); *Shaltemore* (*v.* ***sceald**, **mōr**); *Stodefallemores* ('stud-fold marsh'); *Tainter Yard* 18th VCH (ME *teyntour* 'cloth-stretching frame'); *Umbremores* (*v.* **mōr**, first element perhaps the bird-name *amore*, 'bunting'); *Vestyns* 1540 SAS 54; *Wetemedes* (*v.* **wēt**, **mǣd**); *Wynhetheffeld'* ('heathfield' with ***winn** 'pasture' prefixed).

Minsterley

The parish-name, which means 'wood or clearing belonging to a minster church', is discussed in Part **1**.

CALLOW HILL, 1838 *TA*, *La Calewe* 1271-2 *Ass* (p), *villa de Calewe* 1291-2 *Ass*, *Calewe* 1327 SAS 2/X (p). 'Bare hill', from **calewe*, a derivative of the OE adjective **calu**. VCH has information about the deserted hamlet, mostly from documents at Longleat. Cf. p.306 "The Corbets of Caus constructed a castle on the site of an Iron Age hill-fort on Callow Hill. This --- was disused by c.1274, but its remains were observed by Leland c.1540. --- Two hamlets formerly stood at the foot of the hill. The site of Callow hamlet is not known --- in 1635 it still contained two houses one of which was known as Callow Hill House. Of two cottages recorded in 1766 one stood on the hill to the east of the site of the castle and the other at the foot of the hill to the west." The Leland reference is "In the middle way betwixt the Chirch of Ponsbyri and this Wood [i.e. *Hokstow-Forest*] appere certen Ruines of a Castel or Pile apon longging also to the Lord Powys"

ESTELL. This is the name of a hamlet at a road-junction S.W. of Minsterley. It is *Hedsall* 1836 OS. VCH (297, 324) calls it Etsell (probably the generally accepted local spelling), and cites 18th-19th cent. references. There are three fields called *Etsell* 1838 *TA*. This seems likely to be the place called *Tedestile* 1255-6 *Ass*. In this reference Agnes the widow of Warin de *Tedestile* had a house in *Tedestile*, and men from Wallop, Rowton, Wattlesborough, Bretchel and Eyton were concerned in the case. It is the same name as Tedstill in Chetton (*Tydestighele* 1291-2 *Ass*). 'Tydi's stile or steep place' (*v.* **stigele**) would be a suitable etymology, but the coincidence of two occurrences in the same county (albeit widely separated) naturally raises a suspicion that the first element might be a significant term rather than a pers.n.

HOGSTOW, UPPER AND LOWER HOGSTOW, HOGSTOW HALL

Hocstowe 1294 Par, *Hockestowe* 1329 Pat, *Hokestowe* 1357 Pat, *Hokstow-Forest* c.1540 Leland, *Hockestowe Forest* 1577 Saxton, *Low Hocstowe* 1603 *SBL 6759, Hoc(k)stow* 1712-28 PR(H) 11
Hoxstouwe 1306-7 *Ass, Hexstowe* (? recte *Hox-*) 1347,54 Ipm, *Hoxstowe* 1403,4 Pat
Hogstowe, Hogge- 1399 SAS 3/VI, *Hogstowe* 1567 PR(H) 12, *Low -* 1608 *SBL 6762, Hogg(e)stow* 1703-4 PR(H) 11, *Hogstow Hall Farm* 1725-6 ib
Hockstall 1650 *ShelveMap, Hocston* 1655 SAS I/XLVII
Hucktow Forrest 1695 Morden

The earliest reference is to Peter Corbet's chase, many of the later ones are to a wood or forest. That of 1357 is to the Earl of Stafford's park. Hogstow and Hogstow Hall are in Worthen Parish, Lower and Upper Hogstow in Minsterley. The names are spread over a distance of 2½ miles.

The first element may be **hōc** 'hook', perhaps a name for one of the peaks in the high ground south of Minsterley. There is no obvious reason for the use of **stōw** as the generic. The basic meaning of **stōw** is 'venue for a particular activity'. It is sometimes used of sites associated with saints which were places of pilgrimage, see the discussion of the parish-names Stow and Wistanstow in Part **1**. There could have been a hermitage in the forest.

POULTON, *Pulton'* 1271-2 *Ass, -ton* c.1274, 1379 VCH, *Powlton* 1570 *SBL 92*. 'Pool settlement', *v.* **pōl, tūn**. The farm overlooks marshy ground by a tributary of the Rea Brook. The course of this stream has been straightened, probably draining the pool.

WAGBEACH, *Waggebeche* 1321 *VCH(Hereford)*, *Wagbatch* 1836 OS. There are several -beach names on the high ground which runs from Pontesbury S.W. to Norbury. The only well-recorded one is Beach in More, which is *Bech', La Bech'* in 13th- and 14th-cent. sources. In view of the topography this is likely to be the common element **bæce**, 'stream-valley', though that regularly gives ME

-bache, modern -batch elsewhere in the county. Some local dialect irregularity seems to have affected its development in the region of the Stiperstones. The development is also well-evidenced in Ch (PN Ch 5, 99-100). The first element of Wagbeach is probably a nominal derivative of the ME verb *wag* 'to shake', referring to unfirm ground. It appears to be unique to this p.n., but would be comparable with the use of OE *wicga* in Wigmore (Part **1**).

BANK HOUSE, 1836 OS. BROOKBATCH, *Brockbache* 1546 *VCH* (*Longleat*), *Brook Beach* 1838 *TA*, *v.* **bæce** and cf. Wagbeach *supra*. It is locally called Brogbeach. COLLEGE COPPICE, 1766 VCH 299, 1836 OS. DRURY LANE, a transferred n., from the London street. ESTELL ROUGH, *v. supra*. GREEN FM. THE GROVE. HOGSTOW BANK AND MILL, *v. supra*, the history of the mill is traced in VCH. LADY OAK, *Lady Oak Coppice* 1766 VCH 299. *TAMap* shows a group of fields named from the Lady Oak, which VCH 308 says stood at the cross-roads till 1757, but which A. Morton (*The Trees of Shropshire* p.54) says was felled in the 1950s. There is another ancient oak with this name in Cressage. LITTLE MINSTERLEY (a few houses on the road N.E. of the village). LOWER WORKS. MINSTERLEY PARK, *Minsterley Parke* 1601 *SBL 6755*. VCH 317-8 traces its history. NEW HOUSE FM. OAK HOUSE. OLD TURNPIKE, 1836 OS. PLOXGREEN, -BRIDGE, *Plox Green* 1836 OS, *Plox Green Leasow* 1838 *TA*. VCH cites references to houses here in 1766. From the pl. of *plock*, which is a variant of *pleck*, 'small piece of ground'. THE POPLARS. PROSPECT HOUSE. REABROOK. The house is at some distance from the present course of Rea Brook, but the stream may have been straightened. The name is from ME *atter ee* 'at the river'. ROSE BANK. SNAILBEACH, - FM, - DISTRICT RAILWAY, *Snailbeach* 1836 OS, cf. *The Sneilbach mines* 1799 Townson. 'Snail valley', cf. Wagbeach *supra*. VCH 299 says that a deerleap was constructed here in 1352, but does not quote the name spelling. The places are on the Minsterley/Worthen boundary. SPRING COPPICE, 1836 OS. VCH 299 says this is the *Lady Oak Coppice* of 1766. THE WATERWHEEL. VCH 308 gives the history of the mill here.

Field-Names

Forms in (a) are 1838 *TA*. Early forms dated 1540 are SAS 54, 1546 *VCH*(*Longleat*), and 1590 *SBL 6671*.

(a) Abigails Pce; Aldery Lsw and Mdw; Articles Pce (adjoins Abigails -); Backhouse Croft and Mdw (not adjacent, 'bakehouse'); Ballsters, - Mdw; Banky Fd; Banky Lsw (2); Barley Pce; Barn Lsw; Barn Mdw (3); Barn Yard; Bayleys Pce; Big Coppice; Big Lsw, Far - -; Big Mdw (6); Briary Hayes (2); Brickkiln Pce; Brine Pit Lsw; Broad Mdw; Broadways Mdw; Brook Mdw, Little; Broom over Brook; Broomhill Lsw; The Brooms (2), Great Brooms; Broomy Bank, - - Fd; Broomy Lsw; Calves Lsw; Cinders, Cinder Mdw; Cole Lsw; Coopers Yard; Coppice Lsw; Coppice Pce, Little; Cote Lsw; Cow Lsw (2); Cow Mdw; Cow Pasture (3); Crabtree Lsw (*freq*); Crooked Acres (an irregular shape); Cross Lsw (2, both by road-junctions); Crow Moor; Cuther Croft (2) (dialect *cather* 'hemp'); Dingle; Dip Hedge, Further, Lower and Upper; Dogtree Mdw (probably 'spindle-tree', but perhaps a corruption of *Dodkys Meadow* 1609 *SBL 6762*); Drain Hedge, Lower - - (*Derne Hedge* 1546, 'hidden hedge', *v*. **derne**); Duck Mdw; Far Mdw; Far Pce (2); Feg (rough grass); Five Days Math (i.e. mowing); Flat Mdw; Freeholders Wood; The Furlong (in one of the old common fields, N. of the village); Further Lsw; Further Mdw; Gaily, Big and Little; Gittins Clover; Great Mdw (*Great Medowe or Town Medowe or Comon Medewe* 1590); Grumbreys Lsw; Gutter Mdw; Hands Lsw; Hatty Hall (by Callow Hill, perhaps a sarcastic n. referring to the lost hamlet); Hems, Big - (there is a footpath from Minsterley Park Fm to Hem in Westbury, and these fields are near but not adjacent to it); Hoggins Lsw and Mdw; Holly Croft, Upper; Homer Dale, - Dell (near Long Dale); Honey Mdw; Hope Rough (by Hope in Worthen); Horse Bridge (see Westbury parish); Horse Pce (3); Horse Yd, Lower; House Pce; Jacks Mdw; Johnsons Lsw and Mdw; Ladies Mdw; Lady Hill, Lady Lsw (neither field is near Lady Oak); Lane Pce; Lawn, Lower (near Minsterley Park); Lead Mines; The Leasow; The Lees (*v*. **lǣs**); Level Lsw; Little Lsw; Little Mdw (5); Lloyd Oak (not near Lady Oak); Long Dale (perhaps an irregular development of *dole* referring to shared meadow, there is no question of a valley); Long Lsw (3), Upper and Lower Long Lsw (2); Lower Lsw; Lower Mdw; Lower Pools; Lower Rough; Mansell; The Mares Pce; Margins Lsw (by a road); Mars Mdw; May Pce; Middle Fd; Middle Pce; Milking Fold; Mill Croft; Mill Lsw, Lower and Upper; Millpond Mdw; Miners Big Lsw (near the lead mines); Monk Hays; Moor, Middle and Upper, Moors, Lower (cf. *The More* 1598 *SBL 6753*, *v*. **mōr**); Moor, Little and Near (not adjacent to preceding); Mud Pool; Near Mdw; Nine Ridges (one of a number of furlong-shaped fields E. of Minsterley village); Oak

Lsw (5); Old Ford; Old Mdw; Panton Bank; Parks, Rough Parks, Park Hill, Park Stiles, Parks Lee (*v.* Minsterley Park); Pasture (2); Penadine; Phillips Wood; Pigstie Lsw; Plain, Lower and Upper (by the house called Minsterley Park); Pond Bank; Pool Lsw; Pool(s) Patch; Potato Patch; Poulton Pce (*v. supra*); Price's Fd, Lower; Quat Mdw (perhaps a surname from Quatt near Bridgnorth); Rail Lsw; Resting Hill; Rough End, Far and Near; Rough Lsw (2); Round Bank; Rushy Lsw; Rushy Mdw (2); Ryegrass Lsw; Shop Lsw, Big and Little; Slang (*freq*, 2 of these are narrow strips between a road and the bend in a brook); Slaters Graves; The Sleive (sleeve-shaped); Slip; Square Lsw; Stanage; Storks Nest; Stirrups Lsw; Summer Mdw; Summerhouse Banks and Mdw; Sutch, Little (*v.* Sytch *infra*); Symmonds Mdw; Sytch, Middle and Upper, Sytches, Sytch Mdw (*v.* **sīc**); Tantree Mdw (*tainter*, a frame for stretching cloth); Ten Days Math (adjoins Five - -); Tining, Big, Little and New (*v.* **tȳning** 'enclosure'); Tomlins Mdw; Top of Lady Lane (by Lady Oak); Triangle; Upper Lsw (3); Upper Mdw; Upper Rough; Wagbeach Coppice and Pce (*v. supra*); Walkers Pce; Wall Mdw; Big Ware Lsw, Green Ware Mdw ('weir'); Well Lsw (2); Well Mdw; Wet Reins (i.e. drainage ditches); Whet Mdw; White Lsw, Far and Near; Winberry Top; Woodcock Mdw; Wood Lsw; Yewtree Lsw.

(b) *Asshenshete* 1540 (this and *Highshete* are cockshuts, *v.* ***cocc-scīete**); *Bradbroke, Brodbrooke* 1546 (*v.* **brād**, **brōc**); *Bradenmedowe* 1590 (*v.* **brād**, **mǣd**); *Catbrydge Gate* 1546; *Colyar Lesowe* 1540, *Colliers Leasow* 1609 *SBL 6762*; *Coppys Greve Fyld* 1546 (an open field, *v.* **grǣfe**); *Craneley* 1614 *SBL 6773* (*v.* **crān**, **lēah**); *Gritt Pit* 1590; *Grotemor'* 1306-7 *Ass* (this and preceding n. probably contain **grēot** 'gravel'); *Le Hadwey* 1321 *VCH* (*v.* **hēafod**, **weg**); *Highshete* 1540 *v. Asshenshete supra*); *Hoggesbroke* 1321 *VCH* (*v.* **hogg**, **brōc**); *Hough Medowe* 1590 (*v.* **halh**); *Hurne Lesow* 1546, *Hurmes* 1609 *SBL 6762* (*v.* **hyrne** 'corner'); *Lambeleye* 1546 (*v.* **lamb**, **lēah**); *Lampitt* 1590 ('loam pit'); *Lastley* 1590; *Leyshegge* 1321 *VCH* (*v.* **lǣs**, **hecg**); *Lyes Field* 1546 (an open field); *The Lyttell Field* 1546; *The Myll Brook* 1546; *Nolton More, Noltmore* 1540, *Noltemoreles, Noltemore Meadowe* 1597 *SBL 6751, The Nowltmores Leasow and Meadowe* 1597 *SBL 6752*; *Noalkemoore Meadowe and Leasow* 1618 *SBL 6772* (VCH 300 says this was S. of Rea Brook, near Minsterley Park Fm, *v.* **mōr**, the first element looks like *nolt*, variant of *nowt*, 'cattle', but this is a Scottish and northern English word); *Oak Tree Medowe* 1590; *Peny Butte* 1540; *Pens Hatch Gate* 1546; *Perkisleye* 1540; *Raynbowe* 1590 (*rainbow* is used in f.ns. for land ploughed concentrically with a curved boundary); *Rownde Medowe* 1590; *Rustyng Helde Land* 1540 (*v.* **helde**); *Six Doles* 1590 (*v.* **dāl**); *Slades* 1590 (*v.* **slæd**); *The Swanscyes* 1546; *Wheat Croft* 1590; *Wolstanfiche* 1540.

Pontesbury

The parish-name, which probably means 'Pant's fortified place', is discussed in Part 1.

VCH (p.244) lists 21 townships: Arscott, Asterley, Boycott, Cruckmeole, Cruckton, Edge, Farley, Halston, Hinton, Lea, Little Hanwood, Longden, Malehurst, Newnham, Oaks, Plealey, Polmere, Pontesbury, Pontesford, Sascott and Sibberscot. In the Tithe Apportionment, however, Malehurst is included in Pontesbury and Polmere in Newnham, and this arrangement has been followed here. A portion of Onslow which was in Pontesbury until 1934 will be treated with the rest of Onslow parish as part of the Liberties of Shrewsbury. The southernmost township, Oaks, was in Condover Hundred, not Ford, and Little Hanwood was a member of the Liberties of Shrewsbury, but these townships are treated here, as they are integral parts of Pontesbury parish.

1. ARSCOTT (SJ 437078)

Ardescote 1255 RH (p) *et freq* with variant spellings *-cote, -kote* to 1490 Ipm
Erdeskote 1271-2 *ForProc, -cot* 1271-2 *Ass* (p)
Ardelescote 1291-2 *Ass*
Arsecote 1609 PR(H) 1
Arstecote 1610 PR(H) 1
Arscott 1615 PR(H) 12, *-cot* 1630 PR(H) 1
Ascot 1833 OS

Probably 'Eard's cottage(s)'. The simplex pers.n. is not on record, but *Eard-* is well-evidenced in dithematic names.

On the modern 1" map a house at the crossroads is called Hall (Arscott Hall on 6"), and there is an Arscott Villa ½ mile S.E. The 19th-cent. OS and the *TAMap* show a scatter of houses at the crossroads.

ENGINE COPPICE, cf. *Engine Field* 1840 *TA*, 1853 *SBL 5008*. There are coal mines in the vicinity.

Field-Names

Forms in (a) are 1840 *TA*.

(a) Bowlings Pce; Bradley Mdw; Little Brickkiln Fd; Brickwork; Briery Fd; Broomy Lsw, Great and Little - -; Bunges; Coblees (*v.* **lǣs**, other fields with this name are in Cruckmeole township); Far and Near Coppice Lsw; Cote Leys; Cow Lsw; Cow Pasture; Big and Little Crabtree Close; Fag Lsw; Flat Pce; Garden Fd; Garden Patch; Great Mdw; Hawthorn Stump; Great, Lower and Upper Haymoor, Haymore Mdw; Hovel Patch; The Knolls, Little and Middle Knolls; Lawn (the garden of the largest of the houseplots in the hamlet); Little Fd; Little Hanwood Fd (on the township boundary); Little Mdw; Little Yd; Long Lsw; Long Mdw; Low Hills, Far, Near and Great - -; Middle Ground; New Mdw; Oak Mdw; Oaktree Bank; Ox Lsw; Pitchley Bank; Pit Lsw (by Engine Fd); Pool Mdw; The Pumps, Pump Lsw, Lower Pumps (probably for draining wet land); Round Mdw (a semicircle with the straight edge on a stream); Royal Sitch (*v.* **sīc**); Rushy Lsw; Sawpit Yd; The Seven Butts (a narrow strip on the township boundary); Far and Near Shorthill Bank, Lower and Upper Shorthill Lsw, Shorthill Mdw (Shorthill is in Lea township); Town Mdw; Vetch Croft; Way Lsw; Well Mdw; Wet Mdw; Whixhill Bank (Wixhill is in Cruckmeole Township); Wilcox; Wood Croft; Yewtree Lsw.

(b) *Aukmeadow Furlong* 1670 VCH 249; *The Knorr* 1601 *SBL 12706* (VCH 248 says this is the outcrop of sandstone N. of Arscott, *v.* ***cnearr** 'rugged rock').

2. ASTERLEY (SJ 375070)

Estrelega 1208 SAS 2/X (p), *Esterleg'* 1255-6 *Ass*
Asterlege 1252 MGS (p) *et freq* with variant spellings *-legh, -ley(e)*;
    Astreleye 1291-2 *Ass*
Estleg' 1255 RH
Asturlegh' l.13th *SBL 3836* (p), *Asturley* 1396 Fine, 1555 *SBL 3653*,
    - iuxta Cawes 1398 *SBL 5435*

'Eastern clearing', *v.* **ēasterra, lēah**, identical with Asterleigh PN O 359. In this instance the name probably refers to the position of the settlement in relation to Minsterley, Westley and Winsley. The four items form a close-set cluster of *lēah* names. Caus is over two miles W., and not an obvious choice of affix.

HINWOOD, *Hynewud'* 1261-2 *ForProc* (p), *Inwood* 1799 Townson, *Inwood*, *Hinwood* 1842 *TA*. 'Wood of the religious community', *v*. **hīgna, wudu**. The reference is probably to the priests who served Pontesbury church, which is likely to have been an ancient minster. The church is said in 1254 RH to hold two hides of land in Asterley. The hamlet is a squatter settlement, ascribed by VCH (p.257) to 18th-cent. mining activity.

Field-Names

Forms in (a) are 1842 *TA*.

(a) Asterley Mdw (on township boundary); Back Lsw; Banky Pce; Bannistry Yd; Bark Lsw; Further and Near Barn Lsw; Barn Mdw (2); Further and Near Black Poles (on a stream, *v*. **pōl**); Lower and Upper Botts; Little Brickkiln; Brickyard; Further and Near Broomy Corner; Lower and Upper Calves Patch; Captains Mdw; Lower and Upper Charles's Fd; Coalpit Bank; Coat Mdw (*v*. **cot**); Cow Pasture; Crooky Moor; Curry Croft; Doctor's Mdw; Big and Little Fegg (*feg* is coarse grass); Flat Lsw; Flat Mdw; Four Trees; Hacknells; Hedge Cop, - - Lsw and Mdw (Cop possibly short for 'copyhold', there is a cottage here); Hempyard; Hinwood Mdw; The Homer, Further, Lower and Upper Homer (possibly 'pool in a hollow', *v*. **holh, mere**); Humphreys Fd; Lees Lsw (*v*. **lǣs**); Long Lsw; Marsh Hill, Big, Little and Long - -; Midsummer Oak; Mount; Lower and Upper New Ditches; Nine Bridges (between two streams); Oak Fd (adjoins Midsummer Oak); Oaktree Pce; Pinfold; Pugh's Mdw; Quarry Pce; Big and Little Red Lake (on a tributary of Rea Brook, probably 'reed channel', *v*. **hrēod, lacu**); Ropes; Round Mdw (actually rectangular); Santry Mdw; Shout Pce; Thistly; Three Cornered Mdw (appropriately shaped); Tithe Free Fd; Townsend (at N.E. corner of village); Upper Mdw; Wateridge (by a stream, 'water edge', cf. Habberley f.ns.); Farther and Near Westley Moor (Westley adjoins, in Westbury); White Lsw; Wigley Mdw and Moor (Wigley adjoins, in Westbury); Wisher Fd.

3. BOYCOTT (SJ 387077)

Boycote 1291-2 *Ass*, 1321 AD, *-cott* 1552 PR(H) 12 *et seq*, *-cot* 1697 Morden
Baycott 1582 *SBL 6808*

Probably 'cottage(s) of the servants', *v.* ***boi(a)**. The name occurs also in Bk and Wo, and, in the form Bycott, in D. *Boia* only occurs as a personal name in recorded OE, and this is suspected of being of Continental origin (Feilitzen 205). ME *boie*, however, is well-recorded in much the same senses as modern *boy*. There are place-name compounds with **tūn**, **land** and **wīc**, and the term occurs with a wide range of elements in ME field-names, some of which are listed in PN Ess 426. The existence of the word in OE is probably established by the occurrence of *boiwic* in the bounds of Aldenham Hrt in S 124.

Field-Names

Forms in (a) are 1842 *TA*.

(a) Banky Fd; Boycott Mdw; Boycott Pce; Boycott Wall (possibly 'spring'), Bridge Pce; Burnt Gates (1770 VCH 248), Lower and Upper - -; Coalpit Fd; Coalpit Lsw; Further, Middle and Near Coppice; Cote Fd (*v.* **cot**); Cow Pasture, Lower, Middle and Upper - -; Crabtree Fd; Dimbers Mdw (2 adjacent fields, either side of Rea Brook, one in Boycott township); Engine Lsw; Engine Pce (not adjacent to preceding); The Feg ('rough grass'); Flat Lsw; Fourteen Acres; Horse Lsw; New Lsw; Oaktree Lsw; Peters Lsw; Pontesbury Pce (on township boundary); Rea Mdw (by Rea Brook); Near Rough Ground; Rye Patch; Slang (long and narrow); Sleeve (sleeve-shaped); Walk Lsw; Way Lsw; Weir Lsw; White Lsw.

4. CRUCKMEOLE (SJ 432094)

Mele 1255 RH (p)
Crok(e)mele 1291-2 *Ass*, *Crokkemele* 1340 Pat, *Croke Meole* 1586 *SBL 7065*, *Crocke Meale* 1672 HTR, *Crockmeole* 1700 PR(H) 11
Moele 1308 Ipm, *Moile* 1490 Ipm
Cruckmele 1577 Saxton, 1600 *et freq* PR(H) 1, *Meole Crucke* 1717 PR(H) 12
Crook Meal 1700 PR(H) 15

PR(H) 1, from 1597 onwards, has many variants, including

Crucke meolle, Cruck meele, Cruck(e)meole, Cruckmele, Cruck meale, Cruck Meall, Cruckmeol.

Meole is the OE name of the Rea Brook. In Part 1, under Meole Brace, it was suggested that this might be OE *melu, meolu,* modern *meal,* used figuratively of a stream with cloudy water.

The affix Cruck- is the first element of nearby Cruckton, forms for which are set out below. In both sets of spellings *Croc-, Crok-* is more frequent that *Cruc-, Cruk-,* and a few forms suggest a long vowel. An OE ***crōc** appears in Elements as a possible ancestor of modern *crook.* ON **krókr** could be the origin of the modern word, but it is a reasonable assumption that a corresponding word existed in OE. If the term is a topographical one it must refer to a characteristic of the river, which makes a sharp bend between the two places. If it is not topographical it could refer to the prevalence of buildings made with *cruck* frames; the architectural term is a specialised use of the work *crook.*

Field-Names

Forms in (a) are 1840 *TA.*

(a) Backsides; The Banks, Upper Banks; Bean Croft; Blacksmiths Mdw and Shop; Brickkiln Mdw; Brook Mdw (2); Big and Little Broomy Lsw; Byletts (the Rea Brook has two channels here); Church Mdw; Far, Near and Upper Coblees (*v.* **lǣs**, the fields with this name extend over a wide area); Coffa Gate; Coppice Lsw; Cow Pasture; Crab Close; The Crofts; Cruckton Furlong (scattered fields with Furlong in their names suggest a fair amount of open-field farming in this township: VCH 249 notes a licence to enclose in 1631); Far Croft; Banky, Big and Little Foxholes; Furlongs; Great Furlongs; Little Furlong; The Grove, The Grove Mdw; Near and Upper Halt, Halt Mdw; Harrisells, Bank and Lower -; Horse Pasture; The Hurst (2); Lane Croft; Big and Little Lea Fd; Lawn; Long Heath; Long Mdw; Lower Croft; Lower Mdw; Lower Yd; Marsh, - Mdw; Meole Gate; Meole Gate or Harrow Fd (a corner of preceding, cut off by a road); Middle Croft; Middle Mdw; Mill Hill; The Moor (*v.* **mōr**); The Neaparies (FN 32 suggests that this was a turnip field); Near Croft; Lower and Upper New Inclosures; Lower and Upper Newnham, Turners Lower and Upper Newnham, Newnham Bank (adjoining Newnham township); Patches (a large field); Pleasure Ground; Pound Mdw; Robins Mdw; The Rough; Round Hill; Runsmoors; Far and Near Shop Lsw; Slash Mdw; Stackyard Mdw; Swan Mdw; Lower and Upper

Turnabout Ley; Upper Croft; Upper Mdw; Wixhill or Wixall; Wood (3); The Yeld (*v.* **helde**).

5. CRUCKTON (SJ 430103)

Crotton' 1271-2 *Ass* (p)
Crukton' 1271-2 *ForProc*, 1291-2 *Ass, Cruckon* 1597 *et freq* PR(H) 1, *Cructon* 1601 *et freq* ib
Crokton 1271-2 *Ass* (p), 1308 Ipm, 1339 Pat, *Croctun* ?1273 Ipm, *-ton'* 1306-7 *Ass, -ton* 1308 Ipm, 1551 PR(H) 12, *-tone* 1327 SAS 2/X, *Crockton* 1580 PR(H) 1
Crutton 1274 RH
Creuketon' 1305-6 *Ass*
Criketon 1431 FA
Croketon 1490 Ipm, *-ton'* 1631 *SBL 11047*
Cruckon 1720 PR(L) 20

See the discussion of Cruckmeole. Cruckton could be 'settlement with cruck-framed buildings' or 'settlement near a river-bank'.

BUCK'S COPPICE, 1833 OS, *Buckgate Wood* 1842 *TA, v.* f.ns. CRUCKTON HALL, *Hall* 1833 OS. HANWOOD GATE POOL (on boundary with Great Hanwood), *Hanwood Gate Field* 1842 *TA.* HARE AND HOUNDS P.H. HOLLYBANK, *Holly Bank* 1833 OS. HORTONLANE COPPICE, *Tenches Coppice* 1833 OS (Hortonlane is in Bicton). JENKINS COPPICE, *Jenkins's Coppice* 1833 OS. MOVES COPPICE, *Moose Coppice* 1833 OS, *Moves Coppice, Further, Near* and *Great Moves* 1842 *TA.* NED'S COPPICE, 1833 OS.

Field-Names

Forms in (a) are 1842 *TA*. Forms in (b) and early forms in (a) are 1680 *SBL 996*.

(a) Andrews Yd; Upper Bank; Banky Fd; Banky Pce; Benty Close (refers to bent grass); Further and Near Bicton Pool (*Bricklands als Brickton's Poole,* not adjacent to Bicton); The Bossells; Brickkiln Fd; Brickkiln Lsw; Brickkiln

Mdw; Lower and Upper Bridleroad Pce; Broomy Close; Farther and Near Broomy Lsw; Bucksgate House and Garden (*Buckes Gate, v.* Buck's Coppice *supra*); Bull Fd; The Butts; Cock's Pool; Cockshutt Lsw (*v.* **cocc-sciete**); Coppice Close; Coppice Patch; Lower and Upper Cow Pasture; Crabtree Fd; Cross Lsw (2, both by crossroads); Cruckton Mdw (5); Davies's Yds; Dickens Yd; Dog Kennel; Dovehouse Croft and Pce (by Cruckton Hall); Lower and Upper Dressels (a former open field, *v.* VCH 249); Edwards Lees; Eighteen Swathes (by a brook, *v.* **swæð**); Firgrove, - Pool; Fishpool Lsw (cf. *Stew Leasow infra*); The Flash (a term for a shallow pool); Flat Pce; Further Mdw; Garden Lsw; Lower and Upper Gorsy Fd; Gorsy Patch; Great Fd; Great Furlong (adjoins Furlong names in Sascott township); The Green (a small triangular patch on N. boundary of township); Green Reans (by a stream, drainage furrows); Great and Little Heath Pce; Holt Mdw; Home Pce; Horton Lane Pce, Horton Lsw (Horton is in Bicton parish); House Pce; Hovel Patch; The Hurst; Knox Croft (not near Nox in Pontesbury township); Little Croft; Little Mdw (2); Long Coppice; Lower and Upper Long Mdw; Long Slang; Far and Near Lowe (about GR 424103, probably **hlāw** 'tumulus'); Machine Yd; Marshy Close; Middle Fd; Middle Lsw; Mill Patch; Lower Mill Pool; Mill Pound; Millstone Fd; Medes Gate (the Gate names are on the township boundaries); Moss Pit, Far, Little and Near Moss Pits; New Lsw (3); Newland Close; New Mdw; Great, Lower and Upper Newnhams (adjoining Newnham township); Nicholas's Leys; Noble Croft; Oatalls (this and nearby Wheatalls probably refer to crops); Orchard Patch; Ox Lsw; Paddock Coppice; Great and Little Pit Fd; Pit Fd, Near Pit Lsw (*Pitt Leasow*); Pool Pce; Port Hall Coppice; Prissick's Lsw; Quillet (FN p.8 defines the Sa use of *quillet* for a piece of land in the open field marked off by stones and allotted to a cottager); Rough Hill; Ryegrass Close; Sascot Bank (on the opposite township boundary from Sascott, probably detached meadow); Seven Butts, Further - - (Butts is sometimes used for strips in a furlong); Sheep Pasture; Small Doles (meadowland assigned by lot); Spring Coppice; Spring Fd; Stackyard Lsw; Stockall; Stock(s) Leys; Further and Near Stow (*v.* **stōw**, near where 1" map marks site of Roman villa); Thieves Lane (the road to Hanwoodbank in the E. of the township), Far, Near and Lower Thieves Lane; Thistly Fd; Thornes Leys, Near and Farther - -; Lower and Upper Townsend (immediately N. of the hamlet); Two Pit Furlong; Upper Bank; Upper Mdw; Well Mdw; Wet Moor, Further - -; Wheatalls; Wheat Furlong.

(b) *Bingwing Coppice*, *Black Leys Coppice*, *Bradmore* (*v.* **brād**, **mōr**); *High Stond Gate Croft*; *Marle Leasow*; *The Nooke* (may be the origin of Knox Croft in (a)); *Paradice*; *Passands Yards*; *Rough Hayes Croft*; *Stew Leasow* (*stew*, 'fishpond').

6. EDGE (SJ 399089)

Egge 1255 RH (p) *et freq* to 1308 Ipm
Edge 1555 *SBL 3653 et seq*

v. **ecg**. A sandstone outcrop here has a long, narrow summit, and the village is on the eastern tip of this.

EDGEGROVE.

Field-Names

Forms in (a) are 1842 *TA*. Forms in (b) are c.1700 VCH p.248.

(a) The Bank; Banky Fd (2); Broad Wood; Big and Little Bullring (behind two small houses at GR 397086); Calves Close; Coblers Patch (a shoemaker's cottage was recorded c.1764, VCH 258); Cottage Fd (2); Cow Pasture, - - Fd; Big and Little Crabtree Lsw; Long and Little Doles (meadow assigned by lot); Edge Footway Pce; Farley Fd (on boundary of Farley township); Firtree Fd; Four Acres; Gate Mdw; Hinton Fd and Pce (on boundary of Hinton township); Hollytree Lsw; Horse Pasture; Lawn (2), Bottom Lawn (3 large fields N. and S. of the village); Little Mdw (2), Lower and Upper London (on parish boundary); New Fd; New Pce; Newton Fd (by Newton in Westbury); Orchard Fd; Pontesbury Pce (on boundary of Pontesbury township); Pool Pce; Rea Bank and Mdw (by Rea Brook); Rough Lsw; Roundabout (no discernible reason for the name here); Slang (not a characteristic shape); Stack Fd; Stony Fd (2); Stretton Croft (by road to Stone Stretton); Thistly Fd; Washer Way; Well Mdw; Yockleton Fd (by Yockleton in Westbury).

(b) *Bowers Wood*; *Great Wood*; *Round Turnor Wood*.

7. FARLEY (SJ 386079)

The township-name, which means 'fern clearing', is discussed in Part 1.

Field-Names

Forms in (a) are 1842 *TA*.

(a) Asterley Mdw (on boundary of Asterley township); The Bank; Bank Lsw; Barn Yd; Big Feg (rough grass); Boozy Pasture (a Sa term for land on which an outgoing tenant was allowed to pasture animals for an additional period, ultimately OE **bōsig** 'cow-stall'); Brickkiln; Bridge Mdw; Broad Lsw; Calves Patch; Cow Pasture; Doctors Pce; Farley Throat (bounded by a curving road); Gander Patch; Garden Fd; The Green (in the hamlet); The Harp (triangular); Horse Lsw; Little Mdw; Long Lsw (2); Middle Lsw; New Mdw; Newton Pce (by Newton in Westbury); Oak Lsw; Oat Mdw; Old Lsw; Quarry Fd; Rough Farleys; Round Mdw (not curvilinear); Ryegrass Fd; Ryegrass Mdw; Sleeve (sleeve-shaped); Stackyard Croft; Upper Lsw; Wet Reans (drainage channels); White Dutch; Will Square (a square field).

8. HALSTON (SJ 416078)

Alston' 1255-6 *Ass* (p), *Alston* 1615 *SBL 6839*
Haulston' 1575 *SBL 4023, Hallston alias Haulston* 1672 *SBL 4012*
Hallston 1731 PR(L) 6, 1774 *SBL 5741, Halston* 1787 PR(L) 12
Auston 1552 PR(H) 12, 1600,1 *SBL 6790, 6806,* 1808 Baugh, *Awston* 1581,2,99, 1603 *SBL 6786, 6808, 6787, 6810*
Aulston 1615 PR(H) 12, *SBL 6822, Allston* 1615 *SBL 6822,* 1809 *SBL 5004,* 1809 *SBL 5004*

Possibly '*Ealh's estate'. *v.* **tūn**. The simplex pers.n. is not on record, but *Ealh-* is common in dithematic names. *H-* is not original. The single ME spelling occurs in a list of men of Pontesbury.

LITTLE HALSTON (a building 3¾ miles S.S.W. of Halston).

Field-Names

Forms in (a) are 1842 *TA*.

(a) Banky Fd; Barn Mdw; Big Mdw; Boggy Mdw; Bush Pce; Big and Green Butterbridge (there is a field called Butter Bridge on the other side of the stream, in Pontesford township: the names are several fields away from where the Shrewsbury road crosses the stream); Clayton's Yd; Coppice Lsw; Little, Lower and Upper Earlands; Engine Fd; The Hooks (by bends in Rea Brook); Kitchen; Lawn (one of the fields by Halston Fm); Maidenhall; Mill Green; The Moor; Brook Moor; Upper Moor (*v.* **mōr**); Moor Lane; New Mdw; Nibbs Horn (bounded by a bend in Rea Brook); Old Fd; Old Coppice; Ox Lsw; Paradise (a large field by Rea Brook); Plealey Croft and Ditch (adjacent to Plealey township); Thistly Mdw; Way Lsw; White Fd.

9. HINTON (SJ 410080)

Henton 1272 Ipm
Hunton 1272 Cl
Hynton 1555 *SBL 3653 et passim* with variant spelling *Hin-*

Probably 'estate of the religious community', with the Mercian gen.pl. *hīona, hēona* as first element, *v.* Hinwood *supra*.

HINTON HALL, H. PLANTATION. NEW MILL, *Newe Mills* 1600 *SBL 6807*, *New Mills* 1615 *SBL 6822*, 1783 PR(H) 12. VCH 256 cites a reference from 1464.

Field-Names

Forms in (a) are 1842 *TA*.

(a) Lower and Upper Bank; Barn Lsw; Barn Mdw; Black Moor (*Blackmoore* 1594 *SBL 6794*, *v.* **mōr**); Bran Oak (possibly 'burnt oak'); Lower and Upper Copley; The Coppice; Coppice Lsw; Little Docky Croft, Docky Lsw; Further Pce; Hanley Moor, (*Hanley Moore* 1594 *SBL 6794*); Harmers Pce or Mdw; The Harp (roughly triangular); The Hooks (on other side of Rea Brook from The Hooks in Halston township); House Mdw; House Patch; Lawn (2, on either side of The Hall); Loddy Mdw (FN 26 suggests a connection with dialect *loddle*, 'soft, spongy ground'); Lower Coppice; Lower and Upper Mill Furlong; Mill Mdw (2); Mill Pound; Oak Lsw; Old Coppice; Parry's Wood; Big and Little Rough Lees (*v.* **lǣs**); Big, Further, Middle and Near Rumours (possibly **rūh** and **mōr**); Further, Middle and Near Ryeleys; Sheep Fold; Stony Cross (not a crossroads, possibly a stone cross); Three Acre Pce; Townsend (at S. end of hamlet); Upper Lsw; Watery Lsw; Weir Mdw; Big, Little and Lower Whirlypool (not by a stream and no pool shown on maps: perhaps a figurative term for a messy area); Big Woolaston (a small field called Woolaston is across Rea Brook in Halston township: possibly detached meadow belonging to Wollaston 5 miles N.W.).

(b) *Milward Mills* 1674 *SBL 6545*; *Over Field* 1568 VCH 249 (an open field).

10. LEA (SJ 416085)

Lya 1271-2 *ForProc*
La Lee 1276, 1308 Ipm
Lee 1291-2 *Ass*, 1672 HTR, 1601 *SBL 12706 et seq*

v. **lēah**, probably 'clearing' in this instance.

SHORTHILL, 1783 PR(H) 12, *Schorthull* 1221 SAS 3/VI (FF), *Serthul* 1255 RH, *Sherthill* 1286 Eyton, *Short Hill* 1833 *TA*, *v.* **sc(e)ort, hyll**: 'short' is a rare term in ancient place-names.

CLANBROOK BRIDGE, *Far and Near Clamrocks* occur by the brook in the *TA* for Cruckmeole township (1840). Probably a **brōc** name, earlier forms are needed. LEA CROSS, LEA CROSS BRIDGE, *Lea Crosse* 1638 PR(H) 12. The T-junction here may have been thought of as a crossroads on account of the road to Stapleton joining the A 488 a short distance N. of the junction with the Lea road. LEA HALL. TRAP COTTAGE.

Field-Names

Forms in (a) are 1842 *TA*.

(a) Barley Stubble; Barn Yd (3); Big Lsw; Bran Lsw; Breathing Hill; Bridge Fd; Briery Acres; Broad Lsw; Broomy Lsw; Causeway Mdw (by road from Lea to Lea Cross); Coppice Fd; Corner Lsw; Cow Pasture (2), New - -; Crabtree Fd; The Dale; Little Dale (2, *v.* **dæl**); Diggory's Pce; Doctor Yd; Glaziers Patch; Gravel Hole Fd; Grazing Pce; The Harp (2, triangular fields on either side of Longden road); Hinton Mdw (near Hinton township boundary); House Pce; Kneading Mdw (by Breathing Hill, both obscure); Lea Green (not in the hamlet); Lea Mdw; Leg and Foot (not explicable in terms of shape); The Leys (2); Little Fd; Little Lea Fd; Long Lsw; Lower Lsw; Lower Mdw; Meole (on boundary of Cruckmeole township); Moor Lsw (*v.* **mōr**); New Lsw; Nunnells; Pinfold Lsw; Plough Lsw; Polmer Fd (*v.* Polmere *infra*); Big and Green Pool Lsw, Big Pool Mdw (all by the pool from which Polmere is named); Ranmoors, Lower - (*v.* **mōr**, first el. probably ***rān** 'boundary strip', the fields are on the boundary with Hinton); Raking Bank; Rea Bank Fd; Rea Mdw; Rowley Hill (1601 *SBL 12706*); Shorthill Fd and Mdw (*v. supra*); Sour Lsw; Stackyard Lsw; Thistly Bank; Townend (by site of lost hamlet of Polmere *infra*); Way Lsw; Well Mdw; White Fd.

11. LITTLE HANWOOD (SJ 445078)

The name is discussed in Part **1** under Great Hanwood, with the suggestion that **hān** 'rock' or *Hana* pers.n. are more convincing as possible first elements than **hana** 'cock'. The two settlements, which are a mile apart, are *Muche and Lytyll Hanwoode* 1528 SAS 2/V, and L. Hanwood is *Hanwood Parva* 1614 ib. There is only one farm, and it is called Kennels on modern maps. It was still *Little Hanwood* on the 19th-cent. 1".

PANSON, 1721 PR(H) 1, *Paynston* 1452-3 SAS 2/V, 1604 PR(H) 1, *Painston* 1609 PR(H) 1, *Paynestone alias Pynson* 1621 SAS 2/V, *Peinson* 1636 PR(H) 1, *Painson* 1684,90 ib. There is a moat here, and the name is likely to be a post-Conquest compound of **tūn** with the French pers.n. *Pain*. Such compounds are well-represented in He, but very rare further north.

WOOD HALL is *Wudehus* 1221-2 *Ass*, 1221 SAS 3/VI (FF), *La Wodehus(e)* 1255-6 *Ass* (p), 1271-2 *Ass*, 1299 Eyton, *Wodehalle* 1327 VCH 269, *-hall* 1449 Fine, *Woodhall* 1600 *et seq* PR(H) 1. VCH 269 says that in 1286 Richard de la Halle acquired a quarter virgate in Woodhouse. Assuming that he already lived there, it is possible that the later name, Wood Hall, is a shortened version of **Woodhousehall*, combining the original name of the settlement with a reference to the hall from which Richard took his surname. The name Woodhouse is discussed in Part 1, with the suggestion that it may refer to an establishment for the management of woodland.

COPPICE COTTAGES AND HO. CURTISS COPPICE. GIPSY COPPICE. MOAT HALL, 1833 OS, *Mothall* 1598 PR(H) 1, *Mote Hall* 1599, 1601 ib, *The Motthall* 1651 *SBL 6045*, *Moathall* 1667,9 PR(H) 1. The *TAMap* shows a moat of similar size to that at nearby Panson. PAPERMILL COPPICE, 1833 OS. SLADE LANE (*v.* **slæd**). UPPER AND LOWER WOODHALL COPPICE, *v. supra.*

Field-Names

Forms in (a) are 1840 *TA*. Early forms are e.18th SAS 3/V.

(a) Big, Little and Upper Bakers Fd; Barn Fd (3, one e.18th); Birchy Fd; Brickkiln; Further and Near Brickkilns (cf. *Brickyard Heath*); Broad Lsw; Broomy Fd (cf. *Broomy Croft*); Coalpit Fd; Coppice Fd and Mdw (by Panson); Upper and Lower Coppice, Coppice Mdw and Lsw (by Wood Hall); Lower and Upper Cow Pasture (*Cow-Pasture*); Cross Lsw (*Two Cross Leasowes*, at a junction of three roads); Daiks Croft; Dovehouse Yd; Eleven Acres; Faggy Lsw (a variant of *feggy*, referring to coarse grass); Feeding Pce (e.18th); Five Acres; Flat Mdw; Footway Lsw and Pce (by different roads); Hales Fd (*Great and Little Hails Field*, *v.* **halh**, by Rea Brook); Hall Mdw (by Wood Hall); Hanwood Lsw (by L. Hanwood); Hiles Fd (adjoins Hales Fd); Hopyard; Horse Pasture; House Fd; Hungrell, Little - (perhaps 'hunger hill'); Little Heath; Love Mdw; Lower Lsw (e.18th); Marlpit; Matthews Stable Lsw; Middle Lsw (e.18th); Moat Fd and Mdw (both by Panson); Nine Day Math (i.e. 'mowing'); Orchard Mdw; Ox Lsw (2, one e.18th); Panson Lsw (cf. *Two Pamson Pieces*, *v.* Panson *supra*); The Park (a minute enclosure by Wood Hall, cf. *Park Meadow*); Pit Fd and Lsw (not adjacent); Pitchetts Croft; Pump Fd and Mdw (by Panson); Roundabouts (at Wood Hall, no obvious reason for the n.); Rush Mdw; Shookers Pce; Six Day Math (a smaller field adjoining Nine - -); Slang (2, long, narrow fields); Thistly Lsw; Three Cornered Pce; Upper Fd; Walnut Tree Patch; Well Mdw; Wheat Croft; White Fd; Whitley Fd (adjoins Whitley in Condover); Winter Mdw (e.18th, also - *Field*).

(b) *Little Meadow*; *Long Meadow*; *Rail Meadow*; *Wild-craft*.

12. LONGDEN (SJ 442065)

The township-name, which means 'long hill', is discussed in Part 1.

SYDNALL COTTAGE, *Sydenhale* 1385 Pat, *Sydnall* 1570 *SBL 6906*, *Signal Cottage* 1833 OS. 'Spacious nook', *v.* **sīd**, **halh**, a recurring minor name.

BANK HO. BROOMPATCH. HALL FM, by LONGDEN HALL. HAYS COPPICE, 1833 OS. VCH 247 says this was part of a larger wood known as *Hayes* in the later Middle Ages, *v.* **(ge)hæg** and f.ns *infra*. *Hay Wode* occurs 1351 *SBL 6795* (p). HURST BANK, 1838 *TA*. VCH 247 says this name is mentioned in connection with enclosures made in 1558, *v.* **hyrst**. LINGCROFT POOL AND COPPICE. LONGDEN BRIDGE. LONGDEN COMMON, 1833 OS. LONGDEN COPPICE. LONGDEN MANOR. LONGDENWOOD, 1833 OS. THE POPLARS. RED LION INN. ROCK COTTAGE. ROUNDHOUSE FM. SLANG COPPICE: there are three fields called *Slang* in Longden *TA*; it is a term for a long, narrow piece of ground. WOODHOUSE FM, by Hays Coppice.

Field-Names

Forms in (a) are 1838 *TA*.

(a) Alders Leys, Aldrey - (adjacent); Ashmoor Mdw and Pce; Banky, Big and Little Band Leys (probably **bēan** 'bean'); Bank Fd; Lower, Middle and Upper Banky Lsw; Bare Hill; Barley Butts; Barn Yd (3); Beast Yd; Big Mdw; Bog Leys; Bog Mdw; Brick Lsw; Bridge Wood Mdw; Briery Lsw; Brinsell; Broad Leys; Further and Near Broad Mdw; Brook Lsw; Broomy Lsw; Big, Far and Near Broomy Stile; Bucknalls Mdw; Bungess (Bunges in Arscott *TA*); Bungey Mdw (near preceding); Burnt Gates (another ex. in Boycott); Buslings; Calves Croft; Gardens Ground; Chapel Yd; Old Clover Lsw; Coalpit Mdw and Patch (near but not adjacent, in S..E. of township); Cockshott Wood (*v.* ***cocc-scīete**); Common Ground; Common Lsw (2); Common Pce (2); Common Pool Pce; Lower and Middle Coppice Lsw; Cotley Moor, - - Mdw; Lower and Upper Cow Lsw; Cow Pasture; Crooked Furlong (has a right-angle bend); Cross Lsw (not at a road-junction); Lower and Upper Cross Leys (by the crossroads N. of village); Dennis Croft; Eastons Low (at G.R. 453064, between a road and a stream); Egg Moor, Flat, Little and Lower - - (FN 50 suggests that *egg* refers to the snowberry shrub); The Field; Fishpool Lsw; Foul Cow (earlier *Folkeys*, a common field, VCH 249: an adjoining meadow in Great Lyth is *Fulcheye* c.1230 SAC, perhaps **gehæg** with a pers.n.); Fox's Yd; Further Lsw; Glaze Brook (a possible early n. of Longden Brook); Gorsty Lsw; Gorsty Pce; Hall Yd (a large field E. of village); Hanky Shoots, Big, Little and Upper - - (looks like a common field, but not noted as such in VCH 249); Hare Shakers (earlier *Ash Acres*, part of *Folkeys* Field, VCH 249); The Hatch; Hayes Fd, Lsw and Mdw, Caldrons Hayes (spread round Hays Coppice, Caldrons Hays is mentioned 1576, VCH 247); Hole Mdw (2, on either side of Rug Moors); Home Stile (near village); Horse Lsw; Horse Pce; House Mdw; Hustly Lsw; Kitchen Mdw; Laurences, Lawrences Ground; Lawns Hill, Far - -(by Hall Yd); Leys (2); Leys Mdw; Little Field; Little Meadow; Longden Coppice; Long Headlands (adjoins Hare Shakers); Long Lsw; Long Mdw; Maple Stile; The Marshes; Meadow Furlong (N. of village, near Crooked Furlong); Middle Patch; Middle Yd; Muck Fd; Muncorn Lsw (*muncorn* is a mixture of wheat and rye); Myfords Yd; New Leasow (2); New Mdw; Oaks Hall Lsw and Rough (by Oaks township); Old Coppice; Ox Lsw; Parry's Yd; Penny Moor, Bank - - (Penny refers to rent); Pit Lsw; Pool Lsw; Pool Mdw; Pool Yd; Pound Yd; Powell Fd; Rain Mdw (probably *rean* 'drainage channel'); Rogers Croft; Rough Lsw (3); Rough Pce; Lower and Upper Roundabout (no obvious explanation); Rug Moors (dialect *rug* 'large stone'); Rushy Pce; The Slade (*v.* **slæd**); Slang (3); Big Spring Lsw; Big, Far, Little, Lower, Middle, Near,

Upper Stocking(s), Stocking Mdw (*v.* **stocking**, an arc of names denoting clearings on the E. side of the wood called Hayes); Stone Hill; Stony Ford, Little - - (where the Shrewsbury road crosses Longden Brook); Swathans Mdw; Thistly Lsw (3); Tilley Tree Lsw; Town Mdw; Lower and Upper Turners Lsw; Upper Patch; Upper Yd; Wall Lsw; Well Mdw (2); Well Patch; Well Yd; Wool Mdw; Yew Cross, Big and Little Yewtree Cross (3 fields by a road junction).

(b) *Idekinebroke* 1283 InqMisc (probably the brook on S. boundary of parish); *Le Loueyate at Sydenhale* 1385 Pat (perhaps an early term for a kissing gate); *Withen Furlong* 1528 VCH 249 (*v.* ***wīðigen**). VCH 249 says that there were common fields called *Little High Field* and *Hay Field or Brome Hill Field*, in addition to *Folkeys* noted *supra*.

13. NEWNHAM (SJ 411100) AND POLMERE (SJ 411094)

Newnham 1209-10 MGS (p), 1601 *SBL 12706 et seq*, *Newneham* 1572,7 PR(H) 12
Neunam 1255 RH (p), *Neunham* 1276 Ipm, *Newnum* 1672 HTR
Newenham 1255-6 *Ass* (p), 1308, 1490 Ipm, *Newenam* 1291-2 *Ass*, *Newenam'* c.1380 *SBL 6172*

'New settlement', *v.* **nīwe**, **hām**. The *-n-* is from the dat.sg. inflection of **nīwe**. This place-name is widespread in the country, and it is likely that it continued to be applied to new settlements after **hām** had otherwise gone out of use in place-name formation.

POLMERE. This name, which is a curious compound of **pōl** and **mere**, is discussed in Part **1**. The *TAMap* shows the site of the shrunken settlement lying in Lea township, but the apportionment combines it with Newnham.

MARTON (lost), 1601 *SBL 12706*, *Marton Pool* 1842 *TA*. VCH 244 says this is a deserted hamlet. 'Pond settlement', *v.* **mere**, **tūn**.

NOX, 1783 PR(H) 12, *Nocks* 1768 ib. Named from Richard *Nock* who built an alehouse here in 1653 (VCH 261). The alehouse was called *Star and Ball*; the building is now Nox Ho. An earlier Richard *Noc* appears as a juror for Ford Hundred 1255 RH. The squatter settlement here was the earliest one on the southern fringe of Ford Heath.

NEW HO, *Newhouse* 1833 OS.

Field-Names

Forms in (a) are 1842 *TA*.

(a) The Bank; Bean Croft; Big Fds (a large area by Newnham hamlet-site); Broad Mdw; Calves Close; Cobblebean Yd; Coles Pce (2); Lower Cow Pasture; Dovehouse Lsw; Edge Lsw (on outskirts of Newnham hamlet-site); Fishpool Croft (adjoins preceding); Goblin Styles (by a minor road on parish boundary, about G.R. 406096); Gorsy Pce; Hanging Furlong (1601 VCH 249); Harries's Mdw; Further, Little, Middle and Near Heath; Hinton Mdw (detached from Hinton township); Home Croft; Johnson's Mdw and Nether Bank; Knox Croft and Mdw (*v.* Nox *supra*); Long Close; Merricus; New House Pce (*v. supra*); Newnham Arrow (pointed field on S. township boundary); Old Mdw; Lower and Upper Ox Lsw; Farther, Great, Little, Middle and Near Porthall Lsw (along a minor road on W. boundary of parish); Prill Lsw (not by a stream); Round Lsw (a rectangular field); Ryegrass Pce; Big and Little Southleys (on S. boundary of township); Stony Lsw; The Three Acres; Tiney Croft (probably **tȳning** 'enclosure'); Far and Near Two Furlongs Lsw; Further, Lower, Near and Upper Wall Springs (*wælle*, WMidl form of **welle**); Willmore; Yewtree Lsw; Yockleton Croft (on boundary with Y-).

14. OAKS (SJ 424047)

The township-name, which means 'oak tree', is discussed in Part 1.

CHURCH HILL WOOD, *Church Hill* 1842 *TA*. This is a clear instance of the compound of OE **crūc** (a loan-word from PrW) and **hyll**, which has become Churchill in a number of instances. **crūc** was used both of tumuli and of hills with an abrupt outline, and the latter usage suits this example.

OAKS HALL, 1783 PR(H) 12, OAKSHALL COPPICE. OAKS LODGE. OAKS WOOD, 1833 OS.

Field-Names

Forms in (a) are 1842 *TA*.

(a) Ager's Ley; Big, Far, Little and Near Armsley (along E. side of Oaks Wd, *v.* **lēah**); Bank (2), Upper and Lower Bank; Battenalls; Big Mdw (3); Lower and Upper Big Wood Pce (by Oaks Wd); Bog Moor, Boggy - (adjacent); Briery Fd; Brook Ground and Rough; Butlers Pce; Big and Little Church Hill (*v. supra*); Coltshill; Coppy Lsw ('copyhold'); Cow Pasture; Lower Cross Lsw (not at a road-junction); Lower, Middle and Upper Dew Ley, Dews Ley; End's Leys; Far Lsw (2); Fields Heads; Five Days Math; The Flat (by Church Hill, probably a level area); Further Wood (one of the group of 'wood' names S. of Oaks Wd); Far Giltsitten; Lower Gorsy Bank; Harris's Bank; Little Holly Lane, Holly Lane Lsw (by road to Oaks Wd); Lower House Fd; Hovel Mdw; Lark Leys; Lower Large Wood (by Oaks Wd); Little Fd; Little Mdw (2); Long Lsw (2); Long Rough; Lower Bank (2); The Marsh, Lower and Upper Marsh; New Lsw; Nor Mdw; Old Mdw; Pit Lsw (2); Pit Mill Mdw; Pool Bank; Big and Little Pool Lsw; Prill Slang (by Pontesford Brook); Quabby Croft (cf. *Quebbe Medwe* 14th *SBL 10598*, *v.* ***cwabba**); Far, Further, Little, Long, Near and Upper Rough Ground (scattered over S. part of township); Sheep Pasture; Skinmill Bank (*v.* Skin Mill Cottage in Pontesford township); Slang (4, narrow strips, 3 along Pontesford Brook), Narrow Slang; Lower and Upper Slench (large fields, so unlikely to be variant of *sling* or *slang*); Small Wood (by Oaks Wd); Stony Lsw; Swithins Door (VCH 291 suggests a ref. to the original dedication of Longden Chapel); Little Wallybourne (adjoins Walleybourne); Well Mdw; Big and Little West Mdw; Wood Green and Lsw (by Oaks Wd).

(b) *Edgeheld* 1305 VCH 247 (*v.* **ecg, helde**); *Heselwalleleg'* 14th *SBL 10598* (hazel-spring clearing'); *Knerisselege ib*; *Wassheres Field* 1374 VCH 249.

15. PLEALEY (SJ 423068)

Pleyle 1255-6 *Ass* (p) *et freq* with variant spellings *-ley(e), -legh', -leg* to 1756 PR(H) 12
Pleynlegh' 1271-2 *Ass*
Plalegh 1490 Ipm, *Plailey* 1672 HTR, *Playley* 1749 PR(H) 12
Pleleye 1542 PR(H) 12, 1601 *SBL 12706*, *Plelye* 1564 PR(H) 12
Plealey 1615 PR(H) 12 *et seq*

'Play clearing', *v.* **plega, lēah**. The reference could be to human sports or to animal mating rituals. *Playley* represents the modern pronunciation. The same compound has become Playley in Wo, PN Wo 158.

LITTLE PLEALEY. On 1833 OS this name is given to two separate farms, ¼ mile apart; the southernmost of these is PLEALEY VILLA on *TA* and modern maps. PLEALEY HO. RADLITH, 1840 *TA*, *Ratcliff* 1833 OS. VCH 263 says cottages are recorded here from 1712 onwards. Radlith is one of the **hlið** names which are characteristic of this part of the county, see the discussion of Pontesford Hill *infra*. First el. probably 'red'. RADLITH WD, *Radlith Plantation and Wood* 1840 *TA*. TAG'S GUTTER.

Field-Names

Forms in (a) are 1840 *TA*.

(a) Arscott Croft (by Arscott township); Higher and Lower Bank; The Banks; Upper Bar Lsw; Barn Gate; Bins Fd, Byne Croft (VCH 249 gives the name as Bine Fd and says it was an open field); Bradleys; Lower and Upper Bromden; Broom Fd; Broomy Lsw; Gorsy, Little and Well Cherrytree Lsw; Further, Great, Little and Nearer Chirhayes (*Churcheys* 17th VCH 247, 'church enclosures', *v.* **(ge)hæg**, on the edge of Radlith Wood, perhaps giving name to Cherry Hayes Cottages in Pontesford); Cinder Croft and Mdw; Cockshutt, Middle, Nearer and Upper - (*v.* ***cocc-sciete**); Coffins Yd (contains a chapel); Coppice Fd; Big and Little Cow Lsw; Croft Ashes; Big and Little Cross Hill (near a road-junction on E. side of village); Lower and Upper Dales; Dial Croft (a small field in the village); Docky Reans (drainage channels); Big Dunsdale,

Further and Near Dunsdales (*Dunsdale* 1593 VCH 247); Field Mead; Firtree Mdw; Footway Mdw; Four Gates; Gaudy Ground, Further and Near - - (refers to growing of dyer's greenweed for a yellow dye, OFr *gaude*); Further and Near Gorse Patch; Green Fd; Halston Mdw (adjoins Halston township); The Harp (roughly triangular); Hill Pce, Lower and Upper - -; House Mdw; Lane Croft; Lincroft, - Coppice, Mdw and Pool (probably 'flax croft'); Little Field; Little Piece; Londonderry (a tenement in the village); Long Croft; Long Lsw; Long Moor; Lower Mdw; Marsh Lsw; Melverley (a tiny triangle in a road-junction S.W. of village, no obvious connection with Melverley); New Lsw; The Nine Swaths (*v.* **swæð**, part of Town Meadow); Further, Lower and Upper Oak Moor (by Oaks township); Plealey Coppice; Ponsomer Pool Pce; Pontesford Fd (by Pontesford township); Radlith Bank, Mdw and Patch (*v. supra*); Sawbrooks, Sawbrook Mdw (probably 'willow brook', *v.* **salh**: *TAMap* shows a brook here, forming the N.W. township boundary, but this does not appear on later maps, its place being taken by a railway line); Shop Mead, Shop Mdw (adjoining); Sibberscott Mdw (detached from S-); Slang Mdw; Thorn Tree Mdw; Town Mdw; Upper Mdw; Upper Patch; Wall Lsw, Well Lsw (near but not adjoining); Great and Little Withenall.

16. PONTESBURY (SJ 400060) AND MALEHURST (SJ 383064)

v. supra for Pontesbury. VCH 252 gives some information about street-names. The section of MAIN RD north of the castle-site was *Stanniel Street* in 1831, which can be linked with *Stanwall* c.1540, and may refer to a stone wall enclosing the outer bailey of the castle. The section of MAIN RD west of the church was *Pavement Street* in 1831, and Leland (c.1540) refers to *Castelle Paviment* "on the South side of the Chirche Yard".

MALEHURST

Mathelhurste 1255 RH, *-hurst* c.1274 *VCH(Longleat)*
Mathehurst' 1327 SAS 2/X
Matheleshurst 1378 *SBL 3821* (p)
Malehurst 1378 *SBL 3822* (p) *et seq*, *Maylehurste* 1615 *SBL 6833*
Mealhurst 1842 *TA*

'Speech wood', *v.* **mæðel**, **hyrst**, presumably referring to an ancient meeting-place. The position of the hamlet near a junction of three parishes would be consistent with such a function.

BRIDGLEYS, *Bridge Leys* 1842 *TA*. CROWN P.H. HILL FM. HORSESHOE P.H. MOUNT PLEASANT NURSERY. NILLS HILL, 1842 *TA, Knylls* 1615 *SBL 6822, Knells* 1641 PR(H) 12, *The Knills* 1752 ib, *Nills* 1783 ib, *Knills Hill* 1842 *TA, v.* **cnyll(e)** 'hillock'. POLESGATE, *Poles Gate* 1842 *TA*. PONTESBURY HILL, 1842 *TA*. THE RING (an earthwork on Nills Hill). WOODHOUSE, 1598 *et seq* PR(H) 1, *Wodhouse* 1601 ib. A late-recorded instance of a common name; the possible significance is discussed in Part 1 and under Woodhall *supra*.

A number of houses are named on 6": BROOK HO, CLIFFDALE HO, THE GROVE, LINLEY TERRACE, NEW HO, THE POPLARS, QUARRY VILLA, ROSE VILLA, SOMERVILLE, SOUTH VIEW VILLA, WHITE HALL, WILLOW HO.

Field-Names

Forms in (a) are 1842 *TA*. Early forms dated 1586, 1589, 1594, 1600, 1601, 1602, 1613, 1615, 1616, 1632, 1702, 1783 are *SBL 6785, 6819, 6794, 6807, 12706, 6791, 6813-4, 6822, 6835, 6845, 6841, 6840, 13457, 6546.* It is not certain that all names listed in (b) are in Pontesbury township, some may be elsewhere in the parish.

(a) Lower, Middle and Upper Atwells; Balls Lea and Yds (*Balles Lye and Yarde* 1589); Bank (2); The Barns; Barn Lsw; Barn Mdw; Barnetts Mdw; Big Bank; Big Mead; Big Pce; Blues Yd; Little Bog; Boggy Mdw; Boogy Lane Pce; Bottom Pce; Big, Further, Little and Near Boycott Fd (adjoining Boycott township); Boycott Lane Pce; Boycott Pce (not on township boundary); Branches Mdw; Near Brickkiln Lsw; Brickyard; Bridge Leys; Brook Moor, Further, Lower, Near and Upper - -; Broomy Lsw (2); Big and Little Calico Lees (an obscure allusion to a type of fabric); Chase Hill, Lower and Upper - -; Clover Pce; Lower and Upper Cockshutt Leas (*Cockshutt* 1601, *v.* ***cocc-sciete**); Coppice Pce; Corner Pce; Cottage Pce; Cottons Mdw; Cow Pasture (3); Crosswells; Deanery, Deanery Mdw; Lower and Upper Ditchers Furlong (by Yew Tree Fd); The Dolphins (*dolphin* is a name for a species of aphis); Drury's Lsw; Engine

Fd (2); Big and Long Evans Moor; Little Feg (rough grass); Fishpool; Further and Near Five Acre; Flat Lsw; Flat Mdw; Footway Pce (2); Garden Pce; Big and Little Gin Croft (probably 'engine'); Glebe Lsw; Gorse Patch; Gully Green (Gazetteer lists two other instances); Habberley Mdw, Moor and Slang (all near Habberley boundary); Harpins Pce; Lower Hill Fd (*The Hill* 1601); Big and Little Holly Fd (*Hollinge Field* 1615, a common field (VCH 250), *v.* **holegn**); Horse Pasture; House Fd; House Mdw; House Pce; The Hurst, Lower, Near and Upper Hurst (*Le Hurste* 1594, *v.* **hyrst**); Kings Mdw; Lower and Upper Knolls (*v.* **cnoll**); Lane Mdw; Lane Pce (2); Lawn (inside the oval ring-road which surrounds the oldest part of the village); The Lees (*v.* **lǣs**); Long Mdw (2); Lords Mdw (1600); Lower Mdw; Middle Fd; Mill Lsw; Lower and Upper Moor Lsw (cf. **mōr** names in (b)); Mount Mdw; Nealors Mdw; Further and Near New Mills Pce; New Pce; Nine Holes; Oge Shell Mdw; Orchard Pce; Peartree Lsw; Further and Near Peas Croft; Phillips Mdw; Pit Lsw; Pontesbury Fd (on boundary with Pontesford); Potato Fd; Poulton Croft, Mdw and Pce (adjoining Poulton in Minsterley); Rock; Near Rough Ground; Rough Lsw; Ryegrass Fd; Little Sawney; Sawpit Fd; Sidnall Mdw (cf. Sydnall in Longden *supra*); Slang (4, narrow strips); Further, Little, Middle and Near Slimers Gate (near boundary with Boycott); Smelthouse Yd; Squitchy Fd (refers to scutch grass); Stackyard Fd; Stackyard Mdw (2); Stocking Lsw, Lower Stocking Mdw (cf. *Sto(o)kye* 1586, *Stocky Meadow* 1602, *Stookhey Medowe, Stokeye* - 1613, perhaps a compound of **stocc** 'tree stump' with **(ge)hæg** 'woodland enclosure'); Sturdy Mdw; Tannis Court (along a stream, perhaps a smooth meadow resembling a tennis court); Three Cornered Pce; Three Oaks; Long and Upper Tining (*v.* **tȳning**); Townsend (at W. end of village); Upper Mdw (2); Upper Pce; Big and Little Wallymoor (*Wallymores* 1586, *Wallymoore* 1602, *Wallimore* 1615); Watering Bank; Wheat Lsw; White Lsw; Whitwell Croft (Whitwell was a common field S. of the village, VCH 250); Wildings Yd; Woodside; Workhouse Bank, Croft and Fd; Yewtree Bank (not near following); Big, Little, Lower, Near and Upper Yewtree Fd, Yewtree Mdw and Patch (a group of fields S.E. of the village, perhaps an open field).

(b) *Armore* 1783; *Cadygans Lye* 1589, *Cadigans Ley alias Cardigan's Lye* 1616; *Castlehill, Castle Ringe* 1615 (Gazetteer gives Castle Ring as a modern name); *Cocks Crofte* 1615; *Coults Meadowe* 1601; *Everalls Yard* 1601; *Eyckyns Eyes,* - *Howse* 1615; *Field Ground* 1702; *Gilberts Moor* 1615; *Gorstie Lee* 1601; *The Great Leasow* 1783; *Hare Meadowe* 1601; *The Heald above the Mill* 1601 (*v.* **helde**); *Hemebutts* 1601 ('hemp butts'); *Hue Lie* 1589; *Husons Grounds* 1702; *Hybbos alias Hybbotts Moore* 1615; *Lady Meadowe* 1600 (*v.* **hlǣfdige**); *Lea Furlong* 1601; *Maddoxe Land* 1615, *Madox Furlong* 1616; *Mealinge Field* 1615 (Rea Brook was earlier *Meole*); *Mooredale* 1616, *Moorhead* 1770 VCH 248, *Morewod* 1586,

Moorwoode 1615, *Great and Little Moorewood, Moorewood Meadow* 1632 (*v.* **mōr, dæl, wudu**); *The Neumoores alias The Lords Meadowe* 1602; *Oldes Lye* 1589; *Oxe Leasowe* 1589; *Rowlls Meadowe* 1600; *Trentames Nooke* 1601; *Trevy's Lande* 1616; *Wolpyttes Lane* 1557 VCH 246 ('wolf pits', the road from the village to Gully Green in (a)).

17. PONTESFORD (SJ 410065)

Pontesford' 1255-6 (p), 1291-2 *Ass, -ford* 1308 Ipm *et seq, Pontisford* 1299, 1490 Ipm
Puntesford, Pundes- 1271-2 *Ass* (p)
Ponsforde 1440 Cl (p), *-ford* 1564 *SBL 7031*, 1577 Saxton, 1615 *SBL 6822, Pontesford als Ponsford* 1601 *SBL 12706*
Poinsert 1551 PR(H) 12
Pontsford 1672 HTR
Pontsort 1799 Townson

Probably 'Pant's ford', with the same OE pers.n. as Pontesbury and *Ponslith infra.* The settlement is where the Shrewsbury road crosses a tributary of Rea Brook. The modern pronunciation is [pɔnsət].

PONTESFORD HILL

Ponteslith 1357,78 Pat
Panslith als Yerlys Hill 1539 *VCH(Hereford)*
Ponslithe c.1540 Leland, *-lith* 1589, 1615 *SBL 6819, 6822*, 1637 VCH 254, *Le Ponslythe* 1594 *SBL 6794*
The Ponsort Hill 1799 Townson
Pontesford Hill 1833 OS

The earlier name, *Ponslith*, is 'Pant's concave hill'. Study of **hlith** names in Sa and N.He leaves no doubt that **hlith** is a specialised term used for hills or escarpments which have a large hollow. Pontesford Hill is a striking landscape feature with two peaks and a great hollow in its W. side.

The 1357 and 1378 refs. are to a forest, but the 1589 ref. is to the *mons* called *Ponslith.* The alternative name in the 1539 ref.

has become modern EARL'S HILL, now used of the south peak.

BROOKSIDE HO. CHERRY HAYES COTTAGES, perhaps earlier *Churcheys, Chirhayes v.* Plealey f.ns. EARLSDALE, VCH 254 says the house was *Pool Place* 1810, *Earlsdale* l.19th: probably in imitation of EARL'S HILL, for which *v. supra.* THE GROVE. HILL FM, cf. *Hill Field, Leasow and Piece* 1842 *TA.* LOWER AND UPPER MILL, cf. mill called *Pontisford* 1299 Ipm, *Pontesford Mill* 1783 PR(H) 12, *Ponslyth Mills* 1615 *SBL 6845, v.* VCH 278-9. THE LYD HOLE, *Lyd Hole* 1833 OS, *Lythe Hole Meadow and Piece* 1842 *TA.* This is a deep rocky hollow with a waterfall, at G.R. 415056, another instance of **hlith**, *v.* Pontesford Hill *supra.* NAG'S HEAD P.H. OLD LODGE. THE PLANTATION. SKIN MILL COTTAGE, *Skin Mills* 1782 PR(L) 6, a corn-mill converted to a leather-mill, *v.* VCH 263. SMITHY, 1842 *TA.*

Field-Names

Forms in (a) are 1842 *TA.*

(a) Banky Mdw; Barkers Fd; Barn Yd; Bine Fd (not near Bine Fd in Plealey); Bolt Mdw; Big Bolt Yd (not near preceding); Little Botts; Brad's Croft; Brats Lsw; Brook Mdw; Broomy Mdw; The Bryers; Butterbridge (*v.* Halston f.ns.); Big, Little, Lower and Near Bylets, Little Bylets Bank (Pontesford Brook has two arms here); Calves Croft; Coalpit Mount; Cockshut Yd (perhaps a surname); Cottage Croft; Cross Lsw (by a T-junction); Engine Fd; Feggy Lsw (coarse grass); The Flat; Footway Pce; Front Pce; Gin Patch (probably 'engine'); Gorze; Gritty Mdw; High Trees; Holland Fd; Lady Mdw; The Linleys; Little Mdw; Long Furlong (one of a group of furlong-shaped fields S.E. of village); Long Mdw; Lower Garden; Mill Lsw; Mill Pound (2); New Mill Mdw (by New Mill in Hinton); Pits Lsw; Pool Lsw, Pasture and Place (*v.* Earlsdale *supra*); Prill ('small stream'); Rea Mdw; Ryegrass Fd and Mdw; Sawpit Fd; Slang (3), Further -; Smelthouse Fd; Tanhouse Fd and Pce (*The Tanhouse* 1601 *SBL 12706*); Thistly Mdw; Wheat Fd.

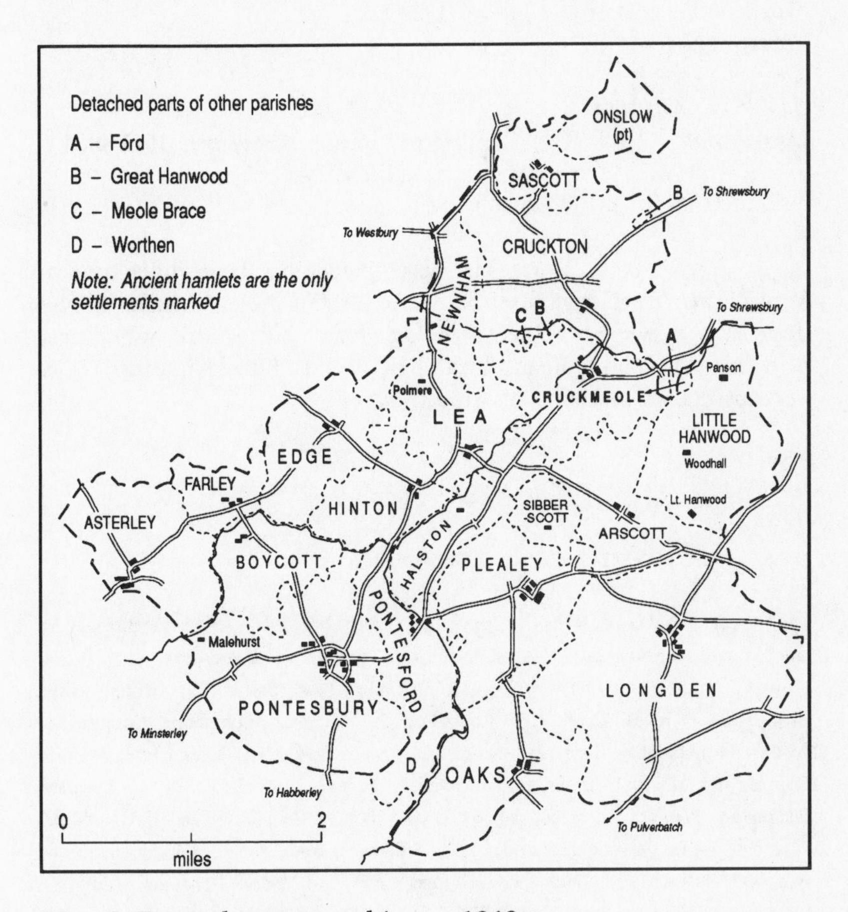

Map 3 Pontesbury townships, c. 1840
(Based on tithe apportionments and maps, 1837-42)

18. SASCOTT (SJ 425119)

Saxcote 1255 RH (p) *et freq* to 1327 SAS 2/X (p)
Sayscot 1274 RH
Saxecote 1308 Ipm
Sassecote 1490 Ipm
Sars(e)coate 1599 PR(H) 1, *Sarsecote* 1607,8 ib, *Sarscote* 1611 ib, *-cott* 1635 *et freq* ib, 1731,83 *SBL 2511*
Sascott 1615 PR(H) 12 *et seq*

'Seaxa's cottage(s)'. The development has been influenced by Welsh *Sais* 'Englishman', a derivative of OE *Seaxe* 'Saxons'. This does not, however, account for the form with *Sars-*, which was obviously the predominant local one in the 17th-18th cent. It is perhaps due to imitation of Arscott *supra.*

Field-Names

Forms in (a) are 1842 *TA*.

(a) Bakehouse Pce; Barnyard; Big Birch Fd, Little Birches, Birches Fd and Mdw (a group of fields in N. tip of township); Boozy Pce (*v.* FN 34, probably referring to pasture rights); Brickkiln Lsw; Briery Fd; Broomy Lsw; Bushy Lsw; Calves Croft (2); Cockshutt Pce (adjoins Longmore Coppice, *v.* ***cocc-sciete**); Coppice Lsw (2); Upper and Lower Cow Lsw; Dairy Close; Dinthill Coppice Fd (Dinthill is in Bicton parish); Farnall Mdw and Pce; Ferny Lsw; Fishpound Pce (by a pond called Sascott Pool); Big Flat Pce; Forty Acres; Furlongs, Little Furlong (adjacent fields S.E. of village); Green Fd; House Mdw; Far and Little Lees, Near Great Lees; Far and Near Longmore Coppice, Longmoor Coppice Mdw; Lower Mdw; Money Lsw (probably referring to rent); Far and Near Onslow Lsw (adjoining O-); Ox Lsw; Pit Lsw; Pool Patch (by Sascott Pool); Stackyard Lsw; Upper Lsw (2); Upper Mdw (2).

(b) *Aldefeld* 1513 VCH 250 (*v.* **eald**).

19. SIBBERSCOT (SJ 427077)

Sibaldescote 1255 RH (p), 1291-2 *Ass*, 1340 Pat, *-kote* 1271-2 *ForProc*, *-cot* 1276 Ipm, 1327 SAS 2/X
Sybescote 1271-2 *Ass*, *Sybascote* 1291-2 *Ass* (p), *Sybaskot alias Sibaldescote* 1308 Ipm, *Sibascote* 1490 Ipm
Sibalscote 1291-2 *Ass*
Siberscot 1551 PR(H) 12, *-cott* 1615 ib, *Sibberscote* 1577 Saxton, 1601 *SBL 12706*, *Sybur-Scoot* 1672 HTR

'Sigebeald's cottage(s)'.

LITTLE COPPICE

Field-Names

Forms in (a) are 1840 *TA*.

(a) Barn Fd, Little - -; Bog Mdw; Lower and Upper Bolus; Brook Mdw; Cinders Lsw, Big and Little Cinders Mdw (a group of fields E. of hamlet-site); The Coppice; Cow Pasture; Crabtree Fd; Footway Fd; Foxholes; Little Mdw; Little Pce; Rail Mdw; Little Shorthill Fd, Shorthill Mdw (Shorthill is in Lea township); Slang (along a stream); Stable Lsw; Wheat Hill; Yewtree Lsw.

(b) VCH 250 mentions a *Lee Field*, recorded in 1493; this was probably a common field adjacent to Lea township.

Westbury

The parish-name, which means 'west fort', is discussed in Part 1.

Westbury contains the townships of Cause, Forest, Lake, Marsh, Newton, Stoney Stretton, Vennington, Wallop, Westbury, Westley, Whitton, Winsley and Yockleton. The VCH account includes Minsterley, but that place is here treated (*supra*) as a separate parish.

1. CAUSE (SJ 340079)

Caus 1134 OrdVit, 1255 RH *et freq* with variant spelling *Kaus*; *Caws* 1394 Pat, *Cause* 1577 Saxton, *Cawse* 1672 HTR
Chaus 1165,98 P, *Chaws* 1274 RH
Caos 1217 Pat, *Kaos* 1255 RH, 1271-2 *ForProc*, 1284-5 FA
Cauz 1246 Ch *et freq* with variant spelling *Kauz* to 1328 Cl
Caures 1255 RH, 1272 Swin, *Caurs* 1301 Ipm, 1392 Pat, 1419 Fine, 1636 *SBL 6573, Caurse* c.1540 Leland, 1618,68 *SBL 6772, 6780, Caourse* c.1540 Leland
Cawes 1255 RH, 1347, 1419,30 Fine, 1549 Pat, *Kawes* 1274 RH, *Caw(e)s* 1308 Ipm
Cowys 1255-6 *Ass*
Cautz 1302,4 Pat
Cauce 1314 Pat, 1404 Cl
Caux 1330 Fine *et freq* to 1453 *SBL 7070*

It is likely that Cause is a French name chosen by the Corbet family for the castle which they built to be the *caput* of their barony. The oft-repeated assertion that the name is a transferred use of that of the Pays de Caux in Normandy must, however, be questioned. It has become general practice to cite Eyton as authority for the statement that the Corbets came from Caux, but Eyton (Vol.VII, p.6) references this to Blakeway's *The Sheriffs of Shropshire* (1831), and Blakeway gives no evidence for it. He says on p.38 that "it seems nearly certain" that the family had resided in Caux, and on p.40 that "Caus Castle [was] newly named from the Pais de Caus", but it seems probable that this is based only on the resemblance of the names.

There is no philological objection to deriving Cause from Caux. The French name was Julius Caesar's *Caletum*, but it had become *Calz* before 1026 (J. Adigard des Gautries, 'Les noms de "pays" normands attestés de 911 à 1066', Festschrift Adolf Bach I, *Rheinische Vierteljahrsblätter* 20, Bonn 1955, ex. inf. Miss C. Clark). Ordericus Vitalis, whose *Ecclesiastical History* provides the earliest reference to the English place, betrays no knowledge of a connection with the French district-name, for which he uses the learned form *Caletensis pagus*. The main objections to the derivation are, however, that a district-name is not so appropriate to the naming of a castle as the name of a Continental castle-site would be, and that no firm evidence appears to be available to connect the Corbets with the Pays de Caux.

Even if it does not derive from the Normandy district-name, Cause is not likely to be English. There are frequent forms with *-z* from 1246 to 1328, and this letter is not normally used in ME place-name spellings for a final voiced *-s*. The sound represented by *-z* is likely to have been [ts], as further indicated by *Cautz* 1302,4. NED, s.n.Z, observes that "Z was used in OE. in the spelling of alien words --- this use was continued in ME."; and that "In French, the reduction of (ts) to (s) brought about a change of spelling from z to s (often alternating with x, e.g. *vois, voix*)". The *Caus, Caux* spellings accord with the last statement.

There are settlement-names in France with the modern form Caux. Some of these are documented and discussed in F.R. Hamlin, *Les Noms de Lieux du Département de l'Hérault* (Nimes 1988). The likely derivation is from *caus*, modern *chaux*, 'chalk, lime'. The Shropshire name could be an independent coinage of this French name, applied to a structure characterised to an unusual extent by the use of lime or chalk.

Cause is a name likely to have been frequently uttered by French speakers. It would also be very familiar to Welsh speakers, and the forms with *-r-*, which cannot bear a regular relationship to the rest of the series, may be a Welsh substitution. R. Morgan (*MorganTs*) takes *Cawres* to be the Welsh word meaning 'giantess', used as a nickname for the castle. The name is listed as "Cawrse (Cawres)" in M. Richards, *Welsh Administrative and Territorial Units*. There was a district called the Welshry of Cause, which consisted of townships in Welsh tenure outside Westbury parish, but for which Cause Castle was an administrative centre. Leland gives a confused account of a district called *Caurs(e)land, Causeland*.

A borough of Cause was planted within the outer ramparts of the castle, and the street-plan could still be made out in the early 19th cent. (VCH, p.310). Cause Castle Fm is the only surviving building. The relationship to 'Old Cause' (Hawcocks Mount) is discussed below.

The DB manor of *Alretone* was formerly considered to be Cause, but it has been demonstrated that it is Trewern in Buttington, Mont.

COTTON (lost), *Cotes juxta Cawes* 1255 RH, *Coten iuxta Caus* 1291-2 *Ass, Cotton* 1574 *VCH*. The hamlet was deserted in 1252 (VCH 317): *v.* **cot(e)**, dat.pl. **cotum**.

HAWCOCKS. The buildings with this name are adjacent to fields called *Great, Long Hawcocks* and *Hawcocks Meadow* 1841 *TA*. VCH (300, 303) says this was a common field called *Aldecaus* Field in 1361 (ref. to *LongleatMSS*). *Aldecaus* has been corrupted to Hawcocks. There is a motte here known as Hawcocks Mount, and this may have been the original site of the Corbets' castle, becoming 'old Cause' when a replacement was built ¾ mile W.

CAUSEBEACH, on the other side of a stream from Whittonbeach, *v.* **bæce**. GROVE COTTAGE: the building is shown, but not named, on *TAMap*. THE KNAPS, *The Knapps, Lower Knaps* 1841 *TA, v.* **cnæpp**. PARK WD, 1841 *TA*, not adjacent to the field called Castle Park in *TA*.

Field-Names

Forms in (a) are 1841 *TA*.

(a) Ashes; Bank; Banky Mdw; Best Fd; The Betch (*v.* **bæce**); Brickkiln Mdw; Broomy Lsw; Calves Croft; Castle Bank, - Park (by the Castle-site cf. *Caus Park* 1540 SAS 54); Cow Pasture; Crabtree Pce; Great, Lower and Upper Dutley; Foggy Pce (*fog* and *feg* are refs. to coarse grass); Big and Little Hook Fd (probably referring to a contour projection); Jacks Pce; Kennets Croft (probably a surname, but it is beside an unnamed stream); Knolls (*v.* **cnoll**); Lower Long Lsw; Long Pce; Lower Fd; Lower Mdw; Mdw Bank; Milking Bank; Mount Lsw (*v.* Hawcocks *supra*); Old Baths (on a small stream); Ox Pasture; Pale Park (N. of Castle Park, the pale may be the park enclosure); Park Fd (near Park Wood, at some distance from the other Park ns.); Peartree Pasture; Peters Bank; Raisin Tree Fd (FN 50 says this is a name for the red currant); Rough Ends; Rough Park, Far - - (S.E. of Castle Park); Round Pce (rectangular); Rushy Mdw; Ryegrass Pce; Thistly Pce; Way Lsw; White Lsw; Wintley, - Fd, - Mdw, - Wood, Lower - (VCH 300 says this was a common field); Far and Near Wood Lsw.

(b) *Bradmershe* 1349-50 *VCH(NLW)* (*v.* **brād, mersc**); *Caldefaresmedwe* 1272 Swin (perhaps a derogatory n., 'cold fare' meaning 'poor food', *v.* **mǣd**); *Cawescastelhul* c.1274 *VCH(Longleat)* ('Cause Castle hill'); *Clicheswey* 1272 Swin; *Le Heth* 1354 Ipm (*v.* **hǣð**); *Malkyn Hyll* 1540 SAS 54; *Wymundesteneslawe* 1272 Swin (possibly **hlāw** 'tumulus' affixed to a n. meaning 'Wīgmund's stone').

2. FOREST (SJ 311086)

The Westbury portion of the Forest of Hayes was accounted a township by 1659 (VCH 295). The forest (a chase in the Middle Ages) was mostly in Wales. It is *boscum qui vocatur Le Hey* 1291-2 *Ass*, (forest of) *La Hey* 1357,78 Pat, (pasture in *Caux* called) *The Haye* 1403 Cl.

DB records four *haiæ* in the adjacent manor of Worthen, and VCH (p.297) suggests that Hayes Forest was one of these. As with Hayes in Alberbury (*supra*), the name is perhaps more likely to be a post-Conquest formation from Latin *haia* 'forest enclosure', than to derive from OE **(ge)hæg**, which had the same meaning.

The settlement is Forest of Hayes on OS maps. Early references are (manor of) *Heye* 1414 Fine, *The Forrest of Heys* 1655 SAS 47, *Forrest of the Hayes* 1672 HTR. VCH (p.307) says the farm is first mentioned in 1564 and cites a Welsh name *Latha-coed*, 'yard of the wood', which is a translation of Hayes.

BREAKNECK DINGLE, 1841 *TA*. BROOMHILL, *Brome Hill* 1540 SAS 54, *Bromehill* 1576,7 VCH, *Broomhill Wood* 1835 OS, *v.* **brōm, hyll**: VCH 306 says a shepherd's hut is recorded here in 1445. COTTAGE DINGLE, *Cottage Meadow* containing a *Dingle* is shown 1841 *TAMap*. FOREST DINGLE, 1841 *TA*. HARE DINGLE. HARBEECH WD, *Harbache* 1564 VCH, *Harbatch, Harbitch Meadow* 1841 *TA*: *v.* **bæce**, first element possibly 'hare', Hare Dingle is nearby. HAYWOOD, *Haywood Meadow* 1841 *TA*, *v.* **(ge)hæg, wudu**. NANT-Y-MYSSELS, - WD, *Nant-y-Musco* 1564 VCH. The house is shown, but not named, on *TAMap*. The Wood, which is some distance E., is *Anti Muscles* 1841 *TA*. A Welsh name with **nant** 'brook'; the farm is by a small stream. OAKLEY WD, 1841 *TA*, *Oykkeleywode* 1349-50 *VCH(NLW)*, *Okeley* 1564 VCH, *v.* **āc, lēah, wudu**. POUND HO, 1835 OS, *Pounds*

Piece 1841 *TA*. QUABBS PLANTATION, *v*. ***cwabba** 'marsh'. WOODLEASOWS, 1835 OS.

Field-Names

Forms in (a) are 1841 *TA*.

(a) Back Lsw; Lower and Upper Bald Hill (VCH 297 says *Baldhill* was one of the Forest walks in 1564); Banky Ground; Banky Mdw; Barn Fd; Black Park (an unremarkable field on N. boundary of township); Bowens Mdw; Big and Little Breakneck (by - Dingle *supra*); Briary Lsw; Broad Pce; Brood Pce; Broomy Lsw; Further, Little, Lower, Near and Upper Carver; Calves Bank; Calves Close; Colliers Moor, - - Dingle; Cow Pasture; Crabtree Lsw; Daisy Fd; Dingle Pce; Face of Ley; Fat House; Flat Lsw; Big and Little Foggy Pce (coarse grass); Garden Mdw; Gorsy Pce; Great Lsw; Hall Mdw; The Harp (not harp-shaped, but field divisions here look like late ones); Lower and Upper Harrow Pce; High Tree Lsw; House Mdw; Kiln Hole; Little Mdw; Long Lsw; Long Mdw (2); Lower Mdw; Lower Pce; Middle Lsw (2); Near Middle Pce; Mountain Pce; New Pce; Oaktree Pce; Over Lsw; Big and Little Ox Lsw; Ox Fd; Ox Pasture; Pepper Hole (6" map shows a spring here, at W. end of Breakneck Dingle); Piggs Clover; Post Pce; Big and Little Quarry Lsw; Red Gate Pce and Pltn; Rough Ground; Round Fd (rectangular); Round Mdw (also rectangular); Big Rowley; Slang (2); Square Mdw (triangular); Stable Pce; Stony Lsw; Top Mdw; Well Lsw (2); Windsors Green (probably *Wynston Feld* 1540 SAS 54, where the building of a house is noted); Lower and Upper Withy Bed.

(b) *Stockings* 1540 SAS 54 (*v*. **stoccing**).

3. LAKE (SJ 371069, 375066)

Lacu 1271-2 *ForProc* (p), *La Lake* 1291-2 *Ass* (p), *Laik* 1579 *SBL 6757*, *Lake* 1608 *SBL 6761 et seq*, *The Lake* 1610 *SBL 6765* *Leeke* 1672 HTR

Richard *de la Lake*, mentioned 1201 P, may have come from this place. *v*. **lacu**, 'small stream, side-channel, drainage ditch': the first sense is the appropriate one in this instance. A small tributary of Rea Brook forms the E. boundary of the township and the parish. The *TAMap* names Upper and Lower Lake, but only the latter is named on the 19th-cent. and modern 1" maps.

The *TA* treats the townships of Westley, Winsley and Lake as a single unit, so the list of field-names is given *infra*, under Winsley.

4. MARSH (SJ 335105)

The township-name is discussed in Part **1** under the form Marche. It derives from OE **mersc** 'marsh'.

BRIAR LEY (1840 *TA*)

Brerlawe 1221-2, 1255-6, 1291-2 *Ass* (p), *Brerlowe* 1274 RH (p), 1291-2 *Ass* (p)
Brerle 1271-2 *Ass* (p)
Breerlowe 1282-1317, 1327 *SRO 840*
Brerelawe 1291-2 *Ass* (p)

'Brier mound', *v.* **brēr**, **hlāw**. The fields called *Brierly* and *Briar Ley* on the *TAMap* surround a small circular earthwork at G.R.343107. If the *hlāw* is this earthwork the structure is likely to be prehistoric or Saxon rather than Norman. VCH 305 says that there was a hamlet, deserted at an unknown date.

PARTONWOOD

Pernedon 1280 InqMisc, 1285 Pat, *-don'* 1291-2 *Ass*
Perendon 1285 Pat, *-done* 1289 Swin
Perndon' 1291-2 *Ass*
Peurendon' 1291-2 *Ass*
Parton Jas I *SBL 4199*, *- Wood* 1840 *TA*

'Pear hill', *v.* **dūn**. First el. an OE adj. ***peren** 'growing with pears'. The same name occurs in Ess in the form Parndon. VCH 305 says that Partonwood was earlier *Little Parton*, recorded 1624 on the site of the deserted hamlet. The farm became Parton Wood in the 18th cent. It was converted into cottages after 1840.

WIGMORE, UPPER and LOWER

This name, which probably means 'unstable marsh', is discussed in Part 1. The names of the two farms have recently been restored to OS maps. The 19th-cent. OS Index to Tithe Survey map gives Marsh and Wigmore as the name of the township.

HALFWAY HO, 1836 OS. VCH 181 describes this as a squatter settlement. The focus may have been a public house with a name which referred to the position on the Shrewsbury to Welshpool road. MARCHE HALL (*Upper Marsh* 1765 VCH, *Marsh Hall* 1801 VCH, *Marsh House* 1840 *TA*), MARCHE MANOR FM, MARCHE LANE, MARSH FM. Marche and Marsh are alternative forms of the township-name. OAK VILLA, the adjacent field is *Oak Piece* 1840 *TA*. SARN. There are fields called *Big* and *Little Sarn* 1840 *TA* on either side of Marche Lane, but the farm called Sarn on the 6" map is beside a parallel road to the E. of this. The name is Welsh *sarn* 'causeway'. SERGEANT'S DINGLE.

Field-Names

Forms in (a) are 1840 *TA*. Earlier forms in (a) and all names in (b) are 1722 *SBL 6195*.

(a) Backhouse Fd and Pce ('bakehouse'); Banky Fd and Pce; Barbers Lsw; Barn Fd (*The Barn Fields*); Barnyard (3) (*The Barn Yards*); Big Fd; Big Mdw (4); Brickkiln Fd; Broomy Bank; Broomy Fd (2) (cf. *The Broomy Park*); Calves Croft; Chandlers Fd; The Closets (*The Clossetts*, of similar size and shape to surrounding fields); Clover Lsw; Common Mdw; Counds Mdw; Cow Pasture; Far, Middle, Near and Upper Eight Acres; Far Mdw; Far Pce; Fishpool Fd (the map shows a pool); Five Acres; Flat Fd; Flat Mdw; Four Acres; Furlong, Lower and Upper; Gay Croft; Gorsy Fd (*The Gorsty Field*); Gravel Pce; Green Hill; Heath Lsw (2); Hill Fd; Holly Bank; Hollybush Mdw (*The Holly Bush Leasow*); House Lsw, Old - - (building shown on map); Intake (land enclosed from heath); Kitchen Mdw; The Lawn (by Marche Hall); Little Fd; Little Mdw (2);

Little Pasture; Long Lsw; Lower Mdw; Marlpit Fd; Middle Fd; Near Mdw (2); Near Pce; Oak Lsw; Orchard Fd; Ox Lsw; Ox Moor; Big Pasture Fd, Little Pasture; Pigeons Bank; Pit Fd (2); Pit Lsw; Pluck Mdw; Plumtree Lsw (*The Plumbtree Leasow*); Pound Pce (2); Big and Little Red Heart (*The Red Hart Ground*, White Heart is nearby, there is no apparent reason for the names); Far Rogers Pce; Rough Ground (2); Rough Mdw; Rushy Mdw (*The Rushy Piece*); Ryegrass Pce (*The Ryegrass Patch*); Slang, Slang Mdw (long, narrow fields); Square Patch (2); Carpenter's Square; Square Mdw (cf. *The Square Croft*); Thistly Fd; Top Fd; Upper Mdw (2); Well Pce (cf. *The Well Leasow*); White Fd (2); White Heart (*v. supra*); White Hill Fd; Wigmore Hill; Wigmore Mdw; Wood Lsw (2).

(b) *The Bank*; *The Bank Leasow*; *The Brand Meadow and Yard*; *The Fold*; *The Goose Close Croft*; *The Little Gorsty Leasow*; *The Green Park Bank*; *The Hemp Butt*; *The Hungry Crofts*; *The Moor*, *- - Meadow*; *The Patch*; *The Rosey Meadow*; *The White Leasow*; *Wigmore Moor Meadow*; *The Yard*.

5. NEWTON (SJ 383084)

Neweton' 1291-2 *Ass*
Neuton' 1291-2 *Ass* (p), *Newton in Cawyslond* 1453 Cl, *Neuton by Westbury* 1492 Ipm, *Newton in Cause* 1500 Ipm

'New settlement', *v.* **nīwe, tūn**, a very common name which occurs more than a dozen times in this county.

The farm called Newton on the 19th-cent. OS map is Lower Newton on the 1961 1"; the 19th-cent. map shows another farm called Upper Newton to the W. The *TAMap* of 1842 gives Upper Newton and Lower Newton as the names of the parts of the township which lie W. and E. of the road on which the farm is situated. VCH 305 says that Lower Newton Fm is likely to be on the site of the earliest hamlet. It is surrounded by a square moat, and there is a reference to it by the name *Broughcastle* in 1839.

NEW LEASOWS, *New Leasow* 1842 *TA*. NEWTON WD: VCH 299 says this is recorded in 1584.

Field-Names

Forms in (a) are 1842 *TA*.

(a) Bank Fd; Banky Lsw; Barn Lsw; Barn Mdw; Big Lsw; Dip Pit Lsw (perhaps a reference to sheep dipping); Doctors Mdw; Big and Little Fag (probably referring to rough grass); Far Old Mdw; Garden Fd; Gorse; Green Lsw; Hightree Lsw; Hopyard; Jones's Lsw; Little Coppice; Little Lsw; Long Lsw; Mans Lsw; Marsh Furlong; Near Mdw; Old Coppice; Rabbit Lsw; Riders Lsw; Rough Lsw; Slang (2); Well Lsw; White Lsw; Wood Lsw; Woodhays Lsw.

6. STONEY STRETTON (SJ 384095)

Stretton' 1255 RH *et freq* with variant spelling *-ton*; *Stretton Parva* 1612,34 PR(H) 6, *Stoney Stretton* 1833 OS, *Stony* - 1842 *TA*
Stratton 1255-6 *Ass* (p)
Strettons 1577 Saxton

'Settlement on a Roman road', *v.* **strǣt, tūn**. *Parva* and Stoney are probably for distinction from Church Stretton, the other example in the county of this common name. The village is a short distance S. of the Roman road from Wroxeter to Trefeglwys, which is called *The Stonye Causeway* 1512 *SRO 0/665.*

ELEPHANT AND CASTLE P.H. NEW BRIDGE, 1836 OS; VCH 301 says this dates from 1767, *v.* Steadford in f.ns. OLDLANE COTTAGES. PATCHES, *patch* is the usual term in this part of Sa for land which has been divided into small allotments. STRETTON HEATH, *Streton's Heath* 1624 PR(H) 6, *Strettons Heath* 1660 *SBL 6124, v.* VCH 308 for the squatter settlement.

The 19th-cent. OS map marks *Oakley Cottage* E. of New Bridge: *TAMap* shows the building but does not name it.

Field-Names

Forms in (a) are 1842 *TA*.

(a) Balls Croft; The Bank; Barnyard (3); Big Lsw; Big, Green and Little Bimes (*v.* Yockleton f.ns.); Black Leys (*Blakelye* 1418-19 *SRO 840, v.* **blæc, lēah**); Blowers Pce; Boars Butts (*Bore Butts* c.1380 *SBL 6172*, first element probably **bār** 'boar', the field-shapes on *TAMap* suggest a small open-field system in this area, *v.* **butte**); Church Bridge, Little and Long - -, Upper Church (probably so named because on the route to Westbury church); Big and Little Cinders (probably referring to slag); Colliers Ley; Coppice, Coppice Lsw, Old Coppice Fd; Crabtree Lsw; Crossways (in one angle of a cross-roads); Big and Little Edge Pce; Farley Pce (by the road to Farley in Pontesbury); Far Patch Lsw; Five Acres; Frog Pole (by the stream); Green Lsw; Hall Mdw; Big Hays, Middle Hay (*v.* **(ge)hæg**); Heath Fd, Pce and Slang (on Stretton Heath); Big, Far and Near Heys (*v.* **(ge)hæg**, not near Hay ns. *supra*); Big and Upper Hicknall (*v.* Yockleton f.ns. *infra*); Humphreys Pce; Little Leys; Linley Mdw; Little Bank; Little Mdw (3); Lower Lsw; Near Patch Lsw; Near Pce; New Fd; New Lsw (2); Big and Little Newton Stiles (by Newton township); North Furlong (this and Upper Furlong might have been parts of an open field N. of the village); Oak Lsw; Ox Lsw; Park Corner (referring to Yockleton Park); Parlour Furlong (this and Brook Furlong are S.E. of the village, the meaning of *parlour* in f.ns. has not been established); Quarry Bank; Ross Moor Pool; Rushy Mdw; Little, Long and Middle Shop Lsw (no building shown on map); Slang (*freq*); Spout Patch (*v.* **spoute**, one of numerous small 'patches' on Stretton Heath); Stable Yd; Steadford Bridge (by New Bridge, where the Roman road crosses the brook which flows through the township); Three Cornered Pce; Top Pce; Upper Furlong; Wain Doors (on S. edge of Stretton Heath, perhaps referring to cart traffic); Way Lsw; Well Mdw; White Lsw; Wood Lsw; Yewtree Lsw (2); Yockleton Yd.

(b) *Gomelyth Grene* c.1380 *SBL 6172* (wrongly printed as *Ganelith Green* VCH 299, middle element probably **hlith**); *Longelye* 1418-19 *SRO 840* (*v.* **lang, lēah**); *More Meadow* 1637 PR(H) 6 (*v.* **mōr**); *Le Myllebroke* 1442-3 *VCH*; *Watkynslye* c.1380 *SBL 6172* (one of several names in this document in which the ME derivative of **lēah** is combined with a pers.n.).

7. VENNINGTON (SJ 339097)

Feniton 1256 Eyton, *Fenyton* 1305 Pat, *Fennyton* 1396 Fine, *Veniton* 1760 PR(H) 7
Feynton' 1291-2 *Ass*
Penyton 1347 Cl, Ipm
Venington alias Fenington 1618 *SBL 9943*, *Fenington* 1649 PR(H) 6, *Venington* 1768 PR(H) 7

'Marshy settlement', *v.* **fennig, tūn.**

HILL FM, 1836 OS, *La Hulle* 1221-2 *Ass* (p), *v.* **hyll.**

VRON GATE, *The Vron* 1600 *VCH(SRO)*, *Vraungate* 1807 PR(H) 7, *Fron Gate* 1836 OS. Welsh *bron* 'breast of a hill'. VCH 307 says that a farm is recorded here in 1609.

BLACKMORE, *Blackmoor Meadow and Piece* 1840 *TA*. CAUSE-MOUNTAIN LANE. DIPTREEHILLS, *Dipter Hill, Lower, Upper and Banky Dipter Hill* 1840 *TA*. GORSTY COVERT: corresponds to *Fallow Piece* 1840 *TA*, *v.* ***gorstig.** QUABBS PLANTATION, *Quags Plantation* 1840 *TA*, probably ***cwabba** 'marsh', in spite of the *TA* spelling. SEVEN STARS P.H., 1840 *TA*.

Field-Names

Forms in (a) are 1840 *TA*.

(a) The Angle (a tiny, funnel-shaped, area); Banky Close; Banky Lsw; Barn Fd; Barn Lsw (2); Bedsmores Mdw; Big Lsw; Big Mdw; Bonny Ford Mdw; Brickkiln Fd; Brook Mdw (2); Broomy Lsw; Burnetts Mdw; Burr Croft; Lower and Upper Butchers Wood; Calves Croft; Big and Little Churns Croft; Clover Seed Pce; Cocketts; Common Fd; Common Pce; Cottage Pce; Cow Pasture (4); Crabtree Fd; Dock Lsw; Dodds Lsw; Eight Acres (2); Far Fd (2); The Fields; Flat Park (two large fields on either side of the brook E. of Half Park *infra*); Four Acres (appreciably smaller than the two Eight Acres); Little, Lower, Middle and Upper Foxholes; Big and Little Friday (*v.* **Frīgedæg**); Garden Pce; Goodalls Patches; Gorsy Lsw; Grazing Pce; Green Bank; Green Lane; Green Lsw; Half Park (two fields by Quabbs Plantation); The Hams (in the bend of a brook, *v.* **hamm**); Harp (harp-shaped); Harpers Pce and Patch; Hill Fd (2); Hill Pce (4); Holly Lsw (2); Hough Mdw, Hough Croft Mdw (*v.* **hōh**, there is a small hill here, N. of the village); Long Leadmoor, Ledmoor Hill, Ledmoor Wall (the last is some distance from the other two); Little Mdw (3); Long Croft; Long Lsw (3); Lower Fd; Lower Lsw; Lower Mdw (3); Big and Little Lowhead, Lowhead Mdw; Marsh Gate Mdw; Middle Bank; Middle Fd (Far, Middle and Near Fd adjoin); Middle Gates; Mounts Hill; Mountain Pce; Near Croft; Near Fd (2); Nelsons Hill; New Bridge, Big and Little - - (by the brook W. of the village); New Inclosure; Owletts Yd; Pen y bryn (Welsh, 'end of the hill', adjoins Vron Gate); Quarry Bank; Quarry Pce (2); The Ridges; Rough Mdw; Round Mdw (not circular); Rushy Fd; Rushy Lsw; Ryegrass Fd; Scotts Fd; Scurry Lsw; Slang (*freq*); The Slieve Mdw (sleeve-shaped); Spring Head; Stackyard Croft; Upper Standleys; Stitches Pce (perhaps a reference to hurdles, *v.* PN Berks 907); Sweet Mdw; The Three Brooks; Three Cornered Pce; Far and Near Top Croft; Upper Fd; Upper Moor (2); Well Mdw; White Lsw; Wigmore Hill, Little, Lower and Upper - - (probably pasture belonging to Wigmore in Marche, *supra*); The Willows.

(b) *The Beche Pasture* 1522 *VCH(SBL)*; *Caldwall ib* (*v.* **cald**, **wælle**); *New Lsw ib* (*v.* **lǣs**).

8. WALLOP (SJ 329077)

Walehope 1255-6 *Ass*, 1403 Cl, 1404 Pat
Walhop' 1255-6 *Ass* (p), *Walhope* 1291-2 *Ass*, 1375-6 *VCH(NLW)*, *Walhop* 1347 Cl
Wallehop' 1255-6 *Ass* (p)
Welhope 1255-6 *Ass* (p)
Walope 1323 BM, *Wallop* 1347 Ipm *et seq*

'Secluded valley with a spring', from **hop** and the West Midland form of **wella**. This is one of three examples, the others being Wallop Ha and Wallhope (in Tidenham) Gl: *v.* DEPN and PN Gl 3, 265.

The medieval settlement is represented by Lower Wallop Fm, which is in a situation typical for the generic **hop**. 'Lower' was probably prefixed for distinction from Wallop Hall, at G.R.316078, which was built 1664-71, demolished 1953 (VCH 303, 307).

LANGLEY WD, 1841 *TA*, *Longlyth* 16th VCH 297, *v.* **lang**, **hlith**, the latter probably in its characteristic Sa sense 'concave hill-side'.

BROOM COVER. HAZELS, 1836 OS. THE NURSERY (a small wood by Wallop Hall). ROOK DINGLE, *Rookery Dingle* 1841 *TA*. TILEDHOUSE WD, *Tiledhouse* 1836 OS, *Tile House* 1841 *TA*. WALLOPHILL PLANTATION.

Field-Names

Forms in (a) are 1841 *TA*.

(a) The Acres (there were three open fields in the township, Oakley, Middle and Langley Fields, and it is clear from the *TAMap* that many of the later fields are enclosed furlongs; acres probably means 'strips' in this list); Ashtree Mdw; Backhouse Mdw (*v.* **bæc-hūs**); Bank Fd; Banners Pce (adjoins Battle Fd); Barn Lsw; Battle Fd (possibly a reference to juridical combat); Big Mdw (2); Broom Mdw and Wood; Broomy Close; Broomy Lsw (2); Little Bryn (adjoins Big Hill Pce, Welsh *bryn* 'hill'); Burgwins Pce; Bush Croft; Calves Close; Coffin, Little - (coffin-shaped); The Coppice; Coppice Mdw; Cote Fd and Lsw (not near each other, *v.* **cot(e)**); Cow Pasture (2); Crabtree Mdw; Dingle Fd; Fish's Back (shaped like a fish viewed from above); Flat Lsw; Foggy Lsw (coarse grass); Furlong (see Acres *supra*); Further Lsw; Garden Fd; Garden Mdw; Gorsy Lsw; The Grove; Hall Mdw (2, by Wallop Hall); New Harp (harp-shaped); Hill Head; Hill Lsw; Big Hill Pce; Lower and Upper Hill Slang (long, narrow strips); Langleys, Further, Little, Middle and Near Langley, Langley Cow Pasture and Mdw (an open field, *v.* Langley Wd *supra* for etymology); Great Laws; Lodwicks Pce; Upper Long Lsw; Long Mdw; Lower Fd; Lower and Upper Middle Fd (an open field); Middle Lsw; Moat Bank (S.W. of Lower Wallop. cf. *Moat Meadow* 1634 VCH 303, there was a moated messuage at Wallop in 1381); Great and Upper Mountain Pce; New Pce; Ninepenny Task (there is another in Mainstone, *v.* FN 60); Middle Oak Lsw; Oaktree Lsw; Orchard Bank and Slang; Park Rogers (by Wallop Hall); Philpots Yd; Pound Pce; Pritchards Cow Pasture; Quarry Lsw; Round Mdw (not circular); Lower, Middle and Upper Rowley (adjoining Rowley in Worthen, which is a **hlith** n.); Shop Mdw (*TAMap* shows a building); Six Acres; Square Pce; Tawney Pce; Ten Butts (*v.* **butte**); Town Mdw; Way Lsw; Well Mdw.

9. WESTBURY (SJ 355095)

v. supra for Westbury.

WIGLEY, 1599 *SBL 7033*, 1609 *SBL 6762*. 1631 *SBL 6942*, *Wigley Farm* 1601 *SBL 6867*. This name occurs in Db and Ha, and there is a better-documented Sa example in Stanton Lacy. 'Beetle wood or clearing', *v.* **wicga**, **lēah**.

BROOK HO. BROXTON WD, *Broxtons Meadow and Wood* 1839 *TA*. VCH 299 ascribes the name to Roger *Broxon*, tenant c.1630. VCH also says that it was formerly *Foxholes Wood*. LION INN, cf. *Lion Meadow* 1839 *TA*. QUARRY WDS. SITELEY, 1836 OS, *Sightley Field* 1839 *TA*. WESTBURY BRIDGE. WOOD FM. WOODSIDE.

Field-Names

Names in (a) are 1839 *TA*. Early forms dated 1343 are *SBL 9335*, 1512 *SRO 0/665*, 1631 *SBL 6889*.

(a) Adders Moor (possibly *Atkynsmore* 1540 SAS 54, *Astons Moores* 1610 *SBL 6768*, *Astomes Moores* 1618,21 *SBL 6774,5,70*); Ash Plantation; Backhouse Lsw (adjoins Wigley, *v.* **bæc-hūs**); Bank (2, immediately N. and S. of Wood Fm); Bank Fd; Banky Fd; Banky Lsw; Barley Bank, Big and Little - -; Barn Croft; Barnyard (2); Big Mdw (3); The Bog; Bog Fd; Big Bonny Fd (adjoins Bonny Ford Mdw in Vennington); Bowyers Lsw and Mdw; Big and Little Brandert (a *brandart* is a trivet, but the fields are not this shape on *TAMap*); Bridge Fd (2); Broad Mdw; Brook Lsw; Broom Mdw; Broomy Lsw; Butts Stiles; Calves Croft (2); Church Bridge; Cinder Lsw; Coalpit Bank; Coalpit Lsw; Cockings Ley (*Corkinges Lee* 1631, *Lee* or *Ley* is often combined with a surname in this Hundred); Cockshut Lsw (*v.* **cocc-sciete**); Colleges Mdw and Moor; Common

Lsw; Company's Moors; Big, Little and Old Coppice; Cow Pasture (3); Far and Near Cross Fd (these and some Cross names in Whitton are near a T-junction on the Vennington-Westbury road); Cureton's Moor; David's Bank; Dingle Marsh; Eight Acres (3: apart from Forty Acres *infra* such ns. correspond reasonably to field-area in this township); Elmtree Patch; Engine Fd and Pce, Old Engine Ground (by coalpits); Far and Upper Fall (adjoining Coppice names, ***(ge)fall** 'clearing'); Far Fd; Feg (coarse grass); Five Acres; Five Strikes Sowing; Flat Lsw (2); Little Flows, Big Flows Green; Forty Acres (a minute patch); Four Acres; Fourteen Acres; The Furlong; Garden Pce; Gilding Gore (together with adjacent Butts Stiles this would be a gore-shaped field); Gorsty Ground (*v.* ***gorstig**); Handleys Coppice and Yd; Big and Little Harp (the two fields together might be considered harp-shaped); Lower and Upper Hill Pce; Hinwood Mdw, Henwood Ground (by Hinwood in Pontesbury); Hollin Graves (*Hellenegreve* c.1265 SAC, 'holly grove', *v.* **holegn, grǣfe**); House Lsw; Hovel Fd; Hurdleys Moor; King Oak, Little - -; Long, Upper and Lower Lady Fd; Lower and Upper Lady Mdw (*Lady Meadow* 1631, *v.* **hlǣfdige**); Big and Little Limmell; Linghams Hayes (1631); Little Mdw (2); Long Lsw (2); Lower Moor; Machine Lsw (2, on either side of Old Coal Pit Road); Big and Little Macknall; Madewell; Middle Pce; Mill Lsw; Mill Mdw; The Moor(s) (*Nether Moore* 1631); Moor Lane Head; Mount Fd; Old Land; Plantation Fd; Pool Fd; Potato Fd; Quarry Bank; Red Lake; Rock Fd; Rossy Pce (possibly 'rosey', cf. *Rosey Meadow* in Marsh); Rough Ground (2); Rough Mdw; Rushy Mdw; Rushy Pce; Ryegrass Fd; Seven Acres; Shed Mdw; Shop Mdw (no building shown); Sitch Mdw, Big Sitch (*v.* **sīc**); Six Acres (2); Slang (2, long, narrow strips); Soil Mdw; Spring Coppice; Spring Lsw; Square Lsw; Stony Croft; Sun Patch; Ten Acres; Three Cornered Fd (2); Townsend (on S. outskirt of village); Big Townsend Mdw, Little Townsend (on N.E. outskirt of village); Two Trees; Upper Mdw; Whites Ground; Far, Lower, Middle and Near Widows Moors; Wier Lsw and Mdw ('weir'); Wigmore Hill (this was a common field, Wigmore is in Marche *supra*), Far and Near Witcher Fd; Wood Lsw; Workhouse Mdw and Pce; Yewtree Lsw.

(b) *Birchemore, - Hurst* 1512; *Brow Cast* 1695 Morden; *The Common Plock* 1768 VCH (a variant of *pleck* 'small piece of ground'); *Depemore* 1450 *VCH(SBL)*, *Dypmore als Lyngers Leys* 1512 (*v.* **dēop, mōr**); *Le Gavelle* 1343 (*v.* **gafol**[2] 'rent'); *The Old Ditch* 1512; *Le Stolkenmedewe* 1343; *Stonihalflond* 1343; *Tydenhale* 1343 (*v.* **halh**); *Vladiggegreneshalflond* 1343 (a 'halfland' by a 'green', first part of n. obscure).

10. WESTLEY (SJ 363070)

Westlegh' 1291-2 *Ass, -ley* 1562 *SBL 13455 et seq, - under Cause* 1649,67 *SBL 13379, 9945*
Woosley 1672 HTR

'West wood or clearing', *v.* **lēah**. Probably named from its position in relation to Asterley *supra*.

HEM, *Hemme* 1430 Fine, 1609 *SBL 6764, Westley Heme* 1597 *SBL 6751, Hem* 1604 *SBL 6756 et seq, Heme* 1604,8,18 *SBL 6758, 6761, 6772, The Yemm* 1610 *SBL 6768A, The Hemm* 1610,21 *SBL 6765, 6770, The Hemme* 1614, *SBL 6773, Ye Hemm* 1671 *SBL 6053, The Hem* 1685 *SBL 4200*. OE **hemm**, 'border', used in p.ns. to indicate position on a boundary. There are several instances in Sa. This place is in an angle of Westbury parish. VCH 307 says there are two farms, Hem Fm and Lower Hem Fm, but the 19th-cent. and later OS maps give the name to a single site.

HORSEBRIDGE, *Horsbrug'* 1291-2 *Ass, Hyrse Brydge Feild* 1546 *VCH(Hereford), v.* **hors**, **brycg**. 19th-cent. and modern maps show Horse Bridge where the Minsterley road crosses Rea Brook. The modern map also shows buildings called Horsebridge a short distance N.

REA (lost), *Ree* 1242 Fees, 1255 RH, *Le Ree* 1346, 1431 FA, *Rea* 1609 *SBL 6762*. Named from Rea Brook, which is OE *æt þǣre īe*, 'at the river'. Eyton (VIII, p.116) identified this settlement with an unnamed DB manor of ½ hide in *Ruesset* Hundred. VCH 306 says that the site may have been the large circular ditched enclosure S.W. of Lower Hem Fm.

KNOLLS COPPICE. MOUNT.

The f.ns. of Westley township are treated with those of Winsley *infra*.

11. WHITTON (SJ 347091)

The township-name is discussed in Part 1. It probably means 'wood settlement', and the estate may have had a specialised function in relation to the ancient woodland marked by the cluster of **lēah** names to the S.E: *v.* Asterley *supra.*

BROOMHILL LANE, Broomhill is in Forest township. GROVE COTTAGE, WHITTON GROVE, *Grove House* 1836 OS, *The Grove* 1840 *TA.* KNOLLS COPPICE, *The Knolls* 1836 OS, *v.* **cnoll**. WHITTONBEACH, *Beech Plantation and Meadow* 1840 *TA*, across the stream from Causebeach. -beach is the local development of **bæce** 'stream-valley', *v.* Wagbeach *supra.* WHITTON FM, GRANGE (1836 OS), HALL (1836 OS), COTTAGES and LANE. WHITTONHILL.

Field-Names

Forms in (a) are 1840 *TA*.

(a) Bath Mdw (by a stream, *bath* is often used of artificial pools); Beech Knap Mdw (by Whittonbeach, *v.* **cnæpp**); Brickkiln Mdw; Burnetts Mdw; Clover Fd; Coalpit Fd; Coppice Lsw; The Cord Hill; Lower and Top Cow Pasture; Cross Lsw, Far, Near and New - - (*v.* Westbury f.ns.); Dutch Clover (a variety of white clover); Eight Acres (2, *Acre* names correspond reasonably to area in this township); Ellis's Pce; Far Fd; Fishpool Lsw and Mdw (not by a stream); Four Acres; Furlongs; Garden Fd; Hall Mdw (by Whitton Hall); Horse Fd; House Fd (by Whitton Grange); Little Hill; Lower Fd; Lower Fd over the Bank; Middle Fd; Middle Lsw; Far, Lower, Near and Top Mountain Fd; Near Fd; Quarry Fd; Quarry Mdw; Rushy Mdw; Scarry Fd; Sheep Pasture; Shop Fd (*TAMap* shows a building); Lower, Near and Upper Shrives (*The Shrives* 1770 VCH 298: FN 35 suggests derivation from OE *scrifan* 'to allot', but this word usually has ecclesiastical connotations and the relevance here would be obscure: the land was Whitton common); Slang; Square Fd (shape spoiled by one irregular side); Stackyard Pce and Fd; Standleys (Upper Standleys is a short distance away in Vennington township); Summerhouse Bank (by Whitton Hall); Triangle Lsw; Twelve Acres; Upper Fd; Water Croft (by Bath Mdw); Well Mdw; The Whale (perhaps with a whale-back-shaped rise); White Lsw.

(b) *Middelestmere, Rattusmere* 1397-8 *VCH*(*SBL*) ('middlemost pond' and possibly 'rats' pond', *v.* **mere**).

12. WINSLEY (SJ 356077)

The township-name, which means 'Wine's clearing', is discussed in Part **1**.

HURST, *Wynnesleyeshurst* 1334 (15th) SAC, *Hurste* 1412 HAC, *The Hurst* 1844 *TA*, 'wooded hill', *v.* **hyrst**.

WINSLEY COTTAGES AND HALL.

Field-Names

Forms in (a) are 1844 *TA*. This award treats "Westley, otherwise Westley Winsley, Lake, Hurst and the Hem" as a single unit. Early forms dated c.1265 are SAC, 1334 are SAC and are (15th), 1349-50 are *VCH*(*NLW*), 1540 are SAS 54.

(a) Alder Tree Lsw; Asterley Mdw (A. is in Pontesbury); Back Lsw; Big and Little Bald Hill (*v.* Forest f.ns. *supra*); Bank Fd (2); Banky Lsw; Big Mdw; Big Yd; Black Pool Mdw; Bradings Pce; Brickkiln Fd (2); Broad Lsw; Broad Mdw (2); Brook Lsw; Broomy Lsw (3); Burlands, Near and Square - (*The Burlynges* 1603 *SBL 6756*); The Butts; Calves Croft; Catch Moor; Cinderland (probably a reference to slag); Clover Pce; Cocks Head Fd (no apparent reason for the n.); Cockshut Fd (by Hurst, *v.* **cocc-sciete**); Coppice Fd and Lsw; Covey Croft (by a tributary of Rea Brook); Cow Pasture; Crabtree Close; Cranley (*Craneley Eastwood* 1615 *SBL 6778*, 'cranes' or 'herons' wood'); Dingle Hole; Dole Mdw (*v.* **dāl**); The Drive (a pasture field, but *TAMap* shows an avenue of trees in it); Field Pce; Flax Butts; Footway Pce; Four Days Math (i.e. mowing); Four Oaks; Gallowstree Lsw (at G.R.353075 by the Westbury-Montgomery road, on the boundary with Worthen parish, VCH 325 suggests that this is a gallows of the Barony of Caus, recorded 1274); Garden Fd (2); Gooseneck Fd (by a sharp bend in the boundary with Minsterley); Goose Pool; Hay Lsw; Hem Fd, Lsw, Mdw, Back Hem (*v.* Hem *supra*); High Tree Lsw; Hill Cop; Hogstow Fd,

Lsw and Mdw (H. is in Minsterley); Hollow Mdw; Further and Near Hook (by a series of squiggles in Rea Brook; the stream has been straightened but the parish boundary shows the old course); House Mdw (by Lower Lake); Hurst Lsw and Pce; Lake Fd and Mdw; Little Lake Turning (where road to Lake leaves Minsterley road); Lawn (by Winsley Hall); Laywell; The Leys; Long Lsw (2); Long Slang; Lower Moor; Lysons Fd; Middle Pce; The Moor, Moor Mdw; New Mdw; New Tining ('new enclosure'); Oaktree Lsw; Overs Pce; Ox Lsw; The Park (a large field by Hurst); Park Lsw (not near preceding); Pit Lsw; Pokers Hole (a marshy area by Lake); Pool Fd (not near following n.); Pool House Lsw (*TAMap* shows two buildings at G.R.363074: there are early refs. to a place called *La Pole*: an entry in 1306-7 *Ass* speaks of the road between Worthen and *La Pole*, and in 1349-50 *VCH(NLW)* land beyond *Wastly* is said to extend to the lordship of *Pole*: 'pool' names are fairly frequent in this part of Sa, however); Puppets Orchard; Quaggy Mdw (i.e. shaking); Red Lsw; Showmakers Lsw and Mdw; Sitch, Further, Lower and Corfield's - (*v.* **sīc**); Slang (2); Spout Lsw; Stackyard Croft; Tenpenny Cut (a tiny field surrounded by larger ones); Three Cornered Pce (2); Townsend (on S.E. outskirt of Westley hamlet); Trefoil Fd; Twaies Mdw; Upper Mdw; Upper Moor; Wainhouse Mdw ('waggon house'); Way Pce; Well Mdw (2); Westbury Lsw; Westley Mdw; White Lsw; Willowery Mdw; Winsley Close; Wood Lsw; Yewtree Fd; Yewtree Yd.

(b) *Bultermedowe* 1540, *The Bought Medow* 1600 *SBL 6754*; *Eywynesacre* c.1265 (the first el. probably a surname); *Godeneshullesfurlong'* c.1265 (possibly 'furlong by Godwin's hill'); *Heme Moores* 1604 *SBL 6758*, *Hemmgreene or Mores* 1609 *SBL 6764*, *Yemmegrene or Moores* 1610 *SBL 6768A*, *Hemm Greene or Moores* 1671 *SBL 6053* (*v.* Hem *supra*); *Limfordesbroc, Lym-* c.1265 (possibly 'lime ford'); *Marshall' Lond* Hy 8 *RentSur* (Thos. *Marchalle* of Hurst leased land in Asterley in 1412 (HAC p.41)); *Monkesbrooke* 1349-50 (Shrewsbury Abbey had land in Winsley); *Mynsterley Medowe* 1540; *Le Peremedewe* 1334 (*v.* **peru**, **mǣd**); *Rawnley or Flashe or Paddock* 1610 *SBL 6768A*; *Tydeswalle* (fishpond called) 1334, *Didewalles Pole, Tydwallespole* 1540, *Tidwallespole* 1542 *VCH(Hereford)*, *Tydwalespole* 1573 *VCH(SBL)*, *Tydwall's Pool* 1702 *SBL 1612* (probably 'pool of Tīdi's spring', *v.* **wælle**, **pōl**, VCH 300 says this was near Hurst and was drained by 1581); *Whitmershe* 1349-50 (*v.* **hwīt**, **mersc**).

13. YOCKLETON (SJ 400101)

The township-name is discussed in Part 1. It is (despite the modern form) a compound of **hyll** with a derivative of the word

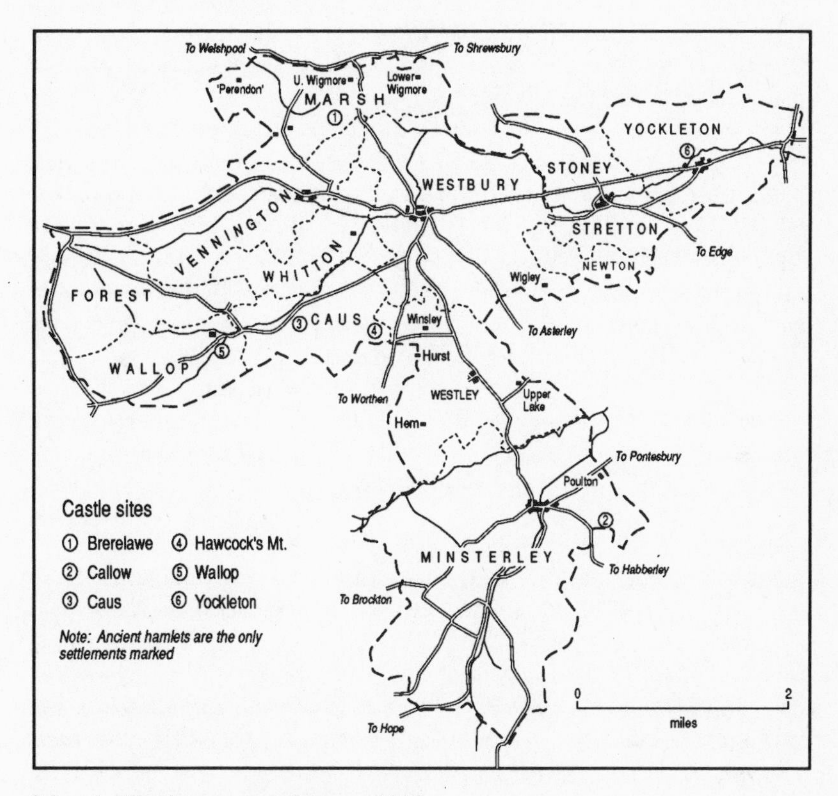

Map 4 Westbury townships, c. 1840
Based on tithe apportionments and maps, 1838-43

yoke; the meaning is obscure.

LYNCHES, 1673 PR(H) 1, *Lynch Meadow* 1654 *SBL 1670*, *The Linches* 1839 *TA*. OE **hlinc** 'terrace'. The farm occupies a large platform on a sloping hill-side.

THE CORNER, by an angle in the parish boundary. FIRLANDS. NICHOLLS COPPICE. NUT ROUGH. PARK FM, *The Parkes* 1600 *SBL 6754*, *The Park* 1839 *TA*. VCH 306 says the farm was established by the late 16th cent., so presumably the park was enclosed by then. The outline can be seen in the field-shapes on *TAMap*. THE ROUGH, 1839 *TA*.

Field-Names

Forms in (a) are 1839 *TA*. Early forms dated c.1380 are *SBL 6172*. Those dated 1787 are from a list in E.W. Bowcock's material, copied in 1939 from a map of Lynches and Yockleton.

(a) Allgreaves (*Aldgraves* 1787, 'old groves', *v.* **grǣfe**); Ash Croft; Bakehouse Yd; The Bank (1787); Banky Fd; Barn Fd; Barn Yard (*The Barne Yord* 1660 *SBL 6124*); Big Fd; Big Mdw (3); Bimes, Bimes Mdw, Big and Little Bimes (possibly *Bymers* 1787, *v.* Hicknall *infra*); Bogs; Upper Brand Stiles (possibly *Barn Stiles* 1787); Broad Lsw; Broad Mdw (1787); Broad Moor; Brook Furlong (1787); Cats Hill Fd; Chapel Fd (*Chappel Field* 1787, the site of a medieval chapel still standing in 1655, VCH 303-4); Clemley Park (2, one in 1787 list, *v.* Cardeston f.ns. *supra*); Old Clover Mill (VCH 304 gives the history of the mill, there is no obvious reason for the name); Coppice, Coppice Fd and Lsw, Far and Lower Coppice (strung out along the N. boundary of the township, Big Coppice is further W. on the same boundary, and Far and Near Coppice are further E.); Cote Lsw, The Cotes (not adjacent, *v.* **cot(e)**); Cow Pasture (3, one in 1787 list); Darby's Coppice; The Field (adjoins Town Fd); Field Patch, Big and Little - -, Field Patch Mdw; Fishpool Lsw (- *Piece* 1787); Gutter Lsw; Bank, Broad, Further, Green, Long and Near Hays (*Upper, Lower and Long Hays* 1787, *v.* **(ge)hæg**, the *TA* fields are W. of The Park); Middle and Upper

Heath Fd, Little Heath Patch, Heath Yd (*Le Hethe c.1380, Yockltons Heath* 1660 *SBL 6124*, on the outskirts of Ford Heath); Hicknall, Big, Broad, Far, Long, Lower and Upper Hicknall (*Hicknals* 1787; Hicknall and Bimes names are intermingled on the S. edge of the township and in the adjacent part of Stoney Stretton: more Hicknall names occur on the N.W. boundary of the township, a mile away); Hoodens Gate; Horse Lsw (2, one in 1787 list); House Mdw (by a mill); Hovel Pce; Middle Isle (not by a stream); Lane Mdw; Little Clover (not near Clover Mill); Little Fd; Little Mdw (2); Long Ground (2: long narrow pieces, but appreciably bigger than the two strips called Slang); Lough Moors; Lower Mdw; Marvels Pool (1787); Mill Mdw (3, one in 1787 list, cf. *Mullemedwe* c.1380; there were two mills in the village); The Moor, Moor Lsw (by Yockleton Brook); Mount Fd (contains a motte, VCH 300); Newcombs Pce (1787); Newnham Fd and Hill (adjoining Newnham in Pontesbury); Oakley Stitch (*stitch* may refer to hurdles); Old Fd Mdw; Outlet (a funnel-shaped track from Park Fm); Ox Lsw; Park Lane and Lsw (referring to Yockleton Park, *v.* Park Fm *supra*); The Patches (2: both average-sized fields); Peak Moor; The Pound (in the village, cf. *Punfold'* c.1380, *v.* **pund-fald**); Pound Slang (not adjoining The Pound); Further, Middle and Near River Land (by Yockleton Brook); Sheny's Mdw; Sherry's Mdw (*Sherry Meadow* 1787); Shop Lsw (adjoins a smithy); Slang (2, one in 1787 list); Tinkers Pool Patch; Town Fd (1787, adjoins village on S.E.); Turnip Pce; Wall Croft; Weir Lsw; Well Lsw; Well Mdw; West Wood; Wether Lsw (1787, probably referring to sheep); Whitening Jacks (*Whitling Jacks* 1787); Wild Moor; The Willows; Yewtree Lsw.

(b) *Bikemonneshale* 1384-5 *VCH* (*v.* **halh**, first el. probably a surname); *Broomy Croft* 1787; *Le Bruche Heth'* c.1380 (*v.* **bryce**, **hǣð**); *Coal Leasow* 1787; *Easmoor* 1787; *Ekins Ground* 1787; *Elysha's Meadow* 1787; *Great Meadow* 1787; *Grene Croft* c.1380; *Halywelmede, Halywellesmore* c.1380 (*v.* **hālig**, **wella**, **mǣd**, **mōr**); *Lyes* (*Forlong' voc'*) c.1380; *New Piece* 1787; *Le Oldeton'* c.1380 (*v.* **ald**, **tūn**, perhaps an abandoned farm); *Ovals Gate; Owlers* 1787 ('alders', *v.* **alor**); *Penyacre* c.1380 (*v.* **pening**, **æcer**); *Wet Meadow* 1787; *Willsmoor* 1787.

Wollaston

The parish-name, which means 'Wīglāf's estate', is discussed in Part 1.

Wollaston was a township of Alberbury at the date of the Tithe Award, but became a civil parish in 1864. It contains the townships of Bulthy, Trefnant, Winnington and Great Wollaston in Shropshire, and it formerly contained Middleton and Uppington in Montgomeryshire. The two Welsh townships were made into a parish of Middleton in 1933.

1. BULTHY FM (SJ 319135)

Bulthey 1608-9 PR(H) 6, *-heye* 1613 ib, *Bullthey* 1658 ib, *Bullthy* 1672 HTR
Balthey 1610 PR(H) 6
Billce 1615 PR(H) 6
Beulhey 1615 PR(H) 6, *Bulheye* 1616-17 ib, *-hey* 1623 ib
Butheye 1616 PR(H) 6, *Butthey* 1651 ib
Bulchey 1619 PR(H) 6, *-hay* 1668,74-5 ib, *-heay* 1678 ib
Bughelley 1656 PR(H) 6
Bulcay 1672 PR(H) 6

MorganTs suggests Welsh *bylchau,* pl. of *bwlch* 'pass'. The farm is at the eastern edge of the Breidden Hills.

BERLEY (lost)

Berlee 1289 Swin, *-ley* PR(H) 6
Bereley 1609 PR(H) 6, *Bearelie* 1612 ib, *Beerely* 1617 ib
Beverley 1840 *TA*

'Barley clearing', *v.* **bere, lēah.** VCH 193 says that three or four houses of this hamlet were still standing in 1685, the last survivor being now an empty cottage. The field called *Beverley* on *TAMap* is at approx. G.R.317141, and VCH says that this marks the site of *Berley.* The development of *Ber(e)-* to *Bever-* is irregular, however.

BRONROTPOL (lost)

Bronrotpol m.13th (1322) Ch, *-poll'* 1291-2 *Ass*
Bromrothpol, Bromrotpol Secunda 1289 Swin

Bronnorampald 1499 Ipm
Brynhopper 1840 *TA*

Perhaps an OE name from **rōt** 'cheerful' and **pōl** 'pool', with Welsh *bron* 'breast of a hill' prefixed.

VCH 194 says that the hamlet was on the site of Plas-y-Court (*infra*). Two fields adjacent to Plas-y-Court are called *Upper, Lower Brynhopper* on *TAMap*, and it seems likely that this is a corruption of *Bronrotpol.*

VCH 193 suggests that *Bromrotpol Secunda* was the hamlet of Bulthy.

PLAS-Y-COURT

Le Place Court 1563 *SBL 2495*, *Place Ye Courte* 1631 PR(H) 6, *Place Y Courte* 1649-50 ib, *Place of Court* 1673-4 ib, *Place-Court* 1714 ib, *Place A Court* 1775 PR(H) 7.

'The large house of the monastic grange', from Welsh *plas* and ME *court*. *MorganTs* points out that *court* is often applied in Wales to monastic granges, and that Plas-y-Court (*Bronrotpol*) was a grange of Strata Marcella Abbey near Welshpool.

BANK, 1836 OS. BULTHY HILL, 1778 PR(H) 6, 1835 OS.

Field-Names

Forms in (a) are 1840 *TA*.

(a) Alder Patch; Bakehouse Mdw; Banky Lsw; Banky Fd and Mdw; Barratts Croft; Beverley (*v. Berley supra*); Big Mdw; Brickkiln Lsw; Brick Mdw; Brook Lsw; Broomy Fd; Browns Yd; Lower and Upper Brunant; Lower and Upper Brynhopper (*v. Bronrotpol supra*); Cae Bella (this and following names have Welsh *cae* 'field' as generic); Cae Hair (1629 VCH 186, probably Welsh *hir* 'long', three long, narrow fields have this name); Cae Harbour; Cae Hill (1629 VCH 186); Calves Croft; Calves Patch (by Cow Pasture); Closet (smaller than surrounding fields); Clover Patch, Lower Clover; Coppice; Little Coppice, Coppice

Mdw; Cow Pasture; Far End; Far Lsw; Far Side; Far Yd; Feggy (rough grass); Feggy Lsw and Meadow; Gooses Pasture; Gorsty Lsw; Gorsty Patch; Gorsy Fd; Big and Little Green; Green Lsw; Hailstones; James Fd; Kruns, Krwns (*The Crimes* 1629 VCH 186, *v.* PN Ch **2**, 171, where a case is made for an OE **cryme*, 'crumb, small piece'); Little Dingle Lsw; Little Mdw; Llanaclodyn (the generic is probably W. *llannerch* 'glade'); Lower Patch; The Meadow, Lower Mdw; Mount Carver; Near Croft; New Inclosure; Old House Mdw; Over Ground; Over Lsw; Ox Lsw; Park (an average-sized field); Petter Patch; Quarry Fd, Stone Quarry; Rocky Fd; Rough; Rough Lsw; Ryegrass Fd; Sheepcote Lsw; Sideland Lsw (by the parish and county boundary); Slang; Long Slang; Sparrow Fd; Stony Ground; Thistly Lsw; Three Cornered Fd; Upper Carn; Upper Leasow (2); Well Fd and Lsw, Well; Welliford Green; Wet Lsw; Wet Mdw; White Lsw; Withy Reynes ('willow drains'); The Wood; Wood Fd; Wood Lsw; Woodside; Over, Upper and Lower Yoed.

(b) *Cae Croyes, Kar r Berllan* 1629 VCH 186 (Welsh 'cross field' and 'field of the orchard'); *Wlveshoo* 1278 VCH 185 (a wood, 'wolf's hill-spur', *v.* **hōh**).

2. TREFNANT FM (SJ 303103)

Trefnant 1265 *NLW Peniarth 231*
Trifnant 1289 Swin
Treuenaunt 1291-2 *Ass, Trevenante* 1613 PR(H) 6, *-nant* 1649 ib, 1672 HTR, 1707 *SBL 6042, Trevanant* 1681-2 PR(H) 6
Treuenant 1650-1 PR(H) 6, *Trewnant* 1664-5 ib
Trevant 1672 PR(H) 6
Traunant 1679 PR(H) 6
Treavnant 1725 PR(H) 7
Trivenant 1675 Ogilby

'Valley farm', from Welsh **tref** and **nant**. This is a common p.n. in Wales. VCH 194 conjectures that the settlement lay to the N.W. of Trefnant Fm, which was formerly Hungerhill Fm. Hungerhill straddles the county boundary to the W.

COUNTY BRIDGE, 1836 OS, on county boundary. DINGLE, D. WD, *The Dingle* 1843 *TA.* DINGLE MILL, *Treuenants Mills* 1644

PR(H) 6, *Trevenant Mill* 1746-7 PR(H) 7. *TAMap* shows *Dingle* here, distinct from the one above. THE HILL, 1836 OS. LOWER TREFNANT, 1843 *TA*. The timber-framed house is probably *Trivenant Halls* 1675 Ogilby; it was *New House* in 1597 (VCH 195). VCH 194 mentions Upper Trefnant, formerly County Brook House. PLANTATION COTTAGE.

Field-Names

Forms in (a) are 1843 *TA*.

(a) Allotment (a number of Allotment fields extend along the eastern extremity of Long Mountain); Bank; Barn Mdw; The Bellands (The Bellons 1831 *SBL 14689*, three fields covering a fairly large area); Big Meadow (3); Brickkiln, Far Kiln Pce; Big Broom; Broomy Lsw (2); Calves Croft; Calves Patch; Cockshot Lsw (*v.* **cocc-sciete**); Long Coppice; Cow Pasture (3); Croft (2); Daisy Lsw (2); Doctor's Yd; Edwards Pce; Field below Meadow; Field below Rickyard; Fishpool Lsw (adjoins Lower Trefnant); Big and Little Flat Lsw; Fold (*freq*); Garden (*freq*); Gorsty Inclosure; Gorsty Lsw (2); Hill Ground, Middle - -, Hill Lsw; Hollow Patch; Holly Fd; House Lsw (by an unnamed building); House Mdw (by Trefnant Fm); Inclosure (*freq*); The Ladder (athwart a steep hill-slope, the contours may form steps); Little Meadow; Long Coppice; Long Leasow (2); Long Meadow; Lower Leasow; The Meadow; Mill Ground, - Mdw, Millers Mdw (by Dingle Mill); Moat, Moat Lsw and Mdw (E. of Dingle Mill, perhaps the site of Trefnant hamlet, *v. supra*); Mountain Pce; Nursery Pce; Big and Little Oat Hill; Orchard; Ox Lsw; Park Mdw (adjoins The Parks in Winnington); Plantation; Pound Lsw; Quarry Hill, Little Quarry Lsw; The Slang (a very narrow strip); Stack Pce (near Brickkiln); White Lsw; The Yard.

3. WINNINGTON (SJ 312105)

Wonyntone 1289 Swin
Winneton' 1291-2 *Ass*
Wenneton' 1291-2 *Ass*
Wynancton 1316 FA
Wonanton 1334 SR
Wynington 1611 PR(H) 6, *Wynnington* Jas I *SBL 4199*, 1703 *SBL 4134*, *Winington* 1650 PR(H) 6, 1737 PR(H) 7, *Winnington* 1672 HTR *et seq*
Wyington 1620 PR(H) 6
Wington 1664 PR(H) 6

Probably an **-ingtūn** compound with a pers.n. such as *Win(n)e* or *Wyn(n)a.* Winnington Ch and St have similar spellings.

The G.R. is for Upper Winnington. VCH 194 says that the site of the medieval hamlet is uncertain.

GLYN, 1609-10 PR(H) 6, *Glyne* 1635 ib, *Gllyn* 1641-2 ib, *The Glin* 1655 ib, *The Glyn* 1703 *SBL 4134*, 1714 PR(H) 6, *The Glynne Farm* 1792 *SBL 4143.* GLYN COMMON is *The Gline Common* 1657-8 PR(H) 6, *The Glynn Common* 1771 PR(H) 7. Welsh **glyn** 'glen', referring to a stream-valley on the county boundary.

HARGREAVES, H. WD, HARGRAVE BANK AND WD, *Haregreve* 1289 Swin, 1291-2 *Ass, Hargreffe* 1536 BM, *Haregreave* 1627 PR(H) 6, *-greve* 1643 ib, *Hargreve* 1651 ib *et freq* with variant spellings *-greave, -greeve*; *Hargrave* 1654 *SBL 2995 et freq* to 1682 *SBL 4201, Hardgrave* 1762 PR(H) 7. The 1654 ref. also mentions *Hargrave Bank* and *Wood.* A *Hargreave Hill* is named Jas I *SBL 4199.* Probably 'grey grove', *v.* **hār**[2], **grǣfe**. Colour adjectives are frequent as qualifiers in 'grove' names.

WHITFIELD, *Withfeld* 1289 Swin, *Whytefeld', Whitefeud, Wytfeld'* 1291-2 *Ass, The Whetfield* 1654 *SBL 2995, -feild* 1682 *SBL 4201.* 'White open land', *v.* **hwīt**, **feld**.

CHESHIRE WD, *The Wood* 1843 *TA.* HALL MILL, 1836 OS, *The Hall Mill* 1768 PR(H) 7; nearby *Winnington Hall* (1842 *TA*) is said in VCH 194 to be recorded in 1593, and *Wilson Hall* 1675 Ogilby (Plate 50) is probably a poor form for this. It is UPPER WINNINGTON on modern maps. THE HILL, 1836 OS. LOWER WINNINGTON. MOUNTAIN FM, *The Mountain Tenement* 1792 *SBL 41433*; VCH 195 says the Fm is known to have existed in 1602. OLD PARR'S COTTAGE, *Parr's House* 1749 PR(H) 7, *Parshouse* 1774 ib. There is a tablet in Wollaston church commemorating Thomas Parr, who died in 1635 and was credited with having been born in 1483. He was buried in Westminster Abbey, and there is a detailed account of him in the *Dictionary of*

National Biography. VCH 195 says that the house, which was burnt down in 1959, is first recorded in 1588. PLANTATION COTTAGE, *Plantation* 1843 *TA.* ROSE AND CROWN, 1767 VCH 195, 1843 *TA.* WINNINGTON GREEN, *Winington Green* 1737 PR(H) 7, *The Green* 1843 *TA.* WINNINGTON LODGE FM, *The Lodge* 1602 VCH 195. WOODLEASOWS, 1836 OS: this farm is called *Cold Hall* 1843 *TA.*

Field-Names

Forms in (a) are 1843 *TA.*

(a) Allotment (*freq*); Bank (*freq*); Banky Fd (2); Banky Lsw; Banky Mdw; Banky Pce; Barn Mdw (3); Barn Patch; Barnyard; The Bibbeys (in an angle of the stream which flows through Upper Winnington, possibly an **ēg** name); Upper Big Mdw; Big Pce (2); Brickkiln Mdw (1779 *SBL 3019*); The Broom; Broomy Lsw; Little Broomy Pce; Cabnal Pce; Calves Croft (2); Clamley Park (*v.* Cardeston f.ns. *supra*); Clover Fd (2); Clover Pce; Common; Common Fd; Common Patch; Common Pce (*freq*); Connells Mdw; Coppice, Little, Further, Hither, Upper Coppice (a series of fields S.W. of Winnington Green); Court Lsw (S. of Hargreaves); Cow Pasture (4); Croft (*freq*); Cross Leys; Ditchers Yd; Dole Wollet, Lower - - (Dole Wallad c.1820 *SBL 6219, v.* **dāl**: *wallet* is used of land in a hollow); Large and Little Duckling (in a stream-bend, perhaps a literal reference to ducklings); The Feg (rough grass); Feg Lsw; The Five Acres; Fold (2); Folly Homestead and Fd (*TAMap* shows a building which is not on 6"); Four Acres; Fowkes's Patch; Foxholes; Garden; Gorst Pce and Plantation; Gorsty Fd; Gorsty Patch (2) (*v.* **gorstig**); Great Mdw; Great Wood; Green Fd and Lsw (by Winnington Green); The Gunna (possibly a corruption of *cunnery* 'rabbit-warren'); Hargrave Fd, Lsw, Paddock (*v. supra*); Far and Near Harp (rectangular fields); Heath Patch; Hill Ground; Hollow; Home Fd; Hop Mdw; Horse Pce; House Fd; Knapps (*v.* **cnæpp**); Little Croft; Little Mdw (5); Little Pasture; Little Patch; Far and Near Little Pce; Long Lsw; Long Mountain (on the slopes of the hill of that name); Long Pce; Lower Mdw (3); Lower Patch; Lower Wood; Middle Lsw; Middle Pce; Middletown (adjoins Middletown Mont); Mountain Pce; Orchard (2); Big Ox Fd; Ox Lsw (*Oxe Leasowe* 1681 *SBL 4201*); Ox Pasture; Ox Pce; Paddock; Paled Mdw; The Parks, Little - (Little Park, Park Fd c.1820 *SBL 6129*, no obvious reason for the name); Pasture Ground; Patch (*freq*); Plantation (*freq*); Rickyard; Road Round (a road curves round one side); Rossy Mdw (cf. Westbury f.ns. *supra*); Rough (*freq*); Rough Ground (3); Rough Lsw;

Rough Rant (on county boundary, possibly **rand** 'border'); Lower and Upper Roundabout (the two fields make a rough oval); Ryegrass Fd (2); Sheepcote Lsw (c.1820 *SBL 6219*); Shop Lsw (building shown); Lower Sideland Pce (c.1820 *SBL 6219*, alongside the Dole Wollet names); Six Acres (2); Slang (3); Spout Lsw; Square Fd; Stackyard; Steep Fd; Little Steepless, Little, Lower and Upper Stepless (*Stepless* 1599 VCH 185, by Steep Fd, possibly 'steep lees', *v.* **lǣs**); Stone Quarry; Sycamore Patch; Three Cornered Patch; Town Fd Mdw (by Winnington Green); Turnip Lsw; Twelve Strike Sowing; Two Acres; Upper Lsw (2); Upper Mdw; Upper Patch; Upper Yd; Lower, Lower Middle and Upper Middle Vrangham (an obscure name, the fields are on S.E. boundary of parish); Well Lsw (3); Little Well Lsw (2); Well Mdw; Wet Mdw; Lower Wheat Fd; Williams Mdw; Wollaston Fd (adjoins W. township); Woodend (adjoins Hargraves Wd); Wood Lsw (3, surrounding Hargrave Wd); Wood Pce.

(b) *Crogen Wladis in ye Glynne* 1696 PR(StA) 5 (apparently 'Gladys's jaw'); *Llanyvellins, Llanyvellinst Meadow* 1681 *SBL 3012* (possibly 'grove of the mill', with *llwyn* as generic); *The Porteway* 1681 *SBL 3012* (*Llanyvellins* adjoins this, perhaps the road N. of Hall Mill); *Pullcough Lane* 1708 *SBL 3047, Pwll Coch Meadow* 1779 *SBL 3019* ('red pool', VCH 187 identifies the lane as the track from Trefnant Fm to Glyn Common).

4. GREAT WOLLASTON (SJ 330124)

v. supra for the township-name.

VACHRIGE (lost), *Baghret, Vagheret, Varegrek', Waregrgh', Waregregk'* 1291-2 *Ass, Vachrige* 16th, 17th VCH 194. The site of this hamlet is not known: VCH 194 says that it seems to have stood near the old Welshpool road. The name is probably Welsh, and the generic may be *bach* 'nook'.

THE ALDERS, *Alders, Alders Field* 1842 *TA*; probably *The Wollars* 1779 *SBL 3019*, *v.* **alor**. LANE FM, *Lane* 1768 PR(H) 7, *The Lane* 1774 ib, 1842 *TA*.

Field-Names

Forms in (a) are 1842 *TA*, except for those dated c.1820, which are *SBL 6219*. Early forms dated 1665-6 are *SBL 3010*, 1779 are *SBL 3019*.

(a) Banky Lsw (3, one named 1779); Big Lsw; Bretchell Fd and Pce (*Burchill Ground and Patches* 1779, adjoins Bretchel in Alberbury); Brook Yd (1779); Calves Croft c.1820; Chapel Fd (1779); Close (*freq*); Collier Pce; Coppice, - Side; Coppice Lsw; Cow Pasture; Crabtree Lsw (1779); Cross Lane Lsw and Mdw (*Crosse Lane* 1657-8 PR(H) 6, *Cross Lane* 1779, by a T-junction); Cross Lsw; Dukes Lsw; Fold (2); Forge; Garden (*freq*); Hazle Lsw (1779); Heath Pce; Hopyard; Little Mdw (1665-6, 1779, c.1820); Long Lsw (1779); Loughnalls (*Soughmall* 1779); Middle Fd (2, one named 1779); Moor Side (*Little Moorside* 1779); New Lsw (1779); New Mdw c.1820; Ox Mdw c.1820; Further Penilpit Lsw; Pugh's Mdw (1779); Red Field (1779, *The Red Feild* 1661 *SBL 3009*); Rough; Rough Lsw; Rough Park Coppice c.1820; Rushy Mdw; Farther and Hither Sideland Pce c.1820 (perhaps to be placed with Lower Sideland Pce in Winnington f.ns.); Slang along Road; Stable Mdw; Townsend, - Croft and Mdw (*The Townsend* 1779, at N.W. end of hamlet); Triangle Fd; Upper Fd (1779); The Vanes Mdw c.1820; White Lsw (1779); Wollaston Lsw (on township boundary); Yard (2).

(b) *Alphyn Moor or Gornellfyn* c.1540 VCH 184 (a **fenn** name may lie behind this); *The Backdore Leasowe* 1665-6; *Banky Field* 1779; *The Barne Orchard* 1665-6; *Bradinemedowe* 1618 PR(H) 6; *The Broomy Croft* 1665-6; *Broomy Feilds* 1661, 1695,9 *SBL 3009, 3043, 3015*; *Calves Meadow* 1779; *Cow Leasow* 1779; *The Crund* 1779 (possibly Kruns in Bulthy f.ns.); *Far Leasow* 1779; *Fat Meadow* 1779; *Field Meadow* 1779; *Goose Patch* 1779; *The Green* 1779; *Heath Ground* 1779; *The Kilvarn* 1661 *SBL 3009, Kilvach* 1695,9 *SBL 3043, 3051* (perhaps a Welsh name with *cil* 'nook'); *The Little Croft* 1665-6; *Long Croft* 1779; *Lyneall Wude* 1668-9 *SBL 3998, Lynial Wude* 1665-6 (there may be a connection with Lyneal in Ellesmere); *Matthew Green* 1779; *The New Inclosure* 1665-6; *Over Bank* 1779; *Pen y Bryn* 1779 (Welsh, 'end of the hill'); *Slang above Green* 1779; *Snalston Hall* 1675 *SBL 4238*; *Upper Field* 1779; *Wonnechnohebret* 1278 VCH 207, *Winchnerchbrook* l.16th ib.

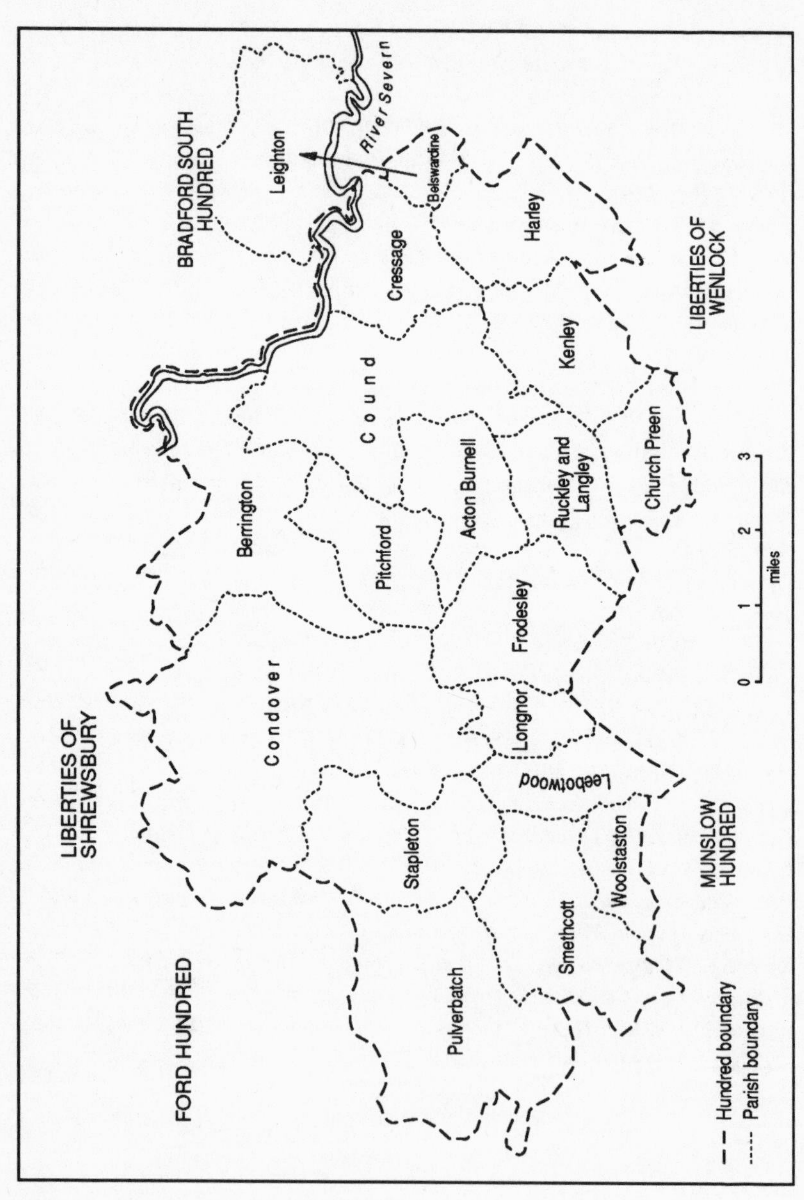

Map 5 The Hundred of Condover

Conodov(o)re 1086 DB, *Conedovre* 1274 RH, 1346 FA, *-overe* 1284-5 FA, *-over* 1316 FA
Cunedoure 1189 CartAntiq, *-ovr'* 1221 Fees, *Cunnedovre* 1255 RH
Gundour 1203-4 *Ass*
Conedovershome 1317 Fine

v. Condover *infra.* For the addition of *-home* in 1317 *v.* the discussion of this phenomenon under Ford *supra.*

This hundred was comparatively little affected by the re-organisation of Shropshire hundreds some time before 1158. VCH 1-2 gives details of manors which were detached from it in the 12th and 13th cents.

Acton Burnell

The name Acton, 'oak settlement', is discussed in Part **1**. The parish comprises the townships of Acton Burnell and Acton Pigott.

1. ACTON BURNELL (SJ 534019)

ACTON BURNELL CASTLE, 1577 Saxton, built 1283-6 by Robert Burnell. ACTON BURNELL HALL, 1739 PR(L) 19. A small stone house was built here by 1731 (VCH 8). ACTON BURNELL PARK, PARK COTTAGE, cf. *The Park Gate* 1745 *et freq* PR(L) 19, *The Park-Head* 1729 ib, *Ye Parkhead* 1741 ib. VCH 5 considers the Park contemporary with the Castle. BARN COTTAGE, *Barn Piece* 1845 *TA* is near. BLACK DICK'S COPPICE AND LAKE, *Black Dick's Coppice and Pool* 1845 *TA.* VCH 5 says that this Lake and Shadwell Lake are probably the fish-ponds recorded in 1292. EASTER HILL (not on map, in Gazetteer), *Ye Easter Hill* 1662 PR(L) 19. Will. *de Asturhull'* mentioned 1364-6 *ForProc* in connection with an inquisition at Bayston Hill may have come from this place. 'Eastern hill', *v.* **ēasterra, hyll.** THE HOLLIES, *Far and Near Hollies* 1845 *TA.* LILLY POOL, 1845 *TA.* LODGE, the house is shown on *TAMap.* SHADWELL COPPICE AND LAKE, *Shadwell Coppice and Pool* 1845 *TA.* The coppice, which is on the

S. boundary of the parish, is given the alternative name *Spring Coppice* in *TA*. 'Boundary spring', *v.* **scēad**. SWISS COTTAGE. WATLING STREET. The portion of this Roman road in Acton Burnell is *Watlyng Streetway* 1612 *LDR*.

Field-Names

Forms in (a) are 1845 *TA* except for those marked *LDR*. Early forms dated 1612, 1685, 1693, 1705, 1718 are *LDR*.

In 1612 the open fields were *the fyld towards Frodsley on the west syde the Towne, the Shoote fyeld* and *ye fyeld towards Acton Piggott*.

(a) Apple Tree Lsw; Ash Furlong; Bargate Lsw, Far and Near; Barn Pce; The Beach (1620 PR(L) 19, *The Batch* 1708 ib, *Ye Beech* 1716 ib, *Ye Bach* 1724 ib: Gazetteer calls this The Batch or The Beach, it is by a small stream-valley and shows the development of **bæce** to Beach which is discussed under Wagbeach in Minsterley); Big Lsw; Brick Kiln Paddock; Broomy Patch; Bucknalls Hatch 1857 *LDR* (1685, *Becknollshatche* 1612, Francis *Bucknoll* mentioned); Butt Mdw (on one side of a block of small, rectangular fields); Calves Croft; Clover Lsw; Cote Lsw (1817 *LDR*, no building shown); Cow Pasture (2); Darwen's Yd; Doctor Pce; Dog Kennel and Yds; Far Lsw (a projecting point on W. boundary); The Field (near Shoots *infra*, probably the central portion of a former open field: this may be the significance of Upper and Lower Field in the N.W. projection of the parish); Finger Post Lsw, New Fingerpost Fd (on either side of Watling St); Fir wood; Galliers Mdw; Goss Lsw; Hadigar; The Harp Pce (slight difference in width between the two narrow ends, cf. *Ye Harpe Furlonge* 1612); Hawfoot, Big and Little Hawpool (*Upper and Lower Hawford* 1685, *Hoofyards* 1698, *Hawford Meadow and Leasow* 1705, 1718, The Holford 1812 *LDR*, Haughfoots or Orfoots 1845 *LDR*, probably from **halh** and **ford**, the ford being a crossing on the stream which forms the boundary with Pitchford); Hill Foot; Holt Rough; Horse Pasture; The Itchings, New Itchings (**hitching* 'place fenced with hurdles', a ModE el. noted PN Ch 5 ii, 225); Kettles Lsw, Lower and Upper; Lady Mdw (1817 *LDR*); Lawn (part of the park); Line Hills, Big and Little - - (*Lynell* 1612, *Linalls Meadow* 1685, *Linolls* 1698, *The Linols* 1705, 1718, by a brook W. of the village which is *Lynell Brooke* 1612, possibly 'flax nook', *v.* **līn**, **halh**); Little Mdw (several, see Townend *infra*); Little Pce, Lower and Upper; Little Tining (*Ye Greate New Tindings, Ye Little* - - 1685, *Great and Little New Tinings* 1718, 'enclosure', *v.* **tȳning**); Little Yewtree Pce; Little Pool Pce (fairly near Shoots Pools); Long Mdw; Long Shrubbery and Sling (a strip along N. end of park); Mill Pool Corner (Mill shown, VCH says it went out of use after 1856); Mintwell, Lower and Upper 1857 *LDR* (*Mynt Walle* 1612, *Mintwell* 1698, a well near the parsonage, *Ye Mynt Furlonge* adjoined in 1612, *v.* **minte**, Gazetteer lists this as a surviving n.); The Moat (2 fields W. of village); Old Mills (1685, *Ould Mylles* 1612); Otleys Heys (*Otles Heyes* 1612, *Ottleys Hays* l.17th, 1805 VCH 3, woodland which had been cleared by 1805, *v.* **(ge)hæg**, the Ottley family had land in Berrington, VCH 22); Ox Lsw (2); Pool Mdw (*Ye Pooles, Ye Poole Meadow* 1612, by Lilly Pool); Radnals Bridge Lsw (*Radnors Bridge* 1612, where Watling St crosses Lynoll Brook, the n. is Radnall in Pitchford *TA*, Radenhurst 1857 *LDR*: abutments of a Roman and a later bridge have been found); Rock's Pce; Rough Patch; The Roundabout (triangular, roads on two sides); Rubbish Mdw; Ruckley Pce (on R. boundary); The Ryall; Rye Grass Lsw; Sheep Pasture; Shoots Lsw, Mdw, Pools and Coppice, Big Shoots (*The Shoots* 1551 VCH 3, *The Shoote Fyeld* 1612, *The Shoot Meadow* 1698, *The Shute* - 1705, *Ye Shyte Medow* 1718, *v.* ***scēot** 'steep slope'); Shrubbery (on edge of park); Skett Butts; Sketts Lsw (not near preceding); Slang Coppice (very narrow); Tall Oak; Thistley Lsw; Townend (VCH 5 suggests that this and one of the two adjacent Little Meadow fields mark the site of the village before the castle was built: this is W. of the present site); Wheat Way (by the Ruckley road); Yeld Bank (*v.* **helde**); Yew Tree Lsw.

(b) *Cumbes* 1270,80 Pat (a wood on the hill S.E. of the village, *v.* **cumb** and VCH 3); *Fulewood* 1274 RH (p), *Fulewode* 1283 Pat ('foul' or 'birds' wood', *v.* **fūl, fugol**); *Ye Highe Landes* 1611 PR(L) 19, *Ye High Lands* 1715 ib; *Kychinge* 1612 (*v.* **cycene**); *Ye Longe Lands* 1612; *Ye Wheate Furlonge* 1612.

2. ACTON PIGOTT (SJ 543027)

ALLCOT (lost) is *Alle(s)cot* 1203-4 *Ass* (p), *Allecot'* 1242 Fees, *Al(l)ecot'* 1255 RH (p), *Alecote* 1269 Ch, 1271-2 *Ass* (p), *Allecote* 1279 Cl, 1291-2 *Ass.* 'Alla's cottages'. The settlement does not appear in records after the 13th cent., and its site has not been established. VCH 6 suggests that it stood near Evenwood, where medieval pottery has been found.

EVENWOOD, E. COMMON, *Evenwood* 1612 *LDR*, 1716 PR(L) 19, 1845 *TA, Evenwood Common* 1817 *LDR.* 'Level wood', *v.* **efn**,

wudu. The squatter settlement on the Common has some 17th-cent. cottages (VCH 6).

Field-Names

Forms in (a) are 1845 *TA* except for those marked *LDR*. Early forms are as indicated under Acton Burnell.

In 1612 the common fields were *ye fielde towards Actonburnell, ye Cross fyld toward Gouldinge* and *Evenwood Field.*

(a) Ash Furlong (1685, one of a group of furlong-shaped fields); Bank, - Mdw; The Banks (lower down on the same stream as preceding ns.); The Bog (adjoins Gutter Mdw, along a stream); Broad Lsw (*Brode Leasowe* 1612, very narrow in 1845); Broom Hill; Chapel Yd (cf. VCH 6, "In the early Middle Ages Acton Pigott was sufficiently populous to have its own chapel, and until the 15th century its own priest"); The Clemley (*v.* Clemley Park in Cardeston *supra*); Cote Lsw (no building shown); Dove Cote Mdw; Eight Butts (athwart adjacent fields); Gig Hole 1817 *LDR*, Giggo Lsw 1857 *LDR* (probably a place where hemp stalks were dried after rotting, *v.* FN 31); The Greens (*The Green or Evenwood Meadow* 1705); Gutter Mdw; Hanging Lees 1857 (*Hanging Lye* 1612,85, *The Hanging Lee* 1698, 1705, 1718, *v.* **hangende**, **lēah**); The Harp (harp-shaped); Hay Brook; Holf Mdw (*The Hough Meadow* 1705, 1718, Houghs 1817 *LDR*, probably **halh**); Holly Moor; Horse Croft; The Knowles 1810 *LDR* (*Knowles* 1612, *Ye Knolls* 1685, *v.* **cnoll**); The Limners, Limners Mdw (*Lymmer Pytt, Lynmere* 1612, *Linmar* 1685, *Limener* 1698, *Limner* 1705, possibly 'flax pond', *v.* **līn**, **mere**); Long Lands, Lane - - (between Wheat Furlong and Eight Butts, part of an open field); The Lords Mdw; The Marl Pits; Milking Bank; New Lsw, Little - - (*Ye Newe Leasowe* 1612); Parkwell 1857 *LDR*; Poplar Mdw (*Popler Meadowe* 1612); Rye Pce; The Stockings (*v.* ***stoccing**); Stockwell; Triangle; Well Lsw; Wheat Furlong; The Yard (adjoining hamlet).

(b) *Brade Meadow* 1718; *Ye Craft* 1685 ('croft'); *Ye Crosse* 1612 (not in Cross Field); *The Crossmeadow* 1705, 1718; *Ye Dale Acre* 1612; *Frydais Furlonge* 1612 (perhaps difficult land, *v.* FN 25); *Ye Longleyes* 1612; *Ye Lords Meadow* 1705; *Tinn Meadow* 1705, *The Tin* - 1718 (probably a short form of *tining*, 'enclosure').

Berrington

The name Berrington, 'fort settlement', is discussed in Part **1**. The parish comprises the townships of Berrington, Betton Abbots, Betton Strange, Brompton, Cantlop and Eaton Mascott. Betton Strange, which was transferred from St Chad's, Shrewsbury, in 1885, has its own *TA*. The other townships are not treated individually in *TA*, but the 1" *Index to Tithe Survey* map marks their boundaries.

1. BERRINGTON (SJ 529070)

BELL HOTEL. BERRINGTON POOL, *Lower or Berrington Pool* 1840 *TA*. CLIFF HO (1776 *VCH*) AND HOLLOW, *Cliffe* 1669 PR(L) 14, *The Cliffe* 1669 *et freq* ib, *Upper, Lower and Middle Cliff Meadow* 1840 *TA*. A bridge over Cound Brook on the site of the present Boreton Bridge was *Cliff Bridge* in 1659 (VCH 16). A steep bank rises immediately behind Cliff Ho, *v.* **clif**. CROSS HOUSES, *v.* Brompton township. GOWTER (not on 6" map, in Gazetteer), *The Goulter Furlong* 1619 VCH, *Gouttard Lane* 1636 *SBL 5135*, *The Gowter Lane* 1779,83 PR(L) 14, *The Gouter* 1797 ib, *The Gowter* 1800 ib, *Gowter* 1833 OS, *Gouter* 1840 *TA*. In *TA* this is a large field by the junction of A458 with the road to Upper Cound. A house here is named Gouters. The name is probably a form of *gutter*, referring to a drain. ME *gote* 'watercourse, channel' sometimes becomes *gowt*, as in Gowts PN L **1**, 24-5. KING-STREET. The 6" map applies this name to a few buildings near a N./S. road (Shrewsbury/Acton Burnell) which it labels "supposed Roman road", but which is not recognised as such by modern authorities. VCH 16 says that a section of this road is known as King Street. On *TAMap*, however, the f.ns. *Upper* and *Lower King Street* occur alongside the Atcham/Condover road, which runs N.E./S.W., and the buildings on the 6" map lie directly on this road. The fields are in Betton, and are listed in a terrier of lands in that township, 1750 *LDR*. RUSSELL PLACE. TOP POOL, *Upper or Top Pool, Upper Pool Leasow* 1840 *TA*.

Field-Names

Forms in (a) are 1840 *TA*. Early forms dated 1292, 1445 are HAC, 1662,98 and 1724,32,76,98 are *VCH*, 1685, 1750 are *LDR*.

VCH 15 says that the open fields of the township in the early 18th century were Atcham, Church and Old Field. The first two are listed 1865 *LDR*, but the third is *Millfeild* there and in later terriers.

(a) Aldery Lsw (1776); The Bank (*Bank Leasow* 1732); Barbadoes (a narrow strip by Cound Brook, on township boundary); Bare Arse (*Barearse Furlonge* 1685, *Bearars* 1698, *Bear Arse* 1732, a ref. to poor land); Bennetts Bank; Binners Pit; Lower Birch Hill (*Birch-hill Meadow* 1693, *Birchill* 1776); Bowens Fd; Brick Kiln Lsw; Bridleway Lse (by Shrewsbury/Bridgnorth road); Church Field (*v. supra*); Church Mdw (a large area N. and E. of church); Clam Croft (perhaps **clām** 'mud'); Clam Moor (not near preceding, probably represents *Cramble(s) Meere* 1662, *Cromsmore Furlong* 1685, 1750, *The Cramps Meers* 1732, *Cramsmoor* 1776, *Cramps Meer* 1798, probably a **mōr** rather than a **mere**: the first el. might be the plural of *crumb*, used in p.ns. for small pieces of land); Coxdale, Coxs' Dale (*Coxtales* 1732, *Cocksdale* 1776, *Coxtails* 1798, apparently 'cocks' tails'); Crop Ground; Cross Ground (by Cross Houses); Foxholes, Lower and Upper; Great Fd (perhaps part of Church Field); Griffiths Yd (perhaps *Giffordesyorde* 1445); Grinders, Big and Little, Grinders Mdw (cf. *Grindow Furlong* 1685, *Grindo* - 1698, 1750, a 1776 survey has several fields called *Grinders*); Hall Yd (a large field S.W. of church); Hawk Moor, Far and Near (*Hawk Moor* 1776); Hawthorn Tree Lsw (*Hawthorn Leasow* 1693, 1750); Kennel Rough (*Big Kennel* 1776); Ladder Stile (1776, cf. Stair Stile in Eaton Mascott); Line Yd; Long Furlong (1776, adjoins Great Fd); Long Lsw (1724); Long Mdw (1776); Lower Mdw (2, one listed 1776); March Lsw (in Cliff Hollow, *v.* **mersc**); Maules Pce; Mill Pce (adjoins Cantlop Mill); Moss Mdw (1776), Little Moss; The Moss; Moss (behind Gouter, in July 1990 the vegetation was vivid green); New Mdw (2); The Oaks, Big and Hither (*Ye Oaks* 1750, *Big Oaks* 1776, *Oaks, The Oakes* 1798); Old Fd (1776, W. of village, probably the central part of the open field of this name); Onslow Bank; Pit Yd (1776); Pool Corner (1776, by Berrington Pool); Pool Ring (1776, between Upper and Lower Pools); Pool Yd (several pools here); Pump Yd (1776, adjoins Pit Yd); Romers, Big and Little (*Roomer* 1776, either side of Moss, perhaps 'rough pond', *v.* **rūh**, **mere**); Rough (1798); Russells Yd; Slip (comparatively narrow); The Slough (1732, *v.* **slōh**); Swine Yd; Tining, New Tinings (adjacent, *New Tining* 1776, 'enclosure', *v.* **tȳning**); Wheat Hill, Whetall Lsw (adjacent, *The Whittalls* 1662, *Wheatall Bank* 1693, *Whittalls* 1732, *Wheathall* 1776, *Big and Little Whittalls* 1798, 'wheat hollow', *v.* **hwǣte, halh**); Warings Ley; Whitefoots Patch (a family named *Whitfoote* appears 1644 PR(L) 14); Wide Pce; The Yard (small enclosure in Church Mdw); The Yelds, Far and Near - (*The Healds* 1662, *Far and Great Yelds* 1776, *v.* **helde**, Plate 1 in FN is a photograph of this field); Yewtree Hill; Yewtree Lsw (1776).

(b) *The Alkmeers* 1662 (*v.* Alkmere *infra*); *Bare Leasow* 1732; *Battery* 1732, *The* - 1798; *Binshill* 1732; *Blackditch* 1776; *Blakemerisfelde* 1445 ('field of the black pool', *v.* **blæc, mere**, perhaps *Blakemoor* 1776); *The Bog, Bog Meadow* 1776; *Crabtree Furlong* 1685, 1750; *Cross Hill* 1798 PR(L) 14; *Depemar'* 1292 (probably 'deep pond', *v.* **dēop, mere**); The Elder *Tree Leasow* 1732; 1732; *The Flat* 1776; *Green Leasow* 1732; *Hales* 1732,98 (*v.* **halh**); *Hallywell Yate* 1662 ('holy well gate'); *Hawfield* 1776; *Hawthorn Bank* 1776; *Island* 1776; *Lady Furlong* 1776; *The Lea Oakes* 1662,85, *Lea Oaks* 1732; *Little Yard* 1732,98; *Longebache* 1292 (*v.* **lang, bæce**); *Longlane* 1644 PR(L) 14; *Lowe Yard* 1776; *Malthouse Yard* 1732; *Manpitt Leasow* 1732; *Marsh Ground* 1776; *Mortimer Pool* 1732; *The Moss* 1732, *Moss* 1798 (possibly identical with some Moss ns. in (a)); *Oakmoors* 1732, *Oakmoor* 1798; *Oatehill Hopyard* 1732; *The Park Leasow* 1693; *The Pool Bank* 1732; *Ye Portway* 1685, 1750; *Rabbit Bank* 1776; *Ryegrass Leasow* 1776; *Scar, Little Scar* 1798 (probably dialect *scar*, one of the meanings being 'bed of rough gravel'); *Shop Field and Furlong* ('shed'); *Stapelmore* 1292 (*v.* **stapol, mōr**, perhaps a marshy area marked out by posts); *Thistly Alkmoor, Thistley Leasow* 1776; *The Thistle Field* 1732; *Weighmoor* 1776; *Wide Piece* 1776.

2. BETTON ABBOTS (SJ 515079)

The township-name is discussed in Part **1**. The suggested etymology, 'beech-tree farm', is, however, far from conclusive.

BETTON COPPICE, *Betton Coppy* 1652 *SBL 5124*, 1840 *TA*. VCH 14 says this is the remnant of a wood which divided Betton Abbot from Betton Strange. BETTON POOL, *Betton Poole* 1652 *SBL 5124*, shown but not named on *TAMap*. FOX FM, *The Fox by Chillton* 1698,9 PR(L) 16, *The Fox, Littel Betton* 1703 PR(L) 15, *The Fox Farm* 1779 PR(L) 14. Possibly from the family of Will. *le Fox*, mentioned 1271-2 *Ass* in connection with Betton, Chilton and Emstrey. It stands on the boundary between the two Bettons and Chilton in Atcham parish. YEWTREE COTTAGES.

Field-Names

Forms in (a) are 1840 *TA*. Early forms dated Hy 8 are *RentSur*, 1692, 1698, 1798 are *VCH*, 1750 are *LDR*.

(a) Barn Mdw; Bean Fd; Betton Bank, Farther and Nearer; Betton Pool (on N. boundary, not near the pool of this name); Bettons Ashes; Bigbrow Pools; Binnals Bank (*Benhill* 1698, *Ye Bean Hills* 1750, *v*. **bēan, hyll**); Birches Mdw and Yd; Birch Hill (*two Berchhills* 1750, 1798); Bog; Brickkiln Pce; Briery Butts (1698, 1750); Britch (1698, 1750, from **bryce**, 'newly-broken-in land', probably also the origin of Birch names *supra*); Calves Patch; Little Chewer (*Chuer* 1698, 1750, the name is sometimes from *tuyère* 'bellows-end', but this field is an unremarkable shape); Colts Patch; Cow Lsw; Cow Pasture, Lower - -; Crab Hedges, Lower and Upper; Croft; The Croft; Crow Lsw, Far and Near; Crow Pool and Park (the 'pool' is a plantation on *TA* and 6"); Dadmoors (*Dademore Feld* Hy 8, *Dadmers* 1750, *v*. **mōr**); Exmoor, Big and Little; Fox Wicket (by Fox Fm); Garden Mdw; Gravelly Pce; The Gores or The Grove (*Old Goors* 1698, *Ye Old Gores* 1750, *v*. **gāra**); Hall Orchard; Hengrove, Little - (*Hengreen* 1698, *Hengrave* 1750); Hovel Lsw (no building shown); John's Yd; King Street, Upper and Lower (*v*. Berrington township); High Langleys (1698, 1750), Lower Langley (fields called Langleys are adjacent in Betton Strange); Long Lsw (2); Marlpit Lsw; Middle Fd; Net House Fd (by Betton Pool); Ox Lsw (2, *Oxlesue* Hy 8); The Park (a tiny triangle in the angle of a crossroads, cf. *Le Parke* Hy 8, *Park Piece* 1692); Pool Lsw (*Pole Lesue* Hy 8, by Betton Pool); Quillet (this word has various senses in Sa f.ns., *v*. FN 8; this instance is a bullet-shaped piece set among rectangular fields); Romers, Romer Mdw (the same name occurs in Berrington township); Shoemere Lsw (by Shomere Pool in Condover, cf. *Shomere Held'* Hy 8, *v*. **helde**); The Slang (adjoins a typical narrow curving piece); Tinkers Mdw (either side of Shrewsbury road); Walk Hill, Lower and Upper; Way Lsw (by Shrewsbury road); Well Mdw; White Fd, Farther and Nearer.

(b) *Ye Ambritch Hook* 1750; *Ye Ash Peices ib*; *Ye Brerely Peice ib*; *Butter Poole, Butterpools ib* (*v*. **butere**, a ref. to good pasture); *Ye Coppy ib* ('coppice'); *Cumbo's, Broomy and Clarks ib*; *Deerne Pole Lesue* Hy 8 ('hidden pool meadow', *v*. **derne, pōl, lǣs** and cf. Pool Lsw in (a)); *Dyademe Feld, Dyadems ib* (presumably 'diadem', but the reference is obscure); *Goldemore ib* (probably a marsh with golden flowers); *Hard Furlong* 1750; *Hares Peice ib*; *Heywood* 1549 *SBL 6731* ('enclosure wood', *v*. **(ge)hæg**); *Hill Leasow* 1750; *Hoddigreave, Hoddy- ib* (*v*. **grǣfe**); *Le Homme* Hy 8 (*v*. **hamm**); *Ye two Judas Furlongs* 1750 (probably referring to poor soil); *Kateryns Yorde* Hy 8 ('Catherine's yard'); *Le Lesue Orchard' ib* (*v.* **lǣs**); *Ye Letchmoor* 1750 (cf. *Letchmere* in Eaton Mascott *infra*, this is a separate example); *Ye Lower Feild ib*; *Le Myddle Lesue* Hy 8 (*v.* **lǣs**); *Nine Butts* 1750 (probably a furlong with 9 strips); *Ye Pairtrees Divide ib*; *Ye Pill in Ye Coppy Leasow ib*; *Ye Pitt ib*; *Scrab Hedges ib* (perhaps 'scrub'); *Venus Bank ib* (*v. infra*, under Lower Cound); *Walles Orchard, Le Walle Yorde* Hy 8 (Ric. *Walle* mentioned); *Ye Well Yard* 1750; *Wett Reans ib* (drainage channels); *Le Weyrehouse* Hy 8 (perhaps on one of the pools, *weir-house* is recorded in 1791 (NED) as a term for a fish-trap).

3. BETTON STRANGE (SJ 507093)

v. Part **1** for a discussion of the township-name.

(BETTON) ALKMERE
Aluedemar c.1280 *SBL 406*
Abrithemere 1291-2 *Ass*
Aluythemere 1291-2 *Ass, Alvichermere* 1301 SAC
Altemere 1380 *SBL 6718 et freq* to 1568 *SBL 6736A*
Althitmere 1391 *SBL 6719*
Almer 1551 Pat, *Almere alias Almer* 1608 *SBL 3455, Allmare* 1705, 13, 16 PR(L) 15
Aulkmaer, Aulkemeare 1567 *SBL 6735, Aulkmere* 1570 *SBL 6747 et freq* with variant spellings *Awlk-* and *-meare* to 1608 *Eyton, Alkmere* 1597 *SBL 6740 et seq* with variant spellings *-mear(e)*, *Alkemere* 1608 *Eyton*, 1618 *SBL 9943*
Aulkemore 1618 PR(L) 6, *Alkmore* 1642 ib, 1670 PR(L) 15, *-moor* 1649 *SBL 13379, Alcmore* 1724 PR(L) 14

Second element **mere**; there are ponds all over this area. The spellings *Aluedemar, Aluythemere, Althitmere* suggest that the first element is the feminine personal name *Ælfgȳð*, but the developments to *Alt-* and *A(u)lk-* are irregular.

Betton Alkmere and Betton Strange were distinct townships, but the area is small, so they have been treated as a single unit.

ASH COPPICE, *Plantation* 1845 *TA*. SUTTON PLANTATION, *Plantation* 1845 *TA*, adjoins Sutton near Shrewsbury.

Field-Names

Forms in (a) are 1845 *TA*.

(a) Barn Yd; Bettons Hedge, Farther and Nearer (on parish boundary); Big Mdw; Boars Den (at G.R. 517096); Bomer Lsw and Pce (by Bomere Pool in Condover parish); Brickkiln Lsw, Big and Little; Briery Lsw; Browns Mdw; Calves Croft and Patch; Clarkes Lsw; Cote Lsw (2 fields, no building shown); Cow Pasture (2); Crabtree Lsw; Croft, Farther, Middle and Near; Dove House Yd; Dry Lsw (2 fields); Eight Acres (much more than twice as Big as Four -); Four Acres (very small); Fox Mdw (by Fox Fm in Betton Abbots); Golds Croft and Pce; Gorsty Pce; Gravelly Bank and Long Lsw; Horse Pasture; Lane Mdw (by Shrewsbury road); Little Mdw (2); Little Way Lsw (not by a road); Long Lsw (2); Long Mdw; Long Yd (large area S. of Betton Alkmere); Lower Mdw; Maiden Well Croft, Big and Little Well Lsw (6" map shows the well by a road 2 miles N.W. of Betton Strange); Moss Mdw, Little and Middle Moss (cf. *Ye Moss Ditch* 1750 *LDR*); New Lsw; Orchard Pce; Ox Mdw, Great and Little; Pig Lsw; Poushill Ground (5 fields); Roundabout (an unremarkable sub-rectangular field); Ryders Pce; Sandy Hill, Banky, Big and Little; Sharpstone Lsw (by Sharpstone Hill in Condover); Six Acres; Six Butts (*Ye Six Butts or Little Croft* 1750 *LDR*); Steppingstone Fd; Three Acres (roughly equal to Six and Eight -); Wheat Lsw; Withy Croft.

(b) *Broomey Leasow* 1677 *SBL 7099*; *The Coppy, Coppy Leasow ib*; *The Little Field* 1608 *Eyton*; *The Roma(y)ne Field ib.*

4. BROMPTON (SJ 548079)

The township-name, which means 'broom settlement', is discussed in Part **1**.

COTONS, 1833 OS, *Ye Cotten, Upper Cotten* 1750 *LDR, The Coatens* 1769, 72, 79 PR(L) 14. *VCH* says that this isolated farm is first mentioned in 1699 (*SRO 112*), the land having previously been a common called *Cound Heath* in 1564 and *Brompton Heath* in 1623 (*ib*). The new farm probably took the name *Cot*(*t*)*ons* from the meadows to which it was applied all along the length of the R. Severn which bounds the township. F.ns. indicative of this usage are set out *infra*. There does not appear to be another instance of

Cot(t)on as a name for river-meadows, and the sense is not obvious. **cot(e)** is used in f.ns. for light-weight animal shelters. The tongue of land along the Severn in which Cotons is the only settlement was transferred to Berrington from Cound in 1654 (VCH 14).

CROSS HOUSES, 1675 Ogilby, 1703 PR(L) 14, *The Crosse House* 1697 PR(L) 14, *Xhouses* 1747 *et freq* ib. In the parish registers for 1635, 1653 and 1758 people are described as "of the Cross(e)". Cross Houses is a squatter settlement on parish and township boundaries, and the n. refers to the T-junction of the Shrewsbury/ Bridgnorth road and the road to Atcham. The settlement-history is given in VCH, p.17. GROTTO COPPICE, 1840 *TA, Grotto* 1833 OS.

Field-Names

Forms in (a) are 1840 *TA*. Early forms dated 1553, 60, 64, 1689, 93, 98, 1729, 98 are *VCH*. Those dated 1750 are *LDR*.

(a) Barn Fd; Barn Yd; Barren Hill (adjoins Groten *infra*); Bearnard Yd (a minute enclosure); Brickwork Ground; Bridges (*Britches* 1698, *Ye Breetches* 1750, *v.* **bryce** 'newly broken-in land', probably also in Birch Pits which adjoins, they are near Heath Lsw); Broad Mdw; Broadway, Little and Lower (*Broadway Croft* 1750, by Bridgnorth road); Broom Hill (*Ye three Broomhills* 1750); Brooms Yd (*Ye Broom Yard* 1750); Claypit Croft (cf. *Ye Claypit Leasow* 1750); Clay Pits; Clem Croft (2, one named 1750, cf. *Clem Furlong* 1724, ***clǣme** 'muddy place'); Corn Yd; Costly (between Heath Lsw and Birch Pits, perhaps a ref. to the need for manure); Cotton Mdw (in the projection of the township which contains Cotons *supra*: the n. probably referred to the riverside meadows before it was given to the farm); Cow Pasture (2); Cross Fd, Low and Upper (*Crossfield* 1693, *Ye Cross, Cross Leasow* 1750, by Crosshouses); Dale Lsw (1750); Diagonal, Far and Near (*Drakenal* 1698, *Drakenall Lane* 1730, perhaps 'dragon nook', *v.* **draca, halh**); The Elms; Forney Cotons (up-river from Cotton Mdw, meadows along the whole length of the Severn which bounds the township were known as Cotons); Green Reams (- *Reans* 1750, 'drains'); Groten (*Crotenffeld'* Hy 8 *RentSur, Grotton Felde* 1553 Pat, *The Grotton* 1564, perhaps a substantival use of the adj. ***grēoten** 'gravelly'); Harbour Lsw (1750, probably 'arbor'); Heath Lsw, Little Heath (VCH 15 says the heath in this area was being enclosed in 1683); Hollings Furlong (*Hollis Furlong, Holly* - 1750, perhaps a surname, but cf. *Holley*

Hy 8 *RentSur, Le Holley* 1553 Pat, *The Hollye* 1564, *v.* **holegn**); Horse Pasture; Hungry Gate (*Hoggy Gate* 1689, *Hoggery Gate* 1750, perhaps 'hog-yard', though *hoggery* is not recorded till 19th); Jonas Croft; Long Yd; Mains Pce, Great and Little ('demesne'); Marsh (*March or Marsh Lane* 1729, *Ye Marsh* 1750); Meadow, Upper, Ford, Big and Lower (in sequence along the Severn); Meers (*Ye two Meers* 1750, on parish boundary, *v.* **(ge)mǣre**); Moor Mdw; Moss, Big and Little (*Ye Moss* 1750, adjoins Slough); New Gate (*Newgate Leasow* 1750); New Tinings (**tȳning** 'enclosure'); Old Cow Pasture; Ox Lsw (2); Perry Hills, Big and Little (**pirige** 'pear tree'); Powells Yd; Priest Mdw; Rugmore Mdw, Far, Near and Middle Rugmore (*Rugmore* 1698, dialect *rug* 'large stone' and **mōr**); Severn Mdw; Slough (2, cf. *Ye Slough* 1750); Stair Stile; Steeple Furlong, Great and Little (*Ye Steple Furlong* 1750, cf. *Steple Croft* 1724, probably referring to the upkeep of the church); Town Mdw (1750, adjoining Brompton); Townsend (adjoins preceding, gates at *Townsend* leading to *Town Meadow* are mentioned 1689); Turner, Great and Little (*Three Turner Gate Leasows* 1750, *Turner* 1798, in a sharp bend of the Severn); Watling Street Fd; Wheat Lsw; Wheat Reans (*recte* Wet Reans, i.e. drains); White Lsw; Withy Plantation; Short Withys (*Short Withies* 1750).

(b) *Bagmore Leasow* 1750; *Brade Meadow and Furlong ib*; *Coppy, Ye Coppy Leasow ib*; *Nether Coton' al' dict' Roxetours Coton'* Hy 8 *RentSur*, (pasture called) *Nethercoton alias Roxcetor Cotton* 1553, *Nether and Over Cotton* 1560, *Wroxeter Cotton* 1564 (common meadow on Severn bank N. of Brompton which was shared between Brompton and Wroxeter, *v.* Cotons *supra*); *Ell Furlong* 1750 (probably L-shaped); *Ferny Furlong ib*; *Hair Furlong ib*; *House Leasow ib*; *Meadow Furlong ib*; *Ye New Inclosure ib*; *Ye New Piece ib*; *Ye Oaks ib*; *Ye Old Reans ib* (cf. Green Reans *supra*); *Ye Orchyard ib*; *Ye Press Meadow ib* (probably 'priest's meadow'); *Ye Upper End ib*; *Ye Upper Leasow ib*; *Whetmore ib*; *Winnye* 1564 (a meadow, perhaps a n. in **-ēg**).

5. CANTLOP (SJ 523058)

The township-name, which is of uncertain derivation, is discussed in Part 1.

CANTLOP BRIDGE. The adjacent field to S. on *TAMap* is *Iron Bridge Field.* The elegant cast-iron bridge over Cound Brook was built by subscription in 1812, to designs approved by Thomas Telford. CANTLOP FM. CANTLOPGROVE, a house built between 1816 and 1845 (VCH 17). CANTLOPLAWN, *The Lawn*

1833 OS. The 19th-cent. 1" and the 6" maps give these names to a house on the W. boundary of the township. *TAMap* does not show this, but marks a field called *The Lawn* on N.E. boundary. CANTLOP MILL, 1748 PR(L) 14, 1833 OS, *Ye Mill* 1685 *LDR*. A mill here is the subject of a grant c.1182 SAC. CANTLOP WD, 1590 *VCH*, 1833 OS, *Boscus de Kontelop* 1235 Eyton, cf. Will. *de La Wode* of Cantlop 1388 *SBL 6686*. LIGHTGREEN COPPICE, 1833 OS, 1840 *TA*, *The Light Green Meadow* 1595 *SBL 9501*, *The Light Greene* 1598 *SBL 7022*, *The Lightgrene* 1602 PR(L) 6, *The Light Green* 1722 *SBL 6946*. 'Light-coloured grassy place', *v.* **lēoht**, **grēne**[2]. WOOD LANE, runs by Cantlop Wd.

Field-Names

Forms in (a) are 1840 *TA*. Early forms dated 1290-1, 1307, 1380, 1418, 1546, 1571, 1573, 1586, 1593, 1595, 1689 are *SBL 6593,4,8, 6688, 6694,5,8, 6702, 6713, 9501, 5142*; and 1316, 1464, 1471, 1635, 1752, 1768, 1780 are *VCH*. The 1316 *VCH* forms are from *AddCh 47247*.

VCH 15 says that in 1316 the common fields were Berrington, Newton (from the lost *Newton* in Pitchford) and Wood Field. In 1418 and till enclosure they were known as Low, High and Barley Fields.

(a) Back Mdw (1768); Bakehouse Yd; Barley Fd (2 separate fields W. of village in the area of the open field; *Berleyeffeld* 1418, *The Barlye Field* 1593, *v.* **bærlic**); Barnwell Lsw (1768); The Binds (1768, *The Bynes* 1752, *Binds Meadow* 1780, 2 fields on *TAMap*: a plant-name, OE **-binde**, used of clinging plants, which occurs several times as an uncompounded p.n. in Sx, PN Sx 185); Brickkiln Fd; Calves Croft (1768); Coal Hill (*Cole Hill* 1595, cf. *The Colepitt Yarde* 1593, but VCH 24 says there is no evidence of coalmining in this parish, so the reference is presumably to charcoal); Cockshutt Lsw (*v.* ***cocc-scīete**); Cocks Pce (1708 *SRO 665*); Cow Pasture; Crackfoot Lsw (1780, a reference to hard soil); Criftin (*Cryftinge* 1595, *Criften* 1768, *v.* ***cryfting** 'small croft'); The Croft (*The Crofts* 1768); Crooked Oak (1752,68,80, *The Croked Oke* 1593); Duckdale, - Croft (*Dukedale* c.1237-40 HAC, *Dogedales Brook* 1418, *Dugdale Croft* 1768, a genuine **dæl**[1] n., unlike Coxdale in Berrington township; first el. **dūce** 'duck'); Far Lsw (1768, on parish boundary); Ferny Bank, Upper and Lower (*Great and Little Ferney Bank* 1752, cf. *Near and Further Ferny Field* 1780); Flat Pce (*Flatt Piece* 1768, near Lightgreen Coppice, perhaps descriptive rather than a ref. to open-field strips); Frogwell, - Mdw and Rough (1768, cf. *Frogmore* 1595);

Gorsty Furlong (1752,68,80, the fields W. of Cantlop are furlong-shaped); Hawthorn Hill (cf. *Hawthorn Stile Field* 1752, *Hawthorn Stile* 1768, *Hawthorn Field* 1780); Heath Lsw ('the heath' is mentioned 1316); High Crofts *(High Croft, Lower - -* 1768); High Lsw (1768); The Hill (1752,68, three fields by a loop in Cound Brook, probably *Milnehull* 1316); Hills Ground (1768, not near The Hill, perhaps *Hill Ground* 1708 *SRO 665*); The Lawn (1768, *Laund Lesow* 1595); Little Fields (*The Litle Field* 1593, *Little Field* 1768, *Little* and *Great Field* are listed 1752); Little Mdw; Long Dole (looks like a furlong in Barley Field); Long Mills; Lower Ground Mdw; Lower Lsw (1768); Mill Ground (1780, by Cantlop Mill); Ox Lsw (2, in one instance Near and Farther, in the other Near and Far; a 1780 list has *Near, Middle* and *Further Ox Leasow*); Patch (used for several very small fields); Pound Mdw; Road Pce; Ryegrass Fd, Lower Ryegrass (*Lower Rye Grass, Ryegrass Patch* 1768); Sheep Lsw, Far and Near (1768); Little Sitch (*v.* **sīc**); Walker Yd (*Walkers -* 1768), Field below Walkers; Wards Yd; Washford (1689, 1768), - Mdw; Well Furlong (the fields S.E. of Cantlop are furlong-shaped); White Lsw (1768); Willowy Patch, Farther - -; Wood Lsw, Lower - - (*Upper and Lower Wood Leasow* 1768); The Yard (2); The Yelds (1768, *La Helde* c.1237-40 HAC, 1316 *SBL 1713, The Held* 1595, *v.* **helde**); Yewtree Lsw (1768).

(b) *Appultre, -londes* 1418 (*v.* **æppeltrēow**); *Bardel'* 1290-1; *The Barme, The Furre and Midle Barmesley* 1593; *Cantelopmere* 1546 (a common or wood adjoining Condover, probably 'Cantlop boundary', *v.* **(ge)mǣre**); *Cantlopps Comon* 1571, *Cantlopp Common* 1593; *Cantlopps Lane* 1593; *Challoorchayes* 1380 (*v.* **(ge)hæg**); *Chirchebrugge* 1418 (at Cantlop Mill, a plank bridge for church-goers, VCH 16); *Codenhull, -medewe* 1418 ('Coda's hill'); *Colonels Meadow* 1752; *Common Leasow* 1768; *Cookes Place* 1593; *Corner Meadow* 1780; *Crooke Ford* 1752 (perhaps **crōc** used of a river-bend); *Field Butts* 1768; *Le Gregrenen* 1316 (obscure); *Le Grenewey* 1307; *Helmwalle* 1290-1 ('elm spring'); *The Highfield* 1593 (a common field); *Lelmdenedore* 1307 (final el. **dōr** 'pass', the first part of the n. may be corrupt); *Le Loghfeld* 1418, *The Lowe Field* 1593 (a common field, 'low' as opposed to *Highfield*); *Long Furlong* 1752; *Make Bridge* 1752, *Magbridge Leasow* 1780 (second el. probably **bryce** 'assart'); *Le Millelone* 1418, *Myll Lone* 1573 ('mill lane'); *Moore* 1586 (*v.* **mōr**); *Neutonstye* ('stye near *Newton*'); *Newfordesmylle* 1464, *Newforemyll* 1471; *New Tineing* 1768 (*v.* **tȳning**); *Le Port(e)wey, Le Smaleportwey* 1418, *The Portway Gate* 1593, *The Portway* 1635 (*v.* **portweg**, one form has **smæl** 'narrow' prefixed; probably the road to Shrewsbury); *Rough Patch* 1768; *The vii Snogges* 1593 (7 of 12 "ridges or lands" which lie beneath "the croked oke" in Highfield; FN 11 notes that *Snog(g)s* occurs elsewhere in Sa, it is perhaps a corruption of nokes, a noke being a measure of land); *Swines Yd* 1768; *Symmehadelond* 1418 (a 'headland' in a field-system, first el. probably a surname); *Symondesyerd* 1418 (*v.* **geard**); *Wallets Yard* 1768; *Wall Lesow* 1595, *Wall Furlong* 1768,80 (probably **wælle** 'spring'); *Wheat Leasow* 1768; *Le Wodedich* 1307 ('wood ditch').

6. EATON MASCOTT (SJ 538059)

The township-name, which means 'river settlement', is discussed in Part **1**. Mascott is a manorial affix.

CLOUD COPPICE. LITTLE CLOUD, *Le Clude* 1221-2 *Ass*, *La Cloude* 1292 HAC, *Le Cloude* 1336 *VCH(AddCh 58775)*, *The Clowde Hill, The Lower and Upper Clowde Meadow* 1636 *SBL 5135*. The early references are to pasture. *TA* gives two woods called *Cloud Coppice* and fields called *Cloud Hill, - Leasow*. These surround an irregularly-shaped massif in the grounds of Eaton Mascott Hall. There is no access to the hill, so no estimate has been made of whether **clūd** refers to a rock outcrop. In Sa, however, the usual term for rock outcrops is **stān**, and it is possible that the name refers rather to the irregular shape of the feature. If it were ME in origin it might be a transferred use of the word *cloud*, rather than a derivative of the OE word, which usually referrred to rocks.

BERRINGTON PLANTATION. THE BOGS, 1840 *TA*. COUNDSTANK, 1840 *TA*, there was a mill-race here (VCH 61), so *stank* probably means 'dam' rather than 'pool'. DIGMORE, MIDDLE AND TOP, *Lower and Upper Digmore* 1840 *TA*. NEWMAN HALL COTTAGES, *Newman Hill* 1687 *SBL 1030*, 1782 PR(L) 14, *Newman Hall* 1785 *et seq* PR(L) 14. Fields called *Croft* and *House Meadow* mark this site on *TAMap*.

Field-Names

Forms in (a) are 1840 *TA*. Early forms dated 1316,36 are *VCH(AddCh 58307, 58775)*, 1556 are *VCH(NLW)*, 1619,79 are *VCH(SRO 1514)*, 1635,6 are *SBL 3303, 5135*, 1689 are *SBL 5142*, 1693, 1702-3 are *VCH(SBL 1033,8)*, 1685, 1750 are *LDR*.

VCH 15 says that in 1316 the common fields were Berrington, Brompton and Cound Field. Berrington was also called Mill Field. Brompton was called *Lechmere Field* in 1556 and *Pool Field* in 1636. They were enclosed between 1556 and 1693.

(a) Aldery Lsw; Black Moor; Boreton Stile (*Burton Stile* 1636, not near a road to Boreton); Brickkiln Lsw; Brook Coppice and Patch (not adjacent, but both by Cound Brook); Broomy Bank; Church Hill (possibly **crūc**); Coneyry Coppice, Further Coneyry, Hither Coneygrey (*The Connygree, The Connygrey Furlonge* 1636, *v.* **coninger**); Cow Pasture; Ferny Lsw; Field, Upper and Middle (perhaps part of the open field called Cound Field); Forge Bank (downstream from Forge Mdw), Forge Mdw (on Cound Brook, *Smithy* and *Forge* are mentioned 1635); Green Lsw; Hollins Townsend (this and Tayleurs - are on the N. and S. edges of the hamlet); Hop Yd; House Mdw (*v.* Newman Hall Cottages *supra*); Mill Stiche (*Mill Sich* 1693, 1702-3; if the earlier form is correct the generic is **sīc** 'small stream'); Oak Hill (*The Oak Hill Head* 1693); Old Hill (1693, 1702-3); Pool Lsw, Upper, Middle and Lower (*The Upper and Lower Poole Leasowe* 1677 *SBL 5138*); Preston Yd, Further and Hither (2 large fields adjoining the hamlet); Pump Yard and The Copy (on Cound Brook); Sand Hill; Sandy Lsw and Fd (not adjacent); Slang Mdw (appropriately shaped); Stonehill Lsw; Stray Mdw; Tayleurs Townsend (landowners named *Tayleur* are mentioned VCH 21); Walk, Lower, Middle and Upper (along the drive of Eaton M. Hall); Well Mdw (cf. *Well Leasowe* 1693, 1702-3).

(b) *Alsteresmor* 1336 (*v.* **mōr**); *Ancresmarfurlong* 1316; *Berringtonfeild* 1636 (an open field); *The Brink* 1636; *The Broome Leasow* 1693; *Byne Furlong* 1693, 1702-3 (cf. The Binds in Cantlop); *The Comon Meadow* 1636; *Coopers Mill* 1619; *Drye Leasowe* 1635, *The Dry Leasow* 1693, *Dry Leasowe* 1702-3; *Eaton Lane* 1798,9 PR(L) 14; *Eton Pool* 1679; *The Gospell Oake* 1636 (a ref. to the beating of the parish bounds); *The Greenway Head* 1693, 1702-3; *The Halpenny Hill* 1693, *The Halfepenny Hill* 1702-3 (probably a ref. to rent); *Harefurlong* 1316 (*v.* **hara** 'hare'); *Herleswall* 1316 (probably **wælle** 'spring' with a pers.n.); *The Hill Copp* 1636; *Hill-furlong* 1685; *The House Yard* 1556; *Lechemorefurlong* 1316, *Lechmerefylde* 1556, *Letchmeare Poole* 1619 (*v.* **mere**, this is a fairly common minor n., the first el. could be **læcc** 'boggy stream' or **lǣce** 'leech', VCH 14 says this was the former name of Eaton M. Pool); *The Little Meadow* 1693; *The Lower Hill* 1636; *The Lower Yarde* 1689; *The Lytlefyld* 1556; *The Ner Leasow* 1693 ('near'); *The Nether Fylde* 1556; *The Peaches* 1556; *The Peartree or The Bannut Tree Yarde* 1689 (a *bannut* is a variety of walnut); *Poole Feild* 1653 (an open field); *The Lower Poole Meadowe* 1636, *The Poole* - 1693; *Pul Acre* 1316 *SBL*

1713 (said to be near *Le Molyn'*, so on Cound Brook, not near other 'pool' ns.); *Rowolowe, Rowolowehull* 1316 ('rough tumulus', *v.* **rūh, hlāw**, VCH 16 says that air photographs show round barrows near Watling Street in this township); *Shutt Yorde* 1635; *The Smiths Yard* 1693; *Le Starveacre* 1336 (a derogatory n.); *Upper Hill* 1693, 1702-3.

Condover

The parish-name, which means 'flat-topped ridge by R. Cound', is discussed in Part 1.

Condover is a large parish containing the townships of Allfield, Bayston, Boreton, Chatford, Condover, Dorrington, Great Lyth, Little Lyth, Norton, Great Ryton, Little Ryton, Westley and Wheatall. Since 1934 the parish has also contained an area on the outskirts of Shrewsbury comprising Hookagate, Pulley, Whitley, Welbatch and part of Bayston Hill. This area was transferred from the ancient parish of Meole Brace. It will be treated under the Liberties of Shrewsbury.

There is, unfortunately, no record of the township boundaries in Condover parish, apart from those of Great Lyth, which are marked on Map no.9 *SRO 665*, box 60. There is a single *TAMap* for the whole parish, and no divisions are marked on the 19th-cent. Index to Tithe Survey map. This problem arises in respect of a few other large parishes in Shropshire, notably Claverley and Shifnal. It seems best to mark out more-or-less arbitrary areas for townships in these parishes, and to treat minor names and field-names within these divisions. This will not occasion serious inconvenience as regards minor names, since these can be located on OS maps. Field-names may not always be listed under the correct township, but this inconvenience is felt to be less than would arise from the presentation of a long list of field-names for the whole parish. The treatment also has the merit of being consistent with that of other large parishes for which the township boundaries are preserved by the *TA*.

Great and Little Lyth and Great and Little Ryton have been treated as single units.

Condover field-names which cannot be assigned to a township are listed at the end of the section devoted to this parish.

1. ALLFIELD (SJ 504072)

Aldefelde 1172-c.1180 HAC *et freq* with variant spellings *-feud, -feld* to 1551 Pat
Haldevelde 1291-2 *Ass* (p)
Aldfyllde 1430 SAS 50, *-field* 1584 *SBL 6631*
A(u)lfeld 1545 *SBL 9077, Allfilde* 1586 *SBL 6883 et freq* with variant spellings *-feild(e), -field*; *Alfeyld* 1587 PR(L) 6, *Alfielde* 1627 ib, *Aulfield* 1767,8,9 ib
Alveyld 1558 *SBL 6585 et freq* with variant spellings *All-* and *-vield, -vilde, -veld(e), -vyeld* to 1697 *SBL 3556, Alfyeld alias Alvyld* 1580 *SBL 6586, Alfild otherwise Alveld* 1655 *SBL 6587, Allfield alias Alveld* 1694 *SBL 9955*
Orlville 1586 *SBL 7035*
Aufyld, -feild 1595 *SBL 9501*
Aldveyld 1598 *SBL 6745*
Awvield 1645 PR(L) 6

The elements are **ald** and **feld**. The meaning of the name is open to conjecture. **ald** 'old' can mean either 'disused' or 'in use from ancient times'. **feld** 'open land' is likely in early settlement-names to refer to land which has been converted to arable from pasture. In the second half of the 10th century, however, **feld** came to be used for the large arable areas of the open-field system of farming (*v.* Gelling, *Place-Names in the Landscape*, 235ff). Allfield could be a name for a place where the arable land was arranged in open fields at a relatively early date, or, if the name is of earlier origin than the 10th century, it could refer to a settlement in an area which had anciently been used for pasture.

There is an identical township-name, Aldfield, in Y (PN ERY 5, 193).

Field-Names

Forms in (a) are 1840 *TA*.

(a) Allfield Eyes, Upper - - (either side of Cound Brook, *Aufeild Eye the lower end* 1595 *SBL 9501, v.* **ēg**); Allfield Hill (*Allfeilds Hill* 1615 *SBL 6848A*);

Backhouse Bank (probably 'behind the house', the field adjoins Allfield Fm); Balls Croft; Betton Bank (adjoins B. Abbots); Big and Little Bomere Mdw (*v.* Bomere in Bayston *infra*); Broad Lsw; Butchers Fd; Bylet (by a sharp bend in Cound Brook); Calves Bank; Cote Mdw (no building shown, perhaps *Coate Meadow* 1705 *SBL 6481*); Lower and Upper Cow Pasture; Crabtree Lsw, Upper Crabtree Fd (near but not adjoining); Eleven Lawns (perhaps *Close called Eleventh Land* 1595 *SBL 9501*); Further and Hither Glebe; Harbour Lsw (*The Harbar Leasowe* 1588 *SBL 6883, Harbur Lesow Close* 1595 *SBL 9501, The Harbour Peice* 1721 *Eyton, v.* **here-beorg**); Hog Yd; Middle Fd (between Crabtree Lsw and Upper Crabtree Fd); Moat Furlongs (W. of Allfield Fm, cf. *The Mote, The Mote Furlonge* 1588 *SBL 6883*); Patch (2 very small enclosures by Allfield Fm); Pool Mdw (3 streams rise here); Prouds Hill; Sandy Bank; Skin Mill Mdw and Yd (a leather mill replaced a fulling mill here in the 16th cent., VCH 48); The Tongues (between Cound Brook and the Condover road, no obvious reason for the name); Turnpike Gate Fd (beside Berrington/Condover road); Weavers Lsw; White Lsw; Widnall (1595, 1615 *SBL 9501, 6848A,* 1706 VCH 52, probably 'wide nook' referring to land in a curve of Cound Brook, *v.* **wīd, halh**); Yewtree Bank.

(b) *Salter's Way* (VCH 31 says this was an old name for the road from Allfield to Hungerhill, which is marked "supposed Roman" on 6" map); *The Wintall or Wintall Bank* 1789 *SBL 1338.*

2. BAYSTON (SJ 492082)

The township-name, which means 'Bēage's stone' (referring to a rock outcrop), is discussed in Part **1**.

BOMERE FM, POOL and WD. (*vivar' de*) *Bolemar, Bulemar'* 1255 RH, (*aqua de*) *Bossemare* (?*recte Bolle-*) 1271-2 *Ass, Bolemeressiche, Bulmeressich* 1301 SAC, *Bulle Mere* 1553 *SBL 6732, Bowmeare* 1583 *SBL 6738A, Bowmer*(*e*) *Leasowe* 1585,98 *SBL 6883, 7022, Bomeare* 1694 *SBL 9955, Bomer 1702 SBL 13457, Beaumere* 1808 Baugh.

OE ***bula** 'bull' is well-evidenced in p.ns., but it perhaps occurs with **mere** 'pond' more often than might be expected. Settlement-names of this origin are Bulmer Ess, Boulmer Nb and Bulmer YN. Two minor names have been noted in addition to the Sa one: these are Bowmoor in Kempsford Gl (PN Gl **1**, 39) and

Bulman Strands in Crook We (PN We 1, 177). It should be noted that Bulmer Ess has the DB form *Bulenemere*, which suggests a gen.pl. This would be especially appropriate if the reference were to an animal (though in the case of bulls the plural should perhaps be understood to refer to successive rather than contemporaneous use of pasture). Also, as regards the Sa name, The Burridges *infra* has the same first el., and it would be difficult to find a qualifier which suited **mere** and **hrycg** better than the animal name. So probably 'bull pond'. The pond is a large one by south-Shropshire standards.

The 19th-cent. 1" shows *Bomer* (Bomere Fm), *Bomer Pool* and *Bomer Coppice* (Bomere Wd). The 1301 SAC reference is to a water-channel (**sīc**).

THE BURRIDGES OR BULRIDGES (not on map). *Bulerugge* c.1160 HAC, *-ruge* 1172-c.1180 SAC, *Boleringe* 1172 (e.14th) HAC, *Bulregg'* 1209 For, *Bolerugh, -rugge* 1301 SAC, *Bull Rudge* 1430 SAS 50, *Bullryche* 1516 *SBL 6727, Bulridge* 1534 *SBL 6728 et seq, Le -* 1553 *SBL 6734, Sayns Marye Bulriche* 1553 *SBL 6732, Seynt Mary Bullrudgis* 1578 *Eyton, The Bulrudge or Bulrudges* 1581,97 *SBL 6745, 6743, Lady Bullrudgis* 1583,6 *SBL 6738A, 6739, Ladie's Bulridges* 1584 *SBL 6738, The Manck Bullridge* 1595 *SBL 9501, Bullridges* 1595 *SBL 9501 et seq, Bullrishes* 1655 SAS I/XLVII, *Bulruch, Lady and Lower Bulruches* 1697 *SBL 3556, The Burridges, Burridge Meadow, Taylors and Little Burridges* 1840 *TA*.

This was an area of rough pasture between Bomere Pool and Sharpstones Hill. The name means 'bull ridge', with the same first el. as Bomere *supra* and **hrycg**. *St Mary* and *Lady* may refer to the Chantry of St Mary in Condover church. *Manck* is obscure.

ALSPATH (a house near Bayston hill). THE BURGS, 1833 OS, *The Berries, Berry Fields and Leasow* 1840 *TA*, a large prehistoric fort on the parish boundary by Baystonhill. The variant forms suggest that derivatives of **burh** and the dat. **byrig** were both current. SHARPSTONE HILL, *Sharpstones* 1840 *TA*. SHOMERE POOL, *pole called Shalmeare* 1549 *SBL 6731* (endorsed *Shamere*), *Shallomere* 1553 *SBL 6732, Shawmeare Moss* 1583 *SBL 6738A, Poole called Shawmere, Shawmere Mosse* 1586 *SBL 6739, Shawmer Mosse and Lesow* 1595 *SBL 9501, Shawmeare Bog and Pools* 1840 *TA*: 'shallow pond', from ME *schalowe* and **mere**. The modern form is anticipated in *Shomere Held'* Hy 8 *RentSur*, in Betton Abbots: *v.* **helde** 'slope'.

Field-Names

Forms in (a) are 1840 *TA*.

(a) The Banks; Barnes Pce; Bears Arse (i.e. Bare Arse, unproductive ground); The Big Banks; Bridge Lsw (by a stream-crossing); Bridge Lsw (by a small stream, not near preceding); Brooky Yd (by a stream); Criften, Big - (*Criftinge Lane, Famers Criftinge* 1595 *SBL 9501* are in Condover but not certain to be in Bayston, *v.* **cryfting*); Croft, Long - (by Bomere Fm); The Doles (meadow-land for which lots were drawn, *v.* **dāl**); Great Fd, Further - - (S.E. of Lower Bayston, Lower Fd adjoins); Great Mdw; Hodges Yd (there was a Hodges family in Condover in 18th, VCH 34); Jennings Lsw; Honey Mdw; Long Moor (*The Longe More* 1552,78 *Eyton* may be this place, *v.* **mōr**); Lower Fd; Lower Lsw; Lower Yd; New Lsw; Pea Lsw; Big and Little Pce (adjacent); Sandy Bank; Stony Furlong (a large field, S.W. of Lower Bayston); Turnpike Mdw and Hole (by the road through Lower Bayston and Norton to Condover: VCH 32 says this was superseded by another route when a turnpike act was passed in 1756, but the f.ns. suggest otherwise); Weather Pool; Well Mdw; Wheat Lsw.

(b) *Clay Furlong* c.1775 VCH 30; *Neare Medow* 1595 *SBL 9501*; *Polehay* 1516,34 *SBL 6727,8* ('pool enclosure', *v.* **(ge)hæg**); *Wood Fd* (VCH 30 says this was a common field).

3. BORETON (SJ 513077)

The township-name, which means 'fort settlement', is discussed in Part 1.

BORETON BRIDGE, *Burtons Bridge* 1595 *SBL 9501, Burton* - 1602 *SBL 7011.* The OS name is on the E. edge of the parish and township. *TA*, however, gives *Upper and Lower Boreton Bridge* as names of fields on the W. side of the township, also by Cound Brook. BORETONBROOK. The 6" map gives this name to some buildings by Cound Brook on the W. boundary of the township, where *TA* map shows 3 buildings in fields called *Upper and Lower Boreton Bridge.*

Field-Names

Forms in (a) are 1840 *TA*.

(a) Barn Yd; Calves Patch; Cantlop Post (by Cantlop road); Church Hill, South - - (no apparent reason for the name); Cockshutt Lsw (*v.* **cocc-sc̄ete**); Lower and Upper Cooks Place (*Cook(e)s Place* 1430 SAS 50, *Cooks* - 1534-5 SAS 2/IX, *Cokes* - 1546 *Eyton, Cookes* - 1595,8, 1649, 1718 *SBL 9501, 7022, 13379, 1718*); Big and Little Cow Lsw; Croggins Yeld(s), Croggin Yelds (*Croggenhelde* 1430, 1580 SAS 50, *Crogen-* 1438-9 SAS 2/IX, a series of fields by Cound Brook, *v.* **helde** 'slope', first el. perhaps *crooken* 'crooked'); Cross Furlong (not by a road, cf. *The Crosse* 1531 *SBL 13448, The Crosse in Condover* 1568 *Eyton, Crossfield* 1580 SAS 50, *Cross(e) Feild* 1595 *SBL 9501, The Cross Feild* 1718 *Eyton*, but these are not certain to be in Boreton township); Dog Mdw; Fish Pits (6" map shows pools); The Five Pools (no pools shown); Little and Near Gorsty Pce, Far Gorsty Lsw (*v.* ***gorstig**); Leys; Little Hales (*v.* **halh**, in a loop of Cound Brook); Hay and Cow Mdw, Upper Hay Mdw; Hollands; Hunger Pit; Far, Middle, Near, Little Loins, Little Loins Mdw (*Long Lynes* 1593 *SBL 6863* may be an earlier form, and *Lonoclye, Longlyes* 1430 SAS 50 may be a corrupt version: probably ME **leyne, lain** 'tract of arable land'); Long Mdw (2); Malthouse Yd; Marlpit Lsw; Marsh; Moor Furlong (*v.* **mōr**); New Heys (probably *The Newe Haye* 1456-7 SAS 2/IX, *The Newe Hey, New(e) Haye* 1586,8 *SBL 6883*, *v.* **(ge)hæg**); Ox Lsw; Poplar Plantation; Potato Fd; Quakers Mdw; Roundabout Mdw (partly enclosed by Cound Brook); Shawbottom; Slang Mdw (narrow strip); Stock Hedge, Stockwells (adjacent); Long and Little Sytch (*v.* **sīc**); Ten Ridges (near Moor Furlong, probably part of an open field S. of Boreton); Townsend (adjoins Boreton); Lower and Upper Wet Lsw; Withy Furlong (near Cross Furlong, probably part of an open field N.W. of Boreton).

(b) *The Abbey Landes* 1588 *SBL 6883, Abbey Lande* 1598, 1604 *SBL 7022,4* (Boreton belonged to Shrewsbury Abbey); *Ales Johnes Horne and Lesow, Ales Johanes Tongge* 1595 *SBL 9501* (said to adjoin Boreton Bridge, pieces of land belonging to Alice Jones); *Burttons Fielde* 1421 SAS 2/IX, *Burton's Field* 1430 SAS 50; *Burtons Pytt* 1595 *SBL 9501*; *Gamelesbrugg'* 1306-7 *Ass, Gainesbridge End* 1377 SAS 2/IX, *The Gannowe Bridge Ende* 1519-20, 1527-8 SAS 2/IX, *The Ganno Bridge Leazowe* 1588 *SBL 6883, Genobridge Leasow and Meadow* 1595 *SBL 9501, Ganns Bridge Leasowe* 1598 *SBL 7022* (the name of a footbridge by the ford at Boretonbrook, *v.* VCH 32: perhaps 'bridge of sport', the first el. of the 14th-cent. forms may be *gamenes*, gen. of **gamen**, *Gaines-* perhaps mistranscribed for *Games-*: the 16th-cent. forms resemble the apparent compound of **hōh** 'hill-spur' with **gamen** which is discussed PN Wo 341: this would be a seventh example).

4. CHATFORD (SJ 473057)

Chattefort 1255 RH, *-ford* 1274 RH (p), *-ford'* 1291-2 *Ass*, 1301 SAC, *-forde* 1430 SAS 50, *-ford* 1410 *SBL 9072*
Chateford' 1255-6 *Ass* (p), 1261-2 *ForProc* (p), 1271-2 *Ass* (p)
Chaddeford' 1271-2 *Ass* (p)
Catford 1483 *SBL 9073*
Chatford 1545 *SBL 9077 et seq* with variant spelling *-forde*; *Chatfurtt* 1615 PR(L) 6, *-fartte* 1619 *SBL 9078*
Chattford 1591 PR(L) 6, 1672 HTR
Chadford 1753,69 PR(L) 6
Chatsford 1753 PR(L) 6

'Ceatta's ford'. The township is traversed by a small tributary of Cound Brook, and a footpath crosses the stream N.W. of the settlement.

CHATBROOK, *a lytle brooke or water co(u)rse called Chatbroke* 1576 *SBL 6667, Chabbrook Meadow* 1595 *SBL 9501, Chatford Brooke* 1724 *SBL 3397.* Probably a shortened form of Chatford Brook. The name appears on the 6" map as that of a house by the stream. *TAMap* shows fields called *Chatbrook Post and Meadow* and *Lower Chatbrook* by a road junction a short distance S. of the house. CHATFORD HO. HUNGER HILL, 1631 PR(L) 6, *Hungerhill* 1615 *et seq* ib, *v.* **hungor**. This is a small hamlet at a cross-roads. NEW BUILDINGS.

Field-Names

Forms in (a) are 1840 *TA*.

(a) Bank; Big Mdw; Bines (probably referring to bindweed); Lower and

Upper Cow Pasture; Crabtree Lsw; Cross (at a road junction); Drakes Mdw; Far Mdw; The Flows (2 neighbouring fields, Flowers Lsw, The Flowers adjoin in Stapleton, *The Flores* 1595 *SBL 9501*, *v.* **flōr** 'pavement', which sometimes refers to ancient remains); Green Yd; Lower and Upper Hill; Hoofs Yd; Langleys Ground; The Lench (*Lench* 1595 *SBL 9501*, dialect *lench* 'rock ledge', Quarry Lsw adjoins); Little Fd; Long Lsw; Long Mdw; March Fd (on parish boundary, but probably from **mersc** 'marsh' rather than **mearc** 'boundary'); The Middle Marsh; New Lsw (2); Oak Mdw; Old Mill Lsw and Coppice (VCH 48 says this is the DB mill in Condover manor, and was known as *Old Mill* from later 14th); Paddock; Pit Lsw; Quarry Lsw (cf. The Lench); Rough Reins (i.e. *reans* 'drainage channels'); Sheepcote Lsw; The Slang (narrow strip); Small Lsw; Span Heat (Spondhurst in Stapleton adjoins, perhaps 'shingle wood', *v.* **spōn**, **hyrst**); Stackyard Close; Lower and Upper Way Bridge (the area is networked by small streams); Lower and Upper Wood Fd (VCH 30 suggests that this and March Fd were open fields).

(b) *Sixe Penny Acre* 1619 *SBL 9078* (referring to rent); *Warreytree Hill* 1580 SAS 50 (VCH 37 says this is the former name of Hunger Hill, *v.* **wearg-trēow** 'gallows').

5. CONDOVER (SJ 495058)

CONDOVER BRIDGE is *pons de Conedo* 1291-2 *Ass.* VCH 31 identifies it with *Hynfordbrigge, Hyne-* 1308 *SBL 6640*, *Hynford's Bridge* 1432-3 SAS 2/IX, and *Endsbridge* 1421 SAS 2/IX, *Endsbridge, Endesbruches, Endyburche, Endbruche* 1430 SAS 50, *Engebruche* 1445 *SBL 9436*, 1542 *Eyton*, *Enshebruge* 1531 *SBL 13448*, *Endesbrydges* 1546 *Eyton*, *The Endsbrochis* 1552 *ib*, *Engesbrige* 1553 *SBL 6854*, *Engebridge* 1588 *SBL 6883*, *Eynsbridge Lane* 1595 *SBL 9501*. *Hynford-* is probably 'ford of the religious community' or 'of the servants', *v.* **hīwan**. *Endsbridge* might be 'bridge at the end of the village', *v.* **ende**. The development of *Endes-* to *Enge-* is similar to that discussed under Frodesley in Part **1**. VCH 31 says the bridge was also known as *Kennel Bridge*.

CONDOVER NEW BRIDGE. VCH 32 says that this was known as *the Great Bridge* until a new stone structure was built 1792-5. Both bridges are over Cound Brook, S. of the village.

CONDOVER GREEN, 1595 SAS 2/IX, 1753 PR(L) 6, *The Greene* 1618 PR(L) 6. At LOWER GREEN two buildings are shown but not named on *TAMap*. CONDOVER GROVE. The house is shown but not named on *TAMap*. CONDOVER HALL, *Hall* 1840 *TA*. CONDOVER PARK. VCH 44 says this was probably formed c.1600. CONDUIT ROUGH, 1840 *TA*. THE GRANGE, buildings are shown but not named on *TAMap*.

Field-Names

Forms in (a) are 1840 *TA*.

(a) Atkinsons Pce or Oakey Lsw; Lower and Upper Besley Hill (*Besill Hill* 1595 *SBL 9501, Bessleye* - 1615 *SBL 6848A*); Brandert (*Le Brandart* 1587 *SBL 9084*, if adjoining Stackyard Pce is included there is a trivet shape); The Brink (*The Brinke* 1652 *Eyton*, ME *brink* 'edge', the field is by Cound Brook); Broad Lsw (1734 *Eyton*); Broomy Lsw (1598 *SBL 7022*, 1734 *Eyton*, *The Bromyeleasowe* 1588 *SBL 6883*); Colley Loton (a very large field); Condover Mdw; Conduit Lsw (adjoins Conduit Rough *supra*); Cow Pasture; Crabtree Fd; The Cross (a lane from The Grange crosses the Stapleton road here); The Furlong (by The Grange); The Horns (3 adjoining fields); The Lawn (by The Grange); Lawn in Front of Hall; Lawn Pce, Near - - (2 very large fields N.E. of village); Lockshutts (2 large fields, possibly *Locsiche* 1604 *SBL 7024*); Lords Lsw; Big and Little Mdw (2 sets of fields, one inside, one outside, the Park); Millers Coppice; Mill Fd (not by Cound Brook); Mill Mdw (by Cound Brook); Pit Lsw; Quarry Lsw; Pinfold Close (*The Pinfowld Close* 1612 *Eyton*, in the village); Pyepit Waste (VCH 34 says a pond called Piepit was drained in 1880 to make the school playground, probably 'magpie pit'); Far, Near, Lower and Upper Reynolds Dale; Rough Mdw; Squires Pce; Stank Lsw (by Cound Brook, probably a pool formed by a dam); Tons Pits; Upper Mdw; Workhouse Plantation.

(b) *Houghton* 1430 SAS 50, 1598 *SBL 7022*, *Manor of* - 1462 *SBL 6609, Howghton Felde, Houghton Feldes,* - *Fields* 1546, 1550, 1570, 1595 *SBL 6616,6, 6625, 13452, Houghtons Grounde* 1568 *Eyton, Houghtons* 1583 *SBL 6631, Haughtons* 1595 *SBL 9501, Houghtons Lane* 1622 PR(L) 6, *Haughtons* - 1634 ib (a manorial name, Richard de Houghton cleared land here in 1308 which was acquired by the lord of the manor in 1565 and became the principal component of Condover Park *supra*); *Parke Feild* 1595 *SBL 9501, Parkes Medowe* Hy 8 *RentSur, The Park Meddow* 1652 *Eyton* (an earlier park than that mentioned VCH 44);

Tadenhurst 1308 *SBL 6640, Taddenhurst* 1580 SAS 50, 1588 *SBL 6883, Taddens Hurst* 1595 *SBL 9501* ('toads' wood', *v.* **tādige**, **tadde** and **hyrst**: in the first ref. it is said to be a field of Condover, i.e. an open field of this township); *Le Walkemulle* 1445 *SBL 9436, Le Walkemyle* 1461 *SBL 6643, Walkemylle* 1542 *Eyton* (a fulling mill, *v.* VCH 49); *Widnold* 1706, 13 *LDR*.

6. DORRINGTON (SJ 478029)

Dodinton' 1198 Fees *et freq* to 1274 RH (p), *Doddinton* 1577 Saxton, *Dodynton* 1619 *SBL 9078*
Dudinton 1255-6 *Ass* (p)
Dodyton' 1291-2 *Ass et freq* with variant spellings *-i-* and *-ton* to 1591 PR(L) 6
Dodyngton 1483 *SBL 9073*, 1629 PR(L) 6, *Dodington* 1545 *SBL 9077 et freq* to 1629 PR(L) 6, *Doddington* 1545 *SBL 9077 et freq* to 1694 *SBL 9955*
Dorington 1584,99, 1619 *SBL 6631, 7007, 9078, Dorrington* 1589 *SBL 7003A et seq, Dodington als Dorington* 1619 *SBL 9083, Dorrington als Dodington* 1652 *Eyton*

'Settlement associated with Doda', one of a group of names formed from **-ingtūn** and this or a closely-related personal name. There are at least 20 in the country, five of them in Sa. The problems associated with them are discussed in Part **1** under Detton. Derrington St has the same origin, and shows the same change to *-rr-*. Forms for the Sa place show that the change occurred in the 16th cent. and that the older form was remembered at least till the end of the 17th century.

CHURCH BRIDGE, *Schertebrugg'* 1388 VCH 32, *Churchbridgefeild* 1599 *SBL 7007, Church Bridge Fields* 1619 *SBL 9078, The Church Bridge* 1621 PR(L) 6. The later name may be a corruption of the earlier, which is probably 'short bridge', *v.* **sceort**, **brycg**. *TAMap* shows eight fields called *Church Bridge* spread over an area on either side of Cound Brook. This was an open field (VCH 30). *TAMap* also has *Church Field* and *Church Yard*, from which *-Bridge-* has probably been dropped.

CROSSBROOK, *The Crosse Brocke* 1612 *LDR, Cross Brook* 1833

OS, 1840 *TA*. The hamlet stands by a bridge over a tributary of Cound Brook, and the bridge is Netley Bridge or Crossbrook Bridge on the 6" map. There is no obvious reason for the name. VCH 100 suggests a connection between the brook-name and *Cress Grange* in Leebotwood *infra*, but this is based on a reading of the 1612 form as **Cresse*. The glebe terrier is written in a vile hand, and certainty is not possible, but *Crosse* is probably the correct form.

BRIDGE INN, by Wayford Bridge in Stapleton. DORRINGTON GROVE, 1833 OS, is said in VCH 34 to have been built between 1786 and 1802, and to have been known as *The Red House* in 1817. PARK TERRACE. *TAMap* gives *Park Meadow* as the name of six fields between the Stapleton road and the stream which forms the boundary with Stapleton. There were two parks in Stapleton. WALFORD HO. The house is shown on *TAMap* and there are two fields called *Walford Meadow* and two called *Walford Bank* in the N. corner of the township. Perhaps 'spring ford', with WMidl **wælle**.

Field-Names

Forms in (a) are 1840 *TA*.

(a) Acre Fd, Big - -; Arch Mdw; Back Yd; Banky Mdw; Barn Fd; Barn Yd; Big Mdw; Birches; Bowen Fd; Brickkiln Lsw (in the same area as Claypits); Brook Lsw (by Cound Brook); Brook Mdw (by a tributary of Cound Brook); Browns Mdw; Bylet (2, between Cound Brook and rivulets); Claypits (4 fields); Clover Pce, Little - -; Cockshutt Hill (*Cockshoot* - 1558 VCH 30, *v.* **cocc-sciete**); Upper and Lower Cow Pasture; Crabtree Lsw; Cuckoo Brook (3 fields by a tiny stream), - - Mdw (cf. *Cuckoo Leasow* c.1620 VCH 30); Dorrington Mdw, - - Nursery; Eighteen Acre (a tiny strip, much smaller than Acre Fd); Ferny Hill; Footway Pce; Forge Fd (adjoins Forge Brook and Lsw in Ryton on the other side of Cound Brook, VCH 49 says the ironworks was known as *Upper Forge* in 1650, for distinction from Longnor Forge, a short distance S.); Gravel Hole, - - Fd; The Green (on S.E. edge of village); Upper Hail (in a bend of Cound Brook, *v.* **halh**); Half Fd; Half Mdw; Hill Head (*Hogshilhead* 1587 *SBL 9084*); Hissicking Mdw; Hodgewood, Upper -; Horseshoe Yd; Jones's Yd; Big and Little Lane End (at a road-junction, probably *Lane End* 1587 *SBL 6893*); Langleys

Mdw; Lawn (this and 2 fields called Lawn Mdw are on the outskirts of the village); Lee Lane Head (by road to Leebotwood); Leys, - Mdw; Little Hill; Long Furland, Little - -; Long Lsw; Long Mdw (by Round Mdw); Milestone (by Ludlow road); Big and Little Moor Mdw (*Moore Medowe* 1619 *SBL 9078*, near the open field called Moor Field, VCH 30, *v.* **mōr**); Nevershall, Lower -; Far and Near New Lsw; Pinfold; Pool Mdw; Poplar Butts; Prices Yd, Upper and Lower - -; Quabby (*v.* ***cwabba**); Big, Little and Lower Rick Leys, Rick Ley Mdw, Big - - -; Round Mdw (a small subcircular piece, still there on 6"); Ryley Fd; Sandy Bank (2, not near each other); Second Fd Lsw (adjoins Third - -); Seven Swathes (i.e. scythe strokes); Shoulder of Mutton (appropriately shaped); Long and Short Sides; Slang Brook and Plantation (by Cound Brook); Slang Mdw (narrow strip); Southerton Hither Mdw, Further Southerton Mdw; Sparks Bridge (near Bridge Inn *supra*); Stackers Fd; Ten Oaks (*The Oak Piece* 1679 *SBL 6748*); Townsend (at N. end of village); Upper Lsw (perhaps *The Upper Leazowe* 1588 *SBL 6883*); Way Lsw (1789 *SBL 1338*), Lower - -; Way Standing; Weeks Croft; Well Mdw; White Lsw; Within, Big, Little and Lower Withins (*Le Great Withins* 1726-7 *SBL 3558*, *v.* **wīðign**, *Park* or *Withen Field* was an open field, VCH 30); Worlds End, Little - -, Big and Little Worlds End Mdw (on parish boundary); The Yard (one of several Yard names in the village).

(b) *Gorstye Lane* 1578 *SBL 7009* (*v.* ***gorstig**); *Kings Lane* 1619 *SBL 9078*; *The Oldetowne* 1599 *Eyton* (probably the site of a deserted hamlet: VCH says it was S. of Crossbrook and that *Aldetonesmedewe* 1323 in Longnor refers to it).

7. GREAT AND LITTLE LYTH (SJ 458072, 479079)

La Lithe 1160-72 HAC (p), *Lithe* c.1175 SAC *et passim* with variant spelling *Lythe* to 1614 PR(L) 6, *Magna Lyth'* 1291-2 *Ass*, *Lythe Magna* 1367 Ipm, *La Lythe* 1507 *SBL 6662*, *Lithe Parva* 1640 *SBL 5820*, *Great Lythe* 1586, 1614 PR(L) 6

La Lya c.1230 SAC, *Magna Lya* 1236 SAS 4/IV(FF), *Maugna, Parva Lya* l.13th *ForProc*, *Lya iuxta Lythwode* l.14th SAC

Magna/Parva Lega/ Leye 1255-6 *Ass*, *Magna Leya* 1271-2 *ForProc*, *Ass* (p)

Parva Leytho 1271-2 *Ass*, *Parva Leyth'* 1291-2 *Ass*

Greatt and Litle Leathe 1586 *SBL 6927*, *Great Leeth* 1597 *SBL 7082*, *Great Leith*, *Greate Lyeth* 1649 SAS 4/VII

Lyth Magna 1667 *SBL 9945*, *Little Lyth* 1666 *SBL 1022*, *Great Lyth* 1745 PR(L) 6, *Lyth Magna* 1746 ib

'Concave hill-side'. Field-work has made it clear that OE **hlið** had this specialised meaning in Sa and north He. The feature referred to in this name is the Lyth Hill escarpment. There is an aerial photograph in VCH VIII, facing p.96, which shows the concave western edge. There is also a hollow on the east side, caused by a scoop in the ground at the foot of the steep slope. The escarpment gave name to a fairly wide area. In addition to these two settlements and the names discussed *infra*, there is DB *Hundeslit*, the earlier name of Stapleton.

The normal development in a simplex name is to **Leeth*, and this is shown in one group of forms. Leith Hill PN Sr 279 may be compared. The modern pronunciation of the Sa name is, however, [liþ]. This may be due to influence from names which have **hlið** as final element (e.g. Evelith, Huglith), these being quite frequent S. of Shrewsbury.

The name has sometimes been misinterpreted as deriving from **lēah**, *v.* Lythwood *infra.*

LYTHWOOD, LYTHWOOD FM AND HALL,
LYTHWOODHALL FM

Lia 1199 P, *Lya* 1201 P *et freq* to 1261-2 *ForProc, La Lye* 1210-12 RBE *et freq* to 1261-2 *ForProc, Lye* 1222 Pat, 1232,3 Cl, 1261-2 *ForProc, La Lya* 1238 Cl, 1395 *SBL 16293*
Leya 1230 P, *La Leg'* 1255-6 *Ass, Leye* 1271-2 *ForProc*
La Lich' (?*recte Lith'*) 1232,41 Cl, *La Lythe* 1264 Cl, *Lythe* 1300 Cl
La Lagh' 1235 Cl
Lythewod' 1250 Cl *et freq* with variant spellings *Lithe-* and *-wod*(*e*) to 1508 AD
Lidewod' 1267 Cl, *Lidwode* 1274 RH, 1289 Cl
Lyde 1270 Cl, *Lide* 1279-88 Cl
Lythwood 1279-88 Cl, 1535 VE *et seq, -wod* 1364-6 *ForProc, -wode* l.14th SAC, *Lithwood* 1601 PR(H) 1 *et freq* to 1735 *SBL 3434*
Leghwode 1399 Pat
Leathwood 1597 PR(H) 1

Early references are to a *haia*, an enclosed area, in the royal forest called the Long Forest. This became an estate, the history of which is set out in VCH 42. The name is that of the Lyth Hill escarpment, with addition of **wudu** in the late 13th cent. The spellings show a greater degree of confusion with **lēah** than is apparent in the settlement names discussed *supra*.

Lythwood Hall is mentioned 1752 PR(L) 6.

ANNSCROFT, *Handcroft* 1833 OS. A row of houses built along one side of a road on the W. boundary of the parish, this was a squatter settlement of the early 19th cent. which housed miners (VCH 37). BAYSTONGROVE. BETLEY HO. Nearby fields are *Bald Eye(s)* 1840 *TA*. VCH 30 says this was *Baillie* in the 15th cent. It is possible that the three names are connected. LONG WD, 1833 OS. LYTHBANK is *Lithbanke* 1625 PR(L) 6. LYTH HILL is (*The*) *Lyth Hill* 1750 PR(L) 6 *et seq.* OLD COPPICE, 1833 OS. SHED COPPICE, 1833 OS. SPRING COPPICE, 1833 OS, 1840 *TA*. WHITE HO, 1833 OS. WREKIN VILLA, the house is shown but not named on *TAMap*.

Field-Names

Forms in (a) are 1840 *TA*. FN 24 gives a list of arbitrary f.ns. from a sale catalogue of 1875, when Lythwood Fm was naming fields after English counties or county-towns.

(a) Alderley Lsw; Allotment (there is a series of these representing ribbon development along the road S.W. from Baystonhill: they are larger than the enclosures called Patch or Croft); Ash Coppy; Bald Eye Mdw (*v.* Betley Ho *supra*); Bell Stile; Lower and Upper Boltons; Brickkiln Lsw (perhaps *Bricky Leasow* 1595 *SBL 9501, Brycky Feild* is also mentioned); Big and Little Briery Furlong (large fields W. of G. Lyth); Broomy Corner; Burnt Croft; Common Plat (similar size and shape to surrounding fields); Coppice Fd (by Spring Coppice); Cow Pasture (2); Croft (*freq* for small enclosures, mostly bigger than those termed Patch); Dock Yd, The Yard (adjoining G. Lyth); Big and Little Field (in L. Lyth, adjoining, and of roughly equal size); Firtree Coppy; Fowks Mdw (to be identified with the meadow called *Fulcheye* c.1230 SAC, both are in G. Lyth: the name became Foul Cow in Longden, Pontesbury, *q.v.*); Gravel Hole Fd; Greasy Butts Mdw (Greasy may be from ME *gresede* 'having been grazed', *v.* PN Ch 4, 25); Hill Lsw (3 large adjoining fields, perhaps *The Hill Leasowe* 1588 *SBL 6883*: Middle and Near Hill Lsw are separated from the others by a field called Province Yeald Hill); Honey Mdw; Kiton Pce; Big and Little Lady Pool; Far and Near Languisheds; Little Field (2, both in G. Lyth, one by Town Fd and the other by Old Fd); Long Acre (a narrow strip, perhaps *The Longe Acre* 1421 SAS 2/IX, *Longe Acres* 1586,88 *SBL 6883*); Long Bank; Far and Near Long Lsw; Longden Lsw (adjoins L-); Lower Mdw; Lower, Upper and Middle Lythe Hodge (perhaps *Hodges Land* 1580 SAS 50, a Hodges family is mentioned in the VCH account of Condover); Marlpit Lsw, Lower - -; Meadow, Big -, New - (on three sides of L. Lyth); Meadow by House; The Moor (cf. *Lythmore* Hy 8 *RentSur*, *v.* **mōr**; Moor Lsw (not near preceding); New Lsw; Old Fd (2 fields S.E. of G. Lyth, Little Fd adjoins); Big and Little Ox Lsw (*The Middle Oxe Leasow* 1705 *SBL 6481*); Ox Pasture; Partridge Furlong, Further - - (near Briery Furlong); Patch (*freq* for very small enclosures); Higher and Lower Piece; Pool Mdw; Province Yeald Hill (Yeald is from **helde** 'slope'); Rock Hole (a tiny enclosure in a corner of Big Lady Pool); Salt Reins (probably *reans* 'drainage channels'); Stannyford (adjoins Stony Ford in Longden, Pontesbury, *q.v.*); The Stocking (stocking-shaped, but this may be coincidence: the bounds of Lythwood (1301 SAC) mention *Le Stockyngesheved* in this area, 'head of the clearing', *v.* **stoccing**); Top Mdw (adjoins Lower Mdw); Near and Far Town Fd (adjoining Annscroft, with several Furlong names in the same corner of the township); Tuslers Yd; Wallebourn Hill; Wattroms Hill; Well Lsw; Winny Croft; Withy Mdw (*v.* **wīðig**); Wood Lsw (3 fields on the other side of a road from Hill Lsw); Woodpile Yd (by L. Lyth); Great and Little Yd (among the Allotments and Patches which run along the road S.W. from Baystonhill); Yewtree Lsw.

(b) *Audulph Shutte, Le Braciesok* 1301 SAS (these occur in a perambulation of the hay of Lythwood which mentions a wood belonging to Audulphus de Bracy, from whom the *Shutte* ('furlong') and oak tree are named); *Burgesses Wood* 1780 *SBL 3398*; *Butte Endes* 1576 *SBL 6667*; *Buttetshute* 1301 SAC (probably **scēat** in the sense 'furlong' with a surname); *Cross Field* e.17th VCH 31 (an open field in L. Lyth); *Goldfynches Meadowe* 1576 *SBL 6667*; *Le Hokesheved* 1301 SAC (perhaps 'headland of the oak'); *Le Horeston* 1301 SAC ('boundary stone', *v.* **hār**[2]); *Hygyns Hey* Hy 8 *RentSur* (VCH 30 says Lythwood Fm was built on the site of this wood, *v.* **(ge)hæg**); *Lith Copie* 1634 PR(L) 6, *Ye Lythe Copys* 1712 ib (possibly Old Coppice *supra*); *Lith Hedge* 1615 *SBL 6848A*; *Lythwoodesheld* 1453 (copy) *SBL 7070* (*v.* **helde** 'slope'); *Lulleyeswey, Lullayeswai* 1301 SAC (*v.* **weg**, first el. perhaps a surname); *Margan's Old and New Coppice* 1780 *SBL 3398*; *The Meare Stone* 1576 *SBL 6667* ('boundary stone'); *Le Morsich, Le Mersigh'* 1301 SAC ('marsh' or 'pond rivulet', *v.* **mōr**, **mere**, **sīc**); *Newhey al' Le Copye of the Lyth' Hill* Hy 8 *RentSur*, *New Haye* 1580 SAS 50,

The - - 1595 *SBL 9501* (*v.* **(ge)hæg**); *Pogh Wenhale, Poghwenhale* 1301 SAC (perhaps containing **pohha** 'bag' and **halh** 'nook', but the middle el. and the structure of the name are obscure); *Protmonegrene* l.13th *ForProc, Pormones Greven*, v.r. *Port-*, 1301 SAC (first el. *portmann* 'burgess', second el. probably **grǣfe** 'grove', cf. *Burgesses Wood supra*); *The Rocke* 1649 SAS 4/VII (a tenement 'on - -' in G. Lyth, presumably 'rock'); *Le Score super Bolerug* 1301 SAC (possibly **scoru**, referring to a boundary mark, *v.* Burridges *supra*); *Twichenilde Greven* 1301 SAC (*v.* **twicen** 'fork, cross-roads', **helde** 'slope', **grǣfe** 'grove'); *Voxake* l.13th *ForProc* (a wood, probably 'fox oak'); *Walkers Medowe* 1576 *SBL 6667*; *Wernardeslegh* 1301 SAC (*v.* **lēah**, first el. perhaps a surname); *Wintle Field* e.17th VCH 31 (open field in L. Lyth); *Wolmereshaystowe* 1301 SAC (first el. pers.n. *Wulfmǣr*, second el. OE *heg(e)stōw*, which occurs four times in Wo charter-boundaries, perhaps 'site of a hedge').

8. NORTON (SJ 495058)

v. Part **1** for the township-name, which refers to the position, N. of Condover. The settlement is *Nortons Farme* 1595 *SBL 9501*. It is incongruously called *Great Norton* 1833 OS.

Field-Names

Forms in (a) are 1840 *TA*. Early forms are 1595 *SBL 9501* except where otherwise stated.

(a) Barn Yd (large field S. of Norton Fm); Bickmoor Mdw, Hither and Great Bickmoor (possibly *Peckmore* 1430 SAS 50, *v.* **mōr**); Big Fd (this and next are appropriately named); Big Lsw; Browns Yd, Big and Little; Little Catty Bridge (6" map shows a rivulet: FN 48 says *catty tree* is a Sa term for the spindle tree); Condover Sword (*recte* Ford, an adjacent field is Great Condover Ford Mdw, and the road to Condover crosses a stream here); Cow Pasture; Crabtree Fd, Little - -; Flax Lsw (*Flaxxe Lesow*); The Foul Hill (N. part of Norton Hill); Gorsty Furlong (this and Kings Furlong lie S.W. of Norton, in an area where field-shapes suggest a small open field); Hole Mdw; Hunting Wicket Pce; Kings Furlong (1635 *Eyton, Le - -* 1729 *SBL 10002*); Lambs Lsw; Lane Pce (by road to Allfield); Latewoods Land (Late Woods - in schedule, probably not a f.n.); Little Mdw; The Lodges Pce (6" map shows building marked Lodge); Norton Hill (*Nortons -*); The Ouses (by the road to Allfield, where the 6" map shows a pool, but no stream; Ouse, from OE **wāse** 'mud', is usually a stream-name in p.ns., see PN Berks 15-16, but here it may refer to a muddy place); Pit Lsw; Primrose; Rough Mdw; Ryegrass Pce; Saffron Butts (1665 *Eyton*); Shadmoor, Far, Near and Little, Big Shady Moor, Near and Far Shadymoor Hodge (VCH 29 calls this Shedmoor, and says that it formed the boundary between L. Lyth, Norton and Bayston townships, cf. *Lower Shedmoor* 1734 *SBL 10015*, *v.* **scēad** 'boundary', probably associated with ModE *shady*: for Hodge *v.* Lyth f.ns. *supra*); Square Fd (rectangular); Stackyard Pce; Little Stony Lake (*Stony Lake* 1595 *SBL 9501, The Stoney* - 1734 *SBL 10015*, probably **lacu** in the sense 'drainage channel', the 6" map shows rivulets); Taylors Croft; Watering Yd (a narrow strip N.W. of Norton Fm, 6" map shows a pool at the far end); The Wet Mdw (adjoins L. Stony Lake); Whitefoot Moor (*Whitefoots Great Meadow and Leyes, Whitefoot Broome* and *Great Leasow, Whitefoote Land Leasow*, Thomas Whitefoot held the manor of Condover in 1545 (VCH 43)).

(b) *Bromy Feild* and *Close*; *Home Croft*; *Wall Croft*, *Lesow* and *Medow* (probably **wælle** 'spring').

9. RYTON, GREAT and LITTLE (SJ 488037, 490032)

Ruiton', - *Superior* 1208-9 *ForProc*, *Ruyton'* 1241 Cl, *Parva Ruyton, Magna* - 1410 *SBL 9072*, *Ruiton* 1783 PR(L) 6
Ruton' 1261-2 *ForProc* (p) *et freq* with variant spellings *-ton(e)* to 1347 Pat, *Magna Ruton', Parva Ruton* 1301 SAC
Rutton 1271-2 *Ass*, *Rutton'* 1291-2 *Ass*
Ryton' 1291-2 *Ass* (p) *et freq* with variant spellings *Ri-* and *-ton*; *Riton Magna*, - *Parva* 1545 *SBL 9077*, 1584 *SBL 6631*, *Lytle Riton* 1581 *Eyton*, *Great Riton*, *Litle* - 1588 *SBL 6645*, *Great Ryton* 1619 *SBL 9078*, *Ryton Magna*, - *Parva* 1694 *SBL 9955*
Rytonne the Lesse, Ruyton the Greate 1430 SAC 50
Rytons 1577 Saxton
Righton Magna 1652 *Eyton*, *Greate Righton* 1658 PR(L) 6
Ritton 1675 Ogilby, *Ritton Manner* 1695 Morden
Reyton 1726 PR(L) 6
Royten 1771 *SBL 10145*

'Rye farm', *v.* **ryge**, **tūn**, one of three instances in this county.

GONSAL, G. COTTAGES, *Gosenhul* 1255 RH (p), *Gosinhull'* 1255-6 *Ass* (p), *Gosenhull'* 1261-2 *ForProc* (p), *Gansell Way* 1595 *SBL 9501, Gonsal* 1833 OS. 'Gōsa's hill'. The first el. is probably the gen. of a weak pers.n. derived from *gōs* 'goose'. The metathesis which occurred in the p.n. did not affect the surname of the Gosnell family, which derives from this place. They were prominent copyholders in Condover manor in the 13th-18th cents (VCH 37).

ASH COVERT. BROOKLYN (a house). CHURCH BRIDGE, 1840 *TA*. The road to Condover crosses Cound Brook here. FORGE VILLA, *Big and Little Forge Leasow, Forge Bank and Meadow* 1840 *TA*. Cf. *Iron Mylls* 1609 PR(L) 6, *Le Iron Fordge* 1619 *SBL 9078*, and *v.* VCH 49. HOLLIES. LITTLE ROW, from Row Brook which forms the parish boundary. *Little* in contrast to Row Fm across the brook in Frodesley. RYTONFIELDS (house shown but not named on *TAMap*). *Ryton Field* in *TA* is not near this house. RYTON GRANGE. RYTON GROVE. SYTCH, *The Sitch otherwise the Seeth* 1749 *SBL 1694, The Seeth* 1789 *SBL 1338, Lower, Middle and Upper Sytch* 1840 *TA*. Probably the name of a rivulet flowing E./W. through the farm-site, since the *TA* fields are some distance to the E. *v.* **sīc** 'small stream'. The building is shown but not named on *TAMap*. For an account of the hamlet *v.* VCH 37.

Field-Names

Forms in (a) are 1840 *TA*.

(a) Bank Yd; Barn Yd; Big Mdw (2); Bog, Middle, Upper and Plantation (*v.* Radmore *infra*); Brickkiln Lsw; Bridge Mdw, Lower and Upper (the road to Stapleton crosses Cound Brook here); Brinset; Brookens (*The Brocken* 1430, 1580 SAS 50, *The Broken* 1580 SAS 2/IX, 1587 *SBL 9084*, 1598 *SBL 7022, Le* - 1587 *SBL 7003A*, the two fields on *TAMap* are beside Cound Brook, and it is possible that the name is a derivative of **brōc**, though nothing of the kind is on record); Brook Lsw; Broomhill; Bylets (in the bends of Cound Brook); Calves Croft; Calves Lane (possibly *Calviland* 1789 *SBL 1338*); Cloleys; Cockshutt Acres (*v.* **cocc-sciete**, Cockshutt in Wheatall *infra* is separated by only 3 fields from this place; Colemoor Slough (*Colemon Sloughe Lane* 1595 *SBL 9501, v.* **slōh**); Coppice

Mdw; The Coppice (not near preceding); Corfields Cloleys, Corfields Ouze Mdw; Corner Patch; Cote Lsw; Cow Pasture; Crabtree Hill; Crumptons Pce; Cuckoo Croft (*Cuckow Croft* 1757 *SBL 1336*); Dorrington Mdw (near Dorrington township); Dunstan; Far Fd (on township boundary); Floating Mdw (refers to irrigation); Gonsal Cover and Lsw (*v. supra*); Gorsty Lsw, Lower and Upper (*v.* **gorstig**); Gravel Hole Fd; Hale (by Row Brook, *v.* **halh**, here perhaps 'river-meadow'); The Heath, Heath Mdw and Slang (a group of fields E. of L. Ryton), Heath, Long Heath, Bicknalls Heath (a group of fields by the Stapleton road) (cf. *The Heaths, The Hethes, Overhethe, Nether Hethe* 1430 SAS 50, *The Heth* 1549 *SBL 7079, Le Nether Heath* 1619 *SBL 9078*, *v.* **hǣð**); Hint Wells (*Little, Middle and Farther Hintwell* 1789 *SBL 1338*); Homers Mdw and Bank, Little Homer (*The Homers* 1757 *SBL 1336*, *Homers Bank and Meadow, Little Homer* 1789 *SBL 1338*, the *TA* fields are W. of L. Ryton, probably 'pond in a hollow', *v.* **holh, mere**); The Hook (one side has a zig-zag outline); Hopyard Mdw; The Knotts (no obvious reason can be deduced from maps); Lawn (large field by L. Ryton village); Lea Heads, Big and Little Leys (adjacent, Leys may be from **lǣs**, Lea - being a false sing.); Lydiad (*The Little Field or The Liddeate* 1789 *SBL 1338*, one of L. Ryton's open fields, *v.* VCH 31, on *TAMap* there are 3 fields lying either side of one of the roads to Condover, *v.* **hlid-geat** 'swing gate'); Marsh Wall (1757 *SBL 1336*, on *TAMap* this is the n. of 4 fields spread out round the S.W. of L. Ryton, in a curve: nothing is shown on the 6" map, but the reference could be to an embankment: *Wallmore* 1430 SAS 50, *The Waull Crofte* 1588 *SBL 6883, The Wall* 1622 PR(L) 6 (p) may belong here, but *Wall* can be from **wælle** 'spring'); Meadow, Big and Lower (up Cound Brook from Mill Mdw); Mill Lsw and Mdw, Lower Mill Lsw, Lower, Middle and Upper Mill Patch, Long Mill Lsw (these occupy a large area between Cound Brook and the Longnor road: one of the open fields of G. Ryton was Mill Field, VCH 31); Moor (2, both on E. boundary of township; Little Moor Mdw and Patch are near the southern field called Moor, E. of L. Ryton, *v.* **mōr**); New Lsw; Nine Butts (by Radmoor, perhaps part of an open field, *v.* **butte**); Normans Coppy Waste and Pasture Pce, Big Normans, Big and Little Normans Mdw (perhaps *recte* Nomans -, the fields are by what is here taken to be the boundary with Wheathall township); Oathill, Little -; One Acre (very small); Ouze Mdw, Little - -, Big, Upper and Rough Ouze (VCH 29 calls this area The Hoos, it is *Le Hoo* 1274 RH, *The Hoo* 1430 SAS 50, 1549 *SBL 7079, The Hooes, The Hooes Medow* 1595 *SBL 9501*, 1668 *Eyton, Ye Hooses* 1688 *Eyton*, cf. also *Rough Hoo, Smethy Hoo* 1430 SAS 50: the name is that of a wide belt of alluvium; it is OE **hōh**, 'spur', and there may be a slightly raised strip of ground for which this term was appropriate: the modern n. is plural because there are a number of fields); Parson Pce; Patch (*freq*, mostly round G. Ryton village);

Pinfold, Lower and Upper (adjoining Pound Lsw); Pit Lsw; Pit Mdw (near Sawpit Croft); Pool Head; Pound Patch and Lsw; Presmoor, Near and In Presmore (*Prestmore Stones* 1586 *SBL 6883*, *Prestmores* 1604 *SBL 7024*, 'priest marsh', *v.* **prēost**, **mōr** : FN 9 says that *in* denotes enclosed as opposed to open-field land); Pump Lsw (by a building); Quillet (a very narrow strip among the Patch ns. E. of G. Ryton); Radmore, - Hill (*Rodmore's Yelde* 1438-9 SAS 2/IX, *Rodmore Hill* 1580 SAS 50, *Radmore* 1586 *SBL 6883 et freq*, *Radmores Grounde* 1595 *SBL 9501*, 'reed marsh', *v.* **hrēod**, **mōr** : the f.ns. cover a wide area but VCH 29 locates the *mōr* N.W. of G. Ryton, where there are Bog ns.; - *Yelde* is from **helde** 'slope'); Rough Lsw; Rushy Patch; Rye Patch; Ryton Fd (perhaps *Ritons Field* 1595 *SBL 9501*, not near either settlement); Sandy Patch; Sawpit Lsw, - Croft (near, but not adjoining); The Slang (adjacent to Heath Slang, narrow curving fields); Square Fd (approximately square); Stackyard Patch and Pce (not near each other); Studleys Fd; Sultans Paddock; Sureland (FN 26 takes this to be a complimentary n.); Teat Lsw (perhaps referring to shape); Tomlins Pce; Well Mdw; Welshman's Hole (*Wallshman's Hole* 1430 SAS 50); Wheathall (adjoins Oathill, both ns. refer to crops); Whitefoot Radmoor (*v.* Norton f.ns. for Whitefoot); Wintel; Woo Gates; Big and Little Yard; The Yard (1789 *SBL 1338*); Yewtree Pce.

(b) *The Nether Annolde* 1545 VCH 31, *Annos* 1595 *SBL 9501*, *Anno Furlong* 1606 VCH 31 (VCH says this was part of Mill Fd); *Cows Long within The Horesfoald*, *Cowrelong Oke* 1619 *SBL 9078*; *Le Cross Lanes* 1729 *SBL 10002*, *The Cross Lane* 1734 *SBL 10015*; *Heath Sale, Lower and Upper* 1789 *SBL 1338* (perhaps *sale* 'division of a wood of which the underwood was sold'); *The Horesfoald* 1619 *SBL 9078* ('horse fold'); *Howefyld ib*; *Manbridges* 1545 VCH 31, *Monbridge* 1588 *SBL 6883*, *Manbruge Leasowe* 1619 *SBL 9078* ('common breach', *v.* **gemǣne**, **bryce**); *Close of Manning* 1595 *SBL 9501*; *Le Oulde Myllnes* 1588 *SBL 6645* (VCH 37 gives an account of mills in Ryton); *Quarry Leasow* 1615 *SBL 6848A*; *Le Roughe* 1619 *SBL 9078*; *The Sixe Penny Acre* 1544 *Eyton*, *Sixpenny Acres* 1580 SAS 50, *Sixe Penny Acres* 1630 *Eyton* (in the first ref. this is said to be arable land in *Greate Rytons Heathes*); *Willerslowe* 1376 SAS 2/IX (perhaps 'Wilhere's tumulus', *v.* **hlāw**).

10. WESTLEY (SJ 470063)

Wesselega 1160-72 HAC (p) *et freq* with variant spellings *-leg'*, *-leg*, *-ley(e)*, *-legh'* to 1620 PR(L) 6

Weseleg' 1208-9 *ForProc*
Wasseley 1230 P, *-leg* 1274 RH
Weslegh 1255-6 *Ass* (p), *Wesley* 1584, 1663 PR(L) 6, *Wessley* 1627 ib
Wesscleg' 1255-6 *Ass*
Westley alias Weseleigh 1576 *SBL 6667, Westley* 1598 *SBL 6753 et seq, -leye* 1600 PR(L) 6, *Westeley* 1599 *SBL 7093*

'Wood or clearing by alluvial land', *v.* **wæsse, lēah**, and see the discussions of Bolas and Buildwas in Part 1. Most p.ns. containing **wæsse** are by major rivers, but there is a small group, of which this is one, which are situated by small streams. Westley overlooks Chat Brook, the course of which has probably been straightened.

EXFORDS GREEN, *Egeforde* 1255 RH, *Eggesfords Grene* 1479 *SBL 6659, Egfordes Greene* 1602,29 PR(L) 6, *Egfoords* - 1627 ib, *Egfords* - 1633 ib, *Egford* - 1639 ib, *Edsford Green* 1749 ib, *Egsford* - 1774 ib, *Edsford* - 1777,82 ib, *Exford* - 1787 ib, *Exfus* - 1803,7 PR(L) 1, *Exfas* - 1805 ib, *Exford* - 1808 ib.

'Ecga's' or 'Ecgi's ford'. Roads converge from all directions on the crossing of Chat Brook here. The addition of **grēne**^{2} by 1479 suggests that settlement was growing in the 15th cent. VCH 37 describes rapid growth from the early 17th.

A point in the bounds of Lythwood Hay in 1301 SAC is *Egesfordesknolle, Eggefordesknolle, v.* **cnoll**.

Field-Names

Forms in (a) are 1840 *TA*. Early forms and those in (b) are 1596 *SBL 6671* unless otherwise stated.

(a) Allotment (several fields near Exfords Green); Boltings; Broomy Lsw; Common Lsw; Coppice; The Coppice Lsw (by Spring Coppice in Lyth); Corner Close (in the angle of a road-junction); Cross Lsw; Lower and Upper Ditches; Fish Croft and Lsw (perhaps referring to fish-ponds); Flat Lsw; The Hail (*v.* **halh**, in the hollow on the S. side of Lyth Hill); Holly Hedges; Large Pits (VCH 31 says this is the area earlier called *Lampit Field*, which was an open field, *v.* **lām** 'loam'); Lashley (*Lastley*); Big and Little Lumkin Bridge (by a crossing place on Chat Brook); The Moor (*v.* **mōr**); Patch (*freq.* for very small enclosures, mostly by Exfords Green); Pinfold (tiny enclosure in Townsend); Pit Lsw, Great - -; Pit Lsw (there are three separate areas with Pit ns.); The Rough; Perkin and Road Sidnall (Sidnall is 'wide nook', *v.* **sīd**, **halh**); Stackyard Close; Stakers Oak (cf. *Oaketree Medowe*); Townsend (adjoins Westley Fm); The Yard, Far and Upper Yd, Yard by Townsend (a group of fields N. of Westley Fm); Lower and Upper Yard (not near preceding); The Yell Bank, Upper Yell Bank, Yells Mdw (*v.* **helde**).

(b) *Brade Medowe*; *Crabtree Butts*; *Greate Medowe*; *The Grittpitt* (*v.* **grēot**, **pytt**, and cf. Pit ns. *supra*); *Hough Medowe* (probably **halh**); *The Knoll* (perhaps *Eggefordesknolle supra*); *The Raynbowe* (land ploughed concentrically with a curved boundary); *Rownd Medow* 1595 *SBL 9501, Rownde Meadowe* 1604 *SBL 7024*); *Sowne Medowe or the Comon Medowe*; *Wheate Crofte* 1596 *SBL 6671, The Wheat Croft* 1652 *Eyton.*

11. WHEATHALL (SJ 497037)

Wethale c.1200 *ForProc et freq* to 1291-2 *Ass, Wethehale* 1208-9 *ForProc* (p), *Wethales* 1301 SAC
Whethal' 1255 RH (p), *Whethall* 1672 HTR, 1765 PR(L) 6
Whetall 1483 *SBL 9073 et freq* to 1628 PR(L) 6, *Whettall* 1545 *SBL 9077*, 1667 *SBL 9945*, 1695 Morden
Whitehales, Whete- 1410 *SBL 9072*
Wheathall 1571 *Eyton et seq, Wheatehall* 1580 SAS 50, 1588 *SBL 6645*
Whithall 1586 *SBL 7094*
Wheatall 1590 PR(L) 6 *et freq* to 1694 *SBL 9955*
Whittall 1592 PR(L) 6

'Nook where wheat is grown', *v.* **hwǣte**, **halh**. Wheathall lies in a slight hollow under the 400 contour.

BERRYWOOD LANE, 1833 OS, *Berriwood* - 1777,97 PR(L) 6. The farm takes its name from a large area of woodland called *Birewude* 1212 Fees, *Biriwode* 13th InqMisc, *Biriewode* 1308 *SBL 6640, Bury Woode* 1421 SAS 2/IX, *Burywode* 1445 *SBL 9436, Buriwode* 1461 *SBL 6643, Bery Wood* 1546 *SBL 6694, Byryewoodde* 1578 *SBL 13433, Burywood, Berry-* 1580 SAS 50. 'Wood by an earthwork', *v.* **byrig, wudu.** VCH 28 suggests that the name refers to a tumulus, now demolished, which stood near Pigeondoor and was called *The Bury* in 1545. The Anglo-Saxons appear to have taken it for a defensive earthwork, and it may be referred to by the later term *castle* in *Castlefield* 1799 VCH 32, near Berrywood Farm.

The wood extended into the adjacent parishes of Berrington and Pitchford. The *TAMap* shows large fields called *Big, Little and Keepers Berrywood* on the E. side of Condover Park. *Birewude* is called a royal forest in 1212 Fees, but it must soon have lost this status. VCH 28 gives an account of woodland clearance here dating from the early 13th to the 16th century.

BULLOCK'S COPPICE, *Bullockes Copye* 1581 *Eyton, Bullocks -* 1588 *SBL 6883, John Bullokes Coppies* 1595 *SBL 9501, Bullocks Coppy* 1840 *TA.* Cf. *Bullock Hoo and Pk* 1549 *SBL 7079, Bullocks Parcke, Bullocks Watte Parcke* 1580 SAS 50, *Bullocks Howe* 1586 *SBL 6883, v.* **hōh, park.** Bullock is still a local surname (*ex. inf.* L.T. Rouse). DUCK HALL, DUCK LANE, cf. *Duckall Meadow and Field* 1840 *TA,* the *TAMap* shows a building. Perhaps a derogatory n. MOUNTSION. VCH 37 suggests that this is an adaptation of an earlier n. in this position, *Monkeye* 1482. On *TAMap* the field containing the house is *Monkeys Patch.* 'Monk island', *v.* **munuc, ēg.** THE PENTRE, probably a modern n. from W. *pentref* 'village', no building is shown on *TAMap.* PIGEON-DOOR, 1840 *TA, Pycham Dore* 16th *SBL 7003A, Pigeon-Dore* 1626 PR(L) 6, *Pigen Doore* 1738 ib, *Pidgeon Door* 1745,77 ib. An obscure n. The earliest form makes it clear that the first element is not *pigeon.* OE **dor** and **duru** are used in p.ns. for passes between hills, but the topography does not warrant such a use here. TEN CHIMNIES. *TAMap* shows two buildings.

Field-Names

Forms in (a) are 1840 *TA.* Forms dated 1308 are *SBL 6640.*

(a) Alders; Barn Yd; Brickkiln Lsw; The Broaches, Big and Little Broaches (probably from **bryce**, 'newly-broken-in land': VCH 31 says *Broach Field* was one of the open fields of Wheathall); Broad Reins (referring to drainage channels, dialect *reans*); Brook Lsw; Broomy Lsw; Church Fd, Lower, Middle and Upper (at S.E. corner of parish, land in this area was given for the repair of the church, *v.* VCH 52); Cockshutt Green, Cockshutts (*Cokshetemedwe* 1410 *SBL 9072*, *Over and Nether Cockshute* 1430 SAS 50, *Cockshute Lane, Nether Cockshute* 1549 *SBL 7079*, *Overcockshute, Cockeshute Feelde, Cockshute Leasowe* 1580 SAS 50, *Cockshott* 1595 *SBL 9501*: *Ley Field or Cockshoot Field* was an open field, *v.* VCH 31 and **cocc-sciete**); Coppice Fd (2); Coppy Lsw (2); Cote Yd, Middle - -; Cudley Croft (*Codlicroft* 1308 *SBL 6640*, obscure); Dakers Lsw (cf. *Dager's Place* 1456-7 SAS 2/IX); The Field, Long Fd (adjacent, E. of hamlet: VCH 31 says these fields were still in strips c.1768); Four Butts (a curving strip, instanced in VCH 31 as a field which preserves the shape of an open-field strip; *butt* may here be used for a cultivation ridge); Gorsty Lsw (*v.* **gorstig**); Hennells, Big, Cross and Long; Kitchen Mdw (adjoining hamlet); Big and Long Leys, Lower Ley (*v.* **lǣs**); Long Mdw; New Lsw; New Mdw; Old House Mdw (by one of the buildings of Condover Green); Orchard Mdw; Peartree Lsw; Pess Lsw (*Pease Lesow* 1595 *SBL 9501*, *v.* **peosu**); Pieces Lsw; Pitwicks, Lower and Upper (*Puttwyche, Palmers Puttwicke* 1430 SAS 50, *Little, Great, Rough and St Mary's Puttwycke* 1580 ib, *Sainct Mary Pitwick(s)* 1621 PR(L) 6, first el. **pytt**, second el. **wīc**, which suggests a settlement: VCH 28 n.18 suggests a reference to the marl-pits which were in use here in the 15th cent.: St Mary's because land here was given for the repair of Condover church); Quillet (a narrow strip); Rowlands Fm; Slang (a narrow strip); Spring Coppy (ME **spring** 'young plantation'); Squires Pce; Stanas Mdw; Stony Croft; Summerhouse Lsw, Lower and Upper; Wall Lsw and Mdw (probably **wælle** 'spring'); Withy Graves (*Wythen Greves* 1545 VCH 31, *Wetherngreves* 1580 SAS 50, 'willow groves', *v.* **wīðign**, **grǣfe**); Withy Moor ('willow marsh'); The Yelds, Old Yelds, Further and Near Yelds Gate (a group of fields on S.E. boundary of parish, cf. *The Held* 1549 *SBL 7079*, *Hellde, The Helde* 1580 SAS 50, *The Healde* 1588,98 *SBL 6883, 7022*, *The Helde Yate* 1623 PR(L) 6, *The Heald-yate* 1628 ib, *The Healds* 1670 *Eyton*, *v.* **helde** 'slope': VCH 28 says this part of Berrywood had been cleared by 1378).

(b) *Biriwod Yate* 1308 (*v.* **geat** and Berrywood *supra*); *The Brandemore* 1308, *Brandomore* 1445 *SBL 9436*, *Brandemoresende* 1461 *SBL 6643*, *Brandemore* 1542 *Eyton* (*v.* **mōr**, first el. uncertain, the medial *-e-* tells against **brand** 'place where there has been burning', and a marsh is in any case not likely to have been cleared by fire); *Bromiehurst* 1410 *SBL 9072* (*v.* **brōmig**, **hyrst**); *Caldewall Hurst* 1308 (*v.* **cald**, **wælle**, **hyrst**); *Hopinghalles More, Hoppingales* - 1308 (**mōr** has been added to the gen. of a p.n. meaning 'nook where hops grow', *v.* **hopping**, **halh**); *Levyng Lane* 1549 *SBL 7079*, *Longacre* 1549 *SBL 7097*, *Longe Acres* 1580 SAS 50, *Long Acres* 1587,98 *SBL 9084*, *7022* (probably a furlong in a field-system); *Neder Place* 1461 *SBL 6643* (probably 'nether place', said to be next to *Buriwode*); *The Newe Place* 1425 SAS 2/IX, *Noweplace* 1445 *SBL 9436, Newplace* 1542 *Eyton*, also said to be next to Berrywood); *Over Field* 1545 VCH 31 (an open field); *Le Parsons Ye* 1308 (*Ye* is probably **ēg** 'island'); *Scharphingeswell* 1308 (perhaps a p.n. **Scearping* 'rough place', with **welle** added to the gen.); *Scott Pk* 1549 *SBL 7079*; *Taylors Pk* 1549 *SBL 7079*, *- Parcke* 1580 SAS 50; *Watts Parcke* 1430 SAS 50, *Watkyn Parcke* 1545-6 SAS 2/IX, *Watt(e) Parke* 1586 *SBL 6883* (probably near Bullock's Coppice *supra*, *q.v.*); *Woodland* 1430 SAS 50, 1549 *SBL 7079*, *Woodlands* 1580 SAS 50, *Le* - 1615 *SBL 6848A* ('newly-cultivated land in or near a wood').

CONDOVER FIELD-NAMES WHICH CANNOT BE ASSIGNED TO TOWNSHIPS

Unless other sources are cited, forms dated 1376, 1421,5,6, 1432-3, 1438-9, 1442-3, 1495-6, 1520-1, 1523-4, 1534-5, 1537-8, 1545-6, 1578, 1581, 1595-6 are SAS 2/IX: 1430, 1580 are SAS 50: 1445, 1461, 1531, 1571, 1586,7,8, 1595,8, 1604, 1610, 1615, 1631, 1702 are *SBL 9436, 6643, 13448, 7036, 6883, 9501, 7022, 7024, 7057, 6848A, 6891, 13394*: 1542, 1571-9, 1624, 1635, 1652, 1665,6,7, 1670,2, 1705, 1718, 1734 are *Eyton*: Hy 8 are *RentSur*.

(b) *Alcie Parcke* 1430; *Alssons Buttlers Ley* 1580; *Arnway* 1595; *Atcham Way* 1595; *Barnmore* 1430; *Beches Hey* Hy 8; *Birke Medowe* 1598; *The Black Buttes* 1430; *Botte Parckyng* 1430; *Bradford* 1595; *The Bricke Copyes and Leasowe* 1586; *The Bright Green Lesow* 1595; *Brochmede* 1580; *Brodeheath* 1430 (*v.* **brād**); *Brodhey* Hy 8 (*v.* **brād**, **(ge)hæg**); *Brome* c.1265 *et seq* VCH 36, *Bromes Cross* 1566 ib (this was a hamlet, stated in 1566 to be near the Shrewsbury road, *v.* **brōm**); *Broomecroft* 1587 *SBL 7003A*, *Bromy Crofte* 1595; *Bromy Hill* 1595; *Brownehurst* 1571, *Brownhurst* 1580; *Browns Meadow* 1734; *Bruchoke* 1595; *Bugebruche* 1461 (*v.* **bryce**); *Burnells Pole* 1595; *Callow Hill* 1631; *Callstocks Sprynge* 1520-1 (probably ME **spring** in the sense 'copse'); *Campions Copye* 1588,98, - *Coppice* 1595; *Cattesleys Yard'* Hy 8, *Catslowes Yarde* 1580; *Catlowe's Lane* 1534-5; *Cawkins Lee* 1624; *Cawmer Long Stole* 1580; *Churmes Grownde* 1588; *Clarcks Place* 1580; *Cloyhale* 1432-3 (*v.* **halh**); *Cokemore* 1430, 1445, 1461, 1580, *Cokmore* 1542, *Taylors Cockmoore* 1595, *Cookes Moore* 1598 (*v.* **cocc**, **mōr**); *Cole Furlonge* 1610, *Cole Hill* 1595, *The Colepitt* 1587 (probably all referring to charcoal); *Collins Leasow* 1705; *Condors Copy* Hy 8; *Conygree Lande* n.d. (16th) *SBL 7003A*, *The Connengrye* 1604 PR(L) 6 (*v.* **coninger**); *The Copie* 1668 PR(L) 6, *Ye Coppy* 1670 ib, *The Coppice* 1734 *SBL 10015*; *Coppice Graves* 1615 *SBL 6848A*, *The Coptie Greave* 1635, *The Copie Greave* 1666 (*v.* **grǣfe**); *Le Cornemilles* 1445, *Lez Cormylles* 1461, *Les*

Cornmylles 1542 (there were a number of mills in the parish); *Cowpers Hey* Hy 8 (*v.* **(ge)hæg**); *Croftes* 1430; *Cross Quary Feild* 1595; *The Crossway* 1734 *SBL 10015*; *Davys Pole* 1430; *The Demeans* 1586 ('demesne'); *Dudmedowe* 1430, *Did Meadow* 1581, *Didmeadowe* 1586 (first el. obscure); *Dingstede* 1430 (a name in **-stede** is unlikely in Sa, and the form is probably corrupt); *Dry Bridge* 1615; *Edge Feild* 1595; *Elmhurste* 1421,6, *-hurst* 1430, 1580, *Elmehurste* 1571, *The Elmhurste, The Ellmehurste* 1571 *Eyton, Ellmast* 1670 (*v.* **elm**, **hyrst**, and cf. *Brownhurst supra*); *The Eys* 1580 *SBL 6586*, *The Eye* 1587, *The Eye(s)* 1588 (*v.* **ēg**); *Ye Meadow* 1430, *Ye Medewe* 1445, *Ymedowe* 1461, *Eymedowe* Hy 8, *Eye Meadow* 1580 (probably a meadow near preceding); *Farmer His Lesow, Farmer His Close, Farmers Barne* 1595; *Fearny Close* 1604; *The Field Ground* 1702; *The Fox Holes* 1734 *SBL 10015; Fradsley High Waye* 1595 (road to Frodesley); *Frekmore* Hy 8, *Frogmor* 1595; *Gabbett, Gabbetts Close and Greate Close, Roger Gabbotts Wood* 1595; *Gorsty Furlong* 1615 *SBL 6848A, The - -* 1666 (*v.* **gorstig**); *The Grasse Lesow* 1595, *Grass Lessows* 1712 PR(L) 6; *The Greate Leasowe* 1588, *- towards Burton* 1598; *The Lesow Greme, The other Greme* 1595 (*Greme* is obscure); *The Hale* 1580, 1587, 1652, *The Greate Hale, The Little Hale, Sukers Hale* 1595 (*v.* **halh**); *Halle Yarde* 1598; *Hallwardyn's Place* 1495-6, *Hallwardens Landes* 1523-4; *Hanger Hill Leasow* 1734 *SBL 10015* (*v.* **hangra**); *Hauck Lesow* 1595, *Hawkes Leasowe* 1598; *Hawrens Medow* 1595; *The Haye, Bettons Haye* 1595; *Haynes House and Orchard, Bayly Heynes Woode* 1595*; The Heath* 1571, 1580, *Overheath and Netherheath* 1580, *Le Nether Heath* 1619 *SBL 9078* (perhaps identical with Heath names in Ryton); *The Heathe Meadowe* 1586,88; *The Henn Eie* 1667 (*v.* **henn**, **ēg**); *Hyllfyeld, The Hyll Leasowe* 1580 *SBL 6586*, *Hill Lesow* 1595, *Hill Leasowe* 1598; *Hockshows Coppice* 1595, *Hockshewe* 1618 *SBL 6899*, *Hogshilhead* 1587; *Hokehey* Hy 8; *The Hoppyard* 1595; *Horshall* 1442-3; *The Horse Leasowe, Horse Meadow(e)* 1588; *Huson's Grounds* 1702; *Inchmore Meadow* 1665; *Kyntons Hey* Hy 8; *The Lay Butts* 1734 *SBL 10015*; *The Little Croft* 1734; *The Little Lessowe* 1635; *Long Medow* 1595, *The Long Meddow* 1652; *Longenors Woodde* (Longnor parish adjoins on S.); *The Longe Yard* 1595; *The Lords Leasow* 1672, 1718; *The Lord's Meadow* 1430; *Lorence Meadowe* 1598; *Lower Lesow* 1595; *Loynstons Coppice* 1595; *The Lymes* 1534-5; *Lyngens Heis* 1624; *Mablyns Crosse* 1581, *Mablin Yate* 1587 *SBL 9084*; *Maggestocking* 1430 (*v.* **stoccing**); *Medow, Upper and Lower* 1595; *The Midle Filde* 1588; *The Myddyll Lye* 1421 (*v.* **lēah**); *The Millnes, Millne Moore* 1586, *The Millcroft* 1595, *Myll Dyche* 1430, *Milnehale* 1604, *Mill Hale* 1615, *The Mill-Hale* 1667, *Mill Lane* 1615; *Le Mill Leasow* 1729 *SBL 10002, The Mill, The Mill Dam, Mill Meadow* 1595, *Myllmore* 1580, *Mill Moore* 1595, *Millne Yarde* 1598 (*v.* **myln**, **mōr**, **halh**, **lǣs**, **geard**, there were a number of mills in the parish); *Moate Furlonge* 1595, *Mote Furlonge and Yarde* 1598 (*v.* **mote**); *The Moore* 1537-8, 1599 *SBL 7007* (*v.* **mōr**); *Newe Leasowe* 1619 *SBL*

9078, The New - 1734 *SBL 10015*; *Newaye* 1438-9 ('new way'); *Nicolles Land* 1579; *Oatleys Mead* 1610; *The Oulde Lesow* 1595; *Owte Park* 1595; *Oxale* 1416 (*v.* **oxa, halh**); *P'kes Medowe* Hy 8, *Parkes Meadowe* 1586; *The Greater Parlor* 1598 (the precise sense of *parlour* in f.ns. has not been established); *The Parrockes* 1430 (*v.* **pearroc**); *Parres Leasow* 1598; *Peare Tree Feild* 1595; *Phidfold Crofte* 1595; *The Porteway leading to Pitcheford* 1579; *The Quar(r)ell* 1586 ('quarry', *v.* **quarrelle**); *Radford* 1595; *The Rough Green Lesow* 1595 (cf. *The Bright - - supra*); *Rowmere Hill alias The Hill* 1595, *Romon Hill* 1604; *Sackenheath* 1430; *Saplyng' Hey* Hy 8; *The Slinge, The Slange* 1670 (both terms denote narrow strips); *Syngers Grene* Hy 8, *Singers Greene* 1586 *SBL 6924*; *Smetheshale* 1426 (*v.* **halh**); *Smythes Lesow* 1595; *Sowes Hill* 1604; *Sprydwycks* 1438-9; *Stanley Medow* 1595; *Stannel Barn* 1702 (perhaps *stān-delf* 'stone quarry'); *Swinnie* 1631; *The Teinter Yard* 1587, *Teinter Yord* 1587 *SBL 7003A*, *Tenterye Yorde* 1588 ('enclosure with cloth-stretching frames'); *Theves Stye* 1442-3 ('thieves' path', *v.* **stīg**); *Thornes Leasowe* 1587, *Thornes Leasow and Meadow* 1595; *Tybbotts Medowe* 1593 *SBL 6863*, *Tibbotts Meadowe* 1598; *Tymothy Furlonge* 1595; *Townsfeildes* 1565 *SBL 6617*; *Uplands* 1694 *SBL 9955*; *Vynes Ground* 1531; *The Wastwater* 1615 *SBL 6848A* (first el. ME **waste** 'wasteland'); *La Well'* 1261-2 *ForProc* (p), *La Walle* 1291-2 *Ass* (p) ('spring', *v.* **welle, wælle**); *Westmore Pitt Feild* 1595; *The Wheat Meadow* 1734; *Whetall Lane* 1595; *White Groves* 1587; *The White Leasow* 1734; *Whitleys Ley* 1553 *SBL 6854*, *Whytleys Lye* 1580 *ib*, *Whitler's Leye* 1586, *Whitsleislye* 1588; *Wilkinsons Leasow* 1705; *Wolder Barrowe* 1580; *Wylckynslye* 1426; *The Wood* 1581, 1617 PR(L) 6; *Woodfield, Woodefelde Greves* 1430 (*v.* **grǣfe**); *Woodenhall* 1430; *The Woode Lesswes* 1578; *Woodward Lee* 1587 *SBL 7003A*; *Upper Yard, Lower Yarde* 1595, *Upper Yarde, Lougher Yorde* 1598, *The Yords betwixt the Lanes* 1588 (*v.* **geard**); *Le Yore* 1445, 1542 (*v.* **gear**, the place is associated with a mill, so this is the sort of enclosure for catching fish by a mill which is referred to in Anglo-Saxon charters by the term *myln-gear*).

Cound

The parish-name, which is a transferred use of the pre-English name of Cound Brook, is discussed in Part 1.

There are four townships: Upper and Lower Cound, Golding and Harnage. The *TAMap* is for the whole parish, but the township boundaries can be recovered approximately from the 19th-cent. *Index to Tithe Survey* OS 1" map. Harnage is very much larger than the others, but it is clear from the bounds of Harnage Grange 1232 Dugdale that the Grange and Moreton were once distinct units in this large area.

1. LOWER COUND (SJ 558050)

v. Part **1**: *Nether* and *Over Cound* are recorded in 1571 and 1572 respectively, and Ogilby (1675) shows *Cund* and *Upper Cund*. There is no hamlet at Lower Cound; The GR given here is that of the church, which was isolated. The hamlet probably stood beside the Cound Brook, along the road leading past the mill to Upper Cound. It was "clearly the primary settlement in the parish", but "seems to have disintegrated in the 18th century" (VCH 60).

BLACK BARN, 1833 OS, is shown but not named on *TAMap*. *Upper and Lower Barn Meadow* adjoin. THE BYLET, *Island* 1842 *TA*, is between two arms of Cound Brook. *Bylet* is the Sa term for land between a river and an artificial channel. This one is unusually large, hence perhaps the *TA* designation. CORN MILL, *Mill* 1842 *TA*. This was in use until c.1930 (VCH 60). Two mills, one perhaps on this site, are noted in DB. COUNDARBOUR, *Cound harbour* 1833 OS, *Windy Harbour* 1842 *TA*. In modern names *harbour* probably implies an exposed situation. The farmhouse, now demolished, was of 19th-cent. date (VCH 61).

Field-Names

Forms in (a) are 1842 *TA*. Early forms dated 1612, 1682, 1700 are *LDR*.

(a) Barn Fd; Baynut Tree Yd (*Banat* - - 1612, *Ye Bannat* - - 1682, a variety of walnut, cf. Golding f.ns. *infra*); Bog Fd; Bottoms (two fields by Coundmoor Brook, *v.* **botm**); Brickkiln Fd and Mdw, Brickyard Office and Waste; The Britch (*v.* **bryce**); Lower Broadway (adjoins Broadway in Brompton *supra*); Brook Lsw; Church Furlong, Little - - (in *Church Feild* 1612, which was an open field, *Little, Middle and Great Church Furlong* occur 1700 *et seq LDR*); Coppice Mdw, Upper - -, Long and Square Coppice Pce; Coppy Lsw (adjoins Coppice names); Cotons Fd, Lower - - (*v.* Cotons in Brompton *supra*); Crabtree

Lsw; Dovehouse Close (cf. *Dovehouse Yard* 1700); Fidlers Heath; Forge Yd (VCH 61 says probably the site of a smithy first recorded 1567); Gorsy Bank; Gravel Hole Bank; Gravel Hole Wd (not near preceding); Hall Garden; Heath Lsw (this and Fidlers Heath are in the area of Cound Heath, which is *Conedehethe* 1271-2 *Ass*, *Cound Heathe* 1573 *SBL 8403*); Horse Pasture; Hownet; Hurst Bank and Mdw (*The Hurst Meadow* 1700, VCH 60 says *Hurst Meadow*, *Oxenhole* and *Weir Meadow* were dole meadows in 17th); Inoculated Mdw (explained FN 34, refers to a method of converting a field to grass); Langfords Mdw; Little Island (adjoins Island, *v.* Bylet *supra*); Maltmans Yd; Marsh, - Coppice (perhaps *Enchmarsh* 1528 VCH 60, *Enchemershe* 1573 *SBL 8403*, perhaps from ME *enche* 'manorial servant'); Middle Mdw (between Coppice Mdw and Little Road Mdw); Little, Middle and Upper Moss (*Mosse* 1573 *SBL 8403*); New Tinings (*v.* U. Cound f.ns.); Oaktree Lsw; Old Fox Cover; Olivers Lsw; Park Mdw (the site of the medieval park, VCH 61); Pasture Patch (a tiny enclosure); Patch (also tiny); Pond Mdw; Rag Fd (*v.* **ragge**); Rail Mdw (by the park); Richards Lsw (cf. *Edmund Richards Yard* 1612); Road Pce, Little Road Mdw (by Shrewsbury road); Rock Mdw (across the Severn from Eytonrock); Great, Little and Lower Rytons (*Rytons Field* 1623-34 *Corn.R.O.*, 1700, *Ryton-field* 1691 PR(L) 2, an open field); Slang (a narrow triangle); Slang along Brook; Stackyard Bank; Three Pit Lsw; Watering Pce Lsw; Lower and Upper Wet Reans (drainage channels); Wheatlands; Wood Mdw.

(b) *Church Brook* 1612, 1700, - *Brooke* 1682; *Boscus de Cunet* 1255-6 *Ass* (VCH 59 says there was manorial woodland on the belt of boulder clay which extends from Venusbank to R. Severn); *Hoggins Croft*; *The Leest Feild Lane* 1612, *Ye Leese Feild* 1682; *Oxen Hole* 1612 (a dole meadow, *v.* Hurst Mdw in (a)).

COUND BRIDGE. COUND HALL, 1833 OS, *Cundhall* 1690-1 *SBL 5230*. COUNDLODGE INN. COUNDSTANK, COUNDSTANK BRIDGE, *Stank Meadow*, *Stanks Leasow* 1842 *TA*, the bridge is so-named 1680, VCH 61. *stank* can mean 'pond', 'waterfilled ditch' or 'dam'. VCH suggests that in this instance it denotes the mill-race for a paper-mill known to have been here in 1616. COUND VILLA, 1833 OS. THE LAWNS, 1783 *et freq* PR(L) 14, *Cound Lawn* 1842 *TA*: this is the park created in the 1740s (VCH 61). LONGDOLE COPPICE, *Longduel* 1833 OS, *Long Dole Coppice* 1842 *TA*. Probably named from adjacent meadowland, *v.* **dāl**. SMITHY, probably moved to this site c.1748 (VCH 61). VENUSBANK, - COPPICE, *Venus Bank* 1833 OS. The name is unexplained. It seems likely that it once referred to the whole length of the ridge of sand and gravel described VCH 14, which ran from here towards Betton Strange in Berrington. A terrier of 1750 (*LDR*) mentions *Venus Bank* under Betton. WATERFALL.

2. UPPER COUND (SJ 553050)

The hamlet was formed in the later Middle Ages and was known as New Street in the later 14th cent. (VCH 61).

COUNDMOOR BROOK, *v.* Coundmoor in Harnage *infra.* COVE COPPICE, by Coundmoor Brook. The wood is shown on *TAMap*, but the schedule says "Wood and Marsh", not giving it a name. The *TAMap* also shows a wood in Harnage, on a tributary of Coundmoor Brook, which is called *Cove Wood.* It is possible that in one of its senses *cove* (OE **cofa**) referred to meanders in a river. It is difficult to explain Coven St ('at the coves') on any other grounds. STEVENSHILL, *Steven's Hill* 1833 OS, *Stephens Hills* 1842 *TA.* The house named from the hill is shown on *TAMap* but not named. Maria *Stevens* is mentioned 1608 PR(L) 2, and Bennian *Stevens* 1746 ib. SUNDAL, *Sand Hill* 1842 *TA.* WORMWOOD COPPICE, - *Coppy* 1842 *TA.*

Field-Names

Forms in (a) are 1842 *TA.* Forms dated 1612, 1748, 1849 are *LDR.* The three common fields of Upper Cound were Sandy Field, Middle Field and Kymry Field, and they covered virtually the whole township (VCH 59-60). *Kymry Feyld* is listed 1612,82 *LDR.*

(a) Little, Lower and Upper Allens Pits; Allotment (a series of fields in the southern extension of the township, along the road which runs by Coundmoor Brook); Banky Pce; Barn Lsw; Barn Mdw; Barn Yd; Berry Bank (cf. *Berry Yate and Yard* 1612); Big Hills (this and Little Hills are on the lower slopes of Stevenshill *supra*); Big Mdw; Brickkiln Fd; Broad Lsw (adjoins Long Lsw and is broader); Far and Near Brook Lsw; Brook Bank; Cambridge Lsw;

Catt Butts (here and elsewhere in the township Butts probably denotes open-field strips); Coppice Lsw; Cow Pasture; Cross Hill, - - Fd (either side of Acton Burnell road, not at a crossroads); Cutlers Lsw; Lower and Upper Eight Butts; Far New Leasow; Footway Lsw; Gorsy Lsw; Govern Hill; Green Pce; Hardy Butts (*Hordibus Leasows* 1748, Hardibutts 1849); Horse Croft, Little - -; House Pce (the house is Stevenshill); Hunger Hill; Leg (narrow strip); Lime Lsw (the limeworks here was producing lime for sale in 1746, VCH 68); Little Fd (small); The Little Hills (*v.* Big Hill *supra*); Little Mdw (2, both very small); Long Lsw (same length as adjacent Broad Lsw, but narrower); Middle Fd (between Upper Fd and Townsend); New Tinings (there is another in Lower Cound, cf. *New Enclosure, alias New Tineing* 1678 *SBL 10083*, *v.* **tȳning**); Old House Ground; Patch (tiny enclosure); Pound Lsw; Pouths Mouths; Quarry Patch, Upper - -; Road Close; Slang (long, narrow strip on slope of Stevenshill); Big and Lesser Swines Lsw; Tillers Bridge and Mdw (*Tillersbridge Furlong* 1612, *Tillersbridge* 1771 VCH 61); Townsend (at S. end of hamlet); Upper Fd (2); Wigleys; Yewtree Pce.

3. GOLDING (SJ 545035)

The township-name, which means 'gold valley', is discussed in Part 1.

BULL ROUGH, 1842 *TA*. FULLWAY, *Fullway Furlong, Upper, Middle and Lower Fullway* 1842 *TA*. The last three fields lie along Coundmoor Brook. The 'foul way' was probably the N./S. road which crosses the brook by a ford, near the house, *v.* **fūl**, **weg**. GOLDING ROUGH, by Bull Rough. WARD'S COPPICE, 1842 *TA*, also - *Leasow*.

Field-Names

Forms in (a) are 1842 *TA*.

(a) Further and Near Ash Grove; Bannut Tree Yd (a walnut tree, cf. L. Cound f.ns.); Big Mdw (larger than Little Mdw); Brook Mdw; Church Fd; Lower and Upper Clay Pits; The Conery (*v.* **coninger**); Cote Mdw (no building shown); Little and Old Cow Pasture; Golding Coppice, Coppice Lsw; Golding

Mdw; Holly Mdw, Big - -; Little Hooked Hill, Big Hooked Hill and Bakehouse; Horse Fd; Little Mdw; May Fd; Moor Head Mdw and Pool (adjoins Walkmill Pool on the brook which forms the W. boundary of the parish); Old Coppice; Great and Little Oney; Big Ostrills; Ox Lsw; Rough Lsw; Sandy Fd; Shutlands (probably *shot*, i.e. 'furlong'); The Slang (same shape as surrounding fields); Spring Coppice (1833 OS, ME **springe** 'young plantation'); The Stitches (perhaps referring to hurdles, OE ***sticce**); Big and Little Tickney; Town Mdw; Walk Fd; Walkmill Pool (e.17th VCH 121, the fulling mill was in Pitchford); Yewtree Lsw.

4. HARNAGE (SJ 567044)

Hernegia, Hernege, Herenegia 1232 Dugdale, *Hernegg'* 1234 Cl, *-ege* 1535 *SBL 7180*
Harenegge 1254 Pat, 1255-6 *Ass*, 1261-2 *ForProc, Harnegge* 1268 MGS, 1271-2, 91-2 *Ass*, *-ege* 1535 VE, *-edge* 1566 *SBL 8384*, 1584 PR(L) 2, 1670,7 *SBL 10144, 10083, Harnedge alias Kinges* - 1665 *SBL 9927*
Arneg' 1255 RH
Harenhegge 1271-2 *ForProc*, *-hegg* c.1291 TN
Harnage 1444 AD, 1567 PR(L) 2, *Harnage otherwise King's Harnedge* 1739,98 *SBL 4135, 3549*
Harin(d)ge 1573 *SBL 8403*
Hernage 1622 PR(L) 6

'Rocky escarpment', *v.* ***hæren, ecg.** The reference is to a ridge of shales which divides the parish into two parts. OE ***hæren** should be regarded as an established p.n. el. despite the doubt expressed in EPN.

King's is presumably for distinction from Harnage Grange *infra.* The manor of Cound was in royal ownership for a time in the 13th cent. (VCH 63), but it is surprising that this should have been remembered in the 17th and 18th cents.

HARNAGE GRANGE, 1739 *SBL 4135, Harnydge* - 1577 Saxton, *Harnedge* - 1580 AD, 1624 PR(L) 2, *Ye Grange* 1699 ib. ME **grange** 'outlying farm belonging to a religious house'. A hamlet here became a dependency of Buildwas Abbey in 1232. In a document of 1232 printed in Dugdale the place is described as a vill, and its bounds are given.

HAYES COPPICE, *Hay* - 1833 OS, *Cowhays* - 1842 *TA*. The wood shown on *TAMap*, which corresponds exactly to Hayes Coppice, is surrounded by fields called *Further, Little and Lower Cow Hays.* The coppice is a remnant of the *boscus qui vocatur Haya* mentioned 1232 Dugdale, which was common to Harnage and Cressage, *v.* **(ge)hæg**.

MORETON, *Mortone* 1232 Dugdale, *-ton'* 1255-6 *Ass, Moorton'* 1381 *SBL 5192* (p), *Morton* 1535 *SBL 7180, Moretons, Murtonfeld* 1573 *SBL 8403.* 'Marsh settlement', *v.* **mōr, tūn**: there are four instances of this name in Sa, *v.* Part **1**. The boundary between the lands of Morton and Harnage Grange is delineated in 1232 Dugdale.

NEWBOLD (lost), *Neubolde* 1255-6 *Ass, Niubold'* 1261-2 *ForProc, Newbolde, Neubaud'* 1271-2 *ForProc, Newball's Lane* 1623-4 *Corn.R.O.* 'New building', *v.* **nīwe**, **bold**. VCH 62 suggests that Bull Fm (*infra*) may be on the site of this hamlet. It is not mentioned in the bounds of Harnage Grange in 1232, so was probably not a township.

There are two instances of the name in Sa, the other being Nobold in Meole Brace. It is the WMidl and La form of the name which became Newbottle or Nobottle in the EMidl and in Scotland. Compounds with **nīwe** greatly outnumber other classes of names containing the related words **bōtl** and **bold**.

BULL FM, 1833 OS, BULLHILL, - BROOK AND COTTAGE. *TA* has *Bull Meadow, Great and Little Bull Field, Bull Hill Coppice.* The building was probably an inn, since PR(L) 2 refers to *The Bull* in 1752, *Ye Bool* in 1769. Perhaps on the site of *Newbold supra.* COUNDMOOR, 1690 PR(L) 2, *Coundmoore* 1670 *SBL 10144, Cound Moor* 1833 OS. 'Marsh belonging to Cound', *v.* **mōr**. Settlement in the area began in the 17th cent., and the marsh was enclosed in 1830 (VCH 59, 63). FOX P.H. GRANGE HILL, 1833 OS, *v.* Harnage Grange *supra.* THE GREEN, 1833 OS, probably *Lycheleys Green* 1567 VCH 59. On *TAMap, Green Lane* is N. of the hamlet, *Little and Upper Leys* are S. of it. *Leys* may represent earlier *Lycheleys.* HARNAGE COVERT, FM AND HO. Houses on the sites of Harnage Ho and Butler's Fm were called *The Lower* and *The Upper House* in the 17th cent. (VCH 61). HIGHLANDS, *Highelands* 1565 PR(L) 2, *The Highlands* 1735 ib. The area is called *Little Lanley and The Highlands* on *TAMap.* VCH 58 says it has been associated with the adjoining manor of Langley since the 13th cent. HOPYARD, *Hop Yard* 1833 OS. LEASOWES, *Well Leasow* 1842 *TA, v.* **lǣs**; VCH 62 traces the history of the house back to 1628. LONG NURSERY, 1842 *TA, House Nursery* 1833 OS. This and Round Nursery are shown but not named on a map of the Harnage Grange estate, 1794, *SRO 1058 box 6.* MOSTERLEY, 1833 OS, LITTLE -. *TA* has fields called *Lower, Near and Upper Mosterley.* This may be an ancient settlement, but no early reference has been noted and VCH does not mention it. NEW PLANTATION. THE QUARRY, 1833 OS, *Quarry Bank, Field, Patch and Slang* 1842 *TA. Quarry Field* is on the 1794 map. This may be *The Quarrey* 1670 *SBL 10144.* ROUND NURSERY, 1833 OS, 1842 *TA,* adjoins Long Nursery *supra.* Partly round with one straight edge on *TAMap,* fully round on 19th cent. OS. WITHY COPPICE. WYLDES QUARRY. A family named *Wild(e)* appears 1715-1808 PR(L) 2.

Field-Names

Forms in (a) are 1842 *TA.* Those marked * are also on a map of Harnage Grange Estate, 1794 *SRO 1058, box 6.* Early forms dated 1232 are Dugdale, those dated 1535, 1670, 1701, 1791 are *SBL 7180, 10144, 10146, 5371,* those dated 1612, 1682, 1700, 1742, 1748 are *LDR.*

(a) Banky Close; *- Fd; - Lsw; - Slang (adjoins 2 fields called Slang); *Barley Close; Barn Fd; Barn Lsw and Yd; Barrett Lsw; Beach, Little and Upper (*The Beach* 1620 VCH 59, *v.* **bæce**, there is a tiny stream); Big Lsw; Big Mdw; Little Mdw (adjacent, Big - being the smaller); *Black Walk (adjacent to Harnage Grange, the 1794 map shows a line of trees, Peartree Walk adjoins); Boozy Pasture (Boosey - on 1794 map, the n. refers to pasture rights); Bottom

(*Botham* on 1794 map, *v.* **boðm**, 6" map shows marsh); Brickkiln Fd; Broad Lsw; Broadwells, Big and Little (*Broadewall Feyld* 1612, *Broadwall* -, *Bradwall Furlong* 1682, 'broad spring', a common field); Bromley Moor, Lower and Upper - - (a large area of wet ground, partly in Cressage); Bromley's Hag (not near preceding, Hag is probably a place where timber is felled); Brook Lsw; Broomy Bank; *Calves Croft (cf. *Calves Close* 1791); *Chimney Pce (refers to shape); Clemley (*v.* Clemley Park in Cardeston, Alberbury); Cleveleys Yd; Clover Fd (cf. *Clover Bank* 1791); Coaling Rough; Coalpit Yd (*The Colpitte, Colpit Furlonge* 1612); Coldwell (*The Cawdall* 1701, *v.* **cald**, **wælle**); Common Pce, Little, Lower and Upper; Coppice, - Lsw; - Ley; *- Mdw; Cove Wd (by a tributary of Coundmoor Brook, *v.* Cove Coppice in U. Cound); Cow Lsw and Pasture; Crabtree Lsw; Crabmill Pool and *Plain (*Crab Mill Bank* 1791, by Harnage Grange: the mill would be for crushing crab apples); The Criftin (1620 VCH 59, *v.* ***cryfting**); Cross Fd (a tiny triangle, not by a road); Dingle (either side of Coundmoor Brook); *Dingle Fd (not near preceding); *Dingle Pce (not near other Dingle ns.); Dinmore (1528, 1612, c.1750 VCH 59, one of the 'marsh' ns. near Moreton *supra*); Ditcher Fd, Far and Near (*Dychefeld* 1528 VCH 59, *Dychen Felde* 1573 *SBL 8403*, *Dychett Feilde* 1701, Wm. *Dychens* is mentioned 1573); The Flash, Lower Flash (a *flash* is a shallow pool); Glazes Yd; Goose Mdw; Gorsy Patch (very tiny); Great Mdw; *Green Court (by Harnage Grange); Green Fd; Green Lane (by the road S. from Harnage, cf. *The Green Lane Leasow* 1670, *v.* The Green *supra*); *Greenley, Lower, Upper and Hollow (*The Three Green Leys* 1791); The Grit (*The Gritt* 1701: an OE **grytte* 'gravelly place' has been postulated to explain f.ns. in Berks (PN Berks 245, 349) and ME surnames in Do and W: to these may be added a name in Rimpton So, which is *Grut* 1224-5, *Grutte* 1252, *Grout* 1722 (*ex.inf.* Mr C. Thornton): in spite of the lateness of the forms this Harnage f.n. is probably another instance); *Hempbutt; *The Hill (*Ye Hill* 1700 PR(L) 2); The Hill, West Hill (not near preceding); Hill Head, Little - -; Hollywells (adjoins Coldwell, cf. *Halliwell Lodge* 1670, perhaps 'holy well'); *Hopyard; House Mdw (by Mosterley); *Kenley Croft (adjoins K. parish); *Large Mdw; Lawn (adjoins Harnage); The Leys (*The Lees* 1700, *v.* **lǣs**); Little and Upper Leys (not near preceding); Limekiln Bank (1837,40 *SBL 6113,4*, the kilns were here in the 18th cent. (VCH 68): the bounds of Harnage Grange in 1232 mention an 'old lime-kiln', but not in this position on the S.W. outskirts of Harnage); Little Lsw; Little Mdw (2, one on 1794 map); Lodge Fd (in the park, cf. *Lodge Bank* 1791); Long Lsw (3, one on 1794 map); Lords Mdw (1528 VCH 60); Meadow; Big, Little and Lower Mdw (not near preceding); Middle Mdw (between Meadow and Harnage Lords Mdw); *Mill Lsw (1791) and Mdw (by Coundmoor Brook); Morton Furlong (*The* - - 1701, *v.* Moreton *supra*); Mortons, Flat, Long and Upper (by Moreton); Nabbs

Hill (*Nabs* - 1791,4, this is probably too far south to be *nab* 'hillock', ultimately from ON: it may be a surname, or a corruption of *Knapp*, from OE **cnæpp** 'hillock'); New Mdw; New Pce; New Tinings (a recurring f.n. in this area, *v.* Loton f.ns. *supra*); Outrack (by Highlands, Outrack is a S. Sa term for an area between cultivated land and hill pasture, FN 35); *Ox Lsw; *Park Mdw, Far and Near, Park Fd, Old Park Pce (there was a park at Harnage Grange, VCH 59); Patch (a tiny enclosure); Upper and Lower Patch (2 small enclosures); *Peartree Walk (*v.* Black Walk *supra*); Peas Croft (*The Peasecroft* 1701); Penny Croft (1678 *SBL 10083, TAMap* shows a small enclosure with a house, the n. probably refers to rent); Pit Lsw (4, not near each other); *Pool Banks and Mdw (*Poole Meadow* 1791); *Pool Mdw (not near preceding); *Pool Pce (not near preceding); Poyners Lsw (2 fields, cf. *Pyners Leasow* 1790 *SBL 5372, The Two Poyners Leasows* 1791: the 1794 estate map shows 3 fields, *Poiners Leasow Pasture, Cow Pasture* and *Tillage*); Quarry Bank, Patch and Slang, *Quarry Fd; Quarry Lsw (not near preceding); Rookery; Roundabout (surrounded by roads); The Rough Mdw; Rudge Wd (*v.* **hrycg**, the wood is shown but not named on the 1" map, S. of Harnage Ho); Rushy Fd; Rye Leys; *Sharmore, Big and Little (*Sciremore, Sciremoresiche* 1232, *v.* **mōr**, **sīc**, first el. **scīr**, here used of a parish boundary: the fields adjoin Cressage); Slang (6, all narrow strips); Spring Well Mdw (*Springwall Meadow* 1670, *Springwell Brook* 1700, *The Springwell Meadow* 1701, by Rudge Wd, perhaps ME *springe* 'copse' and **welle**); Stirchley; The Stocking (*v.* ***stoccing**); Suckley Acre; *Swallowtail, - Mdw, - next Wood (*Swallow Tail Meadow* 1791, the field called Swallowtail has a pointed projection, but the n. does not seem specially apt); Swans Nest; Tainters, Lower and Middle - (cloth-stretching frames); Townsend (adjoins Harnage); Upper Pce; Upton Furlong (at S.E. end of Harnage); Vineyard (1700, 1701, Pool or Vineyard Field was a common field of Harnage (VCH 60)); Wash Mdw (by a pool which was perhaps used for sheep-dipping); Well Lsw (2); Well Mdw; Wet Pits, Big and Little (*Weet pitt* 1612, *Wetpit Field* 1700, *Wetpitt* 1701); *White Fd; Woodcocks; Yard, Lower and Upper Yd, Borders Yd, Bennetts Yd, Pig Yd (all in Harnage village); Lower and Upper Yd, Pig Yd, Powell Yd (a group of fields near Moreton); Yard (by Mosterley); The Yelds ('slopes', *v.* **helde**); Yew Tree Lsw.

(b) *Assartum Reynaldi* 1232 ('Reynald's assart', this and *Wilardesmedwe* were near Sharmore *supra*); *The Brach* 1701 (*v.* **bræc**); *Bryery Furlonge* 1612,82, *The Churche Way* 1612,82; *Condfeild* 1701; *The Crosse Yate Lane* 1612, *Ye Crosse Yate* 1682; *The Eyght Rydges* 1612, *Ye Eight Ridges* 1682; *The Hallowe Rydgwood* 1612, *Ye Hollow Ridg-wood* 1682; *Halloway Meadowe* 1612, *Ye Holloway Meadowe* 1682; *Harnedge Hill Feyld* 1612, *Hill Feild* 1670, *Harnage Hill Feild* 1682, *The Hillfeild* 1701 (a common field); *Hollow Meadow(e)* 1670, 1700, 1701; *The Hollyn*

Style 1612, *Ye Holly Stile* 1682 (*v.* **holegn**); *Kenildebroc* 1232 ('Cynehild's brook', the pers.n. is feminine); *Leekes Yarde* 1612,82; *Meadow Yeards* 1670 (cf. Yard ns. *supra*); *The Newe Leasowe* 1612, *Ye New Leasowe* 1682, *The New Leasow* 1700,42; *Oxnsill Medowe* 1701; *Pistle Furlong* 1612, *Pisle* - 1682, *The Pistle Field* 1700,48 (VCH 60 says that Epistle Field was an alternative n. for Broadwell Field, *supra*: if Epistle refers to a Rogation-tide ceremony the field must have extended further east than the *TA* fields do in order to reach the parish boundary); *Plumtreefurlonge* 1612, *Plum-tree Furlong* 1682; *The Poole Feild* (a common field, *v.* Vineyard in (a)); *Poole Furlong* 1612,82; *The Port Way* 1612,82; *Robynshey* 1535 (*v.* **(ge)hæg**, this was in Moreton: Robins Mdw in Cressage is fairly near); *Rowses Furlonge* 1612,82; *Sowters Buts* 1612,82; *Walkers Pitt* 1670; *Wilardesmedwe* 1232 ('Wilheard's meadow', *v.* **mǣd**); *Yarford Mill* a.1292 VCH 68 (on Bullhill Brook, first el. probably **gear*, used of an enclosure by a mill for catching fish, cf. *Le Yore* in Condover).

COUND FIELD-NAMES WHICH CANNOT BE ASSIGNED TO TOWNSHIPS

These forms are 1573 *SBL 8403*

(b) *Backhowse* ('bakehouse'); *Codnoll*; *Culverhowse* ('dovehouse'); *The Galter* (possibly 'gallows', OE **galg-trēow**); *Hakilmore, Hawkilmore Yards*; *Hoxall*; *Jennett's Hoke* (*v.* **hōc**); *The Ryecroft*.

Cressage

The parish-name, which means 'at Christ's oak', is discussed in Part 1, and it is suggested there that Lady Oak (*infra*) might be the direct descendant of the tree from which the settlement was named. The account of the parish in VCH, however, points out that there were also trees called Gospel Oak and Curst Oak, and in the *VCH* notes for the parish the latter appears as *3 oaks called the Cursed Oaks* from a source dated 1433 (*PRO C 139/67/64*). It is not impossible that *Cristes æc* became *Cursed Oak*. The surviving Lady Oak provides a valuable example of a tree which was accorded special status and allowed to replace itself over a long period, but its relevance to the settlement-name may be less direct than was suggested in Part 1.

The township of Belswardine was transferred to Cressage

from Leighton in 1885.

1. BELSWARDINE (SJ 603033)

The township-name, which means 'Bēdel's enclosed settlement', is discussed in Part **1**.

BELSWARDINE HALL. BROOK HOUSES, BROOKHOUSES PLANTATION, cf. Rob. *Atte Brok'* 1261-2 *ForProc*, Rob. *Attbroke* 1271-2 *ib.* By Sheinton Brook. CHILDE'S PLANTATION, a family named *Childe* occurs 1790 PR(L) 2. JUBILEE PLANTATION. THE MOAT (*Mote* 1848 *TA*), MOAT PLANTATION. NEW PLANTATION. RABBIT WARREN PLANTATION. UPPER SLOPES (1848 *TA*), SLOPES COPPICE. The coppice is shown on *TAMap.* THE TICKNALL, *Ticknall Field and Rough* 1848 *TA*. WITHY BEDS.

Field-Names

Forms in (a) are 1848 *TA* (for Leighton).

(a) Alderley Lsw; Alder Tree Pce (adjoins preceding); Further Apnall, Hither Hapnall; Bare Butts (a large field, *butts* perhaps used of strips); Boggy Mdw; Bogs (adjoins preceding); Brickkiln Mdw; Bullock Lsw, Little - -; Calves Wd Pce, Little Calves Wd; Coney Green (probably a form of **coninger**); Gorsy Fd; Grazing Slang (this and Meadow - lie along Sheinton Brook); Heath Fd; Hither Patch; Holebrooks Pce; Langleys, Great and Little; Mares Lea; Meadow, Lower and Upper; Mdw Slang; New Inclosure; Orchard Pce; Ox Pasture; Big and Little Park (the outline of the park is clearly visible on *TAMap*); Peartree Fd; Tarts Lower and Upper Pce; Thistly Lsw; Wigwigs Hays (adjoins Wigwig in Much Wenlock, *v.* **(ge)hæg**).

2. CRESSAGE (SJ 593040)

LADY OAK. See the discussion of Cressage in Part **1** and *supra* for an account of this tree.

BUTLER'S PLANTATION. CRESSAGE BRIDGE (1833 OS), FM and HO. CROWN INN, *The Crowne Head, The Crown Yard* 1612 *LDR*. FELLEAR COPPICE, *Fell Lea* 1808 *VCH, Fell Lea Coppice* 1842 *TA, Filley Rough* adjoins. LORD'S COPPICE, 1833 OS, 1842 *TA*. THE MOUNT, a large house. NEW BUILDING, 1833 OS. OLD HALL, on the site of the medieval manor house, and in the bailey of a motte-and-bailey castle. PARK COPPICE AND COTTAGE, *Cressage Park* (in Harley) and *Park Coppice* are on 1833 OS, and the *Park* is mentioned 1846 *SRO 168*. ROGERS ROUGH, a family named *Rogers* occurs 1754-1810 PR(L) 2. TUDOR'S PLANTATION, a family named *Tudor* occurs 1811 PR(L) 2. WOOD LANE, 1786 *VCH*.

Field-Names

Forms in (a) are 1842 *TA*, except for those dated 1808, 1813, which are *VCH*. Early forms dated n.d., p.1249, 1269, 1335, 1433, 1469, 1509, 1564, 1586, 1623, 1797 are *VCH*, 1612, 1682, 1700, 1742 are *LDR*, 1746, 1747 are *SRO 168*.

VCH 73 names the common fields as Hurst Field (also called West or Lady Oak), Hay Field (or Field towards Morton) and Lee Field (or Field towards Harley).

(a) Armstrongs Mdw; Barn Fd; Barn Lsw (2, the name occurs 1746); Barn Mdw (2); Barn Yd (*Far and Near - -* 1747); Barras Head (*Barrows Head* 1747, the westernmost of a group of fields which lie between the Shrewsbury road and the Severn: the others are Briary Barras, Big and Little -, Bosom -, Severn -: OFr, ME **barras** 'barrier', here used of flood banks: Bosom may refer to shape); Belswardine Fd and Mdw, Little Belswardine Hill (*Belsadyne Hill* 1612); Bennetts Bower; Bens Lawns (*v.* Long Lawn *infra*); Big Fd; Big Mdw; Blakemoor, Big Little, Pike and Pritchards - (*Blakmore* 1612, *Blakemore* 1682, *Black Moore* 1747, 'black marsh', a tract of land adjoining Bromley Moor: Pike - has a pointed end); Boycotts Mdw; Brickkiln Lsw; Britch Mdw and Well, Lower and Upper Britch (*v.* **bryce**); Broad Croft (adjoins Harley Road Croft *infra*); Broad Lsw (3); Bromley Moor, Big, Little and Grazing - - (*Bromley Moore* 1586, *- Yate* 1612, *Broomley Moore* 1747, *v.* **brōm, lēah, mōr**, the eastern part of a tract which extends into Harnage); Brook Lsw; Broom Lsw; Budge Way 1808; Calves Croft (2); Big and Little Carrotty Lsw; Cocker Hills (*Cockhyll* 1586, *Cocks Hill* 1747, *Cockhol* 1797); Cockrain, Cockerdine 1813; Common Moor, Moor Head, Middle and Farther Moor (adjoins Higgins Moor, - Head is *The*

More Head 1612, *Ye Moorehead* 1682); Coneyry, Flat and Sideland (*Conery, Great* - 1746, *Coneygry* 1797, *v.* **coninger**: Sideland Coneyry is by a stream); Coppice (*Great* -, - *Lsw* 1746, *Little Copy Ground* 1747); Corner Pce (triangular, by a road); Cote Lsw; Cottage Lsw; Criftin 1808 (*Criftins* 1797, *v.* ***cryfting**); Croft (*freq*); Croft below House; Croft by Coppice; Davies Hill; Diamond (very roughly so shaped); The Didgeberry (*Dyddesbury* 1586, *Diche Bery Sych* 1612, *Dick Berry Such* 1682: the 1586 and 1842 forms are consistent, see Part **I**, 136, for the interchange of *-des-* and *-dge-*, the *LDR* forms may have substitution of 'ditch' for first el., -berry may be **beorg** 'tumulus', *Sych, Such* is **sīc** 'small stream'); Far Coppice Lsw; Far End Flg (in the area of Hay Field); Far Fd; Farmers Patch; Far Mdw; Fenny Mdw (Great - - 1808, cf. *Feny House* 1747, *v.* **fennig**); Four Acres (*v.* Seven Acres); Fox Holes (*Foxs Hole* 1746, *Fox's Hole Piece* 1747); Gallow Tree Lsw 1808 (*Gallowestrelesowe* 1586); Gardens (a large field by Wood Lane); Glebe Pce; Goodbys Pit (probably *The Gold Eye Pit* 1612, *Goldey Pitt* 1682, *v.* **golde**, **ēg**); Gorst Fd (2, *v.* **gorst**); The Gospel (two fields away from Leighton boundary); Grange Lane End (1747, by a road to Harnage Grange); Gratenal Bank (*Gridnall Bank* 1700 *et seq LDR*); Gravel Hill; The Grazing and Little Mdw (one field); Greenhill Bank 1808; Green Lsw 1808 (1747); Harley Road Croft, Further Road Croft (two large fields by road to Harley, Croft is unusual for fields of this size: Broad Croft is a small field N. of the other two, and Gardens adjoins on the W.); Harnage Way; Hays Mdw, Far and Near Broad Hays, Long, Near, Rough and Thistly Hays (*Hay* 1232 Ch, *Hey* 1335, *Hayes or Middle Hayes* 1509, *Hayes* 1564, *Hayes Yate* 1612, this area is the eastern part of the 13th-cent. wood called *Haya, v.* Hayes Coppice in Harnage: *Luteheye* 1433 - an assart - may be 'little Hay'); Heart Furlong (roughly heart-shaped); Higgins Lower, Middle and Upper Lsw, Higgins Moor; Hither Dingle, Far - - (between R. Severn and Shrewsbury road, E. of village: the hollow here must be less dramatic than those usually denoted by *dingle*: cf. *Dingell Grange* 1747); The Hurn 1808 (*v.* **hyrne**); Hurst, Far and Near Hurst, Far and Near Hurst Bank (*Over and Lower Hurst, Pigs Yard or The Hurst* 1747, *Upper Hurst* 1797, *v.* **hyrst** 'wooded hill', this gave name to a common field); Isaacs Lsw; Lady Oak, Far and Near (*Lady Oak* 1747, *v. supra*); Little Fd (between Nigher Fd and Near Fd); Little Fd, Far and Near - - (either side of Big Fd); Little Mdw (this, Long Mdw and Severn Mdw adjoin R. Severn); Long Lands (1700,42 *The Longe Lands* 1612), Long Lawn (on either side of Wenlock road, Bens Lawns adjoins Long Lands, cf. *Long Lawns* 1797, the correct form is probably - Lands, as Lawn would be unusual away from buildings); Long Mdw; Low Cow Pasture; Lower Shineton Mdw (near Sheinton boundary); Lower Stile 1808; Marsh Mdw, Big and Little Marsh (*Marche Meadowe* 1612, *Ye March Meadow* 1682, *v.* **mersc**); Meadow (cf. *Over and Lower* - 1747); Mill Croft, Mill

Pool, Mill Pool Croft (*v.* VCH 76 for the history of Cressage Mill); Mill Yd 1808; Moss 1808; New Pasture; New Tyning (3, cf. *New Tinning* 1746, *v.* **tȳning**); Near Fd, Nigher Fd (either side of Little Fd); Nocks Hill (not near Nocks Wd); Nocks Wd, Lower - -, The Woods, Little Wood (adjacent fields W. of the Harley road, cf. *The Nooks, The Nooks or Over Wood, Over Wood, Lower Wood* 1747); No Man's Patch (a tiny field by Bromley Moor); Nursery Fd, Pce under Nursery (6" map shows a small clump of trees); Old Church Yd (the church of St Samson was demolished in 1840); Old Moor 1808; The Omar (*Holemore* 1269, *Homer* 1612, *Holmere* 1742, *Home Moore* 1747, *Homer, Farther and Upper* - 1797, 'hollow marsh', *v.* **holh**, **mōr**); Onion Bed; The Paddock; Park Gate Pce (by Cressage Park); Patch (several); Piece by Glebe; The Pike 1808; Plantation; Plocks Brook, Farther - -, Little New - -, Near, Middle and Upper Plocks (*Le Plokkes, Plokkesbroke* 1433, *The Plock* 1564, *Plocks Brook* 1612, *Plox Brook* 1797; *plock* is a Sa and He word for a small piece of land); Pool Mdw (*Poole Meadowe* 1612); Pool Pce; Pritchards Wd, Big - -; Quillett (a tiny strip of land on the bank of R. Severn); Robins Mdw; Rough Lsw (1747); Rough Mdw; Rough Pasture; Roundabout (two long, narrow fields, no apparent reason for n.); Seven Acres (adjoins Four acres, the comparative sizes are appropriate); Severn Mdw; Shore, Little -, Shore Bank (*Shore Styll* 1612, - *Style* 1682, *Upper and Lower Shore* 1747, apparently *shore* in the sense 'slope', *v.* ***scora**); Sitch 1808 (*Seitch* 1747), Long, Home, Great and Little Sitch 1813 (*v.* **sīc**); Slang Coppice (Coppice Fd, Far Coppice Pce adjoin); The Slangs (two narrow strips); Snape (1747, *The Snape Heade, Snape Meadowe* 1612, *v.* ***snæp** 'boggy place'); Big and Little Spanish Hays (*Spanish Heath* 1746, FN 32 suggests that liquorice was grown here); Spoonless Bank and Mdw, Big Spoonless; Lower and Upper Staff Gates; Stone Mdw; Three Cornered Patch (2); Three Cornered Pce (2); Townsend, Upper - (*Cressage Townesende* 1612, at western end of village); Turnpike Yd (the Shrewsbury road was turnpiked in 1752); Wall Stile (1808); Well Lsw; Wicket Tree Lsw (mountain ash, FN 48); Wills Lea, Big, Far, Little and Near (*Wilsley Hedge, The Wills Lee* 1612, *Ye Wiles Lee, Welsley Hedge* 1682, Wills Leas 1808); Withimoor Pasture, Far Withimoor Pool (*Withy Moor* 1747, adjoins Bromley Moor, 'willow marsh or pond', *v.* **wīðig**, **mōr**, **mere**, *Whitmore Poole* 1612 *et seq LDR* may be the same place); Yewtree Lsw.

(b) *Big Croft* 1747; *Bridgwall* 1612, - *Head and Hedge* 1682; *Brook Feld* 1746; *Broom Close* 1746; *Brotenhulle* p.1249 (associated with the mill); *Bryery Furlonge* 1612, *Briery Furlong* 1682; *Calldwall Headge* 1612, - *Head* 1682 ('cold spring'. *v.* **cald**, **wælle**); *Cauther Croft* 1612, - *Craft* 1682 (probably dialect *cather* 'hemp', *v.* FN 31); *Copped Oake* 1612, 1682 (*v.* **coppede**); *Cows Pasture* 1747; *Cressage Coppice* 1747; *Culver Croft* 1747 (*v.* **culfre**); *The Cursed Oaks* 1433 (*v.*

discussion of Cressage *supra*); *The End Croft* 1787; *The xi Lande* 1586 ('eleven strips'); *Far Moor* 1747; *Fern Meadow, Great, Little and Upper,* 1747; *Fox's Meadow, Little Fox Lsw* 1746; *Grete* 1269 (*v.* **grēot** 'gravel' and cf. Greete in Part **1**); *Hannd Stock* 1612, *Handstock* 1682; *The Harpe* 1612, *Ye Harp* 1682; *Hempbut* 1747; *Heyfeld* 1433 (a common field, *Hey-* could be 'high' or 'hay'); *The Hill, Little, New and Side Hill* 1747; *Home Ground* 1747; *Hook Lsw* 1746; *Horsecroft* 1433; *Hurstfeld* 1433 (a common field, *v.* Hurst in (a)); *Layharesmere* n.d.; *Leefeld* 1433 (a common field, *v.* **lēah**); *Long Brook* 1746; *Long Lsw* 1746; *Longley Meadow* 1469; *Marlederiding* 1269 ('marled clearing', *v.* **rydding**); *Medewebarowe* 1433 (one of three *-barowe* ns. in this source, probably 'grove by a meadow', *v.* **mǣd**, **bearu**); *Mere Tree* 1612, *Ye Mear Tree* 1682 (*v.* **(ge)mǣre**); *Le Meryngdon* 1433; *The Myll Heald* 1612, *Ye Mill Heale* 1682 (*v.* **helde**); *Miller Ross and Lsw* 1747; *Mullards Wood* 1747; *New Piece* 1746; *Oak Lsw* 1747; *Pond Meadow* 1747; *Pound Lsw* 1746; *Prill* 1747 (dialect *prill* 'streamlet'); *Samsons But* 1612, *Sampsons Butt* 1682 (the ancient church was dedicated to St Samson); *Sheep Fold and Lsw* 1746; *Short Croft* 1797; *The xvid Dole* 1612, *Ye Sixteen Peny Dole* 1682 (*v.* **dāl**); *Spring Lsw* 1746; *Stone Lsw* 1797; *Stublebarowe* 1433 (apparently 'stubble grove', but *Stuble-* may be from earlier *stub-hyll*, 'stump-hill'); *Thornybarowe* 1433 ('thorny grove'); *The 3 Corner Lsw* 1747; *Trees Corner Piece* 1746; *Trees Lsw* 1747; *Upper Croft* 1797; *Upperyght Dole* 1433 (*v.* **dāl**, the significance of 'upright' is not clear); *Wayside Lsw* 1747; *Wedershull* 1433; *The Wood* 1747; *Le Wood Lsw* 1623; *Wooller Hill* 1747; *The Yard* 1747.

Frodesley

The parish-name, which means 'Frōd's clearing', is discussed in Part **1**.

BENTLEYFORD 1833 OS. The ford is *vadum de Benetleya* 1221 Eyton. 'Bent-grass clearing', *v.* **beonet**, **lēah**, a common p.n. *TAMap* shows the house but does not name it: a field called *Bently Dingle* is a short distance S.

RAMSHURST (lost)

Romenehurst 1250 Eyton, *Romenhurst* 1306 ib
Bromeshurst 1271-2 *Ass*

Romeshurst 1291-2 *Ass*, 1301 SAC, 1315 Ipm, 1316 Pat, 1346 Cl
Rammeshurst 1317,39,63 Pat
Rameshurst 1416 AD, *Rameshersi or Rameshurt* 1421 Cl

Most of the forms suggest 'wooded hill where wild garlic grows', *v.* **hramsa**, **hyrst**. The *-n-* forms are unexplained. The *Brom-* form may fairly be regarded as a chance aberration.

VCH 81 suggests that the site of this lost settlement is marked by the series of fields called *Romps* in *TA*, E. of Lodge Fm.

ROW BROOK, COPPICE AND FM. A habitation site here is *Fredeleesrowe* l.13th *ForProc* (i.e. 'Frodesley's row'), *The Row* 1614 PR(L) 6, *The Rowe* 1621,40 ib, *Ye Row* 1722 ib, *Rowe Leasow, Garden and Meadow* 1840 *TA*(Wheatall). *v.* **rāw** 'row of houses'. VCH 80 says the Coppice is mentioned in 1460. ROW BROOK was earlier *Kusibroc, Kusybroc* 1221 Eyton. This also became a habitation name: it is *Cussibruck* 1585, *Cussibracke* 1597, *Cosy Brooke* 1621 PR(L) 6. There does not appear to be a parallel for this stream-name. Formally it could consist of the OE pers.n. *Cus(s)a* with **-ing-** and **brōc**.

CAUSEWAYWOOD COPPICE, *v.* Ruckley and Langley *infra.* COPPICE HO, 1810 PR(L) 4, 1833 OS, adjoins preceding. FOX COVERT, the wood is shown, but not named, on *TAMap.* FRODESLEY COTTAGES. FRODESLEY LANE, 1833 OS, the house is shown on *TAMap.* FRODESLEY LODGE, the house (shown on *TAMap*) is described in VCH 81 under the name Lodge Fm. HOBSLEY COPPICE, 1833 OS, 1844 *TA*, *Hobsleys* 1844 *TA.* LODGE HILL, LODGEHILL COPPICE, by Frodesley Lodge. LONGNORGREEN, *Longner Green* 1833 OS, *The Green* 1844 *TA*, on Longnor boundary. PARK FM, *Frodesly Park* 1799 Townson, *Frodesley Park* 1833 OS: two fields called *Park Leasow* adjoin on *TAMap.* *v.* VCH 80 for an account of the park. SWAN INN. WATLING STREET.

Field-Names

Forms in (a) are 1844 *TA*. Early forms are Eyton unless otherwise stated.

(a) Aldery Lsw; Aldery Mdw; Angle Close (between a road and parish boundary); Bakewells Croft; Bank Lsw; Banky Lsw; The Barley, Barley Mdw (*Ber(r)eleg* (an assart) 1221, *Berlegh* (a field) 1298, 'barley clearing', *v.* **bere**, **lēah**); Barn Fd; Barn Lsw and Mdw; Barn Yd (5); Bar Stile; Beggars Bank, Lower and Big - - (the fields straddle Watling Street S.W. of the village, a derogatory term for poor land); Benty Lsw (bent grass); Bottom Lsw; Brickkiln Lsw, Near - - (on either side of Brick Work, *v.* VCH 83); Broad Lsw, Lower and Upper; Brook Lsw; Brook Yd; Butchers Bank; Calves Patch, Big - -; Calves Patch (not near preceding); Caresleys, Lower and Upper; Champions Bury, Far and Near (Bury may be **beorg** 'tumulus', VCH 80 notes that a barrow is recorded elsewhere in the parish); Chesters Lsw (adjoins Watling Street S.W. of the village crossroads); Clover Close; Clover Fd; Coalpit Lsw (*v.* VCH 83 for coalmining in Frodesley); Conduit, Big, Little, Little Lower, Far and Middle; The Coppice, Coppice Fd; Far and Near Coppice; Coppice Fd, Lsw and Mdw; Coppice Lsw, Further - -, Near Coppy Lsw; Copy Pasture, Far and Near, Little Copy Lsw ('coppice'); Cote Lsw and Yd; Cow Lsw (2); Cow Pasture (3); Cross Garden, Great, Little and Far Cross, Far Little Cross (not at a crossroads or junction, VCH 80 says *The Cross Yate* was open-field land in 15th); Big and Little Deerhouse Lsw (within the park wall, VCH 80); Docky Lsw, Near, Middle and Lower; Eight Days Math (i.e. mowing); Far Mdw; Flax Ground; Foggy Pce (coarse grass); Footway Lsw, Lower and Upper; Frodesley Hill, Hill Plantation; The Furlong, Middle and Lower Furlong (adjoining, N.E. of village); Gate Lsw, Far and Upper; Glebe; Gorsty Bank (*v.* **gorstig**); Green Lsw; Green Mdw, Little Green Pce (adjoining Longnorgreen); The Green Reans (drainage channels); Half Close (a small field by the church); Hay Pool (*Heypoll, Over* - 1419 VCH, *v.* **(ge)hæg**, **pōl**, there are small pools in this area: *Hey-* may be *La Haie de Frodesley* 1221); Hemp Yd (2); Hickmans Pce (several large fields); Hobsons Slang (by Row Brook); Big and Little Hollies; Holly Castle (perhaps a jocular n. for a holly thicket); Horse Pasture; Hughes Mdw; Hunts Mdw; Inch Pit and Pool (6" map shows a marlpit); Kempsalls, Long (*Kemeshall* 1222, *Kelmeshale, -hall* 1291-8, *Kelmeshal* 1298, 1323, 'Cēnhelm's nook', *v.* **halh**); Kiln Bank; Kings Yd; Big and Little Kites Pce; Lady Mdw; Lake Lsw and Mdw (*Lakemedewe* 1298, *v.* **lacu**, tiny streams cross the line of Watling Street near here); Lawley Lsw, Far and Near Lawley Pce (from Lawley in Longnor); Lawn, Pleasure Ground (by church: the enclosures round the church are the same on *TAMap* and on the early 20th-cent 6"); Lees Land and Ground (near but not adjacent, *v.* **lǣs**);

Little Calves Patch (adjoins Cow Pasture, not near Calves Patch *supra*); Little Etchley (cf. Longnor f.ns.); Little Mdw (2); Little Orchard; Little Triangle (minute patch in road junction); Long Fd, Far and Near; Longfords Mdw; Long Lsw (2); Longnor Patch (adjoins Longnor); Lower Mdw; Lower Milking Fold; Meadow, Big and Little (adjacent, by Row Brook); The Meadow (2); Middle Fd; Middle Pce (2); Mill Pool Lsw (by Fox Covert, on Row Brook); Morgans Lsw, Lower and Upper; New Inclosure from Hill, New Plantation (adjoining, by Frodesley Hill); New Mdw; The Orchard; Outlet (by Bentleyford, pasture adjoining winter cattle sheds, FN 35); Ox Ground; Ox Lsw (3); Ox Pasture (2); Park Mdw (adjoins Deerhouse Lsw); Parsons Pce (*Parsons Leasow* 1607 VCH); Patch (unusually big for this term); Great and Little Patch (near preceding, also bigger than usual); Peacock Pool (no pool on 6"); Peartree Yd; Pikey Lsw (one pointed end); Pit Ground, Big and Little; Pit Lsw (*v.* Coalpit Lsw); Pool Pce (2); Quarry Lsw; Rail Mdw, Far and Near; The Romps, Upper Middle and Far Romps, The New Romps (probably the site of the lost settlement of *Ramshurst, supra*); Rough, Great and Long, Little Rough, Far and Near, Rough Close, Rough Ground, Lower and Upper (all in N.W. corner of parish); Sadlers Lsw; Saw Pit Yd; Shearas Patch, Shearers - (adjacent fields); Sheep Lsw; Slang (along a road); The Sling (very long and narrow); Smiths Yd; Stakeley (*Le Stakedeleye* 1313 *SBL 3609*, 'staked-out clearing', *v.* **lēah**); Lower Stockings (*v.* ***stoccing**); Thirsty Pce; Thistly Lsw; Three Cornered Pce (not triangular); Town Mdw, Great - - (adjoins village); Townsend Pce (at N. end of village); Tuckers Mdw; Upper Yd; Way Lsw (by Longnor road); Weavers Orchard; Well Croft; Well Mdw (2); Whin Mdw; Wood Green, Far and Near; Wood Lsw, Lower and Upper; Yewtree Lsw.

(b) *Acysvey, Acyswey* 1221 (the first ref. is to a great oak here so the first el. may be 'oaks' though the spelling is unusual, *v.* **weg**); *Aldetonesmedwe* 1323 (perhaps a ref. to a deserted settlement-site, *v.* **ald, tūn, mǣd**); *Barcle* 15th VCH (a wood, *v.* **beorc, lēah**); *Barunde* (?recte *Baruude*) 15th VCH (a wood, possibly 'boar wood'); *Bradleyespolle* ('pool of the broad clearing', cf. *Bradelegesty* e.13th HAC, in the adjacent parish of Longnor, 'path to *Bradley*', *v.* **brād, lēah, pōl, stīg**); *Chepmedue, Keupmedwe* 1221 (*v.* **cȳpe** 'basket for catching fish', **mǣd**); *Crompelegh* 1298 ('crooked clearing', *v.* **crumb, lēah**); *Hewehtsty* 1221, *Hevedsti* 1222 ('chief path', *v.* **hēafod, stīg**); *Hethei* 1310 (John *de Hetheye* appears 1261-2 *ForProc* in Longnor, *v.* **hǣð**, second el. probably **(ge)hæg**); *The Hoo* 1323 (*v.* **hōh**); *Linleye* 1291-2 ('flax clearing', *v.* **līn, lēah**); *Longerhull* 1291-8 (perhaps 'Longnor hill'); *The Lowe* 1323 (*v.* **hlāw**); *Lude, Lude-sparkeheswey* 1221 (*Lude* is the stream-name *Hlȳde* 'loud one', the addition to the second ref. may contain a ME derivative of OE ***spearca** 'brushwood' and **weg**); *Lydehurst* 15th VCH (*v.*

hyrst, the first el. could be the stream-name *Hlȳde*); *The Milnemore* 1291-8 (*v.* **myln**, **mōr**); *Neustokkynge* 1310 (an assart, *v.* **nīwe**, ***stoccing**); *Poklbroc* 1222-c.1230 HAC, *Powelbrok* 1291-8 (*v.* **brōc**, first el. looks like a diminutive in *-el* of **pohha** 'pouch'); *The Russileye* 1291-8 ('rushy clearing', *v.* **lēah**, first el. OE **riscig*); *Shyrmore* 15th VCH (probably 'boundary marsh', cf. the same n. in Harnage *supra*); *Sullakemor* 1221 ('gully stream marsh', *v.* **sulh**, **lacu**, **mōr**); *Swe(t)heley* 1221 (probably 'sweet clearing', *v.* **swēte**, **lēah**); *Thuaheth* 1221 (*v.* **hǣð**, first el. uncertain); *Togthesleye* (*v.* **lēah**, first el. obscure); *Voxhoks-more* 1298 (a wood, *v.* **mōr**, first el. uncertain); *Wisebroc* 1222, *Wisiebrokę* 1222-c.1230 HAC, *Wysebrok* 1291-2 (Ekwall, RN 465-7, suggests that there was an OE river-name *Wise*, related to *wāse* 'mud' and *wisse* 'meadow', and he cites the Sa name in this discussion: *v.* Whissey Brook Lsw and Mdw in Longnor, *infra*).

Harley

The parish-name, which means 'rock wood or clearing', is discussed in Part 1.

BLAKEWAY FM (1833 OS), COPPICE (1714 *VCH*) and HOLLOW. *Blakewey* 1221-2 (p), 1271-2 *Ass*, 1301 SAC, *-weye* 1261-2 *ForProc* (p), *-way* 1281 MGS (p). *v.* **blæc**, **weg**. The surnames Blakeway and Blackway, which are commonest in the west midlands, probably derive from this place.

ROWLEY, *Rouleye* 1331 *VCH*, *Rowley* 1600 *ib*, *Rowley Farm* 1711 *ib*. The first ref. is to a wood, the 1600 one is to the farm. 'Rough wood or clearing', *v.* **rūh**, **lēah**, a fairly common p.n.

YARCHESTER (not on modern maps), *Harechester* 1564,80 *VCH*, *Yarchester Cot* 1833 OS. A Roman villa has been partially excavated here; *v.* **ceaster**, which is used in the imprecise manner characteristic of western counties. The first el. may be **hara** 'hare', in which case this is a mocking name of Owl's Castle type. The site is between Harley Bridge and Red House, by the road from Harley to Much Wenlock.

CASTLEHILL, *Castle Hill* 1799 VCH, 1833 OS, cf. *Castle Pool Leasow* 1841 *TA*. VCH 87 says the name derives from a crenellated tower which was built in 1791. COTTAGE COPPICE. 1833 OS marks *Yarchester Cot* here, *v. supra*, CRESSAGE PK, *The Park* 1841 *TA*, *v.* Park Cottages in Cressage. THE CROW'S NEST. Gazetteer lists three other instances in the county. DOMAS, 1833 OS. This may be an ancient settlement. VCH 87 suggests that it represents one of the four manors which were in Harley before 1066. No early refs. have been noted, however. EDGE WD. Cf. *Mons Eggetop* 1331 *VCH*, *The Edge*, *Mounslowes Edge* 1604 *ib*, *Smiths Edge alias Suttons Edge* 1611 *ib*, *Wenlock Edge in Harley* 1664 *ib*. *v.* **ecg**, **topp**. This is the northern end of Wenlock Edge. FORGE BARN, 1833 OS. This refers to an iron forge (VCH 86, 89). It is *The Smithy* 1564 *VCH*, *The Old Smithy Place* 1628 *ib*, *Harley Forge* 1638 *ib*, *Old Forge* 1833 OS. FEATHERS INN. This is an 18th-cent. house converted to an inn e.19th (VCH 87). HARLEY BRIDGE. HARLEY BROOK. Earlier *Plash Brook*, which is *flumen Plesshe* 1331 *VCH*, *Pleysh Brook* 1564 *ib*, *Plashbrook* 1612 *LDR*. In 1841 *TA*, *Plash Brook* occurs as the n. of a field by the stream. *v.* **plæsc**, which is considered to mean 'shallow piece of standing water'. Perhaps there were shallow pools in the meanders of the brook. HARLEY HILL, cf. *Hill Ground and Piece* 1841 *TA*. This may be the *Eggetop* of the 1331 ref. quoted under Edge Wd *supra*. HARLEY MILL. VCH 89 gives an account of mills in the parish. *TAMap* shows this mill and *Mill Bank and Meadow* adjoining. HARLEY TOWER, 1833 OS, now Harley Court, built early 19th (VCH 87). MERRISHAW, *Merrishwood* 1833 OS, *v.* **mer(i)sc**, **sceaga**. RED HO, 1883 *VCH*.

Field-Names

Forms in (a) are 1841 *TA*, except those dated 1824, which are *LDR*. Early forms dated 1612, 1679 are *LDR*; others for which no source is given are *VCH*.

There are references in 1340 *VCH* to a field towards Wigwig and a field towards Cressage, in 1349 *ib* there is a field towards Blakeway, and n.d. *ib* a field towards Belswardine. In 1612 *LDR* there are references to East Field, West Field and North Field, and these open fields continue to be mentioned until 1734 (VCH 86).

(a) Acre Pce; Bags, Big and Little; Bank Fd (2); Bank Lsw; Bardine Lsw; Barley Lsw; Barn Fd (2); Barn Lsw; Barn Yd; Benbow Fd; Beyond the Green (adjoins Rowley); Big Hales (*v.* **halh**); Big Lsw (two large fields); Blakeway Lsw (*v. supra*); Bogs; The Bogs; Brickkiln Lsw; Brickkiln Mdw; Briery Coppice (1833 OS), - - Lsw (cf. *Briery Meadow* 1714 VCH); Far Brooms, Rocky Broom; Bucks Heap and Lsw; Bulls Grove; Butchers Mdw 1824; Calves Croft (2); Claypit Lsw (*The Claypit* 1659); Cockadine, - Bank (*Cockadine Croft* 1681, 1734, the fields are on either side of Harley Brook, perhaps a **denu** n.); Little Cold Furlong (*Cold Furlong* 1604); Colswet; Coney Burrow, First and Upper (near but not adjacent: VCH 86 says that First - -, which is nearest the village, was earlier *The Conygree* 1598, *Coney Green* 1734-5, *v.* **coninger**); Coppice Lsw; Corn Fd; Cote Lsw, Lsw above the Cote; Cote Lsw, Upper - -, Croft by the Cote (no buildings shown for these two groups of ns.); Cow Lsw (3); Cow Pasture, Great and Lower, Rough Cow Lsw (a plan 1714 *VCH* shows *Cow Leasow* in this area, W. of Blakeway); Crabtree Lsw (*Great and Little Crab Tree Meadow, The Crab Tree Rough* 1714); Croft (*freq*); Croft behind House; Dykes Lsw; Feggy Lsw (*Feggie Lesow* 1537, from dialect *feg* 'coarse grass'); Field; The Field; Field above Barn; Field above the Cote (no building); Five Acre Fd; Flat Fd; Flat Mdw; Furlong, Long - (both S.W. of Harley, cf. *The Furlong* 1664); Glebe Lsw; Gorsty Rock (*v.* ***gorstig**); Gravel Hole Fd; Gully Furlong 1824; Harlands (possibly *Harlow* 1340); Hayes, Great and Rough, Great Rough Hays, Lower and Upper Hay Fd (these fields occupy an area S. of the village, cf. *Rough Hayes* 1595, *Rough Hay* 1600: *v.* **(ge)hæg**, there was much woodland in the S. and W. of the parish (VCH 86)); Hay Fd (2, cf. *The Hey Field* 1612, *The Hayfields, Hayfield Meadow* 1683, *v.* **hēg**); Holding Bank (*Haledene* n.d., *Holden* 1349, perhaps a compound of **halh** and **denu**, there is a small valley here); Horse Fd, Great and Little (*The Horse Pasture* 1714); Horse Pce; House Mdw; Jarmans Lsw; Knocks Lsw; Langleys Croft; Lay Fd (perhaps *The Lea* 1612, *v.* **lǣge**, 'fallow, uncultivated'); The Leasow 1824; Leasow (several); Lewis's Lsw; Lime Kilns, Piece by - -, Piece above - -, Limekiln Pce (these are at the foot of Wenlock Edge: New Work and Lime Quarry on 1833 OS refer to the northern site, the one to the S. is *Lyme Piece* 1714: a 1714 lease of Blakeway Fm refers to a Limekiln at Blakeway Lane head, and Thomas Blakeway pays 20d *pro le lyme kill* in 1522); Little Bank; Little Mdw; Long Fd; Long Hill; Long Lsw; Long and Little Lsw (a single field); Lords Coppice, Far and Near Coppice Lsw; Lower Barn Pce; Lower Fd (Upper Fd adjoins); Lower Pce; Malthouse Mdw; Mare Lsw, Little - -; Meadow (*freq*); Meadow below House; Meadow by Barn Yd; Mill Lsw (by a windmill, which was demolished 1960); Mitland Lsw, Mitland Pool Lsw, Lower Mitland (beside a stream junction, so first el. possibly **gemȳðe**: *Mittenhill* 1664 may be related); Near Allweeds; Near

Croft; Near Lsw; New Inclosure; New Lsw; Orchard; Ox Lsw; Park Lsw, Higher and Lower Park Ground (by Cressage Park); Peartree Lsw (*Peartree Yard* 1714, on a plan which shows *Peartree Mead* on the opposite side of Blakeway Fm); Piece along Road; Piece from Glebe; Pit Marsh; Pool Bank; Quillet (tiny, triangular piece); Radley, - Bank and Ground; Rail Lsw; Rogers Lsw; Rough (*freq*, a series of strips along Harley Brook and a tributary); Round Thorn (*Round Thorny Leasow* 1681); Rowley Lsw (*v. supra*); Rushy Mdw 1824; Sandy Brook, The Sandy Lsw, Sandy Mdw (in northern tip of parish, *Sandebrook, The - Leasow* 1612, *Sandy Brook Bank* 1664, *Sandy Bank Leasow* 1683); Sapling Lsw (1714); Sapper Wing Lsw (*Sapper Whing* - 1714); Schutters Mdw 1824 (*Scutterfurlong* 1612, *The Scutters Furlong* 1679); Sedning Coneyry (adjoins First Coney Burrow, *v. supra*); Sheep Lsw; Slang (3); Slang under Wood (long strip at foot of Wenlock Edge); Smiths Bank; Smiths Lsw; Smiths Mdw 1824; Southern Mdw 1824; Spratts Little and Upper Lsw; Spring Lsw, Great and Little; The Springs, Near, Middle and Grazing Springs (*The Springs* 1564, 1734, *The Springs alias The Forge Leasow* 1638, cf. Upper Springs in Kenley *infra*); Stocking, - Ground, Middle Stocking, Stockings, - Mdw (these fields cover a wide area N. of Harley Brook, S.W. of the village, cf. *The Stockings* 1664 and *Harleyestokyng* 1414-15, *v.* ***stoccing**); Stocking, Great, Little and Long (another series of fields in S. point of parish, *Stockings, The Further* - 1714); Stony Fd (by Stone Ho in Kenley); Stony Stiles; Upper Ground, Far and Near, Upper Pce; Upper Rough; Wall Fd (1714, on a plan which shows four fields, *Wall Field, Upper* - -, *Wall Field Mead and Leasow*, spread out round Blakeway Fm); Way Lsw; Well Lsw; Well Patch; Wenlock Lsw; Wheat Fd; Whitfield, Great and Long (*White Field, Little and Great* - - 1714); Wigwig Gate (by Road to W.); The Yard (2); Yard Mdw.

(b) *Aldithestiele* n.d. ('Aldgȳð's stile', from a fem. pers.n. and **stigel**); *Bankyard* 1681, 1734; *Dudwell Bank and Meadow* 1664; *Ew(e)tree Leasow* 1604 ('yew-tree'); *Golding* 1664; *Hall Woods* 1664; *Hanetrugges* n.d. (perhaps for *Hauet-*, 'head ridges', *v.* **hēafod**, **hrycg**); *Harleyesmed* 1414-15 ('Harley's meadow', *v.* **mǣd**); *Harley Roo* 1610, - *Roe* 1628, - *Rooe* 1641 ('Harley row', *v.* **rāw**); *The Harp* 1612, *Harp Meadow* 1679 (referring to shape); *Hill Leasow* 1637-8; *Le Hyghe ȝate* 1331 (*v.* **hēah**, **geat**); *Kalenge Wood* 1331 ('disputed wood' from OFr **calenge**, cf. Callingwood St (DEPN), Callans Wd PN Wo 218); *Laynnynges* n.d.; *Long Meadow* 1714,34; *The Medewey Acre* 1349 ('meadow way acre'); *Mongetes* 1414-15; *Northcroft* 1414-15; *Nut Meadow* 1664; *Pirifeld* 1414-15 (*v.* **pirige**); *Le Polcroft* 1414-15 ('pool croft'); *Preiscroft* 1414-15; *Pulleys Bank* 1683 (probably a surname from Pulley near Shrewsbury); *Radeweyes Aker* 1340 (*v.* **æcer**, first word perhaps a p.n. 'red way' rather than a surname); *Ruben Mote* 1349 (perhaps referring to

The Moat in Cressage, which is near the parish boundary); *The Spring Gate* 1612; *Le Waretrerewe* 1421 ('gallows row', *v.* **wearg-trēow, rǣwe**); *Wethale* n.d. (probably 'wheat nook', *v.* **hwǣte, halh**); *Ye Wood End* 1747 PR(L) 2; *The Woodhouse or Springs* 1599 (*v.* The Springs *supra*); *Woodleasow* 1612.

Kenley

The parish-name, which means 'Cēna's clearing', is discussed in Part 1.

BROOMCROFT, LITTLE -, 1833 OS, *Bromicroft* 1204 Cur, *Bromcroft* 1242 Fees, *Brom(e)scroft* 1271-2 *Ass*: 'broomy enclosure', *v.* **brōmig, croft**. *Bromycroftelegh'* 1301 SAC has **lēah** added. Cf. Broomey Croft Fm PN Wa 19. VCH 93 suggests that this and Gippols were formerly hamlets.

GIPPOLS, *Gipcnol* c.1200 *ForProc, Giphole* 1261-2 *ib* (p), *Gypholes, Gippoles* (p), *Gyppeholes (p) 1271-2 ib, Gippel', Gippolis* 1274 RH (p), *Gyphole* 1327 SAS 3/VII (p), *Gippoles* 1363 Pat, *The Gibholes* 1628 *VCH, The Gibballs* 1679 *SBL 1329, Gippils* 1833 OS.

Three other instances of this name have been noted, two in Cu and one in L (Kesteven). The Cu names are *Gibholle* 1636 in Hesket in the Forest and *Gibhole* 1677 in Castle Sowerby (PN Cu 207, 248). The L name survives as Gipple Cottages in Syston, N. of Grantham. It is *Gyppehall* 1242-3 Fees, *Grangia de Gypol* 1281 QW, *Gyppole* 1384 Cl, *Gippulgrange* 1384 Pat.

This would appear to be a meaningful compound with **hol** 'hollow' as generic. The *-cnol* of the earliest form for the Sa example is outweighed by the other forms. The first el. is unexplained. The Sa place is by Hughley Brook, the L one on heathland, by Ermine Street.

FETCH HILL, 1841 *TA*. FURNACE LANE, OLD FURNACE (latter 1833 OS): VCH 93 says an iron furnace was erected in 1591. GIPPOLS DINGLE, 1841 *TA, v. supra*. THE GLEBE. KENLEY COMMON, *Lower, Middle, Upper and Far Common*

Piece 1841 *TA.* VCH 93 says this area was becoming known as Kenley Common in the 16th. KENLEY COPPICE, 1841 *TA*, cf. *mess. called The Coppies in Kenley* 1604 *VCH.* KENLEY GORSE. KENLEY HALL, cf. *Hall Leasow and Meadow* 1841 *TA.* VCH 94 says the house was called *The Upper Hall* in 1605. KENLEY PLANTATION. LEASOWS, 1833 OS. The house is shown on *TAMap* and there are many Leasow f.ns. in the vicinity. VCH 94 says the farm is first recorded in 1680. LORD'S POOL, *Lords Pool* 1841 *TA.* LOWER SPRINGS, *v.* Upper Springs *infra.* MAPP FM. A family called *Mapp(e)*, *Mape* appears in the mid-18th cent., PR(L) 1. MAYPOLE BANK, 1833 OS, 1841 *TA.* NEW HALL, 1833 OS, *Newhall* 1716 PR(L) 2. VCH 94 says that it was probably built before 1605, and was 'Mr Lacon's Lower Hall' in 1650, cf. Kenley Hall *supra.* STONE HO, 1833 OS. UPPER SPRINGS (near Lower Springs), cf. 'Thomas Russell of the Spring' 1799 PR(L) 2. The 1833 OS map has a single house called *Springs.* The area called Springs extended into Harley parish, *v.* Harley f.ns. *supra.*

Field-Names

Forms in (a) are 1841 *TA* except where otherwise stated.

(a) Baileys Rough, Large and Small; Bakers Mdw; The Bank, Near Bank (on the Kenley ridge); The Bank (2); Banky Fd; Barn Lsw (4); Barn Mdw (4); Bean Fd; Benty Lsw, Lower and Upper (bent grass); Big Mdw; Birches, Far and Near, Birch Pce, Lower and Upper (adjoining); Birchy Fd; Boggy Lsw, Little - -; Boggy Wall Brooks, The Bog (adjacent, Wall Brooks is further up the same stream); Botany Bay (on S. boundary of parish); Boundary (narrow strip between road and Cressage boundary); Bowling Green 1833 OS; Brickkiln Lsw; Bridge Lsw (2); Broad Lsw (2); Brook Fd; Brook Lsw (2); Bull Mdw; Calves Croft (by Cow Pasture); Calves Yd; Cinder Hearth (near Forge Barn in Harley); Clover Lsw (2); Cobblers Lsw; Cockshutt, Coppice, Footway and Miry - (*v.* ***cocc-sciete**); Coppice; The Coppice; High and Low Coppice; Coppice Lsw (2); Corner Mdw; Cow Lsw (2); Cow Pasture (2); Crabtree Lsw; Dingle, Middle and Upper; Far Big Lsw; Far Lsw (2); Far Yd; Field next Bishops; Feggs, Upper and Lower, The Feggs Lsw (rough grass); Ferny Bank, Upper, Lower and Little - -; Ferny Lsw; Flat Mdw, Lower - -; Footway Lsw (3); Lower Frame Yd, Upper Frame Gate (probably cloth-stretching frames); Franks Mdw; Gate Lsw; Gippols Mdw (*v.*

supra); Goose Mdw; Gorsty Lsw (*v.* **gorstig**); Green Lsw; Hamnetts Lsw; The Hayes (*v.* **gehæg**, Kenley was heavily wooded in the Middle Ages); Highlands Pce (by Highlands in Harnage); The Hill, Big and Little Hill (three fields on the Kenley ridge); Hodgkiss's Pce; Holly Bank; Big and Little Hopes (separated by Big Mdw, probably references to comparative fertility, cf. Small Hopes); Hop Yd; Horse Lsw; Howlerts Mdw and Rough; Jockey Lsw, Far and Near; Johns Lsw, Lower and Upper (Lower and Upper in a number of ns. in this parish indicates S. or N. of the road to New Hall); Kenley Lsw (on outskirts of village); Kings Mdw (*Kingesmed* 1203 SAS 2/X (FF), King's Meadow 1814 *SBL 6232*, Kings Corner is nearby and Queens Lsw adjoins, the significance of the n. is obscure, Kenley was not in royal ownership); Lambs Lsw; The Lawns (not near a house); Lsw above Garden, Lsw below -; Lsw above Madeley; Lsw near Shingless; Leys, Far, Lower and Middle; Little New Lsw; Long Lsw (4); Long Mdw; Long Slang (narrow strip by stream); Lower Lsw; Lower Orchard; Meadow, Upper and Lower; Mdw above House, Mdw below Garden (either side of New Hall); The Meadows; Middle Fd; Middle Ground; Minshulls Mdw, Far and Near; The Nap 1833 OS (*v.* **cnæpp**); New Mdw; Oaky Lsw; Lower and Upper - - (not near preceding); Oats Lsw; Old Clover Lsw; Big Ox Lsw, Little Ox Pasture (adjoining); Ox Lsw, Far and Near; Ox Lsw, Near and Large; Parsons Fd; Peartree Lsw; Pease Lsw; Peters Lsw, Little, Middle and Upper; Pigstye Lsw; Pit Lsw (2); Plowden Close; Pool Lsw (by Lords Pool); Pool Mdw (pool shown); Pool Place (near Upper Springs, 6" map shows unnamed buildings here); Queens Lsw, Lower - - (*v.* Kings Mdw); Road Fd; Road Lsw; Rookery; Rush Mdw, Lower - -; Rushy Bank; Sawpit Lsw; Shoulder of Mutton (2); Skirbish Rough (possibly a mistake for *skirmish*, a form of *scrimmage*: the minor n. Scirmidge near Cold Weston refers to extra-parochial land at the junction of three parishes with a house where parish officials arranged for illegitimate births: the reference might be to disorderly conduct, but it is more probably to ownership disputes: Skirbish Rough is on the S.E. boundary of Kenley); Slade (probably a wet patch, *v.* FN 18); The Slangs (not narrow, perhaps an amalgamation); Small Hopes (an unfertile field); Smiths Lsw; Smiths Mdw; Smouts Lsw; Smouts Yd (not near preceding); Sow Lsw; Sows House; Square Lsw (approximately square); Stack Yd (*freq*); Upper Stangs (by a tributary of Hughley Brook), Stank Lsw and Mdw (by Hughley Brook, another Stank Lsw upstream, *v.* **stank**, but here the meaning will be 'temporary dam' rather than 'pool', *v.* FN 18); The Stocking, Great and Little Stocking (*v.* ***stoccing**, the three fields are all on the Kenley ridge); Thistly Far Land; Three Corner Pce; Three Trees Lsw; Waddy Goose Lane; Wainhouse Lsw, Lower and Upper; The Way Lsw; Well Patch; Wet Lsw; Wet Rough; White Fd; Willow Lsw; Wyres Lsw; The Yard (large field at S. end of the village); Big and Little Yard; Yewtree Lsw; Big and Near - -

(not near preceding); Yewtree Pce; Wall Brooks (*v.* **wælle**); Way Butts; Well Lsw.

Leebotwood

The parish-name is discussed in Part 1. Botwood is 'Botta's wood' and Lee is 'clearing'. Botwood occupied the southern part of the parish; it was enclosed in the 17th and 18th centuries (VCH 98).

LA CRESSE (lost), *La Cresse* 1243-55 HAC, *grange of Crees, Le Crees Parke* 1372 HAC, *ville de Lye - - - et del Crees* 1400 HAC, *Cress Farm alias Cress Grange* 1688 *SRO 567*. Part of Micklewood was assarted by Haughmond Abbey and converted into this grange farm. The bank which marked the site was still recognised in 1688, when the grange was said to have stood on the boundary with Smethcott in the north of Longnor Park (VCH 100).

This is probably a third example of the French name *Dieu l'acreisse*, 'may God increase it', which has become Dieulacres, St (an abbey), and was noted in Clewer, Berks, as the name of a 13th-cent. assart belonging to Salisbury Cathedral (PN Berks 22). The Leebotwood name, however, is only recorded in a truncated form.

MICKLEWOOD

Mittlewode e.13th HAC, *Mitlewod'* 1232 Cl, *Mittelwode* 1232 HAC, *-wodde* 1539 *MinAcc*
Mutlewood e.13th HAC
Mekelewud' 1261-2 *ForProc*
Mydelwood Bosc 1298 Eyton, *Bosc' vocat' Midlewodd* 1539-40 *RentSur*
Mittewode 1323 Eyton
Micklewood Lodge 1833 OS

The name is now attached to a large house of 17th-cent. date, but it earlier denoted a wood which occupied the northern part of the parish. This wood was divided between Haughmond Abbey and the owner of Longnor in the early 13th cent. (HAC 144).

The area of the wood lies between two headstreams of Cound Brook, and the first element may be the term postulated in Part 1 as the origin of Myddle: a derivative with *-el* of **gemȳðe** 'river-junction'. *v.* **wudu.**

ASH COPPICE. THE FIELDS, VCH 99 says that one of the three common fields of the parish lay in this area, near Padmore. LEEBOTWOOD BRIDGE. This replaced a ford over Cound Brook in 1848 (VCH 99). LONGNOR PK, 1833 OS. The part of Micklewood which was allotted to the lord of Longnor c.1221 was formed into Longnor Pk shortly after 1333. It is first named in 1538, and was disparked c.1686 (VCH 99). NEWHOUSE FM. VCH 101 says this was probably built in l.18th. PADMORE, *Padmore Hill* 1619 *SBL 9078*, 'toad marsh', *v.* ***padde, mōr**, the 6" map shows marshy ground. VCH 99 says the settlement was known as *Malliner Green* in the 18th cent. POUND INN, named from the parish pound (VCH 99-100).

Field-Names

Forms in (a) are 1839 *TA* except where otherwise stated. Early forms for which no date or source is given are 1539-40 *RentSur.* 1179, 1340, 1372, 1400, 1458 are HAC.

VCH 99 says that the three common fields lay N. and N.E. of the village. Hill Field was earlier Old Field (*v. infra*), Lower Field was *Midle Yate Felde* (*v.* under (b)), and Malliner or Park Field lay near Padmore and Longnor Pk (*v. supra*).

(a) Back Yd; Bank, Lower and Upper; Banky Lsw and Mdw; Banky Pce; Barn Mdw (2); Big Fd (2); Broad Mdw (*Broad Meddow* 1698 *LDR, The Broad Meadow* 1730 *et seq ib*); Brooms Pce; Broomy Yd; Church Lsw, Patch and Pce (by the church); Clover Lsw; Coalpit Fd, Little - -, Coalpit Mount (Leebotwood colliery was established 1784, VCH 103); Common Lsw; Coopers Mdw, Far and Near - -; The Coppice; Corner Pce (in the angle between two roads); Cote Mdw (no building shown); Engine Pce (by Coalpit Mount); Flat Lsw; Footway Pce;

Four Acre Pce; Frog Pool; Garden Mdw; Gravel Yd; Hemp Yd; Horse Pce; Hotchkiss Pce; Hughes Pce; Hurrow Stocking (*v.* ***stoccing**); Jenny Mdw; Jones Pce; Jordans Mdw; Langfords Yd (*Langfords Piece* 1691 *VCH* (*Smethcott*)); Lee Mdw; The Lees, Big -, Lower, Middle and Upper Lees Mdw (*v.* **lǣs**); Little Mdw (3); Little Pce; Long Furlong (*The Longe Furlonge*, N.E. of village); Long Lsw (2); Lower Lsw; The Meadow; Middle Ground; Middle Lsw (between Lower and Pit -); Milestone Lsw (by Ludlow road); Muck Lsw; New Lsw (2); New Tinding (*v.* **tȳning**); Nine Butts (by Open Fd, *butts* perhaps used of strips); Old Field 1840 VCH 99 (*Alveld* 16th ib, *Auvill* 1777 ib, *v.* **ald**, an open field); Open Fd (on N. boundary, perhaps a patch of late-surviving strip cultivation); Park Lsw (*Parke Lesowe*, by the church); Pease Lands; Pikey Pce (one sharp corner); Pit Lsw; Pool Pce; Postons Pce; The Rough; Ryegrass Pce; Seedley; Slade Pce (probably the Sa dialect use, 'patch of wet ground left as greensward in a ploughed field', *v.* FN 18); Stable Patch (by the colliery); Tantrey Yd, Upper - - (a variant of *tenter* referring to cloth-stretching frames); Tinsleys Pce; Well Lsw; Whitefoots Stile; White Lsw; White Mdw (2); Widows Pce; Wigleys Pce and Yd; The Yard.

(b) *Alwardeshedam* 1179 (a ferry, probably 'Ælfweard's dam', *v.* **damme**, of which this is an early example); *Arrhepytte Medowe* (*v.* **pytt**, **mǣd**); *Le Dichedelye* 1372 ('ditched clearing', *v.* **lēah**); *Esidley, Little, The Fache Furlong* ('vetch furlong', *vache* and *fatch* are 16th-cent. forms of ME *fecche*); *Le Feorrelye* 1372 ('far clearing', *v.* **feor**, **lēah**); *Le Forge* (the smithy at the S. end of the village, demolished 1963, *v.* VCH 100, 104); *Grutterescrofte* 1458 (*v.* **croft**, first el. probably a surname); *The Haines* c.1738 VCH ('enclosures', *v.* **hægen** and cf. Smethcott f.ns.); *Leche Pettes Furlonge, Leche Pitte Furlong* (*v.* ***læc(c)**, **pytt**); *Malkynslye* (*v.* **lēah**, first el. the ME pers.n. *Malkin*); *The Maupas* ('difficult passage', a French n. which gives Malpas Ch and recurs as a minor n., *v.* PN Berks 222: the use of the definite article is noteworthy); *Le Midlehill', Midlehille Coppe* ('middle hill' and '- - coppice'); *Midle Yate Felde* ('middle gate field', an open field); *Les Oldeacres* 1340 (*v.* **ald**, **æcer**, the deed concerns a piece of waste, so **ald** means 'disused' here); *Potterismedewe* 1458 ('potter's meadow', *v.* **mǣd**); *Le Ryddyng* 1539-40 *RentSur, The Riddings* m.17th VCH (*v.* ***rydding**); *Teselerslee* 1400 ('teaseler's clearing', *v.* **lēah**); *Tomley Wauker, Tomlyn Walker, Tumly(e)walker* (presumably the owner's name); *Le Verinhalle* 1372 ('fern nook', *v.* **fearn**, **halh**); *Ysottelyadies* 1458 (perhaps the property of a lady called *Isolde*).

Longnor

The parish-name, which means 'long alder-copse', is discussed in Part 1. The estate was called *Lege* in DB; and in *Longenorlegh'* 1291-2 *Ass, Longnorley* 1586 *SBL 6699* the DB name is preserved with the later name prefixed.

LAWLEY, L. FM, THE LAWLEY, *Lallelyd* 1221 Eyton, (*crofte under*) *The Lawley* 1573 *SBL 8403, Ye Lawley* 1736 PR(L) 4. The Lawley is a long ridge. A row of houses called Lawley is at its N. end, and Lawley Fm (perhaps the croft of 1573) is a third of a mile from its W. edge. The 1221 spelling shows that the final element is **hlið**, used in S. Sa and N. He for hills with concave slopes. In this instance the reference is probably to the hollow between the Lawley and Hoar Edge. The 1221 reference is to a boundary *apud Harlyd et Lallelyd*, which suggests that the whole horse-shoe shaped massif was a **hlið**, and its western and eastern arms were distinguished by first elements. The first el. of Lawley is a pers.n. **Lealla*, which is evidenced in Lawford Ess (*Lalleford* 1045) and Leybourne Sr (*Lelleburne* 1241, *Lalleburne* 1255): *v.* PN Ess 342, Sr 197. The first element of Hoar Edge is **hār** 'grey'.

LYDLEY HAYS (1833 OS). This is a DB manor in the area of Cardington parish which was transferred to Longnor in 1934. The name Lydley (obscure first el. + **lēah**) is discussed in Part 1. It has disappeared from modern maps but is shown 1833 OS adjacent to Day Ho. 1833 OS also shows Heywood Barn a short distance N., *v.* **(ge)hæg**.

BELLEVUE. BIRCH COPPICE, 1833 OS. BLACKHURST, 1833 OS, *v.* **blæc, hyrst**. BLACK POOL. The 1794 *Corbett survey* (*v. infra*) has *Farther and Nearer Black Pool Leasow*, but calls the actual pond *New Pool.* 1833 OS has *Black Pool Coppice.* COURT HO, 1833 OS. DAY HO, 1833 OS, 'dairy-house', *v.* ***dey**. FORGE HO, *The Forge* 1618 *et seq* PR(L) 6, *Longnor Forge* 1833 OS, an iron forge erected in 1605, *v.* VCH 108. HURST BARN, adjoins Blackhurst. LEASOWES, 1833 OS, *Leasows* 1794 *Corbett survey*, pastures', *v.* **lǣs** (dat. *lǣswe*). LITTLE LONGNOR, a group of houses associated with Longnor Forge (VCH 108). LONGNOR HALL, 1772 *LDR*, 1833 OS, *Longnor House* 1794 *Corbett survey*, an account of the house is given in VCH 110. MALT HO, 1730 *LDR*, 1833 OS: the 1794 *Corbett survey* shows a *Malthouse* adjoining *Longnor House*, not where later maps show it. MOAT HO, 1833 OS, *The Mote Yard* 1730 *LDR, The Mote House Gate, Mote Hall* 1772 *LDR*, a large rectangular moat probably 13th-cent. (VCH 108). NELLSYARD. PENKRIDGE HALL, 1833 OS, presumably named from Penkridge St. SMITHY, 1794 *Corbett survey.* WELL HO, 1833 OS.

Field-Names

Except where otherwise stated, forms in (a) are from a survey of the estate of Robert Corbett dated 1794, mapped by H.D.G. Foxall. Early forms dated 1185, e.13th, 1215-c.1230, 1222-c.1230, 1272, 1304 are HAC, those dated 1222 are SAS 3/VII.

VCH 107 gives details of the three common fields. Rea Field lay S. and W. of the village in the area later occupied by the Park. Rea (ME *atter ee* 'at the river') was an alternative name of Cound Brook, which ran through the field. In the N. of the parish was a field variously called Nayles Field, the Field towards Micklewood or the Field towards the Hoo (*v.* Ryton f.ns. for Hoo). S.E. of the village was Wissybrook Field, also called Kempsall Field or the Field towards Lydley. Whissey Brook and Kempsall were in Frodesley, and are discussed under the f.ns. of that parish. For Lydley Hays *v. supra.* The open fields were enclosed by the end of the 17th cent.

(a) Acton's Fd and Mdw; Barnyard (several); Black Acres, Farther, Nearer and Middle (N.E. of the village, probably part of the northern open field); Botwood, Farther and Nearer - (6 fields on S.E. boundary, adjoining Watling Street, for Botwood *v.* Leebotwood *supra*); Bowdler's Pce; Bowling Green (in the village); Brickkiln Lsw; Broad Mdw (adjoins Long Mdw, both names appropriate); Broomy Pce; Calves Patch and Lsw; Clover Patch; Clover Pce; Coachman's Mdw (*v.* Gatehouse Yd); Cockpit (adjoins Smithy, beside Shrewsbury road); Coppice Mdw, Little Coppice; Corfield's Patch; Corfield's Pce (not near preceding); Cote Lsw; Cote Mdw (no buildings shown in either field); Cow Pasture; - -, Old and Nearer; Croft (several, mostly small, but one in S. of parish is a large field); Crowner, - Lane, Crowner(s) Mdw; Docky Lsw; Dole in

Long Sides (*v.* **dāl**, fields called Long and Short Sides lie adjacent in Dorrington township); Gander Neck (if adjacent Lower Mdw were included the two fields are goose-neck shaped); Edwards Ground, Great and Little; Farmers Pce; Field by House; Field Pce; Flat Pce; Forge Lsw and Pool (*v.* Forge Ho *supra*); Gatehouse Yd (adjoins Coachman's Mdw, by Moat Ho); Gorsy Fd, Farther and Nearer; Gough's Mdw; Great Croft (twice as big as adjoining Croft); Great Mdw; Green Lsw (near Longnorgreen in Frodesley); Hall Mdw, - - with Hopyard (N. of Longnor House); Hammer Ditch, Great - - (adjoins Forge); Heath, Great and Little, Pit Heath, Brickkiln Lsw or Heath (a group of fields on E. boundary); High Glat (*glat* is dialect, 'gap in a hedge'); Hitchley, Great and Lower (the adjacent field in Frodesley is Little Etchley, both ns. represent *Edrichesleg'* 1222-c.1230, 'Ēadrīc's clearing', *v.* **lēah**); Hoo Mdw (adjoins Ouze Mdw in Ryton, *q.v.*); Horse Pasture, Upper - -; Horse Pasture (not near preceding); Hungerhill, - Mdw (a reference to poor ground); Lake Mdw (*v.* **lacu**, 'drainage channel'); Lawn or New Park (S. of Longnor House, the park was formed in 18th, VCH 107); Linton Hill, Lower, Middle, Upper and Great - - (a series of fields on W. side of S. tip of parish); Little Close; Little Rails, - - with Cote; Little Yd; Long Mdw; Long Slang (very long and narrow, by a stream); Long Yd, Bayley's and Nearer; Lower Lsw; Lower Pce (2); Messuage (several); Messuage by Old Pool; Micklewood Patch and Lsw (M- is in Leebotwood); Middle Mdw (2); Middle Pce; Nearer Cow Pasture (not near other Cow Pasture fields); New Enclosure; New Pce; New Pool, - - Lsw (*v.* Black Pool *supra*); Moat Yd (*v.* Moat Ho *supra*); Oak Lsw; Page's Yd; Piece, Lower, Middle, Farther, Piece over the Brook, Lower and Upper Pieces (a group of fields on N. boundary); Pit Fd (adjoins Cockpit); Pit Lsw; Plimmer's Fd Pce, Plimmers Fd (both in S. of parish, but not adjoining); Pool Dam (by Forge); Sandy Yd (1730,72 *LDR*); Shutt Yd; Slang (2, one a strip, the other triangular); Upper Ground; Welchman's Yd; Well Lsw; Wet Reyns (drainage channels); Whissey Brook Lsw and Mdw (these are by the eastern channel of the Cound headwater which runs through the centre of the parish, but they probably refer to the open field named from the brook: the brook seems more likely to have been in Frodesley, and early forms are given under that parish); Whiteway, - Head (a road in S. of parish); Wyre Lsw (by Cound Brook, a field lower down the stream is said to be used for "alders for repairing the wyre", a dialect form of *weir*); Yew Tree House 1833 OS.

(b) *Alnetum* (Latin 'alder grove', cf. the parish-n.); *Ancreparrok* ('hermit enclosure', *v.* **ancra**, **pearroc**); *The Barn Lesow* 1730,72 *LDR*; *Birchul* 1222-c.1230 (*v.* **birce**, **hyll**); *The Chapel Yard* 1730 *LDR*; *Cnut(t)ehesel* (a grove) e.13th (second el. **hæsel** 'hazel', probably used collectively like **alor** in the parish-n., the first el. might be a derivative of OE *cnyttan* 'knit', perhaps a past participle meaning 'closely entwined'); *Fulefen* 1185 (*v.* **fūl**, **fenn**); *Fulesloc* 1215-c.1230 (*v.* **fūl**, *-sloc* is unexplained); *Grene* 1215-c.1230 (*v.* **grēne**[2], 'village green'); *Hereberdesmedwe* 1272, 1304 (*v.* **mǣd**, first el. a pers.n. or surname); *The Lady Meadow* 1730,72 *LDR* (*v.* **hlǣfdige**); *molendinum de Langenare* 1185, - - *Longenolre, Le Mulneforlong'* 1222-c.1230 (an account of mills in the parish is given VCH 112); *Noteleg* 1185, *Netelega* e.13th (probably 'nut wood', *v.* **hnutu**, **lēah**); *Ravenesac* 1185 ('raven's oak', *v.* **hræfn**, **āc**); *Rodewey* e.13th ('roadway'); (*altus*) *Ruding'* 1185, *Rudingenorde, Rudingewey* e.13th, *Rudingwey* 1215-c.1230 (*v.* ***rydding**, **weg**, *-norde* is unexplained); *The Steps Yard* 1730 *LDR*, *The Step Yard* 1772 *ib*; *The Tar Pits* 1730 *ib*, *The Tarpit Yard* 1772 *ib*; *Wardemedewe* 1222-c.1230 (*v.* **mǣd**, first el. unexplained, neither **ward** nor **waroð** seems appropriate).

Pitchford

The parish-name is discussed in Part **1**. It means 'pitch ford', and there is a well near the old stream-crossing from which pitch still oozes.

BECHE (lost), *La Beche* c.1200-12 HAC, *Beche* c.1237-40 HAC, (*La*) *Beche* n.d. *SBL 5191*, *Le Beche* 1381 *SBL 5192*, *Le Bache* 1575 *VCH*, *Beitch-juxta-Pitchford* 1583 (copy) *SBL 15759*, *Batchfields* 1611 *SBL 5132*, *The Batches* 1653 *SBL 1124*, *Beaches* 1693 *SBL 1033*, *Beach* 1759 *LDR*. 'Stream valley', *v.* **bæce**, and cf. Wagbeach in Minsterley *supra*.

This lost settlement was in the N. of the parish, on the site of Pitchford Barn, GR 535052 (VCH 117), which stands between two valleys of the sort for which the element **bæce**, **bece** is used. There is a f.n. The Beach on the S. boundary of the parish (*infra*), and another, fairly close, in Acton Burnell.

LITTLE ETON (lost), *Etone* 1086 DB, *Eton, Parva Eton* 13th *SBL 4390* (p). Eyton (VI, p.286) gives references in surnames dating from 1192-4 till 1333. VCH 117 says the place is last mentioned in 1484, but *Newton, Eaton* and *Beach* are listed 1759 *LDR*.

In Part **1** (p.116) the name of this lost DB manor was

associated, perhaps mistakenly, with Eaton Mascott, which is in Berrington parish, immediately adjoining Pitchford parish on the other side of Cound Brook. It is in relation to Easton Mascott that the Pitchford place is 'little', but there is no evidence that the two places were ever a single unit. The location of *Little Eton* is not known. The name (*ēa-tūn*, 'river settlement') demands a position by Cound Brook, since Row Brook is not likely to have been called **ēa**. The area adjoining Cound Brook, however, contained the lost hamlets of *Beche* and *Newton*, and would be over-settled if *Little Eton* were there too. *Little Eton* had a chapel in the early 12th cent., and VCH (117, 123) considers that this was incorporated into Pitchford church, which has 12th-cent. features. But Pitchford must always have been by Row Brook near the pitch well, and *Little Eton* can hardly have occupied the same site, even if Row Brook were big enough to qualify for the term **ēa**. The problem is unresolved.

NEWTON (lost), *Neuthone* c.1200-2 HAC, *Neutona* ?e.13th *SBL 5191, Neutone* 1274 RH (p), 1306-7 *Ass, Neuton* 1316 VCH, *Newton* 1583 (copy) *SBL 15759*, 1759 *LDR*. 'New settlement', *v.* **nīwe**, **tūn**. This was near Little Pitchford Fm (VCH 117).

BIG WD, this and Birch Coppice are remnants of the woodland of Pitchford Pk (VCH 116). BIRCH COPPICE, 1833 OS, 1848 *TA*. HEATHPOOL PLANTATION, cf. *Adam de La Hethe de Pichford'* 1261-2 *ForProc, Bruera de Pycheford'* 1291-2 *Ass, Heath Pool and Leasow* 1848 *TA, v.* **hǣð**. VCH 117 says the pool, a fishpond, was constructed in 1720. KENNELS, *Kennel Yard* 1848 *TA*. LITTLE PITCHFORD, on the site of *Newton, v. supra*. PITCHFORD BARN, on the site of *Beche, v. supra*. PITCHFORD BRIDGE, COTTAGES and FM. PITCHFORD FORGE, 1786 PR(L) 14, 1833 OS, *The Forge or Wyre Mill formerly a Corn Mill* 1759 *LDR*, (*The*) *Forge* 1811 PR(L) 1. Eaton Mascott mill, which was on the S. side of Cound Brook, was converted into an iron forge in 1715 (VCH 121), and later into a wire-mill. PITCHFORD HALL, cf. *Hall Field Coppice* 1833 OS, 1848 *TA, Hall Meadow* 1848 *TA*. For the Hall ("one of the finest timber-framed manor-houses in the county") *v.* VCH 119. PITCHFORD PK, formed 1596, disparked in 1750s (VCH 116). Cf. *Park Gate* 1833 OS. RADNAL

BRIDGE, cf. *Radnor Way* 1673 *LDR*, *v.* Acton Burnell f.ns. STOCKBATCH, - PLANTATION, *The Stockbeaches* 1656 VCH 121, *Stockbeach* 1833 OS, *Near and Middle Stockbatch* 1848 *TA*. A field beside the farm is *The Beach* 1848 *TA*, *v.* **stocc**, **bæce**, and cf. *Beche supra.* The farm overlooks the valley of Row Brook. THE TREE WITH THE HOUSE IN IT, *v.* A. Morton, *The Trees of Shropshire*, p. 73. There has been a house in this lime tree since 1692, and Queen Victoria visited it in 1832.

Field-Names

Forms in (a) are 1848 *TA* except where otherwise stated; those dated 1857 are *LDR*. Early forms dated 1612,73, 82, 85, 98, 1736, 59, 72, 79 are *LDR*.

VCH 116 says that the three common fields were all E. of Row Brook, which bisects the parish. Stockwell Field ran E. from the village, Standell Field lay N. of it, and Quarrell Field (also named from a quarry) lay S. of the village. Bradfield may also have been a common field, *v. infra* for these names.

(a) Baileys Fd; Bank, Upper, Rowling and Wildes; Banky Lsw; Barn Fd (3); Big Lsw; Big Mdw; Birchen Harbour (in the park, probably an arbour with birch trees); Black Pits; Blind Bridge (*The Blinde Bridge* 1702-3 *SBL 1038*, on Row Brook, *v.* **blind**, probably referring in this instance to the absence of a footpath); Bradfield, Lower, Middle and Upper 1857 (*The Parsons Brodefield, Bradfield Gate* 1612, *Bradefield* 1673 *et seq*, *v.* **brād**, **feld**: *TAMap* shows 4 fields in the N .E. corner of the parish, between Row Brook and a smaller stream: it may have been a fourth open field); Brickkiln Lsw, Lower, Middle and Upper (small building shown); Bridle Way (by road to Cound); Broad Lsw (2); Calves Close; Calves Patch; Church Pool (Fish Pond on 6"); Church Stile; Clappers, Near and Farther (on the other side of Row Brook from Blind Bridge, *v.* **clapper**); Claypit Lsw; Cockshoots, Lower and Upper 1857 (*Cockshutt* 1759, 1848 *TA*, *v.* ***cocc-scīete**); Colliers Pce (by Wood Lsw); Common, Upper, Middle and Lower (on the N.W. boundary); Common, Upper and Lower (in S.W. of parish: VCH 116 gives an account of these commons); Coppice Mdw (by Pitchford Coppice); Cote Lsw (a small enclosure in a corner of this is Patch Cote); Cound Coppice and Little Coppice, Cound Pool, Lower and Upper (all by Row Brook and nowhere near Cound Brook, perhaps referring to a connection with Cound parish); Cound Stank (on Cound Brook downstream from Stank Lsw); Cover, Upper, Lower and Wood (probably a ref. to hunting); Two Crabtree Pieces 1857

(*The Crab Tree Furlong, The Two Crab Tree Pieces* 1673, *The Upper and Lower Crab Tree Furlongs* 1685, *The Crabtree-pieces* 1759: *TA* has 2 fields called Crabtree Lsw, not near each other); The Croft 1857 (1759, *The Craft* 1673,82,85, perhaps *TA* Croft, a tiny enclosure by the village); Cross Greaves (*v.* **grǣfe**, the cross is a road-junction); Ditch Nook (*The Dyched Nooke* 1612, *Ditch-nooke* 1673); The Dugdales, Near Dugdale (*v.* Duckdale in Cantlop f.ns. *supra*); Field below Barn; Fingerpost Lsw (by road-junction S. of village); Fishpond Yd (the manor had a number of fishponds); The Fold 1857 (1682 *et seq*); Footway Mdw; Forge Fd and Mdw (*v.* Pitchford Forge *supra*); Furlongs, Long - (in the area of common field E. of village, cf. *The Furlong* 1702-3 *SBL 1038*); Glydol, Parrs - (*Glide Hole* 1673, perhaps 'kite hollow', *v.* **gleoda**, **hol**[1]); Goughs Yd; Halford (not by a stream); Half Pce; Hancock's Yd 1857 (1772, 1801); Heath Lsw, Lower and Upper (not near Heath Pool); The Held 1857 (1759, The Yeld 1848 *TA*, 'slope', *v.* **helde**); The Hempbut 1857 (*The Hemp Butt* 1673,82,85); Hills Corner; Knoll Lsw, Upper - -, Knolls Patch (*v.* **cnoll**, VCH 118 says that a small squatter settlement is recorded here in 1638, but the houses were demolished after 1800); Lawns, Lower and Upper (by Park Mdw); Lee Mdw, Lower and Upper; Light Green (adjoining Lightgreen Coppice in Cantlop, *supra*); Lilly Pool Rough, Upper Lilly Pool Lsw (by Lilly Pool in Acton Burnell); Little Mdw (2); Lodge Croft and Pce; Long Lsw (longer than its neighbours); Longs Coppice; Malthouse Yd; The Meadow, Lower Mdw; Meadow Platt (*v.* **plat**[2]); New Lsw; Nook Shotton Quarry (the field is a narrow triangle between two converging roads: *nook-shotten*, defined by NED as 'running into corners or angles', is first recorded in Shakespeare); Oil Rock Mdw (by Pitchford Bridge, a short distance N. of the bituminous well); Orchard; Orchard Mdw; Orchard Patch; Ox Lsw; Paddock (2); Parrs Mdw (Parrs Glydol and Parrs Standel are fairly close); Parrs Pinnacle Hill (also in E. of parish); Piller Brook 1968 VCH (*Pyller Brooke* 1612, VCH 115 says this is the n. of the brook which bounds Pitchford on the E.); Pinfold; Pitchford Coppice; Plains, Lower and Upper (on W. boundary, perhaps a level piece of ground); Pool Pce (by the westernmost of three fishponds); Quarry Fd, Field above Quarry (*The Quarry* 1673, in S. of parish; Quarrell Field, from ME **quarrelle** 'quarry', was in this area); Quarry Lsw (2); The Rookery; Roundabout, Little - (on either side of a road-junction); Russells Pools; Sandy Furlong (W. of Row Brook, so not in an open field); Sheep Lsw, Far and Near; Spring Coppice (perhaps **spring** in the sense 'coppice'); Stable Yd; Stackyard Mdw; Standel, Big and Parrs (*Standile Field* 1673, *Standel* - 1682, 'quarry', *v.* **stān**, **(ge)delf**, an open field); Stank Lsw (by Cound Brook, perhaps **stank** in the Sa sense of a temporary dam, FN 19); Stockbatch Dingle Plantations, Upper and Lower Coppice Stockbatch, Row Stockbatch, Lower - - (*v.* Stockbatch *supra*); Stockwell Yd (*Stockwell Fields* 1673, *v.* **stocc**, **w(i)elle**, an open field); The Straits (*The Strayte Lane* 1612, by Watling Street, *v.* **stræt**); Twopenny Yd; Ucle Bridge (*Hucklebridge* 1612, a haunch-shaped bridge, *v.* NED s.v. *huckle*: a footpath to Stockbatch crosses a stream at N.W. corner of this field); Upper Castle Lsw (the adjacent field in Acton Burnell has a moat); Walkmill Pool Mdw (VCH 121 says the pool was so called e.17th, and connected with a fulling mill recorded in 1284, it is *Le Walkmulnepole* n.d. *SBL MS2*); Warmer Fd; Weir Fd (by Row Brook); Weir Mdw, Far and Near - - (by Cound Brook); Well Bank; Wibberley (this small field on E. boundary is described as 'part of Wibberley', but the name has not been noted in Cound or Acton Burnell, the adjacent parishes); Windy Monday 1968 VCH (VCH 117 says this is the name of a pair of derelict cottages on the site of a park lodge; Gazetteer gives it as Windy Mundy); Wood Lsw, Further and Near; Yewtree Lsw (2).

Church Preen

As stated in Part **1**, the forms for this name point to OE **prēon** 'brooch' as the origin. This word has not otherwise been noted in place-names. A transferred topographical sense would perhaps be most likely to refer to a hill. Church Preen stands among a cluster of hill-peaks, but none of them today presents a distinctive outline. The peak which overlooks the church and manor may be the relevant one, if Preen be, in fact, a hill-name.

There were two settlements, Church (Magna) and Holt (Parva) Preen. Holt Preen is now in Cardington, but it was in Church Preen until the 13th cent. (VCH 124).

BIG WD. BROOK HO, 1833 OS, BROOKHOUSE COPPICE. DRY ROUGH. HIGH FIELDS. HOLLYGROVE, cf. *Holly Bank* 1814 *SBL 6232*. HOLT COPPICE, 1833 OS, LARGEHOLT COPPICE: this is the **holt** from which Holt Preen is named. THE LAUNDRY. MANOR FM. MEREOAK, 1833 OS, 'boundary oak', *v.* **gemǣre, āc**, at northern tip of parish. NEW HO. POOL FM, Edward Corfield "of the pool" was buried in 1706, PR(H) 16. PREEN COTTAGE AND MANOR, latter on site of priory (VCH 125). SPOUT HO, *v.* **spoute**.

Field-Names

There is no surviving *TA* for Church Preen.

(b) *Clawley Field* 1754 VCH (a common field); *Preen Common* 1789 PR(H) 16 (VCH 125 gives an account of this); *Preneway* 1576 *SBL 1174*; *Seven Pools* 1652 *SBL 6231.*

Church Pulverbatch

The name Pulverbatch is discussed in Part 1. It consists of **bæce** 'stream-valley', with a qualifying element **pulfre* which has not been explained.

The parish contains the five townships of Cothercott, Castle Pulverbatch, Church Pulverbatch, Wilderley and Wrentnall.

1. COTHERCOTT (SJ 420016)

The township-name, which means 'cottage(s) associated with Cūðheard', is discussed in Part 1.

SHEPPEN FIELDS, *Shupene* 1291-2 *Ass* (p), 1301 SAC, *La Shupene* 1339 *SBL 3616* (p), *Chepinfelde* 1464 HAC, *Shippen Fields* 1688 *SBL 3469A, - Feilds* 1722 *SBL 3451, Sheppenfields, Shepherds Fields* 1735 *SBL 3459, Shippon Field* 1756 *SBL 3496, Shopanffields* 1780 *SBL 3398, Lower and Upper Shopen Fields* 1789 *SBL 6581, Shepton Fields, Sheppen -, Shippen Field Hedge* c.1790 *SBL 6579.*

OE **scypen**, 'cattle-shed'. The Latin equivalent, *Boveria*, is used in HAC for an extensive farm which was set up here in 1204 (HAC 10-11). Both sheep and cattle were managed from this centre. *Upper Shopen Fields* in the 1789 ref. was a farmhouse higher up Cothercott Hill (VCH 133).

BANK, *New Bank Homestead* 1839 *TA*. COTHERCOTT COTTAGE, - HILL (1839 *TA*), - HILL FM. LONG ROUGH. OUTRACK, 1839 *TA, Wilderley Outrack* 1788 *SBL 3496.* The farm lies beside a drift-way leading to common land on Cothercott Hill. FN 35 defines the Sa usage of *outrack* as 'an area between cultivated land and the open common or hill pasture where the various farmers' animals were sorted out on return from the hills'.

Field-Names

Forms in (a) are 1839 *TA*.

(a) Big Lsw; Brickkiln Lsw; Broad Pce; Broomy Lsw, Big and Little; Church Acre; Clover Pce; Coat Green, Further and Near (*TAMap* shows a building in adjacent field, still there on 6"); Cooks Rough; Cote Lsw; Croft (*freq*, very small enclosures); The Dale; Dead Man's Brook and Ford (1666 *SBL 3496*, 1756 *SBL 3496*, *Deadmansford, Deadmans Skull* 1789 *SBL 6581, Deadman's Skull and Brook* c.1789 *SBL 6579*, the ford is at GR 427007, Gazetteer cites the Brook name as still known); The Dingle, Little Dingle (two stream valleys); Field below House; The Flat; Footway Pce; Gorsy Dingle, Big and Little (upstream from The Dingle); Harp Mdw and Lsw (the meadow is harp-shaped); The Hemp Yd; Hill Lsw, Lower and Upper; Hole Mdw (6" map shows a small area of rough ground); Home Croft; Inclosure (fields on Cothercott Hill are First, Second, Third, Fourth, Near and Far -); Lambs Lsw; Leys, Near and Further, The Leys Bank (in a tongue of cultivated land running up Cothercott Hill) ; Little Clover; Long Moor Mdw; Lower Mdw; Marsh Mdw, First, Second and Third; Meadow, Big and Little; Meadow, Home, Further and Near; Middle Hurst; Mountain Pce, Further, Middle and Near Mountain Pce Bottom (in the tongue of fields running up Cothercott Hill); New Lsw; Nut Croft; Orchard; Pearces Mdw, Far and Near Pearce Mdw; Pulleys Fd, Long, Broomy, Upper and Rough (*Le Polehous, Polehows iuxta Codarcott* 1327 HAC, *Le Polhous* 1334 HAC, *Polehowse Felde, Polehowselande, Pollehowse Grene* 1539-40 *RentSur, Polehouse, Polehouseland, Polehousegrene* 1615 *SBL 3465*,6, *v.* **pōl**, **hūs**, *TAMap* shows no building, but VCH 133 says there were houses here in 1534: the fields are by a stream junction, where there might have been a pool); The Ravish Hill; Rough Mdw, - - Top; Square Mdw (nearly square); Stable Close; Stocking, Little and Long (*v.* ***stoccing**); Stony Pce, Big and Litttle; Townsend Mdw (adjoins hamlet); Upper Pikes (has two sharp corners); Wheat Lsw, Big and Little; Wheatley, Farther, Hither and Upper; Lower Willys Fd, Upper Willys Lsw; The Wood, Cockshutt Wd, Fur Wd; Wynnes Fd, Big and Upper; The Yard.

(b) *Boozy Thorne, The Boozie* 1666 *SBL 3496*, *The Boozie or Bovaria* 1756 *ib* (land by a cattle-shed, or land on which outgoing tenants had grazing rights, FN 34); *Le Bradmedwe* m.13 HAC, *Brodmedewe* c.1270-90 HAC, *Brodemedowe* 1477 HAC (*v.* **brād, mǣd**); *Cothercott Park* 1788 *SBL 6165* (it is not likely that Cothercott had a park in the usual sense); *Coudretum* 1281-4 HAC (this Latin term means 'hazel-grove', *v.* Cecily Clark's discussion in *Leeds Studies in English* 18, 101ff: it is wrongly transcribed *Condretum* in HAC and taken to be a tributary of the R. Cound); *Cranmersihe, Cranmerswal(l)* c.1270-90 HAC, *Cranmere Wall, Cranmer(e) Sich* 1666, 1756 *SBL 3490* ('crane pond', *v.* **cran, mere**, to which have been added **sīc** 'small stream' and **wælle** 'spring'); *Hakefens Medowe* 1539-40 *RentSur, Hangman's Nap* (*v.* **cnæpp**, on Cothercott Hill); *Hardeheselmedewe* c.1250-80 HAC ('hard hazel meadow', *v.* **heard, hæsel, mǣd**: **heard** may be used of nuts, as it is of pears in Hartpury PN Gl 3, 155); *Hazler* 1756, *Haseler Bank* 1788, *Hasler* 1789 *SBL 3496, 6581* (probably the same name as Hazler in Church Stretton, from **hæsel, ofer**); *Le Longeforlonge* m.13 HAC; *Lorde Medowe* 1539-40 *RentSur, Mechells Boosie* 1666, 1756 *SBL 3496, Michels Bosie or Bovaria* c.1790 *SBL 6579* (*v.* The Boozie *supra*); *Midelhurstesbrok, Middelhurtbroke, Middelhurste* c.1270-90 HAC, *Middlehurst (Brow)* 1666, 1756 *SBL 3496* (*v.* **middel, hyrst, brōc**); *Parva Munede* ('little Mynd', perhaps a term for the hills at the N. end of the Long Mynd massif); *Overelidihet* c.1270-90 HAC ('higher swing-gate', *v.* **hlidgeat**); *Paynes Bank* 1788 *SBL 3496, Pere Medowe* 1539-40 *RentSur* ('pear meadow'); *Post Bank* 1788 *SBL 3496, Renegeteshul* c.1250-80 HAC (*v.* **hyll**, first el. uncertain); *Roberts Cottage on Cothercot Hill* 1789 *SBL 6581*; *Saltarsthorn* c.1270-90 HAC, *Salters Thorn* 1756,9 *SBL 3496* (the 13th-cent. ref. occurs in boundaries of land at Sheppen Fields: the thorn was regarded as special in 1790, when instructions were given for a replacement to be planted (*SBL 3496*); salt is mentioned also in Wilderley f.ns. *infra*: perhaps there was a minor, local salt way over Cothercott Hill); *Sparugenhul(l)* 1281-4 HAC (*v.* **hyll**, first el. uncertain); *Stanlawesbroke* c.1270-90 HAC, *Stanley or Stanlowe Browe, Stanlows Brow* 1666 *SBL 3496, Stanly or Stanlowe Brow* 1756 *ib, Stanley Bank* 1788 *ib*, 'stone tumulus', *v.* **stān, hlāw**, to which **brōc** and modern *brow* and *bank* have been added); *Le Stevyn Pytte* 1539-40 *RentSur* (*v.* **pytt**, first el. uncertain); *Stotfeld* 1539-40 *RentSur* (*v.* **stōdfald**); *Wellersley* 1539-40 *RentSur, Witernarlesihc* c.1270-90 HAC, *Withenhalresich* 1281-4 ib, *Whitnerle Sitch, Witnerle Sich* 1666 *SBL 3496, Whitnerle Sitch* 1756 *ib* (probably 'white alder stream', *v.* **hwīt, alor, sīc**); *Yatelee* m.13 HAC (*v.* **geat, lēah**).

2. CASTLE PULVERBATCH (SJ 424023)

The castle is an impressive motte and bailey. VCH 131 says it was still occupied in 1205, but was not regarded as a manor house in 1292. The village has obviously been laid out at the foot of the castle.

GATTENSHELVE is *Gathovereshelde* a.1244 HAC, *Gathershell or Gatherhead Brook* 1756 *SBL 3496.* 'Slope of the goat ridge', *v.* **gāt, ofer, helde.**

HUGLITH

Hughelith a.1244 HAC
Huggelith' 1291-2 *Ass, -lith* 1314 BM, 1342 Cl
Hagelith' 1291-2 *Ass*
Hockelyth 1292 Ipm
Hoglith 1453 (copy) *SBL 7070*
Huglyth 1715 *SBL 6900*

The second element is **hlið**, used in He and Sa for hills with a large concavity. Huglith Fm lies in a deep recess in a semi-circle of high ground, the two peaks of which are Huglith Hill and Lawn Hill. Huglith is a wood in most early references, but it was a habitation site in 1291-2 *Ass.* The present farm was formed in the late 16th-cent. (VCH 133), so it is not certain to be on an ancient site; but the great hollow in which it lies would be a likely settlement-site at an earlier period.

The first element is identical with that of the names Higford (earlier *Hug(g)eford*) and Highley (earlier *Hug(g)eleye*), which are discussed in Part 1. Ekwall's suggestion of a pers.n. **Hugga* offers the likeliest explanation. Dodgson, PN Ch 5 xiv-xv, however, lists a number of minor names and field-names in Ch which have *Hugge-* and suggests an OE **hucg,* **hycg* meaning 'hill, mound'.

PRESTLEY FM, cf. *Presteleyesmor'* 1382 *SBL 6172* (in the adjacent parish of Habberley), *Presley Field and Bank* c.1790 *SBL 6579.*

'Priests' clearing', *v.* **prēost, lēah.** The Habberley land was marsh, *v.* **mōr.**

BANK, 1839 *TA.* BROOK COTTAGES. An adjoining field is *Cotton* 1839 *TA*, from *cotum*, dat.pl. of **cot(e).** BROWN'S COPPICE, 1830 *TA, Brown(e)s Coppy* 1629,49 *SBL 6892, 13379.* HUGLITH HILL, *v. supra.* LAWN, L. HILL, *The Lawne* 1649 *SBL 13379, Lawn Field and Leasow* 1839 *TA.* The house is shown on *TAMap. Lawn* is generally used in Sa for parkland. Perhaps the land round Lawn Fm had unusually smooth grass. Woodland on the hill was called *Huglith Wood* c.1780 (VCH 130), so Lawn is likely to have been the name of the farm-site, transferred in recent times to the hill. LOW COTTAGE. RIDDLES WD, cf. *Ryddeslugh, Ryddeslesicheshed* 1453 (copy) *SBL 7070. v.* **sīc, hēafod,** the etymology of the basic name is uncertain as the two forms are inconsistent. SPRING COPPICE. WOODCOCK INN, named from an early-19th-cent. licensee, Samuel *Woodcock* (VCH 132).

Field-Names

Forms in (a) are 1839 *TA.* VCH 131 says that the three common fields of the township, Staple Field, Broad or Okeover Field and Huglith Field, lay on boulder clay to the N. and W. of the village.

(a) Bank above House (a building on the 1000' contour is shown on 6" map and on *TAMap*, perhaps the house called *Pennsylvania* 1783 VCH 133); Banky Lsw and Bog; Barn Yd (2); Black Venns (*v.* **fenn**); Brickkiln Lsw; Briggage; Brook Fd; The Broom; Broomy Bank, Little Broomy Lsw; The Burrington, Parson's Burwarton (separated by a narrow strip of rough: reminiscent of the group of names discussed in Part 1 under Berrington, but there is no evidence that the f.n. is ancient); Butchers Bank, The Banks; Claypit Mdw; Close (several); Clover, Near and Further; Coppice Fd and Yd (by Browns Coppice); Cote Lsw, Upper - -; Cote and Walls Mdw (3 fields W. of Huglith); Cow Ground; Cow Pasture; The Crest (the road to Bishop's Castle crosses the 1000 contour here); Cross Lsw and Harolds Croft, Cross Mdw (the last is in a road fork); Five Acres Glebe; Gallows Tree Mdw (GR 426028, by road to Shrewsbury); Gauntlessley, Further -; Gittins Fd (*Gittins Leasowe* 1615 *SBL 3466*);

Golden Lsw; Gorsty Bank (*v.* **gorstig**); Hey Lsw; Honeydale Mdw; Hotley Bank; Ingles Lsw; Jones's Fd; Leasow, Near and Broad; Level Mouth; The Leys (2); Little Fd; Long Furlong (*v.* Ten Butts); Lower Pce; Marsh Fd, Little Marsh; Meadow, Lower and Upper; Mill Lsw (by Habberley Mill); Mill Mdw, Millpond Lsw (these relate to Pulverbatch Mill, mentioned a.1221 HAC, *v.* VCH 137); New Mdw; New Pce; Oaken Top; Open Hurst; Oswells Mdw; Parnall; Patch (*freq*, used for very small enclosures); Patch before Door (by the house called Bank); Peas Croft; Peascroft (not near preceding); Pinfold Close; Pitts Mdw; Pool Mdw; Prestley Mdw (*v. supra*); Profit (W. of the castle); Quakers (a ref. to quaking grass); The Rail; Rogers Broom; Round Duck Lsw (*Duckelesowe* 1539-40 *RentSur*, *v.* **dūce**, the *TA* field is not round); Sharpstones (on either side of a road W. of Huglith); Sheen Bank; Shop Lsw (by Smithy on 6" map, *v.* **sceoppa**); Slang, Long, Upper, Little Long and Lower Little; Spy Bank (possibly ***spǣg** a side-form of ***sprǣg** 'brushwood, twigs'); Stepping Stone; Ten Butts (probably strips in an open field, Long Furlong adjoins); Turnabout (perhaps referring to the turning of the plough, *v.* FN 35, one of a group of small, furlong-shaped fields); Upper Ground and Kitchen Mdw (by Huglith); Wall Lsw; White Lsw, East, West and Upper; Withy Mdw; Wood Lsw (10 fields between Pulverbatch Brook and the Bishop's Castle road); Yewtree Lsw.

(b) *Achovere* a.1244 HAC, *Okeveresfeld* 1342 Cl ('oak ridge', *v.* **āc**, **ofer**, the first ref. is to the feature, the 1342 ref. is to an open field); *Drench Yate* 17th *VCH*, *Drench Lane Gate* 1756,89 *SBL 3496, 6581, Drenish Lane Gate* c.1790 *SBL 6579* (Gazetteer gives Drench Lane as an extant name); *Oxeleasow* 1715 *SBL 6900*; *Stapelfeld* 1342 Cl (an open field, probably named from proximity to *Stepelwood, q.v.* under Church Pulverbatch).

3. CHURCH PULVERBATCH (SJ 431029)

The local name, Churton, is abbreviated from *Chirchetona de Pulrebeche* 1221 HAC, *v.* Part 1.

STEPLEWOOD (lost), *Stepelwud'* 1261-2 *ForProc*, *Stepelwod* (*and Werkwod*) 1342 Cl, *Stepulwode* 1385 Pat, *Stepple Woodd* 1601 *SBL 6848B*. Probably a shortened form of 'Stapleton wood'. Stapleton (*infra*) adjoins Pulverbatch to the east, and had a disputed boundary with it till 1610 (VCH 129). The wood extended N. into Wrentnall township, where *Werkwod* lay.

CHURCH COTTAGES. HOLLYGROVE, H. COTTAGES, *Grove* 1833 OS.

Field-Names

Forms in (a) are 1839 *TA*.

(a) The Acres (E. of village, not near other f.ns. indicative of a field-system); Alder Lsw; Barn Fd; The Beach (in Wilderley), Beach Bank, Lower and Upper (either side of a brook, *v.* **bæce**); Big Lsw; The Brink (overlooking a brook); Broach (perhaps a form of Brutch, from **bryce**); Close (*freq*); Clover Ley; Corn Rudges (on E. boundary, perhaps ridges in a common field); Cow Lsw; East Fd, Near and Further; East Mdw; Elmtree Close; Feg (rough grass); Ferny Hill; The Furlongs (VCH 131 suggests that this, together with East Fd and Near Fd, may indicate common fields S. of the village); The Knowle, Knowle Mdw, Lower and Upper (*v.* **cnoll**); Leys, Austins, Long, Middle and Upper, Bottom of Leys; Little Coppice; Little Fd; Little Wd; Meadow, Big and Little; Meadow, Lower and Upper; Meadow, Upper and Little; Morgans Close; Morhalls Mdw; New Lsw; North Fd (a small field N. of Pulverbatch Brook); Pinfold Mdw (*Pynfold Leasowe and Meadowe* 1699 *SBL 3427*); Rick Mdw (-*Meadowe ib*); Rye Lsw; Slough (*v.* **slōh**); Timber Sich, Further Sich Mdw (*v.* **sīc**); Two Meadows; Washford (*v.* **(ge)wæsc**); Way Lsw (by Stapleton road); Weston Fold and Yd (in village); Wood, Lower and Upper; Yewtree Lsw.

(b) *Ry-medow-ford upon Wilderley Broock* c.1597 *SBL Plan 47, The Rye Meadowe Foorde* c.1597 *SBL 6848A.*

4. WILDERLEY (SJ 434018)

The township-name, which means 'Wilþryð's clearing', is discussed in Part 1.

LEA, *The Lea* 1718 *VCH*: this may be *The Lea in Churton parish* 1810 PR(L) 1. On *TAMap* the buildings are shown but not named, and there is a large field called *Long Leys* adjoining. This last (the plural form) can be linked with *The Lees* 1615 *SBL 3466.* LEASOWS, *Wilderly Leasowes* 1833 OS. TINLIE: the farm and associated enclosures are shown on *TAMap*. WILDERLEY HALL: this is the sole survivor of the former hamlet (VCH 132). WILDERLEY HILL, 1788 *SBL 6165*. WILDERLEY LANE FM, *Wilderly Lane* 1833 OS.

Field-Names

Forms in (a) are 1839 *TA*. Early forms for which no source is given are HAC.

(a) Backside, Big and Little (adjoining Wilderley Lane Fm); Bamthale, Far and Near; The Banks, Little Banks; Barn Mdw; Barn Yd Croft; Big Mdw (2); Broad Mdw (*Brode Medowe* 1539-40 *RentSur*); Calves Close; Calves Croft; Church Fd (a tiny field in N.W. corner of township, possibly *Church Field* 1589 *SBL 7073*); Clover Pce, Near and Upper; Coalpit Top (on E. boundary, the colliery was in Stapleton); Cow Pasture (2); Crabtree Lsw; Croft (*freq.* small fields E. and W. of Tinlie are Near, Far, Lower, Garden, Long, Square Croft, etc.); Dunmore, First, Second, Near and Further; The Field (near Stapleton boundary, with Rough Mdw separating it from Wilderley Fd); The Field (a large field near Lea); Garden Croft (by Wilderley Lane Fm); Gorsy Ley; Goughs Ground, Big, Little and Further; Greens Ground, Far and Near; Halls Mdw, Further - -; Harnalls, Big and Little -, - Bank; Hollow Mdw; Home Croft (by a small building shown on 6", S.W. of Tinlie); Home Croft (adjoins a small building); Home Yd (by Lea); The Knowles, Knowles Mdw (*The Knowle* 1615 *SBL 3466*, *v.* **cnoll**, 6" map shows a small hill of 600); Little Lsw; Little Ryegrass Pce; Little Town Mdw (by Wilderley Hall); Long Leys (*v.* Lea *supra*); Long Mdw; Lower Fd; Lower Pce, Far and Near; Margery Ley; Near Croft; Oak Fd; Old House Lsw (no building shown); Parsons Yd; The Patch (very small); Pike Mdw (not unusually pointed); Pool Green Mdw (*Pool Green* 1718 *VCH*, 6" map shows pools); Pool Lsw; Postgate Yd; Road Fd (by a footpath); Rocking Mdw; Rough Mdw; Salt Furlong, Big, Little, Lower and Upper (*v.* Cothercott f.ns.); Shut Hays, Big and Little; Slang (narrow strip by a stream); Stank Lsw (*v.* **stank**, beside the stock funnel which leads from Wilderley Green to the hamlet, probably a pond for watering cattle); The Stocking (*v.* ***stoccing**); Tidders, Little and Upper; Turning Lsw (a large field in a road fork); Under Mdw; Washington Yd (the largest of a line of rectangular fields stretching S.W. from Tinlie); Well Mdw; Wilderley Fd (a tiny field in N.W. corner of township); Wilderley Fd, First, Second, Third, Fourth and Fifth (along Stapleton boundary); Wilderley Green (rough ground on the N. slope of Cothercott Hill connected via a stock funnel to Wilderley Hall: 1833 OS gives the name to a group of cottages on the Cothercott side of the boundary); Wilderley Mdw (by Hall); Wilderley Outrack (enclosure on W. Hill *v.* p. 167).

(b) *Abbotte Hey* c.1597 *SBL Plan 47*, *Abbotts Hey Corner* 1601 *SBL 6848B* (*v.* **(ge)hæg**, an enclosure on the Abbot of Haughmond's land); *Abbotsknott* 1615,16 *SBL 3465, 3450* (presumably a hillock on the abbot's land, *v.* **cnotta**); *vadum Anfredi* 1227 ('Anfred's ford'); *Brokemeadowe* 1615 *SBL 3465* (*v.* **brōc**, **mǣd**); *Church Hill Meadow* 1589 *SBL 7073*; (*quercum que vocatur*) *Cunrue(d)hac* 1227 (*v.* **āc**, the obscure first el. is probably an adjective); *Galkewyn* l.15th (a croft, probably a pers.n.); *Malkyn(s)heyes* 1539-40 *RentSur*, *Malkinshey* 1615 *SBL 3465* (*v.* **(ge)hæg**, first el. a surname); *Middelyort at le Hedacre* 1324 (*v.* **middel**, **geard**, **hēafod**, **æcer**); *Mil(l)inhey* 1615 *SBL 3465,6* (*v.* **(ge)hæg**, first el. uncertain); *Monkesplace* l.15th; *Poetacre* 1324 (*v.* **æcer**, first el. obscure); *Portyatehole* 1615 *SBL 3466* ('port gate hollow', but a town-gate, taken literally, is out of the question here: the term is perhaps used fancifully); *Pyndleys* 1539-40 *RentSur* (probably a surname); *Qubboldsitch* 1615 *SBL 3466* (*v.* **sīc**, first el. obscure); *Revesnehac* 1227 (possibly 'raven's oak', *v.* **hræfn**, **āc**); *Sadewalle* 1227 (apparently 'sad spring', *v.* **wælle**, but none of the early senses of *sad* seems appropriate to a spring, so perhaps from **scēad** 'boundary', *v.* Shadymoor in Stapleton); *Sondesleg* 1227 (apparently 'clearing of sand', *v.* **sand**, **lēah**); *Swetenacre* 1324 ('sweet plough-land', *v.* **swēte**, **æcer**); *Uplidone* 1329; *Upnete Lye* 1539-40 *RentSur*, *Upnethlee* 1615 *SBL 3465* (*v.* **lēah**, first el. obscure); *Walshemanniscrofte* l.15th ('Welshman's croft'); *Wylderleybrok* 1385 Pat, *Wilderley Brooke* c.1597 *SBL 6848A*; *Wynyats Meadow* 1615 *SBL 3466*.

5. WRENTNALL (SJ 426037)

The discussion of this name in Part **1** requires some qualification. As regards the first element, a spelling which was not taken into account is *Wrontenhal'* c.1216-30 *SBL 6903*. This is the grant of Walleybourne to John Walensis, and the occurrence of a clear *-o-* in the first syllable of the name in this local deed suggests that the later *Wronten-* spellings (1271-2,91-2, 1346) should be taken seriously. An element **wreonta* seems to be indicated. A full run of spellings for Wrentham Sf may help.

As regards the second element, the sense of **halh** here has not been ascertained. Position on the N. boundary of the parish was postulated, rather desperately, in Part **1**, but this is not convincing. The curve in the parish boundary is following a stream, and the township is not an administrative outlier.

WALLEYBOURNE

Walibourne c.1216-30 *SBL 6903*, 1338-9 *ForProc* (p), 1346 FA (p), *-burn'* 1272 Cl, *Walyburn* 1417 Fine, *-burne* 1431 FA, *-borne* 1528 *SBL 4001*
Walyngborne 1327 SAS 2/X (p), 1364-6 *ForProc* (p), *-bourne* 1342 Cl (p), 1594 *SBL 6794*, *-born* 1438 Fine
Walynbourne 1346 FA (p), *-borne* 1364-6 *ForProc*
Walliborne 1577 Saxton, 1602 *SBL 13450*, *-bourne* 1602 *SBL 7075*, *Wallyburne* 1602 *SBL 6907*, *Walliborn* 1694 *SBL 9955*, *Wallybourn* 1712 PR(L) 6
Wallingbourne 1594 *SBL 6794*, *Walliborne alias Wallingbourne* 1605 *SBL 6909*, *Wallingebourne* 1610 *SBL 7057*, *Wallingborow* 1631 PR(L) 6
Wallaburne 1604 *SBL 7067*
Wallesbourn 1807 PR(L) 1

The forms suggest OE **Walingburna*, which could be explained as 'stream associated with Walh ('Welshman')', *v.* **burna**, **-ing-**[4]. Compounds of **burna** with personal names are rather rare, however. Walburn PN NRY 270 is 'stream of the Welshmen', but the Walleybourne forms require a connective *-ing-*, and this is most appropriate with a personal name.

It is probably only a coincidence that an estate here was granted to John *Walensis* in the early 13th cent. (*SBL 6903*). An **-ing-** formation would not be coined at that date, and in any case the place-name was in existence at the date of the grant. An earlier owner named *Walh* seems the likeliest explanation.

BLACK LION FM, *Black Lion* 1833 OS. VCH 133 says the name is first recorded c.1780, and the place was an ale-house till the late 19th cent. BROOM HILL, EAST AND NORTH BROOMHILL PLANTATION, *Broomhill* 1715 *SBL 6900*, *Broom Hill*, *North Broomhill* 1839 *TA*. CASTLE PLACE, 1833 OS, *Topynescastell* 1385 Pat, *Toppings Castle* 1601 *SBL 6848B*, *the greate ditche called Topins Castle* 1612 *LDR*, *Toppins Bank* 1839 *TA*. *Topping* is a surname. The 'castle' is a large natural depression surrounding the house (VCH 132). COALPIT LANE, 1833 OS. There was coalmining in Pulverbatch in 18th-19th cents (VCH 129). FURZY COTTAGE. THE GORSE, this is *Gorsy Field* 1839 *TA.* HOLLY COTTAGE, *Leaden Hollies* 1839 *TA.* NEW HO, 1833 OS, LOWER - -. Cf. *Near Newhouse Piece* 1839 *TA.* Lower New Ho is shown but not named on *TAMap.* OUTRACK, *Outracks* 1839 *TA, v.* Outrack in Cothercott *supra.* On *TAMap* and on 6" this is a narrow strip of wooded ground near the W. boundary of the township. It is still there on the 1965 1". WRENTNALL COTTAGE AND HO.

Field-Names

Forms in (a) are 1839 *TA.* Early forms dated c.1597, 1601, 1615, 1707, 1715 are *SBL Plan 47, 6848B, 6848A, 5823, 6900.*

(a) Alder Bank; Banky Lsw; Barkers Garden and Croft; Barley Pce; Barn Lsw; Barn Mdw; Beech Close; Broad Lsw; Brook Close; Brook Lsw, Lower and Upper; Broomcroft; Broomy Bank; Broomy Fd; Burnett Fd and Mdw (possibly **bærnet** 'land cleared by burning'); Burn Mdw; Burstons Leys (*Burstowes Lye, Burstow Meadow* 1601, *Bustorsley* 1615, *Bustyns Lye* (*v.* **lēah**, first el. probably a surname, *Bristol Meadowe* 1699 *SBL 3427* may belong here); The Butts (perhaps cultivation strips); Calves Close; Calves Slang; Campians Mdw; Close (*freq,* used of normal-sized fields); Clover Hill; Coalpit Lsw (cf. Coalpit Lane *supra*); Coppice, Long, Little and Spring (in N.E. corner of parish, no trees shown on any map); Copwell; Cow Lsw; Crowpers Lsw; Dairy House Pce, Near, Middle and Further, Dairy House Lsw (Dairy House 1833 OS); Dalacres Croft; Fallybourn, Lower, Middle and Upper, Fallybourn Plantation (*Walliborns, Fallibrons Field* 1715, here are three furlong-shaped fields, perhaps part of a field-system belonging to Walleybourne, of which Fallybourn may be a corruption); Far Lsw (2); Feg Lsw (rough grass); The Field; Flatt Pce; Foxglove Pce; Further Coalpit Fd (near E. boundary); Further Leys (by Burstons Leys); Gin Lsw (near Further Coalpit Fd, probably 'engine'); Gorsy Lsw; Gorsy Mdw; Great Lsw; Great Well Lsw (separated by two fields from Little - -); Green Pce; Green Rudge (*v.* **hrycg**); Harrow Close (a small triangle); Hayside, Lower -; Hughes Pce; Hush Greaves, - - Mdw (*v.* **grǣfe**); Jaspers Coppice; Little Coppice; Little Lsw (2); Little Mdw; Little Moor and Hemp Yard; Little Well Lsw; Lord Pce; Lords Lsw; Lower Croft and Rushy Mdw; Lower Lsw; Lower Mdw; Malls

Pce; Marlpit, - Lsw; Mdw adjoining House (by Sydnall Cottage in Longden); Middle Fd; Middle Lsw (2); Moor, Lower and Upper; Morgans Close; Morgans Pce (not near preceding); Muncorn Furlong (adjoins Windmill Fd, muncorn is a mixture of wheat and rye); New Bank (by Broomy Bank); Newhouse Lsw (not near New Ho); New Lsw; New Mdw; Old Fd; Old Mdw; Ox Mdw and Ground; Patch above Garden, Lower Patch (by Lower New Ho); Pike Mdw, Great and Little (not exceptionally spiky); Pool Lsw; Red Barn Lsw; Rough Lsw; Rough Mdw Bank; Rushy Mdw; Salop Fd (by Shrewsbury road); Shoulder of Mutton (not appropriately shaped); Sittlery Spy Bank, Wallybourn Sittlery (Spy Bank is in Castle Pulverbatch *supra*, Sittlery is obscure); Skinners, Pce by -; The Slang (narrow strip by brook); Spring Coppice; Stamwell; Sunny Bank and Green Lsw; Tin Mdw (probably short for *tining* 'enclosure'); Tompkys Pce; Upper Mdw; Wall Fd (perhaps an open field of Walleybourne, VCH 131); Washford, - Fd (two converging roads cross a stream here, *v.* **(ge)wæsc**); Well Lsw; Wharstone ('hoar stone', usually a boundary marker, but this field is in the central part of the township); Windmill Fd, Lower and Upper (perhaps, like Wall Fd, an element in a Walleybourne field-system); White Lsw; Wood Lsw (1615, *The Woodleasowe* 1707); Yard, Barn, Green, Upper, Lower, Lane and Walkers (enclosures in the village); Yard above House, Burnetts Yd, Further Yd (by Lower New Ho); Yewtree Pce.

(b) *Almly Brock* c.1597 (*v.* **brōc**, probably on E. boundary); *The Challenge Land* 1610 VCH 129 (in dispute with Stapleton until transferred to Pulverbatch); *The Person's Lie Corner adoinyng to Burstowes Lye* (part of Burstons Leys, *supra*, belonging to the parson); *Rie Meadow* 1601 (perhaps a reference to wild rye); *Rose Hurst* c.1597; *Werekwude* 1235 Eyton, *Werkwod* 1342 Cl (VCH 130 says probably on Broom Hill, 'wood from which building material is obtained', *v.* **weorc**, **wudu**, Walkwood PN Wo 321 is identical); *Wilde Beache* 1615, *Wildbechbrooke* 1715 (VCH 129 says this is the brook which divides Wrentnall from Church Pulverbatch, 'uncultivated stream-valley', *v.* **wilde**, **bæce**); *Wrentnor's Gate* 1601, *Wrentnalls Wood Yate* 1615, *Wood Yate* 1715.

PULVERBATCH FIELD-NAMES NOT ASSIGNABLE TO TOWNSHIPS

Forms dated 1507, 1528, 1570, c.1597 and 1615, 1601, 1699, 1715, 1756, 1789, c.1790 are *SBL 6662, 4001, 6906, 6848A, 6848B, 3427, 6900, 3496, 6581, 6579.*

(b) *Allenlye* 1601 (several f.ns. in the parish consist of reflexes of **lēah** with a surname); *Birchin Brook* 1756 (*v.* **bircen**); *The Black Close* 1601; *Blokes*

Gate 1789; *Brabenshelde* 1507 (*v.* **helde**, first el. probably a surname); *Brown Hill Top* 1756; *Castleway ib*; *Coopers Yard* 1699; *Corbetts Wood Leasow* 1601; *Danley Vallet ib* (a *vallet* is a portion of wood felled annually, OE ***fællet**); *Derneford* 1385 Pat, *The Dearne Foorde* c.1597 ('hidden ford', *v.* **dierne**); *Edenhawnyng* 1570; *Furlong Leasowe* 1699; *The Greene Yord alias the Pyrle Yorde or the Pyerle Yord* 1570; *Gwilliams's Inclosure* 1789; *Henley Knap ib*; *Haraldesoke* 1385 Pat ('Harold's oak', near *Derneford supra*); *Hawkins's Inclosures and Tump* 1789 (the *tump* may be a tumulus); *Heylys* 1528; *The Hurst* 1601 (*v.* **hyrst**); *Irelands Post* c.1790; *Limekiln Road ib*; *Litle Parke, The Litle Parke Ende* c.1597; *Longdons Woode* 1601 (i.e. belonging to Longden in Pontesbury); *The Mere Ashe* c.1597, *The Mear Oake* 1601 ('boundary ash and oak', *v.* **(ge)mǣre**); *Oken Held* 1589 ('oak-covered slope', *v.* **ācen**, **helde**); *Porbiler(s) Bache* 1601 (*v.* **bæce**); *Portfield Gate* 1789; *Poulderbache Woode* 1601, *Powderbatch Wood* 1615 ('Pulverbatch wood'); *Quatfordes Oute Park*, *Quatfords Lane End* c.1597 (*Quatford* is probably a surname); *Rachel's Garden* c.1790; *Rieslye* 1715; *Sidney Brook* 1601; *Stanleys Brow* c.1790; *Starrs Yard* 1699; *Twiseledeake* 1280-84 HAC ('forked oak' with the past participle of OE *twislian*: *SBL 6848A*, c.1597, refers to several oaks with special characteristics, one being *the twiste oke*, which may be this tree); *Le Wildeland* 1342 Cl (said to be a plot which lies by itself, *v.* **wilde** 'uncultivated'); *Witake* 1280-84 HAC (*v.* **hwīt**, **āc**).

Ruckley and Langley

The parish-names, which mean 'rook clearing' and 'long clearing', are discussed in Part **1**.

HAWKSLEY (lost)

Avochelie 1086 DB, *Avekelegh* 1229 Cur
Havekelega c.1190 SAC *et freq* with variant spellings *Haueke-*, *Haveche-* and *-leg'*, *-ley(e)* to 1439-40 *SBL MS2*
Hawkesley 1535 VE, Hy 8 *RentSur*

'Hawk wood', *v.* **hafoc**, **lēah**. The DB form was mistakenly said to be unidentified in Part **1** xii.

The manor was waste in 1086. Later references are to cultivated land and to a wood, the latter being *Boscus de Hauekelee* 1197 FF. A deed of 1269 in SAC says that the cultivated land called *Havekeleye* lies between Ruckley and Langley, and in VE the place is said to lie in Langley Park.

HOTHALES (lost)

Hothale 1250 Fees, *-hal'* 1251 Cl, 1255-6 *Ass*, *-hall* 1253 InqMisc, *-hales* 1261-2 *ForProc*, 1269 SAC, 1291-2 *Ass* (p), 1329 *SBL MS2*
Hokehales 1216 Pat
Hoteile 1255-6 *Ass*, *Hotales* 1265 Cl, 1304 MGS (p), *Hotall* 1411-12 *SBL MS2*, *Hotalles* 1479-80 *ib*
Othales 1347-8 *SBL MS2*, *Ottehale* 1394-5 *ib*

In spite of the scarcity of forms without *H-* this is probably 'oat nook', *v.* **āte**, **halh**. The place was a hamlet with its own common fields, probably situated between Ruckley and Causeway Wood (VCH 142). *Whethalls Meadow* 1848 *TA* probably preserves the name. A deed of 1570-71 in *SBL MS2* speaks of *Ruccley, Whettalls* and *Causey.*

BALLSHILL COPPICE, 1848 *TA*. BROOKHOUSES (lost), Roger *de Brochous* is mentioned 1327 SAS 2/XI, and a deed of 1376-7 copied in *SBL MS2* concerning *les Brochouses in Langley* is dated *apud Brochouses*. 'Houses by the brook', *v.* **brōc**, **hūs**. VCH 142 suggests that this is the hamlet later known as Causeway Wood. CAUSEWAYWOOD, DEVIL'S CAUSEWAY, *Ye Causie Head* 1699, *The Cause-Way* 1708, *Ye Causeway Wood* 1731, *The Cawsea Wood* 1755, *The Gossywood* 1768, *The Gorsey Wood* 1801, *The Causey Wood* 1808, all PR(L) 19. A settlement here is *Causey* 1570-71 *SBL MS2*. A road from Acton Burnell crosses Coundmoor Brook here. It is marked on the 1903 6" map as 'supposed Roman road', but it is not recognised as such. It diverges from Watling Street S. of Pitchford, and follows a meandering course to Plaish and Longville in the Dale. There may have been a raised bank at the stream crossing, which was called *Causey*, ultimately from French **caucie**. To this, *way* was added, and the name was sometimes misinterpreted as 'gorsy'. LANGLEY HALL, *v.* VCH 14. LITTLE HOLLIES, *The Hollies, Far, Little and Lower Hollies* 1848 *TA*. Hollies in Acton Burnell is nearby. NETHERWOOD

COPPICE, *Nether Wood, Netherwood Piece* 1848 *TA*. PARKGATE, *Park-gate* 1751 PR(L) 19. The history of Langley Park is given in VCH 141-2.

Field-Names

Forms in (a) are 1848 *TA*. Ruckley, Langley and *Hothales* each had their own common fields.

(a) Banky Lsw; Banky Pce, Big, Little and Lower - -; Barn Mdw (*TAMap* shows a building, which is larger on 6"); Barn Pce; Big Close (between Pool and Lower Closes, all of them very small); Big Mdw; Brickkiln Rough, Little - -; Broad Lsw; Broom Bank (by Broome in Cardington); Carroty Lsw (there is an unexplained Carrot Tree Lsw in Buildwas, *v*. FN 48); Causely, Little - (by Devil's Causeway, obviously a corruption); Chapel Mdw (the 1903 6" map shows a disused church in this field: this is Langley Chapel, for which *v*. VCH 145: there was another chapel W. of Ruckley, and *Le Chapel Feld in campo de Hothales* 1319-20 *SBL MS2* may refer to that); Close, Far Close (tiny enclosures by the Devil's Causeway); Clover Lsw; Common Pce; Coppice, Coppice Lsw and Mdw (by Nether Wood); Cote Bank; Cote Mdw; Cow Lsw (2); Cow Pasture, Far, Lower and Upper; Crabtree Lsw; Cone Park, Lower (a large field E. of Ruckley hamlet: it is cone-shaped); Cromhill Mdw; Drumbles, Little, Lower and Upper (the sort of hollow frequently called a dingle, *v*. FN 18); Far Pce (2); Faulkes's Pit; Goss Mdw and Yd (a corruption of Causeway, *v*. *supra*); Grangers Cow Pasture; Great Ruckley Pce; Green Pce; Halls Cow Pasture; Harpers Yd; Hemp Yd (in Ruckley hamlet); Henhouse Mdw; Hill Mdw; The Holt, Little Holt (*v*. **holt**, the fields adjoin The Hollies: they are shown as rough ground on 6"); Home Close (2, one by a building on S.E. boundary which is not on 6", the other by Parkgate); Hopyard Mdw; Line Hill (several fields in N.E. of parish are shown as Inclosures from Line Hill, and VCH 142 says that this tract of waste land was enclosed between 1805 and 1846: this is a wooded hill slope, and Line may be from **lind** 'lime-tree'); Long Mdw (2); Long Sides (a narrow field); Lower Close; Lower Lsw and Mdw; Middle Lsw; New Hill Lsw, Lower and Upper; New Lsw; New Mdw; Orchard; Owens Yd; Ox Lsw, Lower and Upper; The Park, Big and Little Park, Park Lsw, Middle Little Park Mdw (these fields cover the large area of Langley Park, disparked in 1805, *v*. Parkgate *supra*); Park Lsw and Pce (by Frodesley Park); Pit Lsw; The Pool (by Bullhill Brook, which runs N.E./S.W. through the parish); Pool Close (2, both higher up on the same stream); Pool Lsw (*TAMap* shows a pond at one corner); Pool

Pce, Lower - - (not by a stream); Poston Fegg (6" map shows rough ground here, *feg* refers to long, rank grass); Pound Mdw (by Ruckley hamlet); Rail Pce, Lower and Upper; Ralphs Croft; Round Mdw, "part of" (adjoins Cardington, but Round Mdw does not appear on that *TAMap*); Round Pce (not circular); Rushy Pce; Sankey Lsw; Sheep Walk and Pasture; Slade (*v.* **slæd**); Slang (a narrow strip); Small Patch (one of a group of tiny enclosures by buildings beside the Devil's Causeway); Spring Lsw and Mdw (close but not adjoining); Square Lsw (adjoins Round Pce and is not square); Square Pce (approximately square); Summer Appletree Close, Near - - -; Swans Nest; Thistley Lsw, Big and Little Thistly Lsw; Town Mdw (in Ruckley hamlet); Two Days' Math (adjoins Long Mdw); Upper Barn Mdw; Upper Lsw; Weavers Croft; Westhope Mdw, Little and Lower (a connection with Westhope in Diddlebury parish seems unlikely); Whetalls Mdw (probably named from the lost settlement of *Hothales, supra*); Widows Mdw, Great - -; Wood Close; Yard, Lower and Upper; Yewtree Close.

(b) *Herburhalle* 1318-19 *SBL MS2* (said to be in the common field of Ruckley, 'shelter nook', *v.* **here-beorg, halh**); *Mabotesstokyng* 1411-12 *ib* (said to be near *Hotall*: 'clearing', *v.* **stoccing**, with a fem. pers.n.); *Ye Meare Ocke* 1602, *The Mere Oak* 1749,51 PR(L) 19 ('boundary oak', said to be near Parkgate); *Mershaleswey* 1274 InqMisc (VCH 142 equates this with the Causeway road discussed *supra*, 'marshall', ME *mareschal*, may have NED sense 1a, 'tender of horses'); *Le Redpole* 1413-14 *SBL MS2* (a pond near Langley, probably 'reed pool', *v.* **hrēod, pōl**); *Tywleshey* 1274 InqMisc (a wood below *Mershaleswey*, *v.* **(ge)hæg**, first el. possibly the ME pl. of **tigel** 'tile').

Smethcott

The parish-name, which means 'cottage(s) of the smiths', is discussed in Part 1.

There were three townships, Smethcott, Betchcott and Picklescott. The bounds of Betchcott are shown on the Tithe Survey Index map, but the division between Picklescott and Smethcott is not observed in *TA*, so the assignment of areas to these two is an approximate one, based on hints in VCH 146ff.

This is an area in which clearing, enclosure and settlement was proceeding in the 12th and 13th centuries, and **cot(e)** must have seemed the appropriate habitative term. A fourth example, *Hollycot*, is discussed under Smethcott *infra*.

1. BETCHCOTT (SO 435986)

Becchecota 1163-6 HAC, *Bechecot'* 1212 Fees *et freq* to 1320 Ch
Bechcot 1255 RH
Bachecot' 1261-2 *ForProc*
Beccheton 1301 SAC
Betchcot 1620 PR(L) 1, *-cott* 1622,88, 1722,25 ib
Betchscott 1735 *SBL 3459*
Beatchcott 1833 OS

'Cottage(s) near a stream-valley', *v.* **bæce, cot(e)**. Betchcott Brook flows in an appropriate hollow. In spite of the spelling and the paucity of *-a-* forms the modern pronunciation is [bætʃkɔt].

BETCHCOTT BROOK, B. HALL (*Hall* 1833 OS), B. HILLS (*Betchcott Hill* 1788 *SBL 6165, Batchcott Hill* c.1790 *SBL 6579*), B. HOLLOW (*Beatchcott Hollow* 1833 OS). HAWKHAM HOLLOW, cf. *Ockham Bank* 1788 *SBL 3496, Ockham Beach and Gutter* 1789 *SBL 6579*. VCH calls the brook here Oakham Brook. Possibly *ācum*, dat.pl. of *āc* 'oak'.

Field-Names

The *TAMap* for Smethcott parish leaves Betchcott township blank, but a few modern and 19th-cent. names are mentioned in VCH and *VCH*. Early forms dated 1722, 1725 and 1775, 1727, 1788 are *SBL 3451, 3387, 3440, 3496*.

(a) Bone Furlong 1968 VCH (cf. *The Bonmore* 1722, *The Banmore* 1725,75, possibly 'bone', referring to the use of bone-dust for manure); Lower Butts 1968 VCH (this and preceding may not be modern names, they are cited VCH 148 as showing that one of Betchcott's three common fields lay N.W. of Middle Betchcott Fm); Callow Batch 1833 OS (*Callow Helde* 17th VCH, *Callow Bank and Betch* 1788, *v.* **calu, helde, bæce**); Orration Fd 1968 VCH (*Orrington Furlong* 1675 *VCH, Orington Field* 1725,7,75, an open field E. of Betchcott Hall, perhaps *oration* in the sense 'prayer' referring to Rogationtide ceremonies); Ross 1808 *VCH* (*The Roest, Roost Butts* 1601 *VCH, The Rost* 1722,5,7: two names in Picklescott, *Le Rosteisheede* 1445-6 HAC and *Rostefeld* 1464 *VCH*, are obviously connected: apparently the word *roost* in some sense, perhaps a place where birds congregated).

(b) *Birds Acre* 1725,7; *The Black Pool* 17th *VCH*; *The Doles* 1722, *The Doles Hall* 1725, (*v.* **dāl**); *Field Ground* 1722,7; *Goseforde* 1253 HAC (*v.* **gōs, ford**); *Hauedwey* ib (*v.* **hēafod, weg**); *High Furlong* 1722,5,7; *Holly Tree Leasow* 1722, *Holley* - - 1725,7,75; *Horne Meadow, Hill Horne* 1722,5,7,75 (*v.* **horn**); *Lower Leasow* 1722,5,7; *Lower Yard* 1722,7, *The Loweryard* 1725; *Lydes* 1722,5,75; *Mansells Tenement* 1722,7; *The Moore Acre* 1722,5, *Moor Acre Farm* 1788 (*v.* **mōr, æcer**); *Stephens Pitts* 1722,5,7; *The Tweengates ib*; *Upper Field* 1722,7 (a common field, VCH 148); *Wareings Tenement* 1717 *VCH, Warings* - 1722, *Warings Land* 1722,75; *Wawmas Knowle* 17th *VCH*; *Wooley ib* (probably a hill: the boundary between Wilderley and Picklescott follows the 'skirt' of *Wooley* after the 'skirt' of Thorny Knoll in Ratlinghope).

2. PICKLESCOTT (SO 435996)

Pikelescote 1204-c.1220 HAC *et freq* with variant spellings *Pykeles-* to 1397 InqMisc
Pikescote c.1220-30 HAC, *Pykescote* 1271-2 *Ass*
Piclescot 1255 RH, *Pyclescote* 1255-6 *Ass*
Pychelecote 1271-2 *Ass*
Pykclescote 1301 SAS, *Pyckelscott* 1549 Pat, *Pykelscote* 1569 *SBL 6621, Picklescott, Pikkles-* 1615 PR(L) 1
Pyllestowe alias Piklescott 1551 Pat, *Pillescote alias Picklescoote* 1596-7 *SBL 3463*
Pigglescote 1617 PR(L) 1
Piddlescott 1740 *SBL 993*

Probably 'Pīcel's cottage(s)', but the first el. could be the genitive of a hill-name **Pīcel*, a diminutive of **pīc** 'point'. As is frequently the case in Sa, shortened forms have failed to oust the original longer one.

BIRCH COPPICE. PARKGATE, *v.* Underhill *infra.* PEASE

LANE, 1833 OS. *TAMap* shows two houses here. PICKLESCOTT HILL, c.1790 *SBL 6579.* POGAN HALL, 1802 PR(L) 1, *TAMap* shows the house. THE SLADE, 1844 *TA*, *v.* **slæd**. UNDERHILL HALL, 1774 *et seq* PR(L) 1, *Underhill* 1833 OS. Cf. *Underhill Park* 1789, c.1790 *SBL 6581, 6579.* The history of the house and park is given in VCH, p.151. WILDRECK, *The Wolrich* 1718, *Willriche* 1724, *The Woolrack* 1735, *Wilreck Common* 1737, *Willreck* 1739, *The Wilrack* 1741 (all *VCH), Wool rake* 1833 OS. There may have been association of the second el. with ME **rake** 'hill-path', but the forms with *-rich(e)* suggest a compound with ***ric**, 'narrow strip', which usually refers to a straight ridge or bank. In the absence of earlier forms only conjectures can be offered. The first el. could be **wulf**.

Field-Names

Forms in (a) are 1844 *TA*. Early forms dated 1621, 1685, 1772, 1788, c.1789 are *SBL 5120, 10345, 3496, 6579.* Others for which no source is given are *VCH.*

(a) Ash Stubbs, Ash Run Stubbs (*Ashen Stub Acre* 1601); Banky Lsw (3); Barn Pce; The Beach (2, by streams, *v.* **bæce**); Big Hill Pce; Big New Lsw; Birch Lsw (2); Bottom Mdw; Bowens Yd (by a house); Broad Lsw; Brooky Lsw, Lower and Upper; Buttrey Beach (*The Buttering Patch* 1685, *Butterings Beaches* 1772, *v.* **bæce**, the field is by the stream which divides Picklescott from Betchcott: the first el. refers to good pasture, *v.* **butere**); Close (*freq*, used for very small fields S. of Parkgate and W. of Pease Lane); Cockshutt Hill, Lower - - (*Cockeschoteisfelde* 1445-6 HAC, *Cokshotfeld* 1464, *Cockshutt Field, Hill and Gate* 1601, Cockshutt Mdw, Lower Cockshutt Hill 1808, *v.* ***cocc-sciete**, this was an open field); Common Ground and Pce; Coppice Ground (7 adjacent fields); Cow Pasture, Lower and Upper; Crabtree Lsw; Crabtree Patch; Cross Acre (2 fields by a road junction, an open field here was *Cross Field*, VCH 148); Crowthers Yd; The Dale Acre (*The Dallecke Ridge* 1601, *Dalliacre* 1772, *v.* **dæl**, **æcer**, the *TA* field is by an indentation in the 900'c ontour); The Dale End (there is another indentation in the 900'contou r here); Ellds (*Le Held Ground* 1532, *The Helde End* 1601, *v.* **helde**); Far Pce; The Far Pce; Fawn Bank; Ferny Acre; Field Mdw; Flat Mdw; Fold Close (by a house which is still there on 6"); Gate Pce; Gilbers Ley, Guilsbury (*Gilbarts Lowe* 1601, *Gilbersley* 1777, Gilberts Lay, Upper - - 1808, probably 'Gilbert's tumulus': the *TA* fields adjoin in the S.W. corner of the township, and the n. is identical with *Le Silbardeislowe* 1445-6 HAC, said to be in *Hullegrenefeld*, of which this area was part: *v.* **hlāw**, first el. the OG pers.n. *Gislebert*, here probably that of a ME tenant); Gorsty Patch; The Hale, Big Hale Mdw, Hall Mdw (*v.* **halh**, the fields lie between converging roads E. of the village: this may be *land called The Hall* 1685, *The Hale* 1772); Hardwicks Head (Hardway Head 1777, 1808); Hill Ground and Lsw; Hill Pce; Hobs Pike 1808; Hollow Lsw; Horse Close; Inch Pinch (*v.* Smethcott f.ns. *infra*); James' Yd 1839 *LDR* (*James Yard* 1612 *et seq* to 1767 *ib*); Lawleys Lsw; Little Mdw; Little Park (adjoins Underhill Hall); Long Furlong (adjoins The Dale Acre, both are furlong-shaped); Long Pce; Meadow, Piece below -; The Mole Acre; Morgan's Mdw; New Pce 1808 (1772); Orchard Hill; Owens Mdw; Patch (each of a group of small enclosures by the road near W. boundary of parish is called Patch); Piece, Upper, Middle and Lower; Pinches Lsw (2); Pool Pce, Close and Mdw (a pool is shown on 6" S. of Pease Lane); Post Fd; Rocky Lsw; Rushy Mdw; Rushy Patch; Sandy Hill; School Yd (adjoins village on W.); Square Pce, Near - - (both square); The Yard (on edge of village); Yard House (building on N. edge of village); Yewtree Lsw.

(b) *Adams Castle Field* c.1789; *The Andritch Hill* 1685, *The Andrith Hill* 1772; *Appeltresfelde* 1445-6 HAC, *Apple Tree Lands* 1601 (both said to be in Cockshutt Field); *Ash Furlong* 1772; *Barnyard* 1601, 1772; *Beche* 1445-6 HAC (possibly identical with one of the Beach ns. in (a)); *Birchin Land* 1601; *Brodmore's Corner* 1524, *Bradmores* - 1603,5, *Broadmoor* - 1681; *Brown Hill* 1788; *Le Bruches, Le Brucheistile* 1445-6 HAC, *The Brooches* 1601 (*v.* **bryce, stigel**); *Le Bynne End* 1535; *Chirmacr'* e.14th HAC, *Churchmays Acre* 1601; *The Crosswey* 1532; *Doles Meadow* 1601 (*v.* **dāl**); *Duns Yard Head* 1601; *Eyneshamstile* 1340, *Eyshams Meadow* 1601 (first el. probably a surname); *Farmer's Piece* 1788; *Field beneath the town* 1601 (open field, also known as *Cross Field*, VCH 148); *Gapit Syche* 1601 (*v.* **sīc**); *Haddestomsmedew* 1445-6 HAC (*v.* **mǣd**, first el. probably a surname); *Hakestone Meadowe* 1551 Pat, *Hakestons Meadow* 1621 (perhaps identical with preceding); *Le Haale* 1445-6 HAC (in *Hullegrenefelde*, so not connected with Hale ns. in (a), *v.* **halh**); *Hale Pike* 1524, *Le Haylepyke* 1535, *Hale Pyke* 1601 (*v.* **halh, pīc**); *Hardoms Head* 1601 (perhaps identical with Hardwicks Head in (a)); *Hillons Style* 1525; *Hullegrenefelde* 1445-6 HAC (an open field), *Hill Grenes Acre* 1601 (*v.* **hyll, grēne**[2]); *Le Hurst Stile* 1524 (*v.* **hyrst, stigel**); *Hyndebache* e.14th HAC, *Hynde Beeche* 1601 (*v.* **hind, bæce**); *Lampitts Acre* 1601 ('loam pit'); *Limekiln Road* c.1789; *The Lowe* 1601 (in Cockshutt Field, which was N. of the village, *v.* **hlāw**, this is a second 'tumulus' name in the township); *Lower Gorsty Bank* 1788; *Le Marsh* 1537; *The Mary Acre* 1601 (in Cockshutt Field, perhaps dedicated to the maintenance of a shrine); *The Meer Oak* 1741 ('boundary oak'); *Merxhacr'* e.14th HAC (possibly 'marsh acre'); *The Old* 1551 Pat (a toft called - -); *Parkesheld* 1524 ('slope near the park'. *v.*

helde); *Le Porte Weye* 1445-6 HAC (in *Hullegrenefeld*, so apparently the road from Picklescott to Betchcott, for which the term does not seem appropriate); *Les Rowetinges* 1340 (perhaps referring to ground disturbed by rooting pigs); *Silvann Hill's Cottage* 1741; *Stevens Pits* 1532; *Thorny Acre* 1601 (in Cockshutt Field); *Wall Meadow* 1772; *Ware Hedges* 1788; *Wheat Butts* 1601; *Wilardewic, Wylardewyk* 1340 (this was a wood in 1340, but there may earlier have been a settlement, 'Wilheard's **wīc**': the resemblance to Wilderley is probably coincidental); *Wildings Brook* 1741; *Winter Field* 1524.

3. SMETHCOTT (SO 449994)

HOLLYCOT (lost), *Holicote, Neweholicote* 1340 *VCH, Hollycot* 1624 PR(L) 1, *Le Hollycote* 1636 *VCH.* Associated names are *Holicotescrosse, Holicotes Netherford, Holicotesbrook* 1340 *VCH, Holycots Bach* 1585, 1615 *VCH, Hollicots Brook* 1618 *VCH.* The *TAMap* shows fields called Big, Little and Lower Hollycot lying between Pease Lane and Smethcott Common. This was probably once a hamlet, though it is only recorded as a name for a cultivated area (VCH 153-4). Associated names contain **bæce, brōc, ford,** and ME *cross,* which may here (as regularly in later Sa f.ns.) refer to a road-junction. *Hollycot* is 'holly cottage(s)', *v.* **holegn, cot.**

BANK FM, 1808 *VCH,* 1833 OS, *The Bank* 1844 *TA.* Cf. *The Bank House* 1781 PR(L) 1. The name refers to a large rectangular earthwork N.E. of the farm. BIRCH COPPICE, *Birchin Copies* c.1619 *VCH.* BRANMILL, *Brandmills, Brandmill Meadow* 1675 *VCH, Brand Mill* 1777 VCH 149: 'burnt mill', *v.* **brende**.[2] COPPICE HO, 1833 OS, *The Coppy House* 1649 SAS 4/VII: first recorded in 1585 (VCH 150). FACTORY DINGLE. This is a wooded stream-valley by Parkhead. The corresponding strips of land are *Scoltocks Yard* and *Scoltocks Dingle* on *TAMap.* GREENFIELDS, 1870 VCH, called *Shady Moor* 1833 OS, *v.* Shadymoor in Stapleton. LAWLEY VIEW. LONG COPPICE. NEW HALL, 1751 PR(L) 1, 1833 OS, first recorded in 1583 (VCH 150). NEW HO. NIGHT SHELL DINGLE (Gazetteer), *The Knyghts Held* 1496 *VCH, Knyghts Helde* 1532 *VCH, Knights Heald* 1617 *VCH, - Held* 1675 *VCH, The Knightshill* 1763 *LDR, Nightshield, - Coppice* 1777 *VCH, Night Shell* 1833 OS. 'Gentle slope belonging to a family named Knight', *v.* **helde**. The name is not shown on 20th-cent. OS maps. PARISH HO, *Parish House Field* 1844 *TA*, shown as *Poor Houses* 1833 OS. PARKHEAD, 1833 OS, *The Park Head* 1619 *VCH*, 1749 PR(L) 1, *Parke Head* 1652 *SRO 567*, perhaps referring to the larger of the two parks in Stapleton. SMETHCOTT COMMON, 1755 *SBL 3515*, *v.* VCH 146-7. SMETHCOTT DINGLE. SMETHCOTT POOL, 1844 *TA*. This was a fishpond called *Froggepol* 1320 *VCH*, *Frogpool* 1720 *VCH*, *v.* **frogga, pōl**. TUMULUS. This designation is wrongly given on 6" and 1" maps to the motte and bailey castle W. of the church, *v.* VCH 149. WALKMILLS, 1782 *et freq* to 1811 PR(L) 1: fulling mills were probably established here by e.14th (VCH 100, 150). There is a reference 1676 VCH to "2 walk mills called the Upper Mills".

Field-Names

Forms in (a) are 1844 *TA* except for those dated 1808, 1817, which are *VCH*, those dated 1839, which are *LDR*, and a few others which are individually sourced. Early forms dated 1445-6, l.15th are HAC, those dated 1612, 1692, 1698, 1705, 1763, 1767 are *LDR*. All others for which no source is given are *VCH*.

(a) The Acre 1808; Addys Butts (*Adys Gate* 1496, 1617, *Adys Furlong* 1675, *Adys Butt and Furlong* 1777, a unit in the common field called Cross or Linch Field, first el. probably a surname); The Bank (not near Bank Fm); Barley Fd; Barn Fd, Far and Near; Barn Mdw (2); The Barn Lesow or Barnyard 1839 (*Barnes Leasow* 1647, *Barnyard* 1653, *The Barn Lesow* 1763); Bartlams Yd (1777); Beaches, Beach Rough 1808 (1777, *v.* **bæce**); Big Lsw; Bonsty Rough; Boosey Pasture, Lower and Upper (land with special pasture rights for an outgoing tenant, *v.* FN 34); Brandarts Bank (adjoins a small triangular field which was probably called 'the trivet'); Brandmarsh 1808 (1675, 1777, *The Brand Marsh* e.17th, *Branmarshe Hedge* c.1635, in the 1777 ref. the name follows Brandmill in a list, so perhaps shortened from **Brandmill Marsh*, *v.* Branmill *supra*); Brickkiln Lsw, Lower and Upper; Broad Mdw (2); The Broomy Lsw 1839 (1685); Browns Close; Buggy Brook (by the brook which forms the N.W. boundary of the parish); Burgoines Mdw; Calves Patch (1817); Castle Fd 1808 (1653), The Castle Fd Acre 1839 (*The Castle Field Ackar* 1705, *The Castle Acre near the Church* 1763, *The Castle Acre or The Castle Field Acre* 1767, a common field named from the motte and bailey W. of the church); Churns

Head, Little; Close (several tiny enclosures by a house near E. boundary); Coalpit Fd (in N.E. tip of parish); Cockshutt Fd (- *Leasow* 1653,75); Common Pce, Upper and Lower, Common Land and Lsw, Upper Common Fd (on Smethcott Common); Common Pce, Far and Near, Common Lsw (in E. of parish, not near preceding); Coppice (*The Copies* 1763); Coppice Bank, The Bank (adjoining in S.E. corner of parish); Cottage Land; Cow Pasture, Lower and Upper; Croft (*freq* for small enclosures in the village); Crow Pool (no pool shown); David's Patch (*Davids* - 1681, a normal-sized field); Dicks Hill; Dingle, Lower -; Dole Mdw 1808 (*Doles* - 1777, *v.* **dāl**); Dyers Mdw (Ric. Davies 'dyer' is mentioned 1634, and cf. "the Dyhouse lately rebuilt" c.1796); Field before Rectory House; Flat Lsw; Flat Pce; Four Turnings Fd and Pce (by a crossroads); Foxholes (*Voxhole* l.15th, *v.* **fox-hol**); Franks Lsw; Gorsty Patch; Gorsy Bank and Rough; Grilpit, Lower and Upper (a corruption of *Gritt Pitt* 1675, 1705, *Gritpit* 1698, *The Gritt Pitts* 1763,67, The Gritt Pits 1839, 'gravel pit', *v.* **grēot**); Hain Bank (*Hene Furlong* 1660, *Heane, - Bank* 1675, *Haynes Bank, Hean, - Furlong* 1681, *Hayne, - Bank, Haynes Rough* 1777, ***hægen** 'enclosure', ME *hain*, a rather rare p.n. el: Hain Bank is on the Leebotwood boundary, and *The Haines* occurs c.1738 in that parish); Hales Yd 1808; Harringtons Furlong; Hawthorn Bank; Hazeler Mdw (a number of 'hazel' names occur in Smethcott records, cf. *Hasylhurst* 1496, *Haselhurst Moore* 1532, *Haslehurst* 1617, *Haslemore Meadow* 1653, *Hasells, Hasellwood Moor* 1675, *Hasles* 1719 *SBL 4094, Hazles, Hazle Meadow, Hazlemoor Meadow* 1777, *v.* **hæsel, hyrst, mōr**); The Held 1839 (*The Healde* 1705, *v.* **helde**); Horse Lsw (1685); Horse Pasture; Horse Pce, Little; Horestone Lsw (*The Hoarstons* 1612, *Hoarstone* 1675, *Hoarestone Lesow* 1777, *v.* **hār**[2], **stān**, not on a boundary); Hungerhill (1653,75, 1777); Hurst Bank; Inch Pinch (there is an adjoining field with this name in Picklescott, the two fields are on either side of a sharp road bend); Lamberts Butt 1808 (*Lampus Butt* 1777, perhaps 'loam pit'); Lane Pce; Langfords Bank; Lenacre (*Linacres* 1675, *The Lynacre, Lynaker* 1681, *Linacre* 1777, 'flax acre', *v.* **līn**); Little Lightmoor, Big Lightnor (*Laytnor, - Coppice* 1777, possibly *Lightnoll, Leighknoll* 1653, first el. **lēoht** 'light-coloured', second el. uncertain); Linch Mdw and Slang, Upper and Lower Lynches (*Le Lynche* 1496, 1532, *Lynches* 1617, *Le Lynch* 1636, *Linches, Linch Coppice* 1675, Lynch Bank, Long Lynch 1817: *v.* **hlinc**, the *TAMap* shows the names on either side of the road E. of the village, so the sense may be 'terrace way': an open field here was Cross or Lynch Field, it is *The Lynch Fyeld* 1612); Little Fd and Mdw (adjoining, *Little Meadow* 1675); Long Bank (1685, also *Middle* - and *Great* -); Long Furlong (1660, 1777, in the first ref. it is said to be in *Stockin Field*); Long Lsw (2); Lower Lsw (*Lower and Over Leasow* 1675, *Lower and Upper* - 1777); Lower Low, High or Low (*Le Lowe* 1636, *The Low(e)* 1653, *Over, Middle and Lower Lowe* 1675, *The Lowe* 1777, 1817, *v.* **hlāw**, the *TA* fields are E. of the village, High or Low is a corruption of Higher Low: there are 2 tumulus names in Picklescott township); Lye Lsw and Mdw (*Lye, Lye Meadow* 1777); Marlpits (*The Marlepytt* 1612, *The Marle Pitt* 1698, 1705); Meadow, Lower and Upper; Middle Mdw; The Moat 1808 (1625, 1777, *Le Mote* 1428, *Over and Lower Moat* 1675, probably referring to the motte and bailey castle W. of the church); The Moor 1839 (*Moores Pool* 1675, *Ye Moore* 1692, *The Moore* 1698, 1705, 1767, *The Moore Lesow* 1763, *v.* **mōr**); Myttons Bank; Myttons Lsw (not near preceding); The Netch-hills 1839 (*The Netch Hill* 1767, Netchells 1808, possibly ***ēcels** 'additional land' with *-n* from ME *atten*); New Lsw (*The New Leasowe* 1612); New Mdw; Old House Pce (a large field, no house shown); Old Womans Mdw; Ox Lsw, - - Rough; Parson's Patch; Patch (a number of small enclosures near the church, one being Patch opposite Church); Patch (*freq*, mostly very small); Piece before Gwilliams; The Pike (pointed at one end); Plumers Fd, Plunners (*Plontenal* m.13th, *Pluntnall* e.17th, *Pluntners Coppice* 1625, *Pluntnoll* 1653, *Pluntner, Pluntners Coppy* 1675, *Plunners Coppy* 1747, second el. **halh**, first el. perhaps OE *plante* 'plant' in the sense 'sapling'); Pool House 1808; Pool Pce (4); Preeces Berry; Rabbit Borough; Rabbit Burrow Fd (not near preceding); Rabbit Hole Lsw (2); Rail Lsw (*Raile* - 1675); Rich Lsw and Mdw; Riddle Door (*Riddlesdoor* 1777); Roberts Patch (cf. Roberts Mead 1817); Rocky Fd; Rocky Lsw; Rookery Lsw; Rough Fd; Rough Lsw, Lower and Upper; Ryegrass Fd; Sawpit Lsw (1777); Scoltock's Yd and Dingle; Simons Hill (*Samon Hill* 1675, *Samons* - 1777); Spout Lsw; Slang Mdw (long, narrow strip); Snails Yd 1808 (1777, *Snailes* - 1675); Southertons Rough; Stayleys Slang (narrow strip); Tithers Lsw; Tranter Yd (*Tanter Yard* 1681, 1777, probably from a cloth-stretching frame); Trantums Copy 1812 PR(H) 1 (*Trenthams Wood alias Smethcott Wood* 1584, *Trentham Copy alias Trentham Wood* 1585, *Trenthams Coppice* 1615, *Trentam Wood* 1675, named from a family called Trentham, VCH 152: Gazetteer gives Trantum's Coppy as an extant name); Turnip Fd; Upper Cow Lsw; Upper Croft; Upper Lsw; Upper Mdw; Upper Pce; Wassells Dale (a large field N.E. of the Rectory, Wassell is sometimes from **weard-setl** 'watch house', used of prehistoric fortifications); Well Lsw (1685 VCH); White Lsw, Big and Little; Wilcocks Lye, Wilcocks Lee or Lee House 1817 (*Wilcocks Lee* 1521, *Wylcocks Lye* 1527); Wilcocks Horne 1839 (*The Wilcoxhorne* 1612, *Wilcocks-Horne* 1692, *Willcox Horen* 1698, 'grassland and horn of land belonging to a family named Wilcox'); Wood Lsw and Rough; The Yard (several enclosures between the village and the church have Yard names); Yewtree Bank (1817); Yewtree Lsw; Yewtree Patch.

(b) *Anscroft* 1340; *Aysome Yate* 1681 (perhaps to be associated with *Eyshams Meadow* in Picklescott); *Barkus Furlong* 1777; *Blakemore Meadow* 1675 (*v.* **blæc, mōr**); *Bradackes Wood, Bradocks Wood* 1619 (from a surname);

Brandgreave 1675, *Brand Greaves* 1777 ('burnt grove', *v.* **græfe**); *Le Bredeles Acre* 1496, *Breadlers Acre* 1617; *Brodfyld, Le Brodfeld* 1496, *Broad Field* 1617 (an alternative name for Stocking Field, VCH 148); *Broomy Peece* 1698; *Bruchers Glatt* 1681 (the same source mentions *Coppy Glatt* in Woolstaston Wood, second el. dialect *glat* 'gap in hedge' recorded from We, Wo, Sa, Mont, He, Rad, Gl, cf. High Glat in Longnor *supra*: it is surprising that this word is not more common in f.ns.); *Brusty, Over and Lower* 1675; *Chessell Bank* 1675 (*v.* **ceosol**); *Chircheweishull'* 1445-6, 'church way's hill'); *Le Coliere(s)ford* 1340, *Colliers Ford* 1674 ('charcoal-burner's ford'); *Croisfelde* 1445-6, *Crossfield* 1636 (an open field, 'cross' may mean road-junction: it was E. of the church and alternatively called Lynch Field); *Cross(ed) Leasow* 1691 *SRO 567*; *La Crufting* 1340, *Criftines* 1660, *Le Criftings* 1691, *The Cryftyn* 1701, *Criftin* 1777 (*v.* ***cryfting** 'small croft': VCH 147 locates this N.E. of Smethcott Pool, and the curved road here may be going round some ancient enclosures); *Echleys Meadowe* 1612; *Fallow Moor* 1685; *Fearney Banck* 1698; *Le Fernyhale in Brodfyld* 1496, *Le Fernehole* 1532, *The Fearnyhale* 1612, *Ferny Hole in Broad Field* 1617, *Le Fernyhall* 1636 ('ferny hollow', *v.* **halh, hol**[1]); *The Field* 1777; *Foxes Rails* 1747; *The Green* 1747; *Grethesforde* 1340 (perhaps 'ford of the gravelly place', *v.* ***grēote**); *Halehedde* 1445-6 ('nook head', *v.* **halh, hēafod**, it was in *Croisfelde*); *Hardemedowe* 1445-6 (*v.* **heard, mǣd**); *Le Helde* 1445-6 ('slope', in *Croisfelde*); *Hesters, - Moor* 1636; *The Hill Pool Rough* 1763; *Hollies* 1740 PR(L) 1; *Holemedo* 1496, *Le Holle Meadow* 1532, *v.* **hol**[2]); *Home Meadowe* 1612, *Homedow* 1705 ('meadow near the farm'); *Horscroft* 1340; *Jennys Lee, Jennis Ley* 1653, *Jennings Lye* 1675, 1777; *The Lower Field* 1612, *Lower Field* 1777; *Lyd Yeat* 1612 (*v.* **hlidgeat**); *Lyes Coppy* 1675, *The Lye, Lyes Wood* 1681 (*lye* is probably a form of *lea* 'grassland'); *The Lyme Myers* 1619; *Marsh Lane* 1608,19; *Mill Meadow* 1777; *The Nether Field* 1608; *New Furlong* 1675; *Newehokcok* 1340; *The Ollers below the Well* 1763 ('alders'); *The Orchard* 1636; *The Ould Coppye* 1595 *SBL 7085*; *Ould Mills* 1694 *SBL 9955*; *Over Wood* 1629; *Peas Bank* 1777; *Pellystyle* 1496, 1617, *Pellyns Marlepitt* 1532, *Pellyne* 1612 PR(L) 1, *Pellien Bank* 1651, 1660, *Pelline Bank* 1675, *Pelline* 1777 (the stile, marlpit and bank were probably at a place called *Pelline*, but the origin of that name is totally obscure); *Pennes Well* 1651, *Penis Well* 1660; *Picts Meadow* 1675; (*The*) *Pinfold Yard* 1701,19; *Port Yate, - - Meadow* 1651,60, *Portgate* 1681, *Portgate Meadow* 1777 ('town gate', no more appropriate in Smethcott than *Port Way* is in Picklescott, cf. *Portyatehole* in Wilderley, *supra*); *Ronnockslye* 1675, *Ronhooks Lye* 1777 (probably 'grassland' with a surname); *The Rudd Way on the west side of Longnor Park* 1651 *SRO 567, Ruddway* 1652 *ib, Ruding Way* 1675 *ib, Rudding Way and Slang, Rid(e)ing Way, Ruding Way* 1688 *ib, Rudding Way, Rudy or Ridding Way* 1691 *ib* ('clearing way', *v.* ***ryding**); *The Sandy Lesow* 1763; *Shitters Moor* 1618; *Smallway* 1777 ('narrow way', *v.* **smæl**); *Smethcott Wood* c.1619, 1636;

Le Stonyegge 1340 (*v.* **stānig, ecg**); *Le Stokkyng* 1496, *Stockynge Hill* 1532, *Stocking* 1617, *Stocken* 1675, *Stocken Field* 1747, *Stocking* 1777 (*v.* ***stoccing**, an open field); *Strete Meadow* 1777; *Tews Yard* 1777; *Tymbryng(k)esbechesbrok* 1340 (a garbled form, the name probably contains **timber**, **bæce**, **brōc**); *Upper Field* 1777; *Warands Dale* 1675, *Weddings Dale* 1777 (perhaps to be identified with Wassells Dale in (a)); *Wheat Furlong* 1777; *Wilderdeleyes-brok* 1340 ('Wilderley brook'); *The Willer* 1747; *Wodewalle* 1340 ('wood spring').

Stapleton

The parish-name is discussed in Part **1**. It probably means 'settlement at a steep place', though the topography is not dramatic. There are two townships, Netley and Stapleton, Netley being the southern part of the parish. In Part **1** (p.222) it was erroneously stated that the two were combined in one Tithe Award. In fact Netley has its own *TA*.

On the 1967 OS Combined Index map, which shows civil parishes, Stapleton is included in the area of Condover. It is shown as a separate parish on the 1" map of 1961.

1. NETLEY (SJ 474017)

The township-name, which means 'nettle clearing', is discussed in Part **1**.

ASH COPPICE, *Ash Cover* 1844 *TA*. BEECHCROFT, 1844 *TA*. NETLEY HALL, NETLEY OLD HALL. The two houses are ½ mile apart. On 1833 OS the former is *Netley* and the latter *Netley Hall*. On 1844 *TAMap* the former is not named and the latter is *Netley*. *Netley Hall* is mentioned 1748 *LDR*. HIGHER AND LOWER NETLEY are so named 1833 OS. No early forms have been found for SIDE NETLEY, but this and all the Netley sites listed here have buildings shown on *TAMap*. SIGNAL BANK, 1833 OS, *Signall or Whitnell Bank* 1844 *TA*. UPPER WD, *Upper Cover* 1844 *TA*.

Field-Names

Forms in (a) are 1844 *TA*.

(a) Allens Mdw; Almshouse Croft and Pce; Arley, Lower and Upper; Banky Fd; Barn Fd, Upper, Middle, Lower; Barn Patch; Barn Patch and Yd, Upper and Lower Barn Cow Lsw (adjoining fields on S. boundary); Barnyard, Lower and Upper; Big Bank; Birch Lsw; Brick Fd; Broomy Lsw, Big and Little; The Butts (N. of Higher Netley, probably not referring to arable strips in this instance); Chone Hill, - - Mdw; Colliers Mdw; Coppice, Near and Farther (adjoining Upper Wd); Coppice, Near, Middle, Old, Little, Far Great (a row of fields between Ash Coppice and Beechcroft); Cow Pasture; Dorsetts Mdw; Dovehouse Yd; Dry Pce; Foxholes; Garden Mdw; Garden Paddock; Gooseberry Lsw; Great Gorsty Bank; Great Lsw (2); Great Mdw; Green Pce, Little - -; Hardings Pce, Far and Near; Heynes's Mdw; Hightree Lsw, Lower and Upper; Hill Pce; Horse Pasture; Lawn, Upper and Lower (by Netley Hall); Leasow, Upper, Lower, Great, Long (adjoining fields); Leys, Gorsy and Lower; Long Lsw; Long Mdw; Mixen Mdw (*v.* **mixen**); New Lsw; New Mdw; North Paddock; Old Well Lsw; Orchard, Upper -; Ox Lsw; The Park (by Netley Old Hall); Pikes, Lower, Middle, Little (between a brook and a road which converge to make a point at one place); Pond Cover (in grounds of Netley Hall, pond shown on 6" map); Road Lsw; Sir Roger's Lsw; Spout Mdw; Stackyard Pce; Sweet Bank; Thistly Fd; Thistly Pce; Three Cornered Croft; Waterpit Lsw, Lower and Upper; Way Lsw; Well Lsw; White Lsw (2); World's End (on parish boundary).

(b) *Hetheshall Field* 1453 VCH 162; *Hurst Field* ib.

2. STAPLETON (SJ 472045)

LOWER AND UPPER SHADYMOOR FM, MIDDLE SHADYMOOR. The three farms lie beside a road which runs between BIG and LITTLE SHADYMOOR COPPICE. Corfield's Coppice (*infra*) is N. of Lower Shadymoor Fm, so the area so named was a mile long. Early forms are *The Wood Shedmore* 1635 *Eyton, Shedmore, Shedmore Wood* 1666 *ib, Shaddow Moor* 1729 *SBL 3396, The Pitshed Moore* 1734 *Eyton* (perhaps referring to coalpits), *Shadow Moor* 1788 *SBL 3496, Shady Moor* 1791 PR(L) 1, *The Shadymoore* 1808 ib, *Shadymoor* 1810 ib. LOWER SHADYMOOR FM is *Lower Shadymoor* 1839 *TA*, and BIG SHADYMOOR

COPPICE is *Upper Shadymoor Wood ib.* All three farms are marked *Shady Moor* on 1833 OS. 'Boundary marsh', *v.* **scēad, mōr**. There has been association with the words *shadow* and *shady.* The same name occurs in Norton in Condover, *supra.*

VCH 161 equates this with *Stanleymor* 1311 Pat (named from Richard *de Stanleye* 1327 SAS 2/XI), and *Shadwell Moor,* mentioned in 1547.

VINNALS, *The Vinnals* 1453 VCH 162, 1800 PR(L) 1, *The Vennors* 1651 PR(L) 6. *TA* has *Vinnals* as the name of a building, and fields called *Upper and Lower -, Shakers -, Tomkiss -* and *Vinnals Patch.* These fields are spread out over the N.W. of the parish, not all adjoining. There was an open field called *Vinnals* here. There is an obvious similarity to the He name High Vinnalls, which is that of a wooded massif S.W. of Ludlow. No etymology can be suggested, and the name has not been noted in other counties.

WAYFORD BRIDGE, 1726 *LDR, Weyvord* 1586 PR(L) 6, *Weyfforde Brydge* 1612 *LDR, Wayford* 1614 PR(L) 6, 1681 *LDR, Weiford* 1626 PR(L) 6, *Weavord Gate* 1685 *LDR, Wayford Farm* 1730 *LDR. TA* has *N. and S. Wayford Hill* and *Big and Little Wayford Leasow* (*Wayford Lessow* 1693 *LDR*). VCH 162 cites refs. to Sybil de Wayford in 1353 and to a smithy here in 1356. VCH 31 says that the Shrewsbury/Hereford road was described as from Wayford to Shrewsbury in 1466. *v.* **weg, ford**: the road crosses a tributary of the Cound.

BLACK FIRS. BRIDGE FM. CORFIELD'S COPPICE, this is *Lower Shadymoor Wood* 1839 *TA, v. supra.* MANOR FM. MEOLES MEADOW PLANTATION, this is *Moat Lane Plantation* 1839 *TA.* MOAT, MOAT COTTAGES AND FM, UPPER MOAT, UPPER MOAT COTTAGES: *Ye Moate* 1601 *SBL 6848B, Ye Mote Farm* 1726 *LDR, The Moat otherwise The Moat Farm* 1755 *SBL 3515, Moat Farm* 1765 *SBL 3489, The Mote* 1762 PR(L) 1, *The Moat* 1793 ib, 1839 *TA, The Moat Lane* 1802 PR(L) 1, *Upper Moat* 1810 ib. The 1833 OS map marks *Lower* and *Upper Moat.* The Moat is at Moat Fm, which corresponds to *Upper Moat.* The

6" map shows nothing corresponding to *Lower Moat* (which is by Meoles Meadow Plantation), and there is no building here on *TAMap.* VCH 162 says the house at Moat Fm is first recorded in m.14th, when it was occupied by a son of the lord of the manor. *v.* Park in f.ns. *infra.* OLDE FM, possibly *Olde Stepelton'* 1306-7 *Ass.* OLD MILLS, *Oulde Mylles* 1610 *SBL 7057, The Oolde Mylles* 1612 *LDR, Ould Mills* 1694 *SBL 9955, Old Mills* 1667 *SBL 9945, Ye Old Mills* 1726 *LDR.* The name is included in this section on the strength of an entry in Gazetteer. It has not been found on any map, and VCH does not mention it. VCH 166 does, however, give an account of mills on the Cound, in the N.E. corner of the parish, which were called *Clee Mills* in 1453. WETREANS, *Wetrains* 1833 OS: 'wet furrows', a common Sa f.n., frequent also in Ch.

Field-Names

Forms in (a) are 1839 *TA* except where otherwise stated. Forms dated 1612, 1681, 1685, 1693, 1718, 1726, 1730, 1748, 1768, 1805, 1825 are *LDR*, those dated 1729, 1768b are *SBL 3396, 3472.*

(a) Aldery Lsw and Patch; Bakers Yd; The Bank; Bank Fd; Barn Lsw; Barn Lsw and Yd (by Upper Moat); Barn Mdw and Yd (by Lower Shadymoor Fm); Big Mdw; Bolt Patches; Bowling Alley, Little - - (adjoins 'Park' fields *infra*); Braziers Patch; Brickkiln Fd, Lower, Upper, Little; Brickkiln Fd, Lower and Upper Brickkiln (not near preceding); Brickkiln Mdw (not near either of preceding); Brook Croft; Burnt Tree Fd; Burnt Tree Lsw (this, Hightree Lsw and Yewtree Lsw adjoin); Calves Croft (*The Calves Croft* 1729, 1768b); Chatford Fd, Big and Little (adjoins Chatford in Condover); Clover Ley; Coalpit Lsw, Old Coalpit Fd (a colliery here is known to have been in operation c.1764-82, VCH 167); Cockshutt Mdw (*Cockshut Lessow* 1718, *Ye Cock-shut Leasow* 1730, *v.* ***cocc-sciete**); Colliers Lsw; The Combs 1825 (1748, *The Combes* 1681, *The Combis* 1685, *Ye Combes* 1718,30, *v.* **cumb**); Coneyrie, First, Second, Third (*Howels Cunnary* 1718, *The Coneygree* 1729, *Ye Cunnary* 1730, *The Coneygree, Coneygree Lane* 1768b, *v.* **coninger**: the *TA* names refer to 3 fields in a triangular space between roads E. of the village: VCH 161 says there was a rabbit-warren here in 1327: VCH 162 says *Conigree Field* was an open field); Coppice, Further and Hither; Coppice Bank and Lsw (separated by The Field); Coppice Lsw; Cow Pasture (2); Crabtree Lsw; Croft (a number of small enclosures in a projection of the parish by Stapleton Common, also some enclosures in the village);

Crumps Lsw, Near and Far; Engine Fd (adjoins Brickkiln Fd); Far New Lsw; Feggy Fd (rough grass); Field, Far, Near and Middle (in N.E. corner of parish); The Field (2 fields a short distance apart N.E. of village); Flat Fd; Flat Lsw, Far and Near; Flem Mdw (by a tributary of the Cound, *fle(a)m* is a dialect word for a mill-stream); The Flowers, Flowers Lsw (*The Floes* 1612, probably *flow* NED sb^2 'watery moss': the 2 fields, on N. boundary of parish, are shown as rough ground on 6" map); Foxholes Lsw, Big and Little; Garden Lsw, North and South; Georges Yd; Gonsell Yd (adjoins Gonsal in Condover); Gorsy Bank; Gorsy Fd; Gorsy Lawn, Upper and Middle Gorsy Lands (adjoining); Little Gotherage; Great Mdw; Great Orchard; Green Fd; Green Lane (a short lane leading from Upper Shadymoor Fm to where the 6" map marks a footbridge over a brook); The Half Field 1805 (1685, *Ye Halfe Field* 1681, *The Half Field* 1693, 1748, *Ye - -* 1718,26,30: VCH 162 equates this with *The Haulle Feylde* 1612, a common field S. of the village: the etymology is uncertain); Hay, Big and Little (*v.* **(ge)hæg**); Hemp Patch; Hemp Yd Patch; Hendall Mdw; High Tree Lsw; Home Fd, Near and Far (by Bridge Fm); Home Mdw (3, respectively by a house in N.E. corner of parish, near Middle Shadymoor, and by Upper Moat); The Horns, Great and Little Horns (the shape of the combined fields has two sharp points: cf. *Sukars Great Wall-horn* 1718); Horse Lsw; House Croft (by the building called Vinnals on 6" map); House Pasture and Pce (by Upper Shadymoor Fm); Hurst, Big, Little, Lower, Upper, Near, Further (adjoining fields S. of Vinnals, cf. *common called The Hurste* 1612, *v.* **hyrst**); Jones Croft; Leasows Wood; Leys, Further, Near, Middle, Upper, Leys Mdw (adjoining fields S. of the village, *The Leas* 1729, 1768b, *v.* **lǣs**); Little Dairy; Little Mdw; Long Lsw (4); Long Wd, Lower and Upper; Lower Ground, Far and Near; Lower Mdw; Marsh, Lower, Upper, Far Middle, Near Middle, Furthermost, Little (6 adjoining fields S. of village, cf. *The Marshes* 1729, 1768b); Marshes Pce (not near preceding); Meadow, Big and Little; Meadow, Far and Near; Moat Lane Plantation (*v.* Moat *supra*); The Nandmans, Far, Near, Little and Great Nornhams (5 adjoining fields along a brook, N.W. of Lower Shadymoor Fm, second el. possibly **hamm**); New Lsw; Oak Lsw; Old Bank Pce; Old Fd; Old Yd; Orchard Patch; Orchard Pce; The Park (2 fields between Little and Big Shadymoor Coppice); The Park, Big, Little and Far Park Fd, Park Lsw and Lane (adjoining fields N.W. of Moat Fm: VCH 162 says that the smaller of the two medieval parks was here, and Moat Fm may have been associated with it); The Parks, North, South and Lower Park Lsw (near Lower Shadymoor Fm: the larger of 2 medieval parks, known as Great Park, seems to have occupied most of Shadymoor (VCH 161): cf. *The Parkes or The Park Ground* 1729); Patch (several, very small enclosures); Patch, Home, Boundary, Road (by the building called Vinnals on 6" map); Peartreee Croft and Fd, Upper Peartree Mdw (adjoining); Piece above Way Close; Piece below Coppice, - above - (either side of Big Shadymoor Coppice); Piece beyond Brook; Pool Fd; Quaggs; Little, Long and Upper Quaggs (not near preceding); Quaggy Mdw, Big and Little Quaggy Lsw (*quag* and *quaggy* are both in NED, used of quaking bogs, but the term is not common in field-names); Rail Lsw; The Rainbow (the field has curved sides); Rebecca's Mdw; Road Mdw; Road Pce (2); Rockall Fd and Patch; Rogers Rough; Scoringers Hill; Seat Lsw; Shaws Pce, Far and Near; Slade (*v.* **slæd**); Slang (a narrow strip); Smiths Croft; The Span Gate 1825 (*The Spoone Yatte* 1612, *Ye Span Yate* 1681, 1718,26,30, *The Spawn Yate* 1685, *v.* **geat**, first el. **spōn** 'wood-shaving': the common field here was Spanyate or Vinnals Field); Spondhurst (on N. boundary of parish and of Spanyate Field, *v.* **spōn, hyrst**); Stackyard Croft; Stony Lsw; Tary Lsw (infested by *Vicia hirsuta*, the Hairy Tare); Thistly Fd; Townsend (2, on edge of village); Upper Mdw; Upper Pce; Way Close; Way Lsw (2); Well Lsw (2); Wheathill, Far and Near; White Lsw, First, Second, Lower; Winter Furlong (in the area of Spangate Field); Woodcocks Ditches; Wood Lsw; Woolbank, Further - (cf. *Reynolds Wool Leasow* 1718,20); Yard, Big, Little, Upper, Yewtree, Doctors (adjoining, in village); Yard, Near, Olivers (adjoining fields by Bridge Fm); Yewtree Fd; Yewtree Mdw.

(b) *Alsleys Furlong* 1718; *Alsemore* 1284 VCH 161, *Alissemor* 1311 Pat ('Alice's marsh', *v.* **mōr**); *Badleyeslaine* 1612; *La Broke* 1291-2 *Ass* (p) (*v.* **brōc**); *The Bylett* 1729, 1768b (an island between river-channels); *The Churchyard Leasow* 1729, 1768b; *Colleyes Forde* 1612; *The Collimore* 1729, *The Collimore Shell* 1768b (*v.* **mōr**, first el. perhaps ***colig**, referring either to charcoal or to pit coal); *Daymore* 1612 (probably 'dairy marsh', *v.* ***dey, mōr**); *Dodmyses Feyld Hedge* 1612; *The Farther Bank* 1729, - *Further* - 1768b; *Fewtrills Upper Yard* 1718; *The Field Lands* 1768b; *The Hayme Yatte* 1612 (*v.* **geat**); *The Little Leasow* 1729, 1768b; *The Middle Field ib*; *Howells Pris-hill* 1718, *Pris-hill* 1729, *Prishill* 1768b (the Church Stretton *TA* has a Priss Hill and there is a Press Hill in the *TA* for Tarvin Ch (PN Ch **3**. 284)); *The Rie Medowe Heade* 1612; *Stanleymor* 1311 Pat (*v.* Shadymoor *supra*); *Teynter Mede* 1453 VCH 167 (referring to cloth-stretching); *Ye Three Butts* 1730; *The Weye Meare* (*brocke called*) 1612 (*v.* **weg, (ge)mǣre**); *The Wheat Furlong* 1729, 1768b; *The Would Coppice* 1768b; *The Hither and Further Yards* (*two broomy pieces of land*), *The Upper Yard* 1729, *The Hither and Further Yord, The Upper Yord* 1768b.

Woolstaston

The parish-name, which means 'Wulfstān's estate', is discussed in Part 1.

BLACKPOOL COPPICE, *Wood* 1840 *TA*. CASTLE BANK, a motte and bailey beside the church, *v.* VCH 171. CASTLE HILL, 1833 OS, 1840 *TA*, a natural mound in N.E. corner of parish. The lady of the manor built a house here in e.13th, and the name may be to some extent a transfer from Castle Bank. VCH 170 says this is the earliest recorded assart in the parish, and on the *TA* and 6" maps the mound is surrounded by a cluster of small, irregularly-shaped fields of the sort characteristic of early assarting. COLLIERSLEY, 1840 *TA*, *Colliersleigh* 1701 PR(H) 8, *Collier's Lye* 1741 ib. PINE COTTAGE. SPRING COPPICE. WOOLSTASTON HALL. VCH 171 says the hall is first recorded c.1589. YEWTREE COTTAGE.

Field-Names

Forms in (a) are 1840 *TA* except where otherwise stated. VCH 171-2 says the common fields were *Beech Field, Stanklees or Stankley Field* and *Lower Field*, respectively W., S. and N. of the village.

(a) The Bank (site of motte and bailey, *v.* Castle Bank *supra*); Bank Pce; The Banks; Bank Yd; Barn Moor (VCH 170 calls this Brandmoor); Bartham Yd; Batches 1833 OS (*v.* **bæce**); Beach Fd, Far, Upper and Little (an open field, probably **bæce**, referring to the valley of Betchcott Brook); Big Fd (very small); Birches, Big and Long (in this area probably a corruption of *Britches, from **bryce**); Bowers Lsw; Brickkiln Bank; Brickkiln Mdw; Briers Wall; Broad Brook 1968 VCH 170 (VCH gives this as the name of the brook which bounds Woolstaston on the S., but it is not on maps or in Gazetteer: it is *Broadbrooke* c.1789 *SBL 6579*); Broad Mdw, - - Head; Byletts (by Walkmill Brook, land between a stream and a side-channel); Catmere, Big and Little (*Catmore* VCH 170, *TAMap* shows the pool, *v.* **cat, mere**); Church Pce, Little - - (adjoins St Mary's Church in Leebotwood); Close (a group of fields on S. boundary are all called Close); Clover Lsw (2); Clover Ley, Big Clover Fd (adjoining); Common Pce, Upper and Little - - (a group of fields in N.E. corner of parish); Condover Lee (*Condovers Leyes* 1621 PR(L) 6, the rent was dedicated to the repair of Condover church, VCH 52); Coppy Lsw (by Blackpool Coppice); Corn Stubble; Crabtree Bank; Dale Acre (adjoins North Furlong); Dickens Coppy; Dods Yd (by a house W. of Castle Hill, which is still there on 6" map); Far Pit Fd; Field (2); Fir Tree (a small conical field, probably a shape name); Flat Pce (2), Flat Lsw (these are 3 adjoining fields); Footway Pce; Garbetts Mdw; Gorsty Lsw (2); Haxnells; Haydness; Hill, Lower and Upper; Hobbins Oak; Hop Yd; House Yd (by Woolstaston Hall); Hungerhill (*TAMap* shows a cottage, there are 2 on 6"); Four Wickets (possibly referring to mountain ash trees, *v.* FN 48); Holly Pce; Honey Mdw; Lady Mdw (*The Lady Meadow in Wostansson* 1621 PR(L) 6: the rent was dedicated to the repair of St Mary's Church at Condover, *v.* VCH 52); Leasow, Upper, Middle, Well (a group of small fields by Castle Hill); Leizure Hill, Big and Little (Leisure Hill Gazetteer, Lazar Hill VCH 170: FN 9 classifies this as a form of *leasow*, but corruption of that word is not likely in Sa, where it is ubiquitous in f.ns.: the word may be *leisure*, there is a class of field-names which refer to recreational pursuits); Ley Lsw; Long Lsw; Long Lsw and Mdw (adjoining); Lucas's Bank; Mapps Ford (near the junction of Betchcott and Walkmill Brooks, possibly *malpas* 'difficult crossing', *v.* PN Berks 222); Meadow, Lower and Upper -; Meadow; The Meadow (2); Mill Ground (3 fields by Branmill in Smethcott); Mill Mdw, Upper - - (by mills on Walkmill Brook); Moutherwalls; New Lsw; New Lsw Bank; North Furlong (one of several furlong-shaped fields N.E. of the village); Oaks Mdw; Old House Pce (no building shown); Old Mdw, Near and Lower; Orchard, Pce above -; Orchard Pool; Outrack and Rough (by a track leading to The Long Mynd); Paddock and Rough; The Parks, Green Parks (VCH 170 says The Parks was so called e.17th, the n. constitutes the only evidence for a medieval park); Patch (*freq*, of tiny enclosures); Piece above Hall (near Woolstaston Hall); Pieces Yd; Pool Lsw and Mdw (S. of Castle Hill); Pool Lsw and Mdw (N. of village, pool and Boat House shown on 6" map); Postan Mdw; Quobbs (*v.* ***cwabba**); Rail Lsw; Road (a narrow strip S. of Castle Hill); Rough (several); Rough Bank; Rough Ground; Rye Grass Fd; Seeding Wall, Little - - (VCH 170 calls this Seething Well: 'seething spring', the n. occurs 3 times in Ch, *v.* PN Ch 5, 335-6); The Sitch (*v.* **sīc**); Slang (2, narrow strips); Stank Mdw, Bank and Lsw (FN 19 discusses the Sa uses of **stank**: it may be a temporary dam to form a drinking-place for cattle); Stockhalls Bank; Sunny Bank (2); Townsend Mdw (on E. edge of village); Turnabout Mdw (the explanation of *turnabout* in FN 35, 'land on which a plough may be turned', does not seem appropriate to a meadow); Twin Yets, Far and Near (small fields on W. edge of village, perhaps 'between gates'); Upper Cow Pasture; Water's Lee; Well Lsw; Wilding Fd, Big, Little and Far, Wilding Mdw; Wildings Ground (not near preceding: Francis Wilding was the owner of a fulling mill in 1757, VCH 175); Wolstaston Summerhouse 1812 PR(H) 1; Wood Pce, Upper and Lower (by Blackpool Coppice); The Yard, Middle Yd (by Yewtree Cottage); The Yard; Yewtree Lsw.

(b) *Monkesplokes* l.15 HAC ('monks' plots', second el. a variant of **plek**); *Stanckleys Gate* 1656 *SBL 6570, Stankleys Lane* 1777 VCH 171 (the lane was the road to Church Stretton, named from one of the common fields, *v.* **stank, lǣs**); *Trhawareshede* l.15 HAC (the end of something, *v.* **hēafod**, but the first part of the n. is probably corrupt); *Way Meadow* 1679 *VCH(Smethcott)*; *Woolaston Lane Head* c.1790 *SBL 6579.*

INDEX TO THE PLACE-NAMES OF SHROPSHIRE PART 2

In cases of identical or nearly identical names the relevant township is cited, except for the two townships called Westley, which are ascribed to their parishes.

THE ENGLISH PLACE-NAME SOCIETY

COUNTY VOLUMES

**ENGLISH PLACE-NAME SOCIETY, DEPARTMENT OF ENGLISH,
UNIVERSITY OF NOTTINGHAM , NOTTINGHAM NG7 2RD**